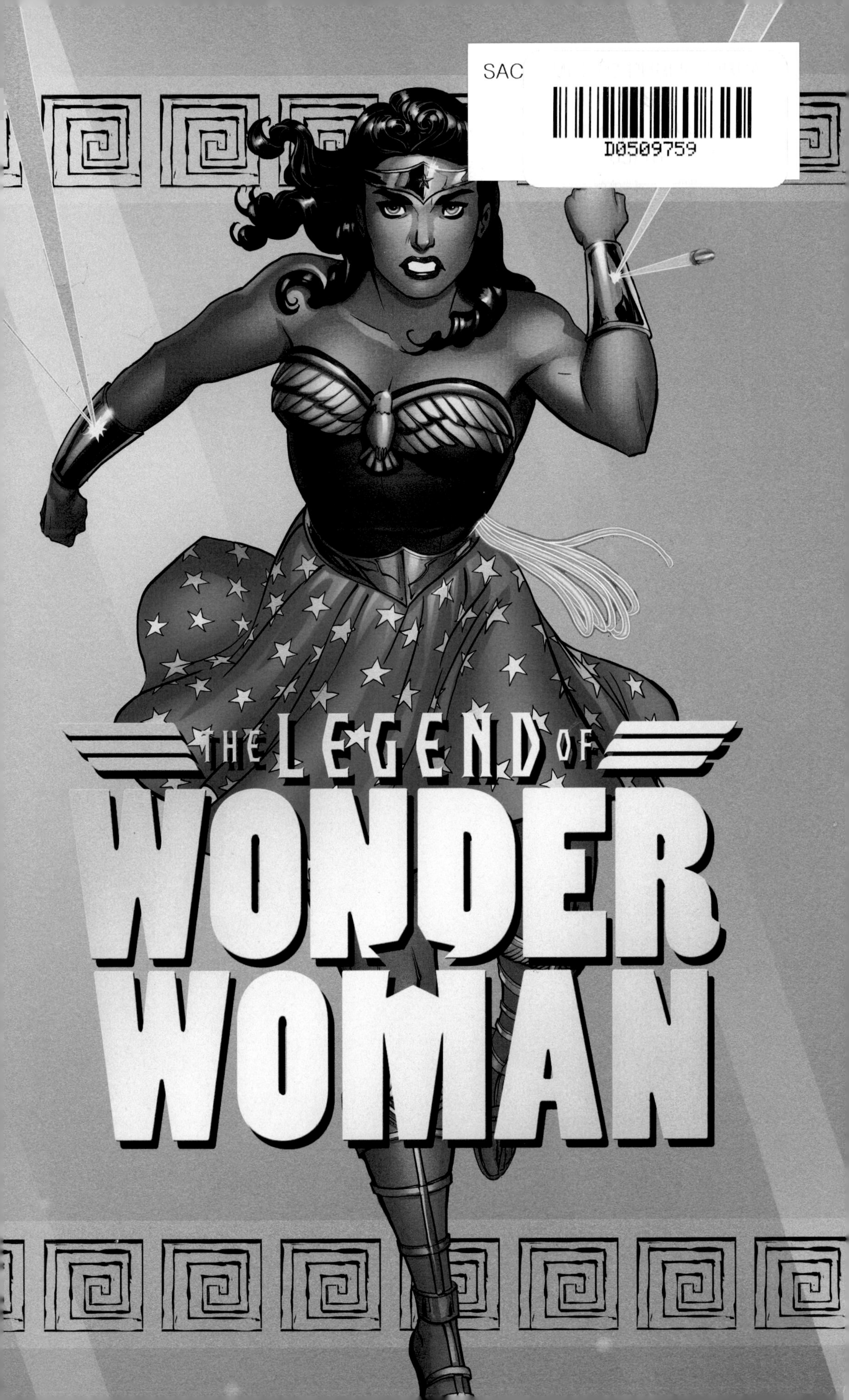
THE LEGEND OF
WONDER
WOMAN

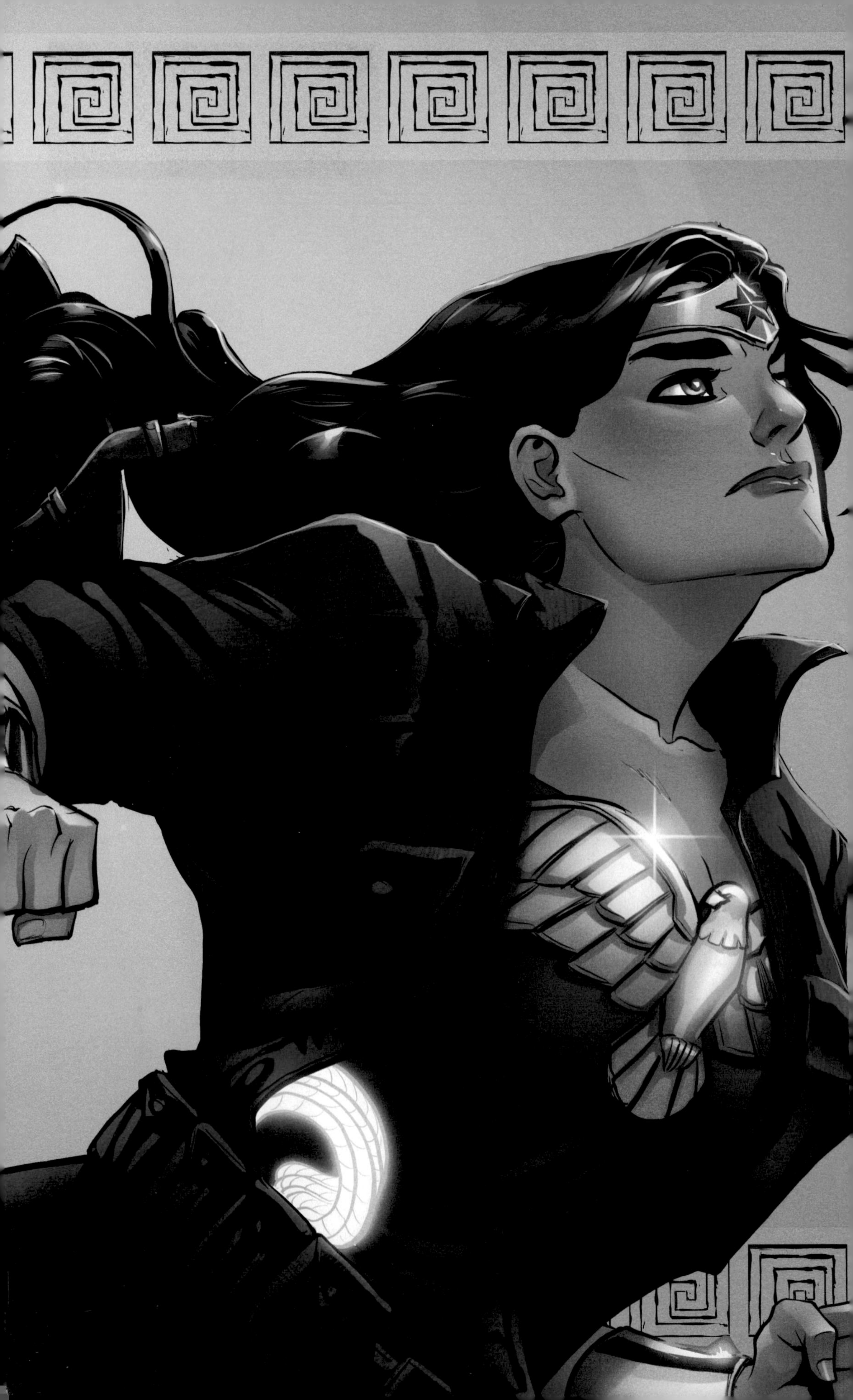

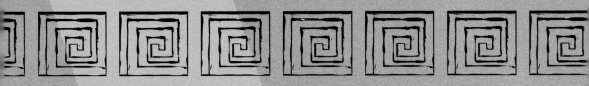

THE LEGEND OF WONDER WOMAN

Story and Pencils by
RENAE DE LIZ

Inks, Colors and Letters by
RAY DILLON

WONDER WOMAN
created by
WILLIAM MOULTON MARSTON

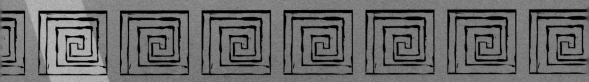

THE LEGEND OF WONDER WOMAN: ORIGINS

DC Comics, 2900 West Alameda Ave., Burbank, CA 91505
Printed by LSC Communications, Kendallville, IN, USA. 10/13/17. First Printing.
ISBN: 978-1-4012-7425-2
Library of Congress Cataloging-in-Publication Data is available.

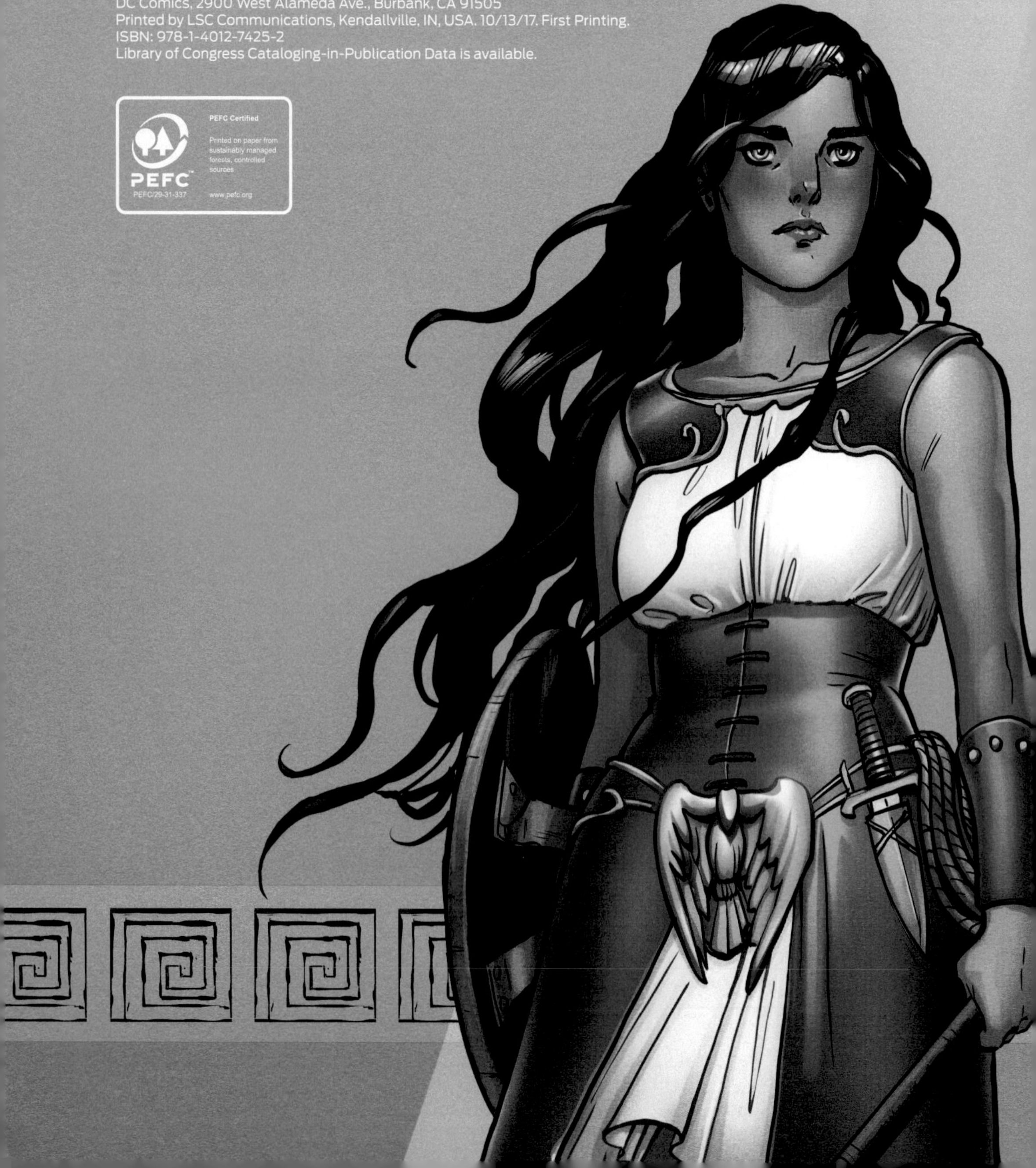

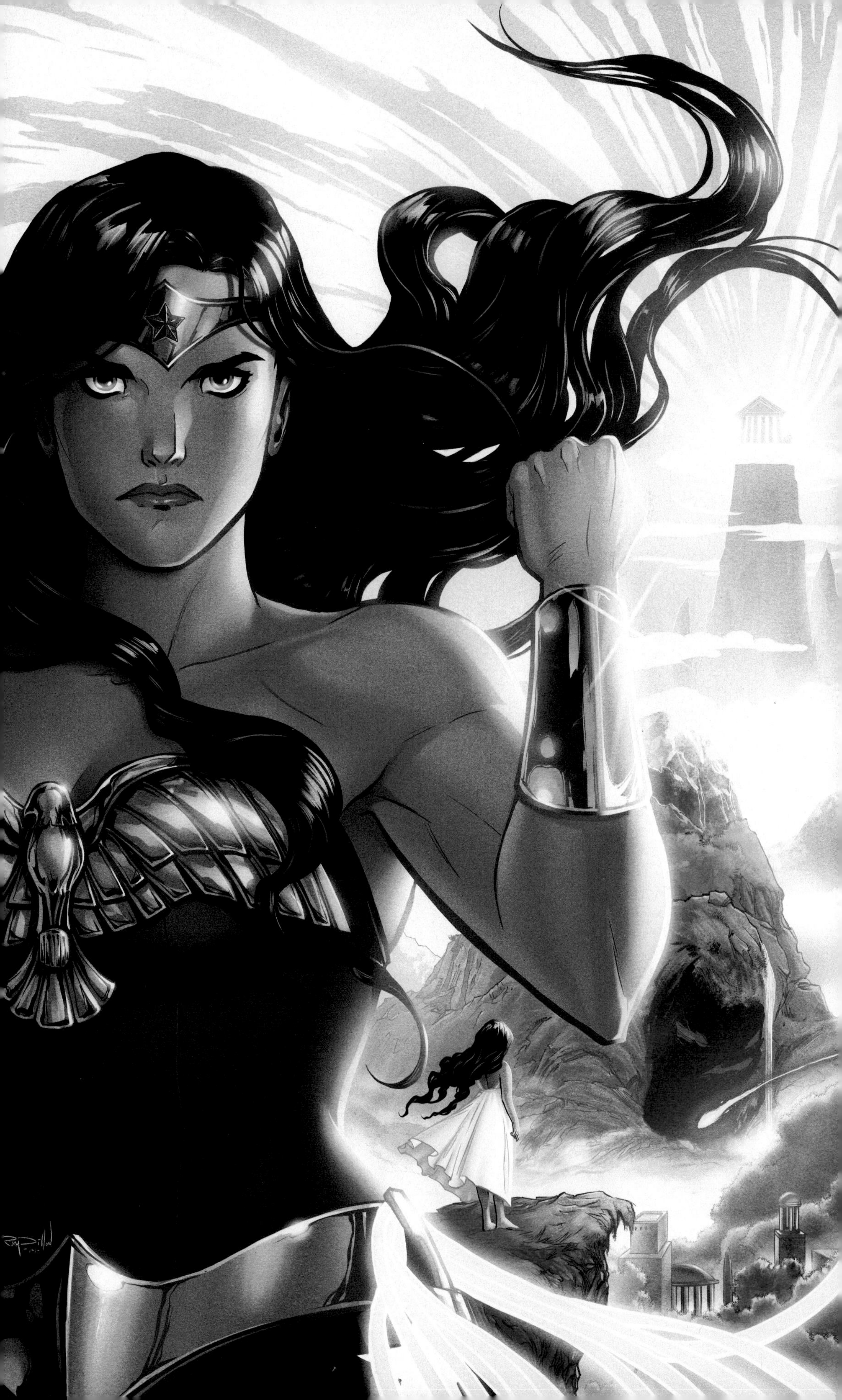

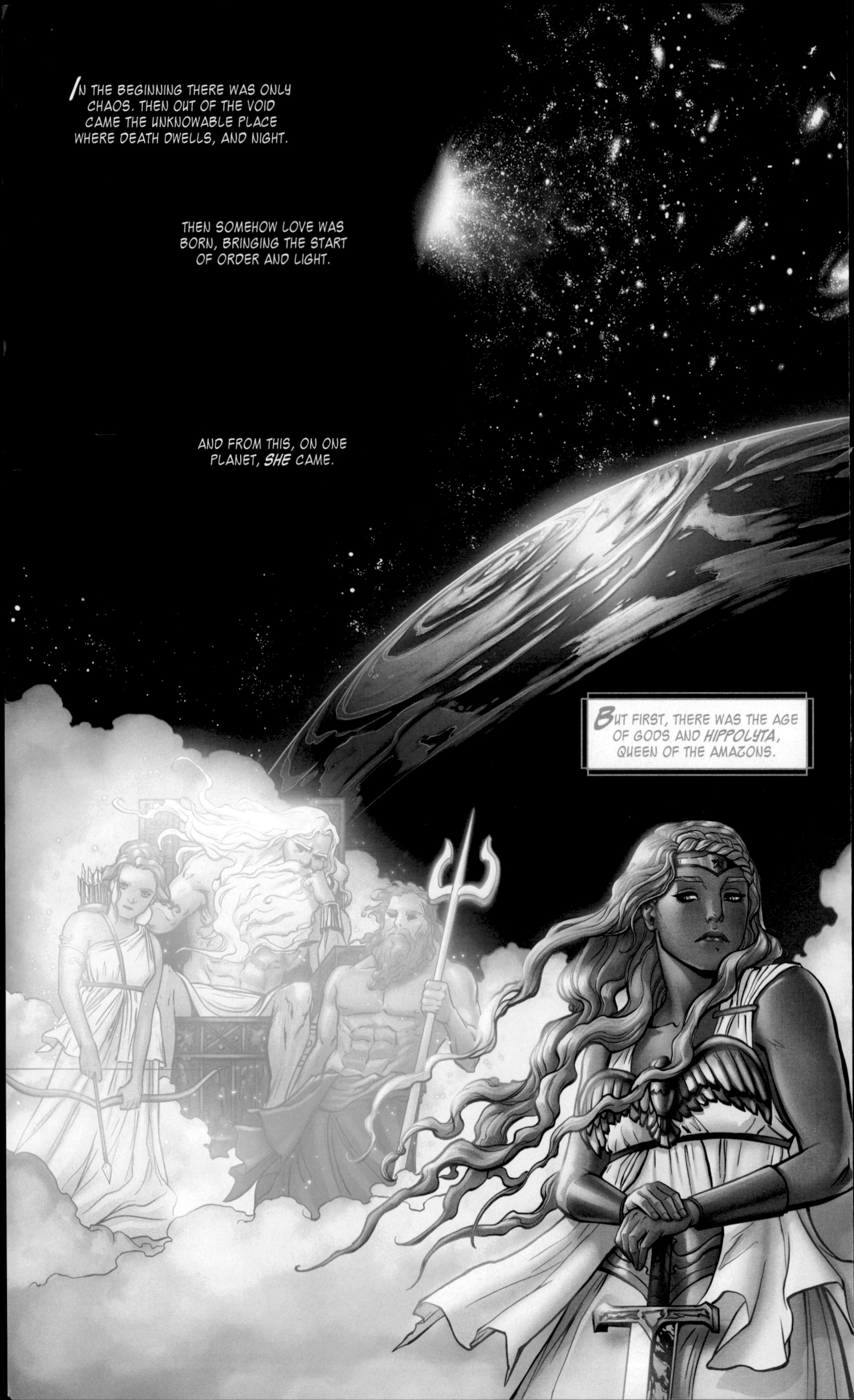
IN THE BEGINNING THERE WAS ONLY CHAOS. THEN OUT OF THE VOID CAME THE UNKNOWABLE PLACE WHERE DEATH DWELLS, AND NIGHT.
THEN SOMEHOW LOVE WAS BORN, BRINGING THE START OF ORDER AND LIGHT.
AND FROM THIS, ON ONE PLANET, SHE CAME.
BUT FIRST, THERE WAS THE AGE OF GODS AND HIPPOLYTA, QUEEN OF THE AMAZONS.

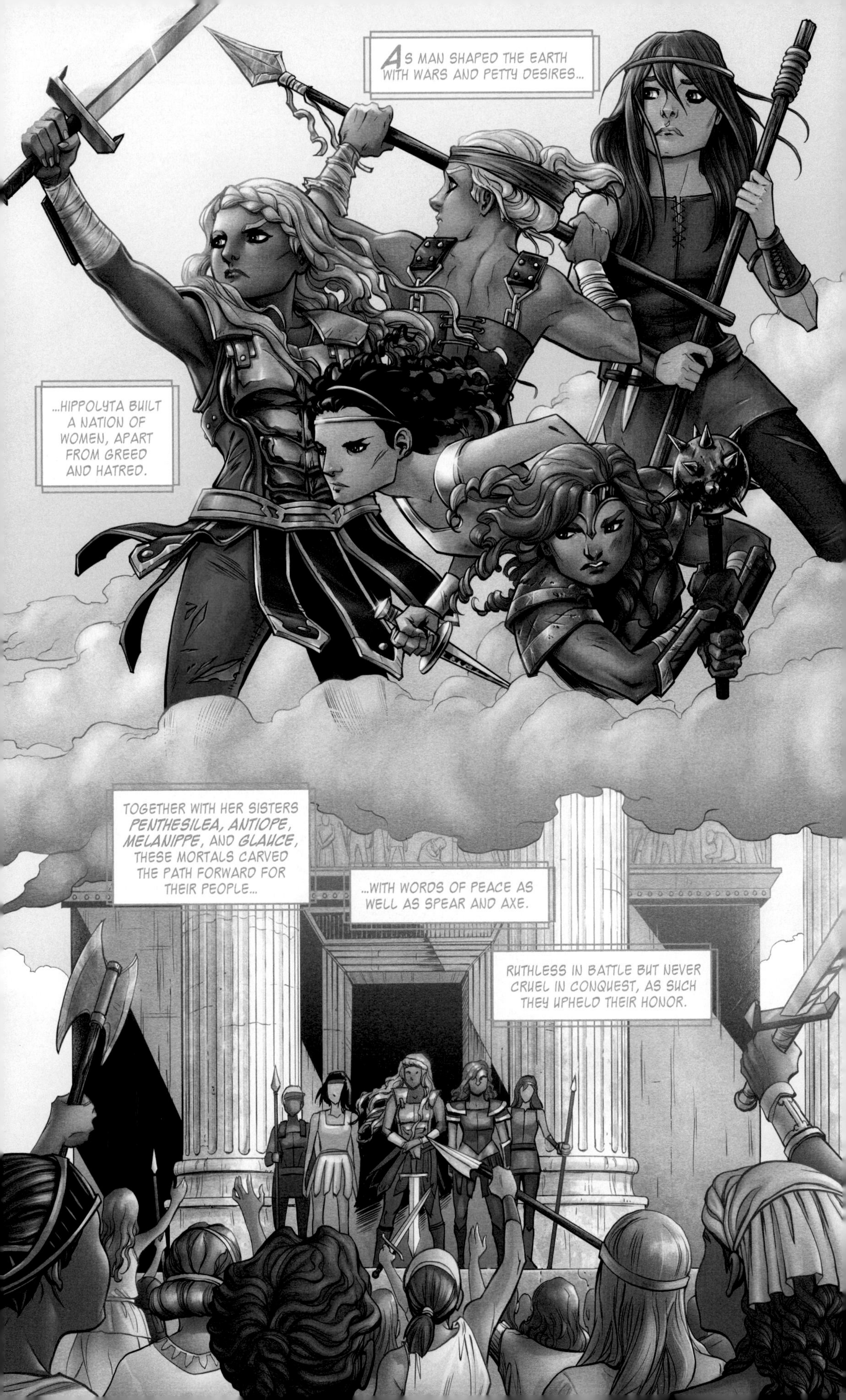
AS MAN SHAPED THE EARTH WITH WARS AND PETTY DESIRES...
...HIPPOLYTA BUILT A NATION OF WOMEN, APART FROM GREED AND HATRED.
TOGETHER WITH HER SISTERS PENTHESILEA, ANTIOPE, MELANIPPE, AND GLAUCE, THESE MORTALS CARVED THE PATH FORWARD FOR THEIR PEOPLE...
...WITH WORDS OF PEACE AS WELL AS SPEAR AND AXE.
RUTHLESS IN BATTLE BUT NEVER CRUEL IN CONQUEST, AS SUCH THEY UPHELD THEIR HONOR.

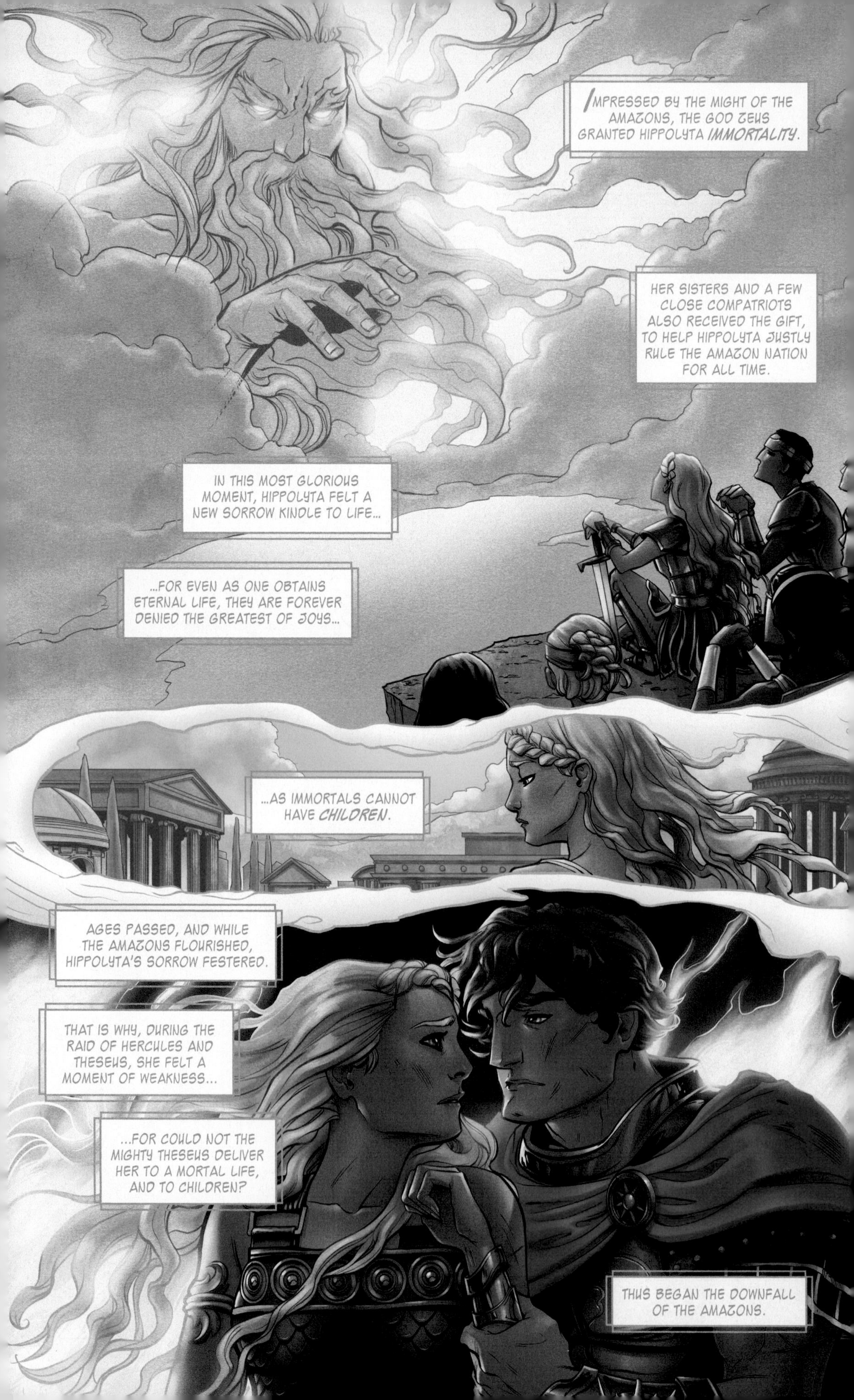
IMPRESSED BY THE MIGHT OF THE AMAZONS, THE GOD ZEUS GRANTED HIPPOLYTA *IMMORTALITY*.
HER SISTERS AND A FEW CLOSE COMPATRIOTS ALSO RECEIVED THE GIFT, TO HELP HIPPOLYTA JUSTLY RULE THE AMAZON NATION FOR ALL TIME.
IN THIS MOST GLORIOUS MOMENT, HIPPOLYTA FELT A NEW SORROW KINDLE TO LIFE...
...FOR EVEN AS ONE OBTAINS ETERNAL LIFE, THEY ARE FOREVER DENIED THE GREATEST OF JOYS...
...AS IMMORTALS CANNOT HAVE *CHILDREN*.
AGES PASSED, AND WHILE THE AMAZONS FLOURISHED, HIPPOLYTA'S SORROW FESTERED.
THAT IS WHY, DURING THE RAID OF HERCULES AND THESEUS, SHE FELT A MOMENT OF WEAKNESS...
...FOR COULD NOT THE MIGHTY THESEUS DELIVER HER TO A MORTAL LIFE, AND TO CHILDREN?
THUS BEGAN THE DOWNFALL OF THE AMAZONS.

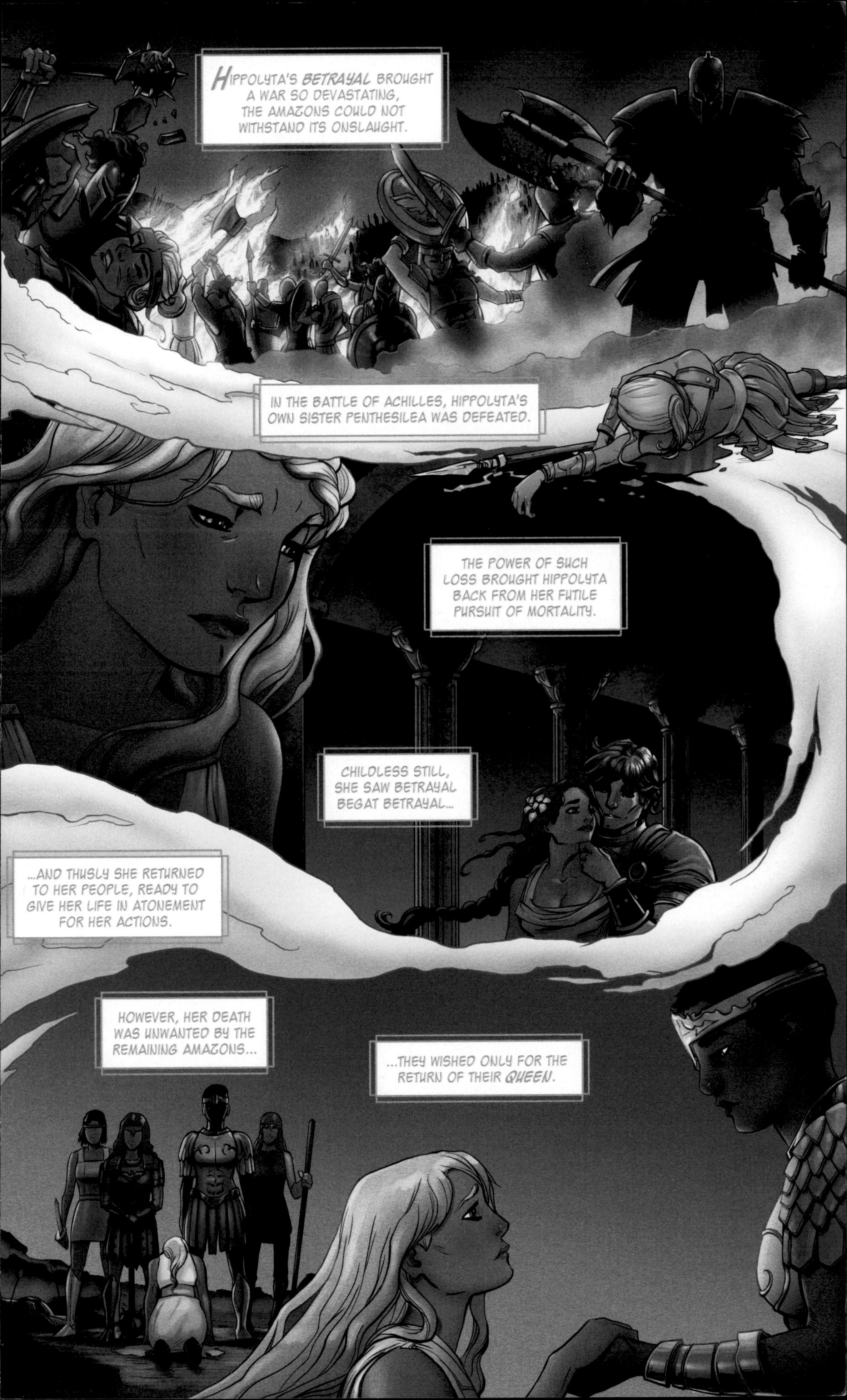
HIPPOLYTA'S BETRAYAL BROUGHT A WAR SO DEVASTATING, THE AMAZONS COULD NOT WITHSTAND ITS ONSLAUGHT.
IN THE BATTLE OF ACHILLES, HIPPOLYTA'S OWN SISTER PENTHESILEA WAS DEFEATED.
THE POWER OF SUCH LOSS BROUGHT HIPPOLYTA BACK FROM HER FUTILE PURSUIT OF MORTALITY.
CHILDLESS STILL, SHE SAW BETRAYAL BEGAT BETRAYAL...
...AND THUSLY SHE RETURNED TO HER PEOPLE, READY TO GIVE HER LIFE IN ATONEMENT FOR HER ACTIONS.
HOWEVER, HER DEATH WAS UNWANTED BY THE REMAINING AMAZONS...
...THEY WISHED ONLY FOR THE RETURN OF THEIR QUEEN.

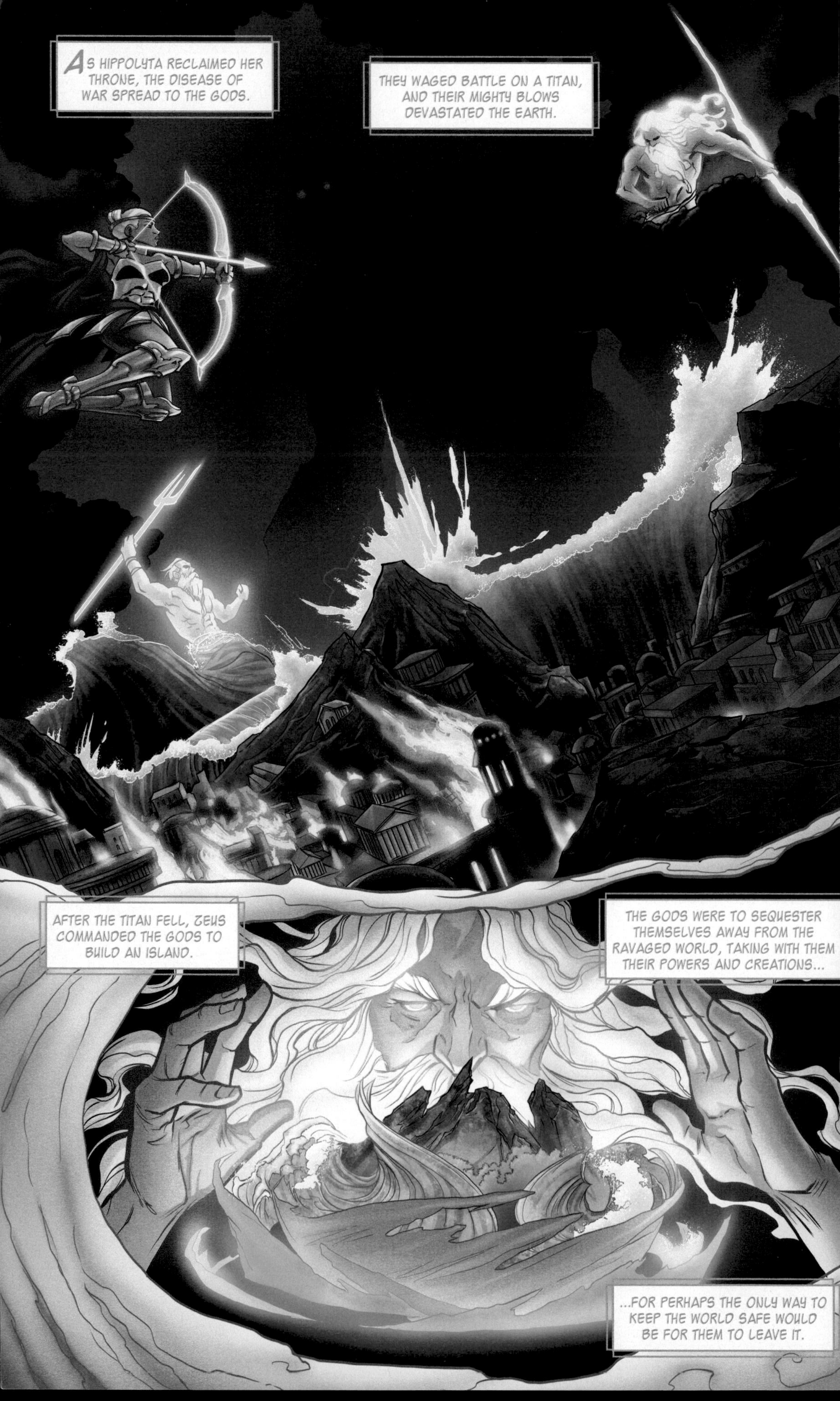
AS HIPPOLYTA RECLAIMED HER THRONE, THE DISEASE OF WAR SPREAD TO THE GODS.
THEY WAGED BATTLE ON A TITAN, AND THEIR MIGHTY BLOWS DEVASTATED THE EARTH.
AFTER THE TITAN FELL, ZEUS COMMANDED THE GODS TO BUILD AN ISLAND.
THE GODS WERE TO SEQUESTER THEMSELVES AWAY FROM THE RAVAGED WORLD, TAKING WITH THEM THEIR POWERS AND CREATIONS...
...FOR PERHAPS THE ONLY WAY TO KEEP THE WORLD SAFE WOULD BE FOR THEM TO LEAVE IT.

DESPITE HIPPOLYTA'S BETRAYAL, ZEUS OFFERED HER A PLACE ON THEIR ISLAND, CALLED *THEMYSCIRA*.

HERE THE AMAZONS WOULD BUILD A CITY OF ETERNAL PEACE, AND PROVIDE WORSHIP FOR THE MANY GODS.

IN RETURN, THE GODS WOULD PROVIDE SOULS OF DAUGHTERS TO CHOSEN MORTAL AMAZONS EVERY TEN YEARS TO HELP THEIR PEOPLE FLOURISH, AND WOULD PROVIDE WATCHFUL GUARD OVER THEM FOR ETERNITY.

CENTURIES PASSED. HIPPOLYTA OBEYED THE GODS' WISHES, AND ON THEMYSCIRA HER PEOPLE KNEW ONLY LIGHT AND HAPPINESS.

AND YET...

...DESPITE THE PROSPERITY OF THE AMAZONS, HER SORROW REMAINED.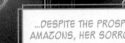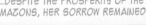

THIS VAST EMPTINESS WAS THE ONLY THING THE GREAT QUEEN TRULY FEARED.

IN HER MOST DESPERATE MOMENT SHE FLED.

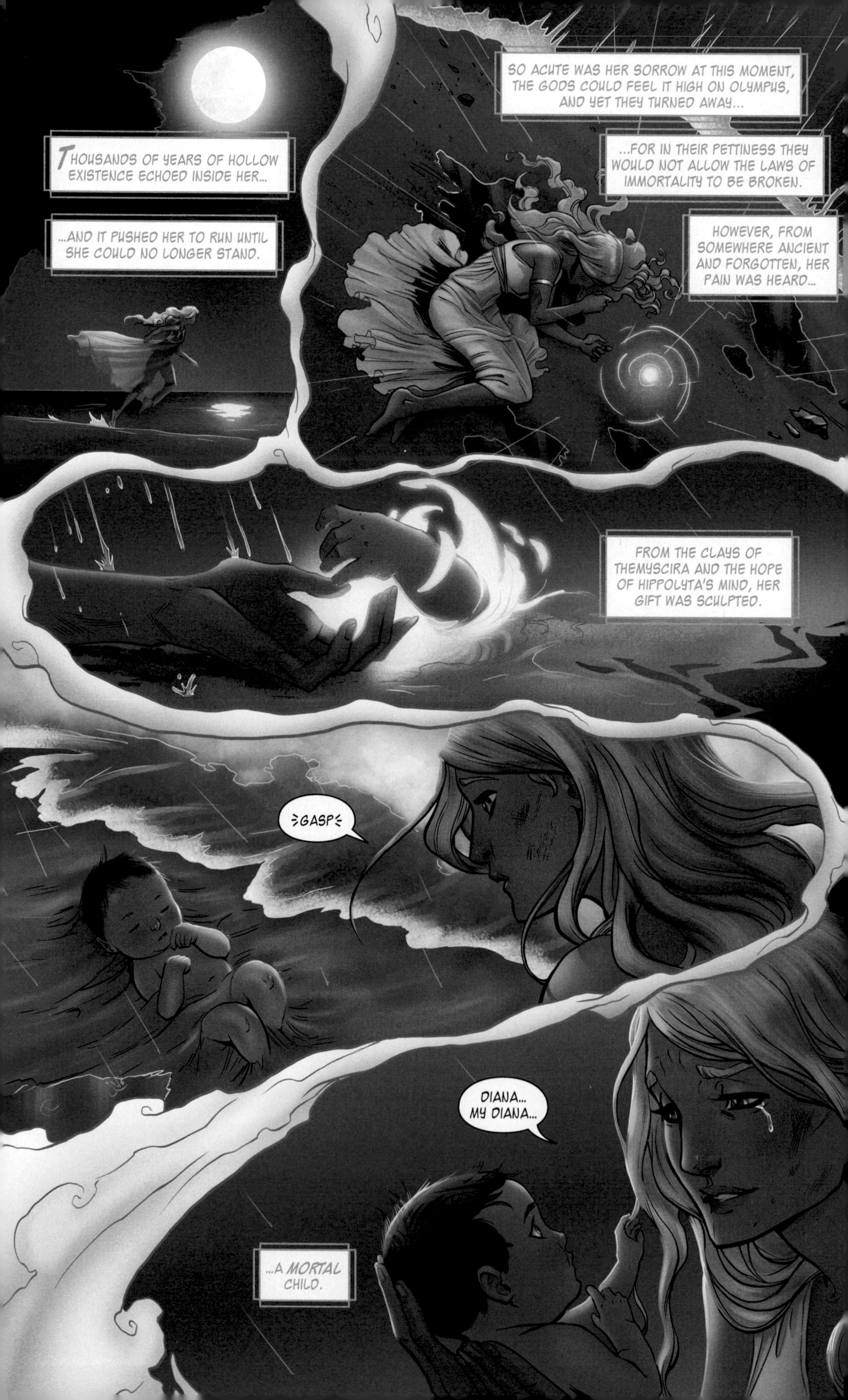
THOUSANDS OF YEARS OF HOLLOW EXISTENCE ECHOED INSIDE HER...
...AND IT PUSHED HER TO RUN UNTIL SHE COULD NO LONGER STAND.
SO ACUTE WAS HER SORROW AT THIS MOMENT, THE GODS COULD FEEL IT HIGH ON OLYMPUS, AND YET THEY TURNED AWAY...
...FOR IN THEIR PETTINESS THEY WOULD NOT ALLOW THE LAWS OF IMMORTALITY TO BE BROKEN.
HOWEVER, FROM SOMEWHERE ANCIENT AND FORGOTTEN, HER PAIN WAS HEARD...
FROM THE CLAYS OF THEMYSCIRA AND THE HOPE OF HIPPOLYTA'S MIND, HER GIFT WAS SCULPTED.
GASP
DIANA... MY DIANA...
...A *MORTAL* CHILD.

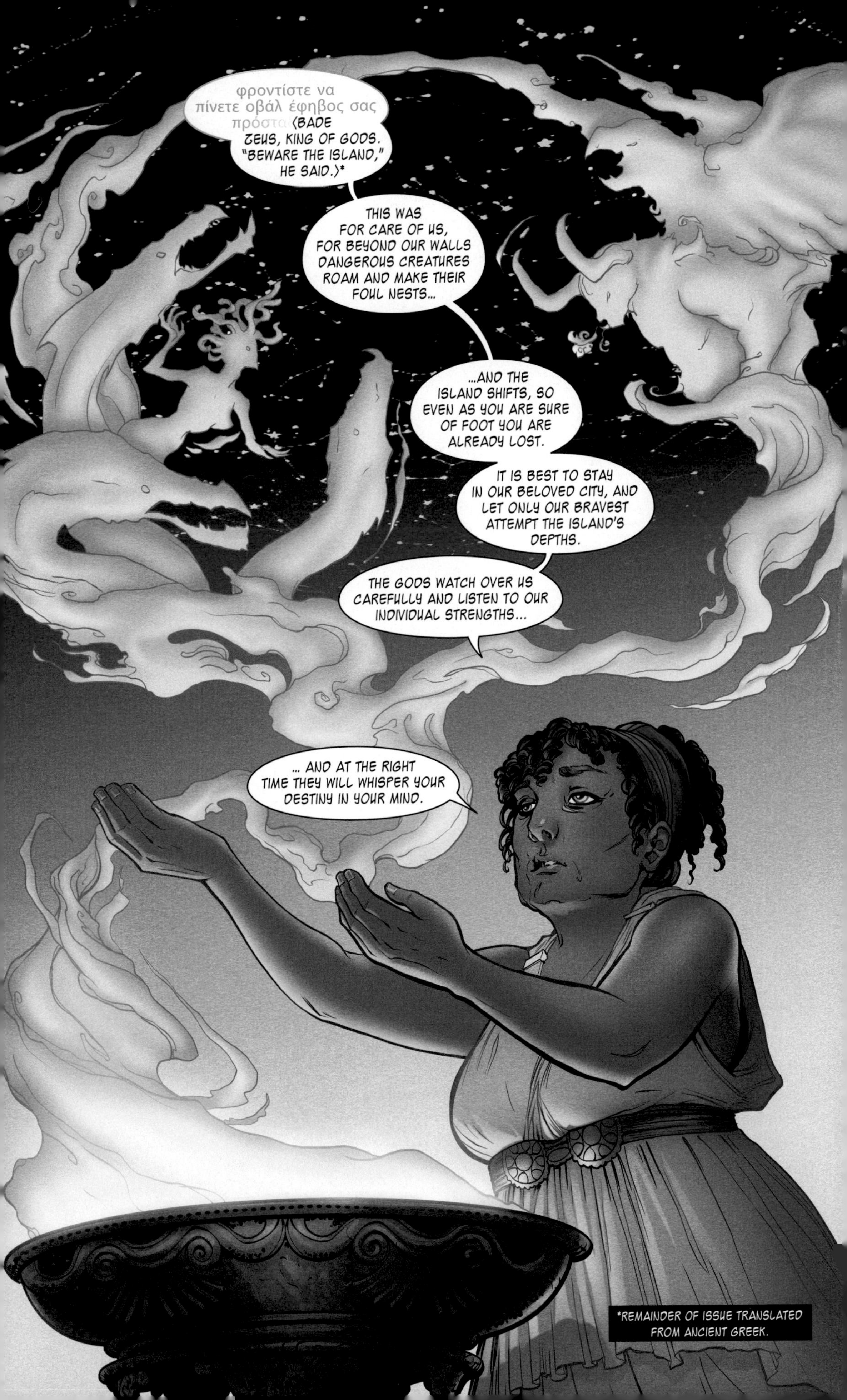
φροντίστε να πίνετε οβάλ έφηβος σας πρόστα (BADE ZEUS, KING OF GODS. "BEWARE THE ISLAND," HE SAID.)*
THIS WAS FOR CARE OF US, FOR BEYOND OUR WALLS DANGEROUS CREATURES ROAM AND MAKE THEIR FOUL NESTS...
...AND THE ISLAND SHIFTS, SO EVEN AS YOU ARE SURE OF FOOT YOU ARE ALREADY LOST.
IT IS BEST TO STAY IN OUR BELOVED CITY, AND LET ONLY OUR BRAVEST ATTEMPT THE ISLAND'S DEPTHS.
THE GODS WATCH OVER US CAREFULLY AND LISTEN TO OUR INDIVIDUAL STRENGTHS...
... AND AT THE RIGHT TIME THEY WILL WHISPER YOUR DESTINY IN YOUR MIND.
*REMAINDER OF ISSUE TRANSLATED FROM ANCIENT GREEK.

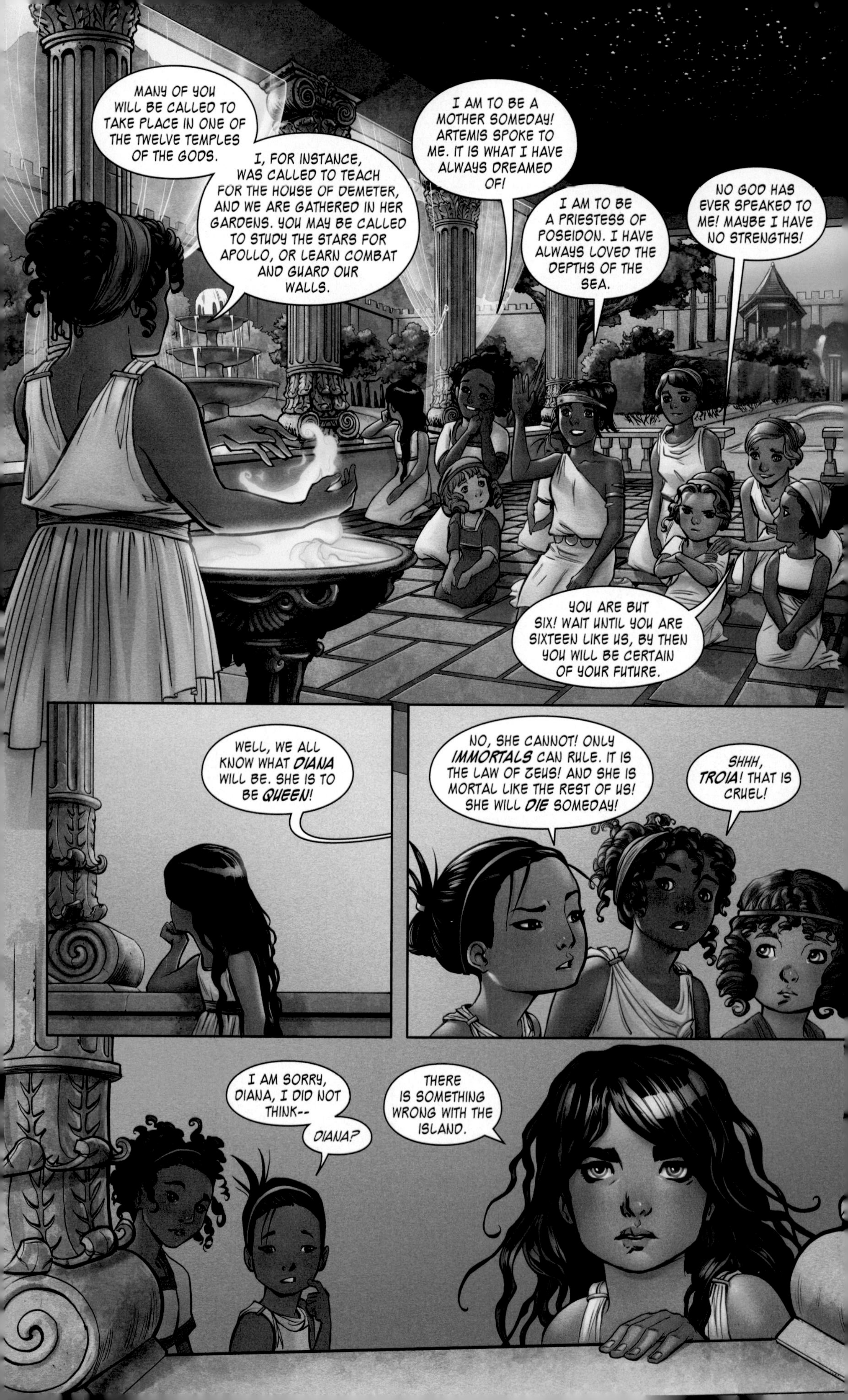
MANY OF YOU WILL BE CALLED TO TAKE PLACE IN ONE OF THE TWELVE TEMPLES OF THE GODS.
I, FOR INSTANCE, WAS CALLED TO TEACH FOR THE HOUSE OF DEMETER, AND WE ARE GATHERED IN HER GARDENS. YOU MAY BE CALLED TO STUDY THE STARS FOR APOLLO, OR LEARN COMBAT AND GUARD OUR WALLS.
I AM TO BE A MOTHER SOMEDAY! ARTEMIS SPOKE TO ME. IT IS WHAT I HAVE ALWAYS DREAMED OF!
I AM TO BE A PRIESTESS OF POSEIDON. I HAVE ALWAYS LOVED THE DEPTHS OF THE SEA.
NO GOD HAS EVER SPEAKED TO ME! MAYBE I HAVE NO STRENGTHS!
YOU ARE BUT SIX! WAIT UNTIL YOU ARE SIXTEEN LIKE US, BY THEN YOU WILL BE CERTAIN OF YOUR FUTURE.
WELL, WE ALL KNOW WHAT DIANA WILL BE. SHE IS TO BE QUEEN!
NO, SHE CANNOT! ONLY IMMORTALS CAN RULE. IT IS THE LAW OF ZEUS! AND SHE IS MORTAL LIKE THE REST OF US! SHE WILL DIE SOMEDAY!
SHHH, TROIA! THAT IS CRUEL!
I AM SORRY, DIANA, I DID NOT THINK--
DIANA?
THERE IS SOMETHING WRONG WITH THE ISLAND.

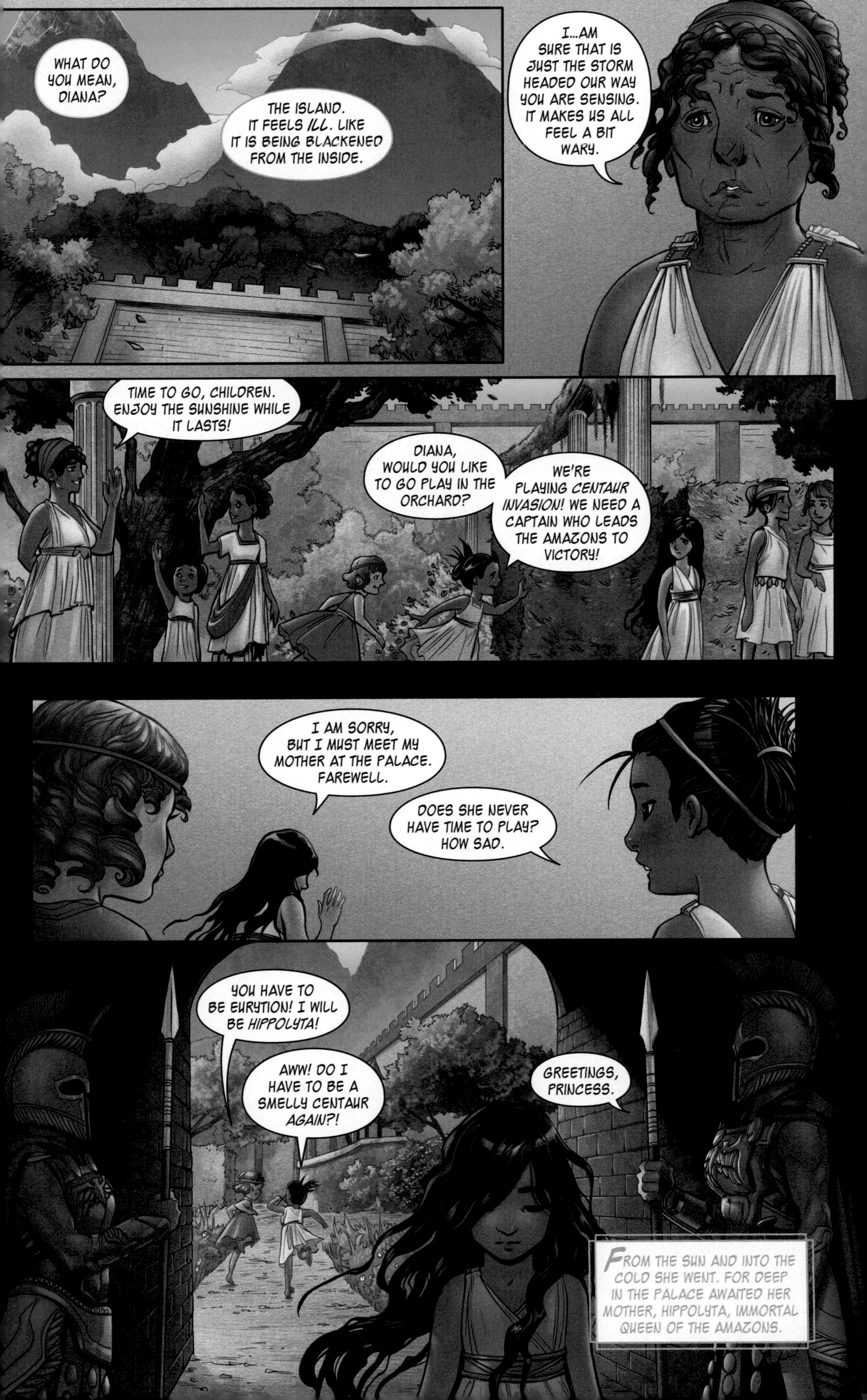
WHAT DO YOU MEAN, DIANA?
THE ISLAND. IT FEELS *ILL*. LIKE IT IS BEING BLACKENED FROM THE INSIDE.
I...AM SURE THAT IS JUST THE STORM HEADED OUR WAY YOU ARE SENSING. IT MAKES US ALL FEEL A BIT WARY.
TIME TO GO, CHILDREN. ENJOY THE SUNSHINE WHILE IT LASTS!
DIANA, WOULD YOU LIKE TO GO PLAY IN THE ORCHARD?
WE'RE PLAYING *CENTAUR INVASION*! WE NEED A CAPTAIN WHO LEADS THE AMAZONS TO VICTORY!
I AM SORRY, BUT I MUST MEET MY MOTHER AT THE PALACE. FAREWELL.
DOES SHE NEVER HAVE TIME TO PLAY? HOW SAD.
YOU HAVE TO BE EURYTION! I WILL BE *HIPPOLYTA*!
AWW! DO I HAVE TO BE A SMELLY CENTAUR *AGAIN*?!
GREETINGS, PRINCESS.
FROM THE SUN AND INTO THE COLD SHE WENT. FOR DEEP IN THE PALACE AWAITED HER MOTHER, HIPPOLYTA, IMMORTAL QUEEN OF THE AMAZONS.

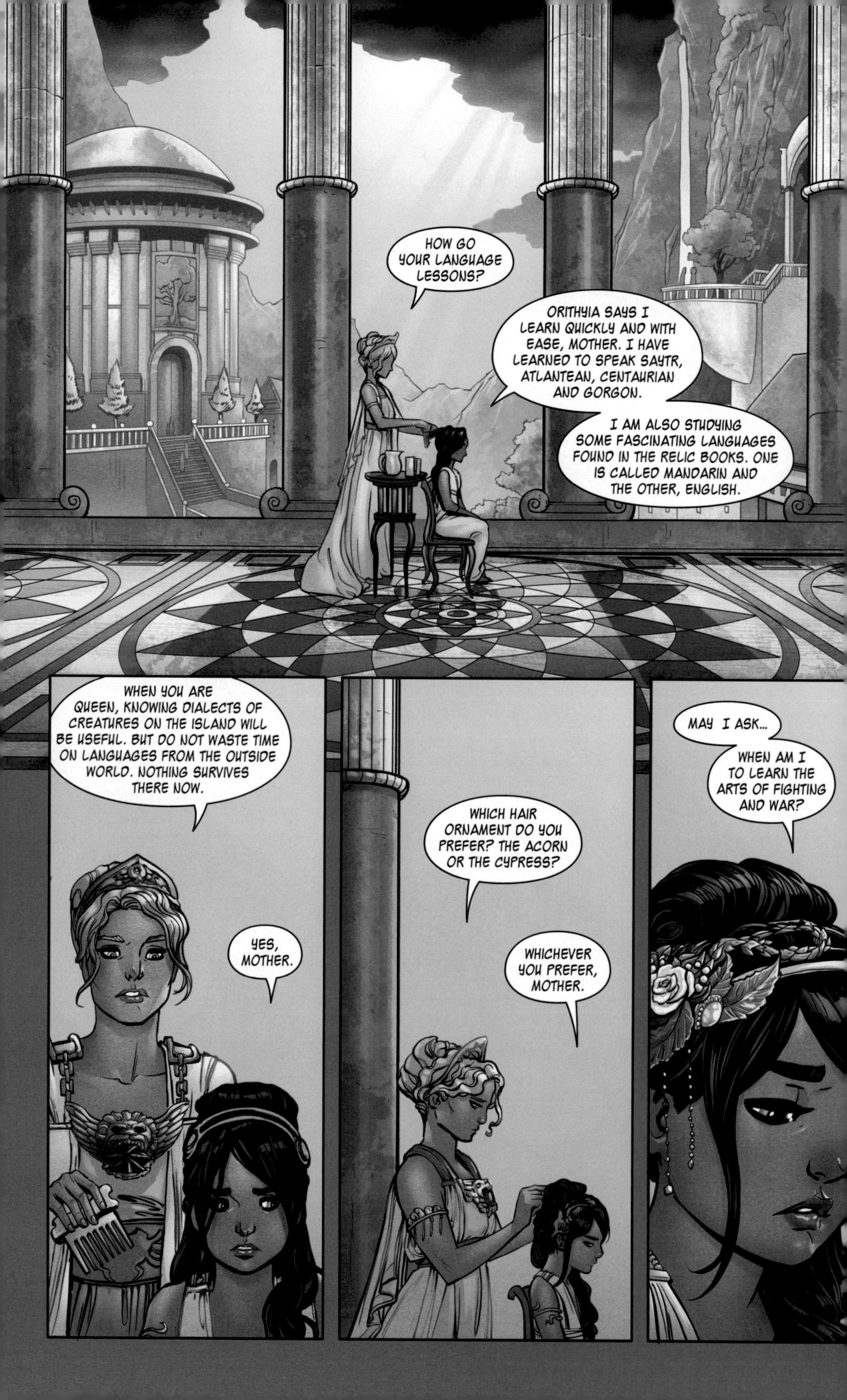
HOW GO YOUR LANGUAGE LESSONS?
ORITHYIA SAYS I LEARN QUICKLY AND WITH EASE, MOTHER. I HAVE LEARNED TO SPEAK SAYTR, ATLANTEAN, CENTAURIAN AND GORGON.
I AM ALSO STUDYING SOME FASCINATING LANGUAGES FOUND IN THE RELIC BOOKS. ONE IS CALLED MANDARIN AND THE OTHER, ENGLISH.
WHEN YOU ARE QUEEN, KNOWING DIALECTS OF CREATURES ON THE ISLAND WILL BE USEFUL. BUT DO NOT WASTE TIME ON LANGUAGES FROM THE OUTSIDE WORLD. NOTHING SURVIVES THERE NOW.
YES, MOTHER.
WHICH HAIR ORNAMENT DO YOU PREFER? THE ACORN OR THE CYPRESS?
WHICHEVER YOU PREFER, MOTHER.
MAY I ASK...
WHEN AM I TO LEARN THE ARTS OF FIGHTING AND WAR?

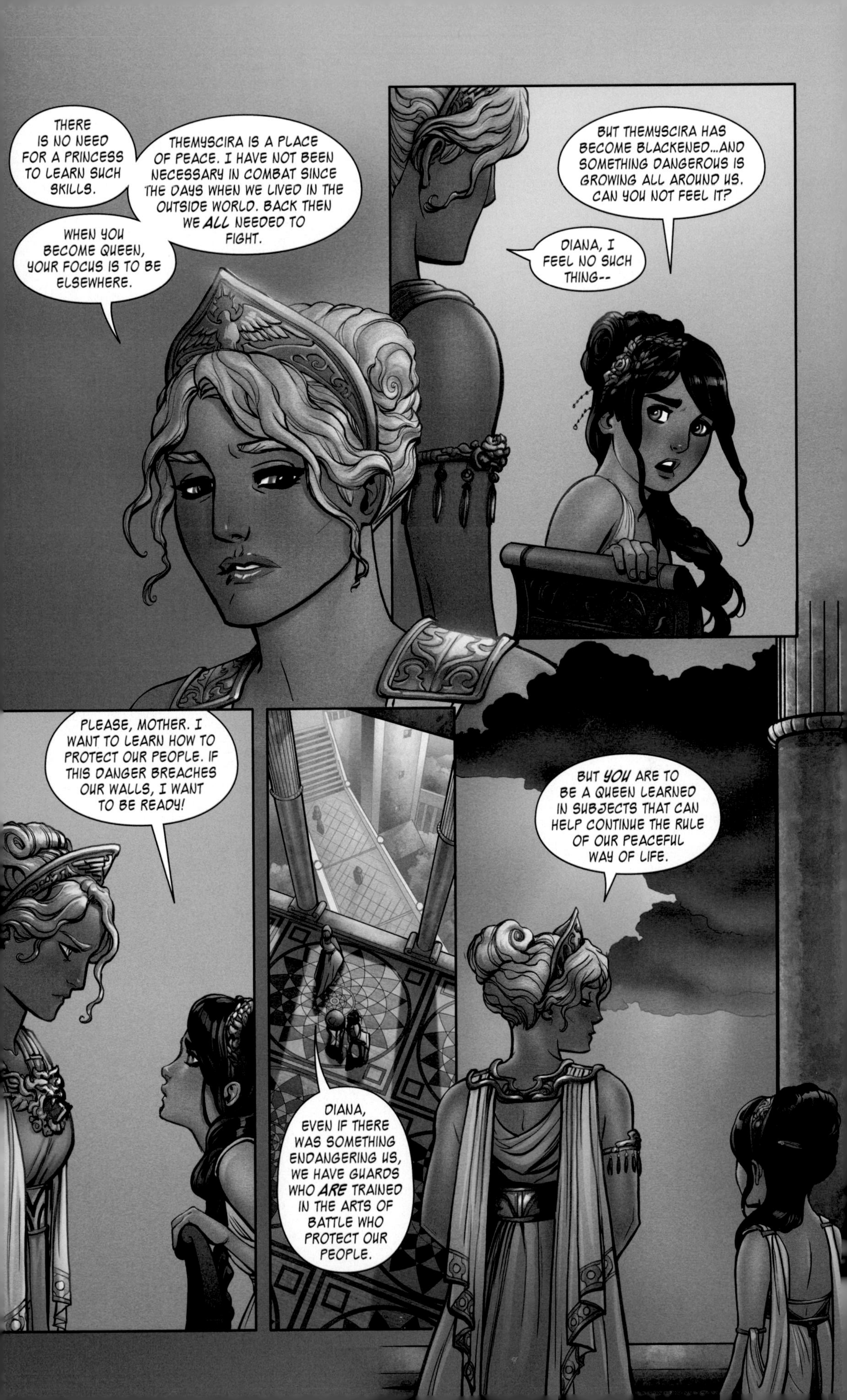
THERE IS NO NEED FOR A PRINCESS TO LEARN SUCH SKILLS.
THEMYSCIRA IS A PLACE OF PEACE. I HAVE NOT BEEN NECESSARY IN COMBAT SINCE THE DAYS WHEN WE LIVED IN THE OUTSIDE WORLD. BACK THEN WE ALL NEEDED TO FIGHT.
WHEN YOU BECOME QUEEN, YOUR FOCUS IS TO BE ELSEWHERE.
BUT THEMYSCIRA HAS BECOME BLACKENED...AND SOMETHING DANGEROUS IS GROWING ALL AROUND US. CAN YOU NOT FEEL IT?
DIANA, I FEEL NO SUCH THING--
PLEASE, MOTHER. I WANT TO LEARN HOW TO PROTECT OUR PEOPLE. IF THIS DANGER BREACHES OUR WALLS, I WANT TO BE READY!
DIANA, EVEN IF THERE WAS SOMETHING ENDANGERING US, WE HAVE GUARDS WHO ARE TRAINED IN THE ARTS OF BATTLE WHO PROTECT OUR PEOPLE.
BUT YOU ARE TO BE A QUEEN LEARNED IN SUBJECTS THAT CAN HELP CONTINUE THE RULE OF OUR PEACEFUL WAY OF LIFE.

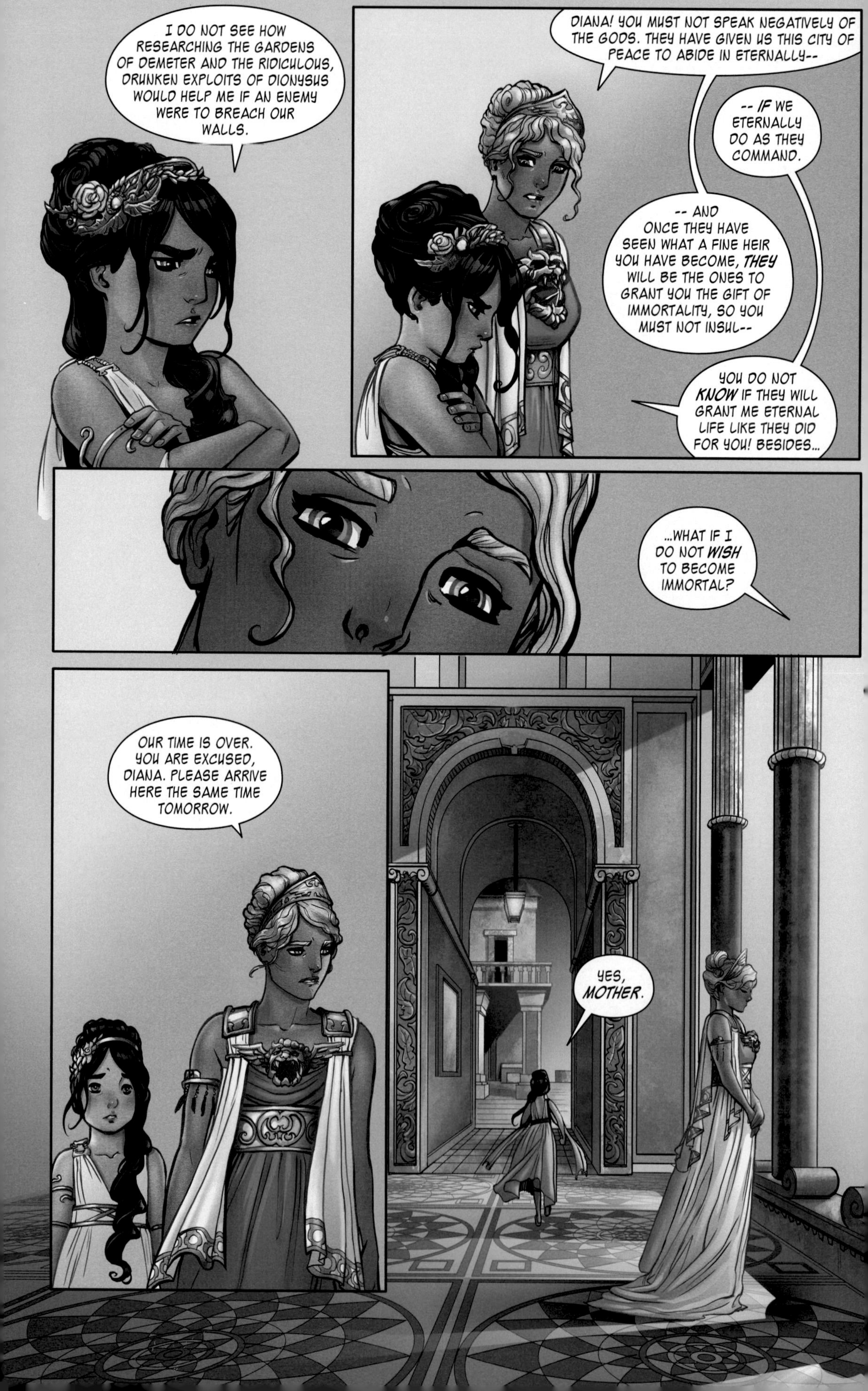
I DO NOT SEE HOW RESEARCHING THE GARDENS OF DEMETER AND THE RIDICULOUS, DRUNKEN EXPLOITS OF DIONYSUS WOULD HELP ME IF AN ENEMY WERE TO BREACH OUR WALLS.
DIANA! YOU MUST NOT SPEAK NEGATIVELY OF THE GODS. THEY HAVE GIVEN US THIS CITY OF PEACE TO ABIDE IN ETERNALLY--
-- IF WE ETERNALLY DO AS THEY COMMAND.
-- AND ONCE THEY HAVE SEEN WHAT A FINE HEIR YOU HAVE BECOME, THEY WILL BE THE ONES TO GRANT YOU THE GIFT OF IMMORTALITY, SO YOU MUST NOT INSUL--
YOU DO NOT KNOW IF THEY WILL GRANT ME ETERNAL LIFE LIKE THEY DID FOR YOU! BESIDES...
...WHAT IF I DO NOT WISH TO BECOME IMMORTAL?
OUR TIME IS OVER. YOU ARE EXCUSED, DIANA. PLEASE ARRIVE HERE THE SAME TIME TOMORROW.
YES, MOTHER.

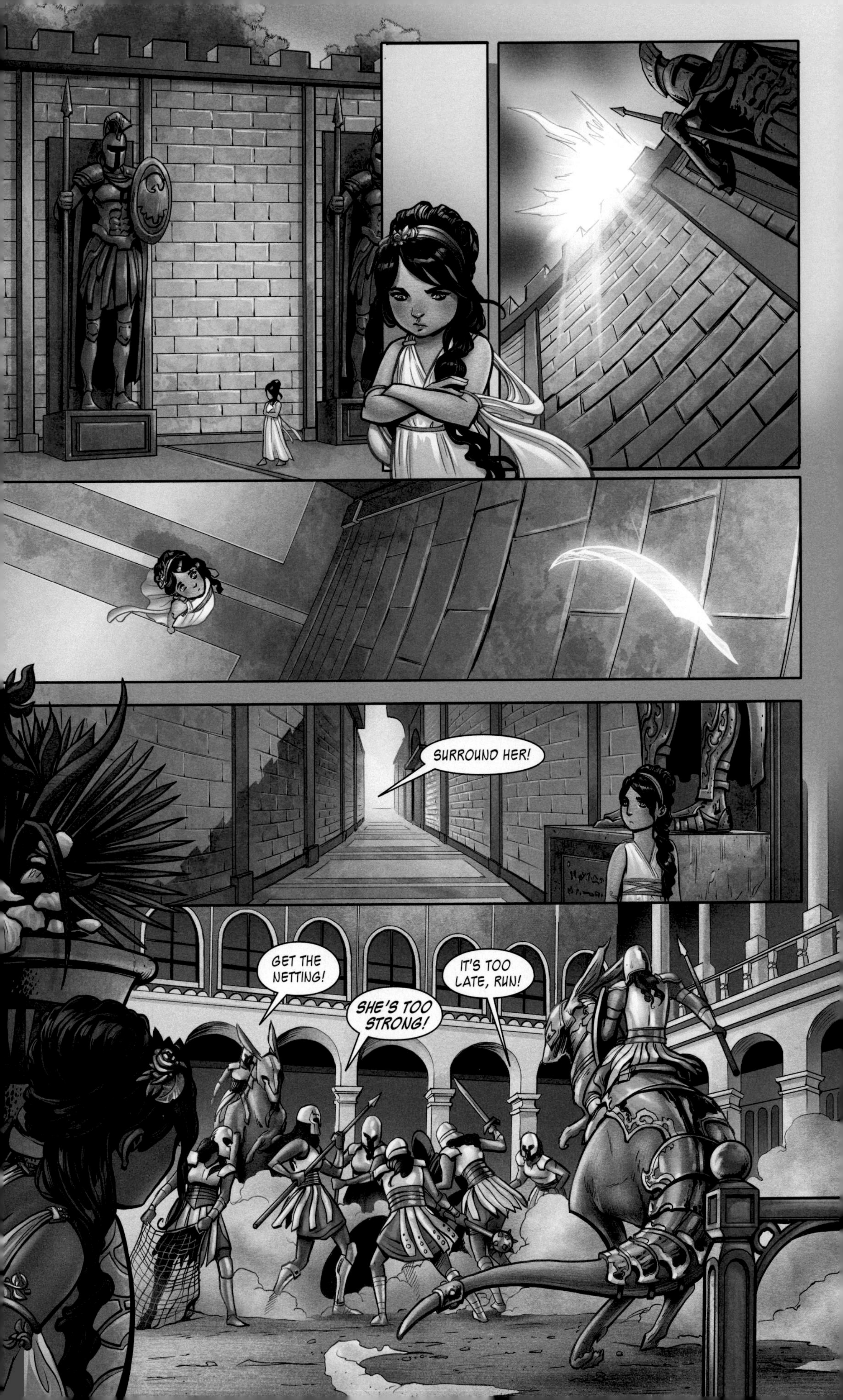
SURROUND HER!
GET THE NETTING!
SHE'S TOO STRONG!
IT'S TOO LATE, RUN!

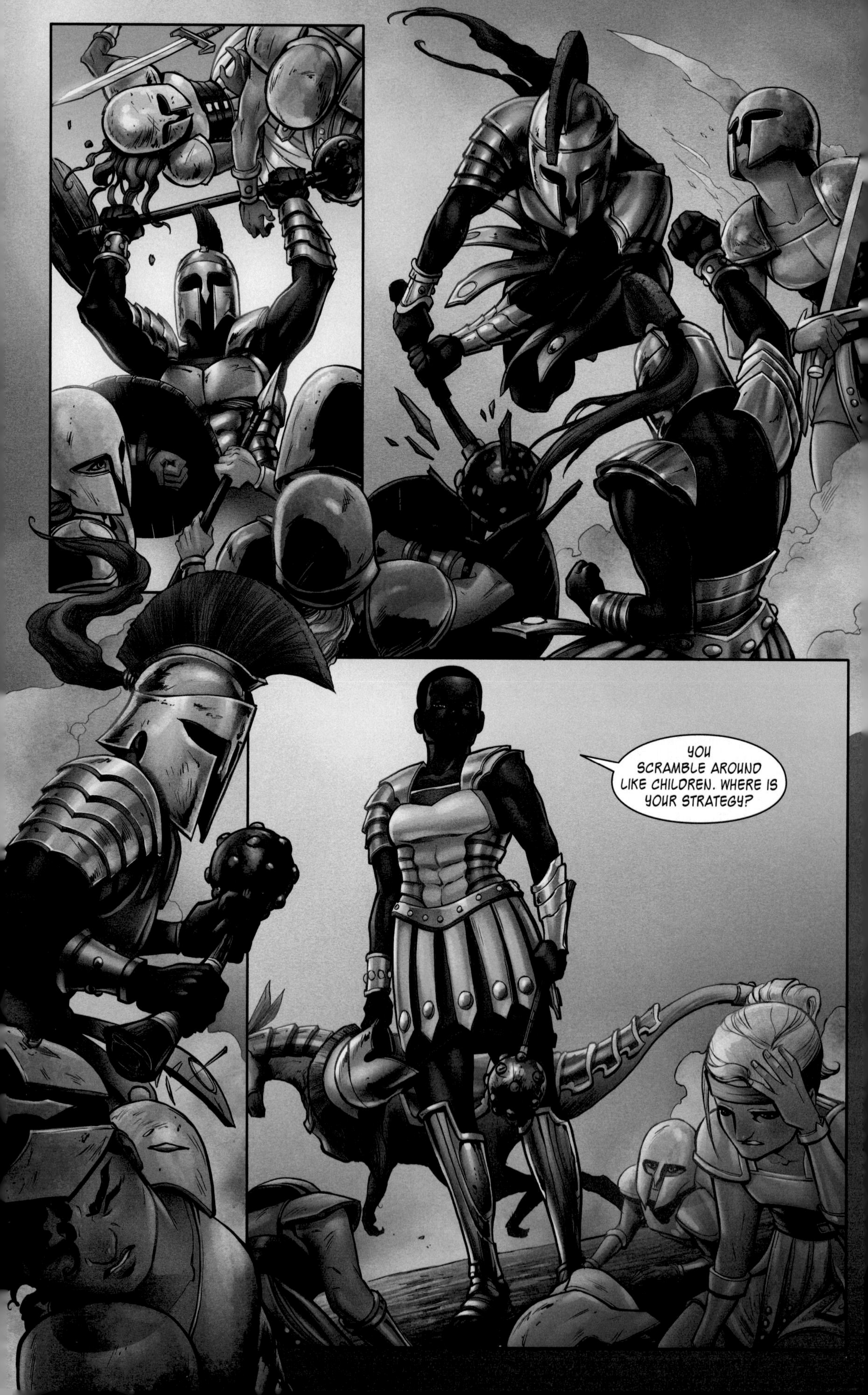
YOU SCRAMBLE AROUND LIKE CHILDREN. WHERE IS YOUR STRATEGY?

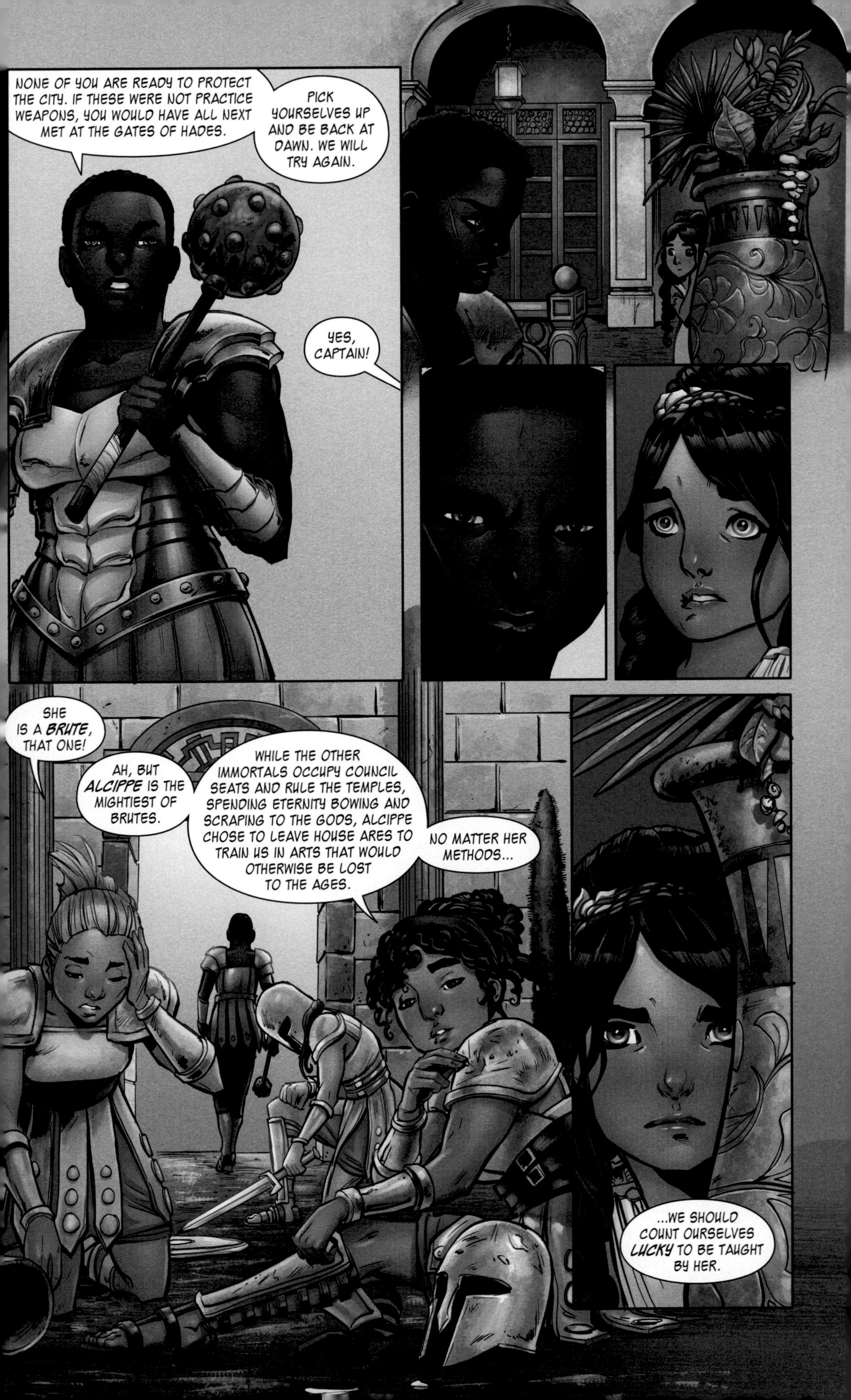
NONE OF YOU ARE READY TO PROTECT THE CITY. IF THESE WERE NOT PRACTICE WEAPONS, YOU WOULD HAVE ALL NEXT MET AT THE GATES OF HADES.
PICK YOURSELVES UP AND BE BACK AT DAWN. WE WILL TRY AGAIN.
YES, CAPTAIN!
SHE IS A BRUTE, THAT ONE!
AH, BUT ALCIPPE IS THE MIGHTIEST OF BRUTES.
WHILE THE OTHER IMMORTALS OCCUPY COUNCIL SEATS AND RULE THE TEMPLES, SPENDING ETERNITY BOWING AND SCRAPING TO THE GODS, ALCIPPE CHOSE TO LEAVE HOUSE ARES TO TRAIN US IN ARTS THAT WOULD OTHERWISE BE LOST TO THE AGES.
NO MATTER HER METHODS...
...WE SHOULD COUNT OURSELVES LUCKY TO BE TAUGHT BY HER.

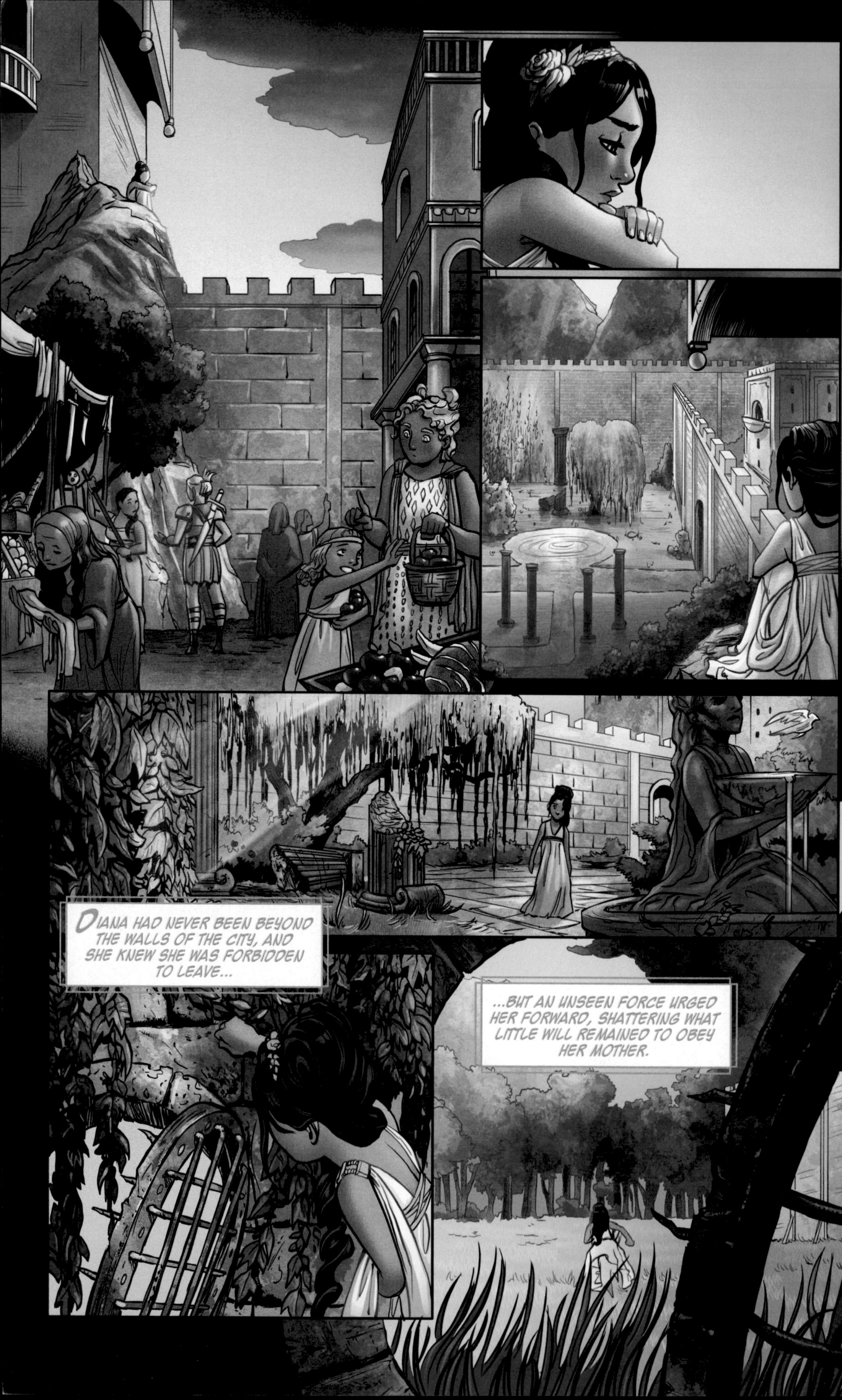
DIANA HAD NEVER BEEN BEYOND THE WALLS OF THE CITY, AND SHE KNEW SHE WAS FORBIDDEN TO LEAVE...
...BUT AN UNSEEN FORCE URGED HER FORWARD, SHATTERING WHAT LITTLE WILL REMAINED TO OBEY HER MOTHER.

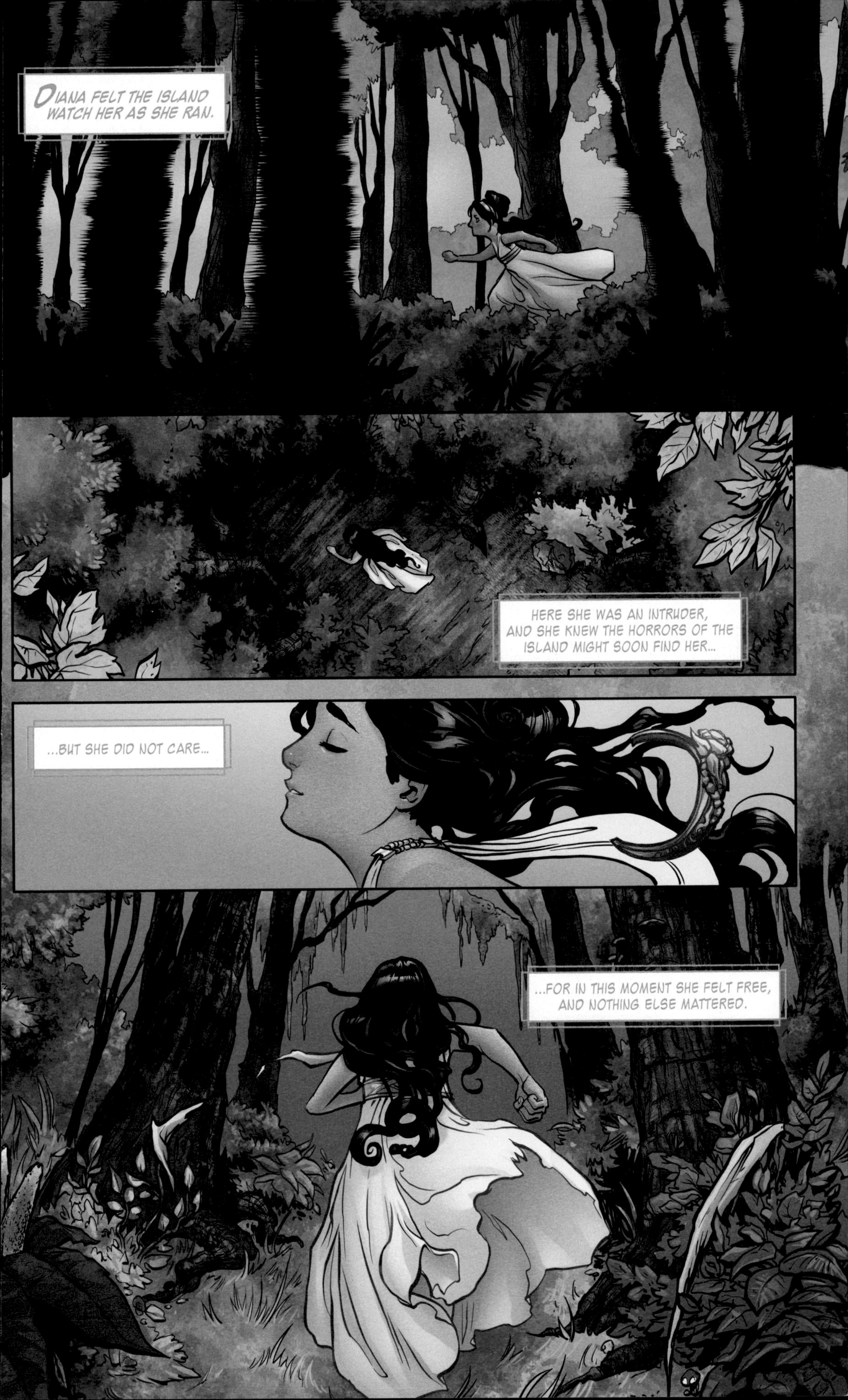
DIANA FELT THE ISLAND WATCH HER AS SHE RAN.
HERE SHE WAS AN INTRUDER, AND SHE KNEW THE HORRORS OF THE ISLAND MIGHT SOON FIND HER...
...BUT SHE DID NOT CARE...
...FOR IN THIS MOMENT SHE FELT FREE, AND NOTHING ELSE MATTERED.

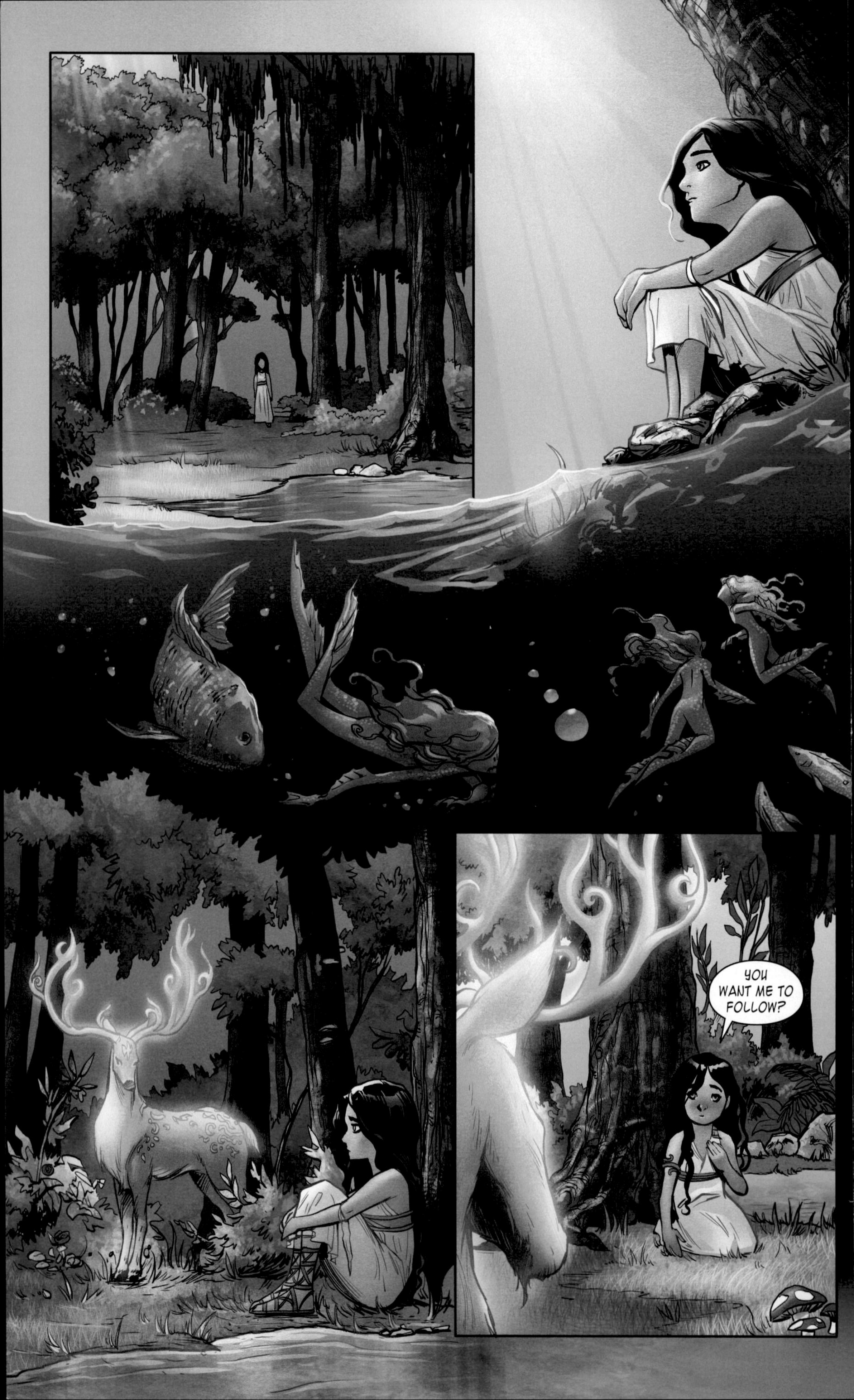
YOU WANT ME TO FOLLOW?

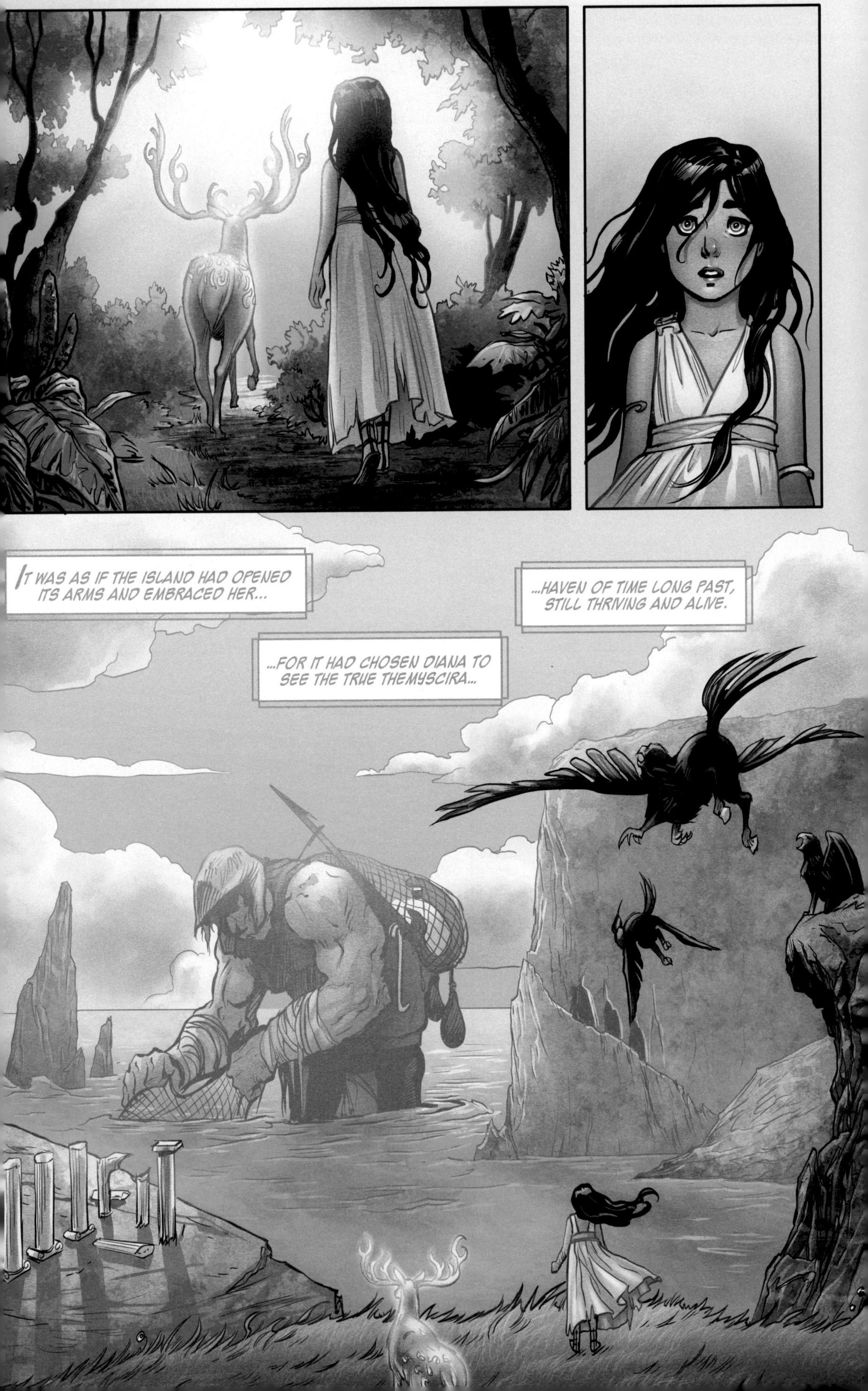
IT WAS AS IF THE ISLAND HAD OPENED ITS ARMS AND EMBRACED HER...
...FOR IT HAD CHOSEN DIANA TO SEE THE TRUE THEMYSCIRA...
...HAVEN OF TIME LONG PAST, STILL THRIVING AND ALIVE.

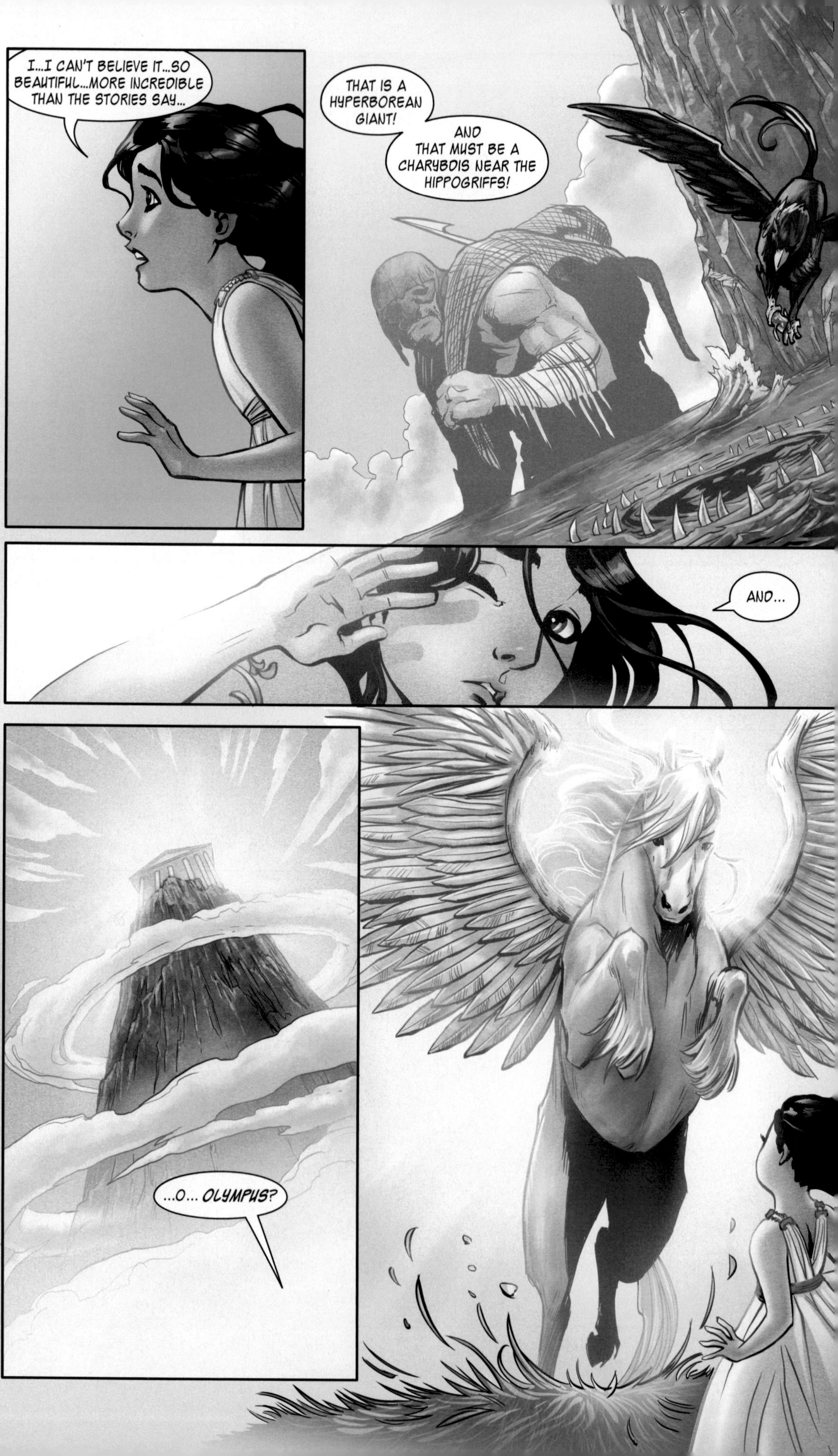
I...I CAN'T BELIEVE IT...SO BEAUTIFUL...MORE INCREDIBLE THAN THE STORIES SAY...
THAT IS A HYPERBOREAN GIANT!
AND THAT MUST BE A CHARYBOIS NEAR THE HIPPOGRIFFS!
AND...
...O... OLYMPUS?

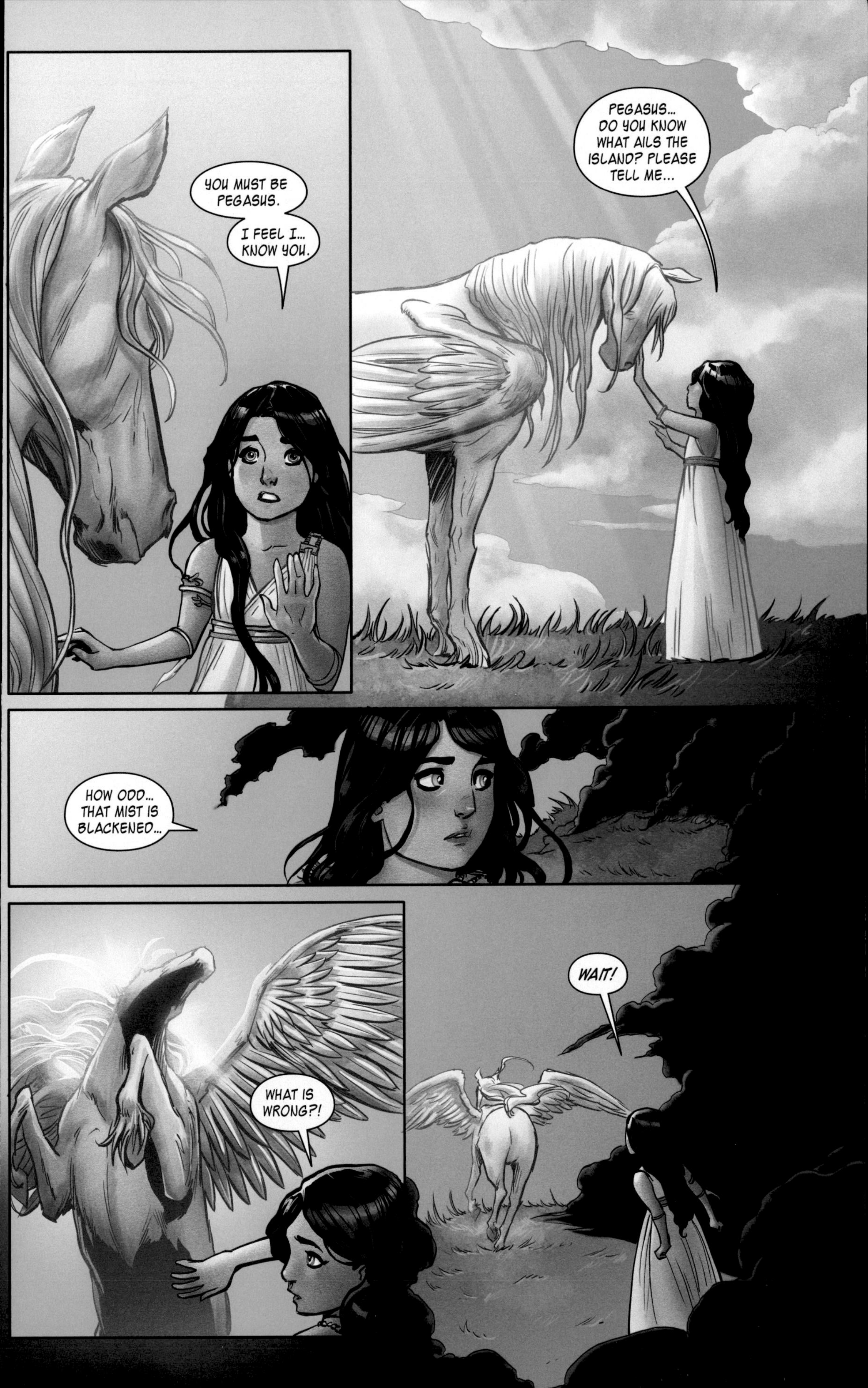
YOU MUST BE PEGASUS.
I FEEL I... KNOW YOU.
PEGASUS... DO YOU KNOW WHAT AILS THE ISLAND? PLEASE TELL ME...
HOW ODD... THAT MIST IS BLACKENED...
WHAT IS WRONG?!
WAIT!

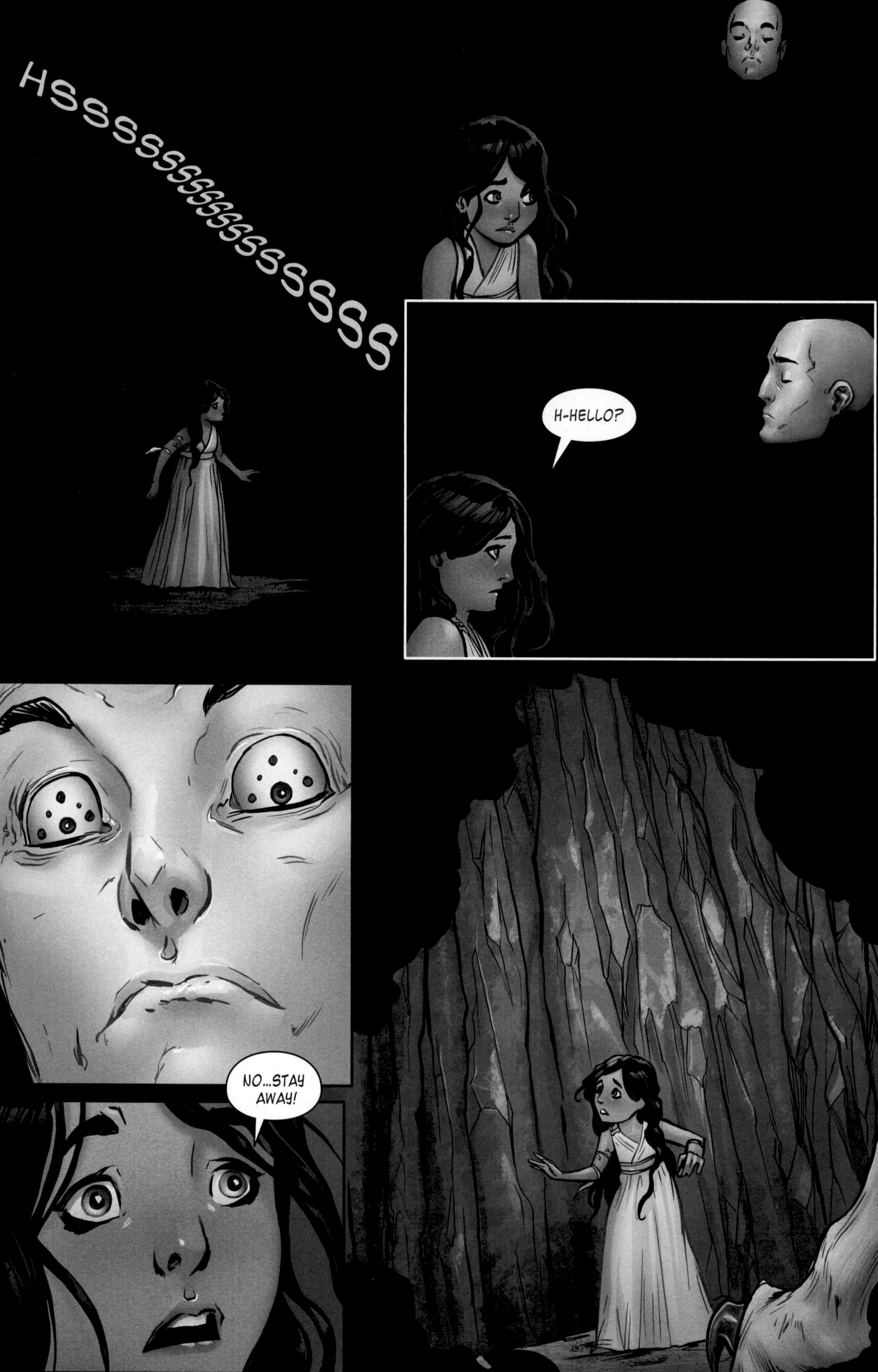
HSSSSSSSSSSSSSSSSSSS
H-HELLO?
NO...STAY AWAY!

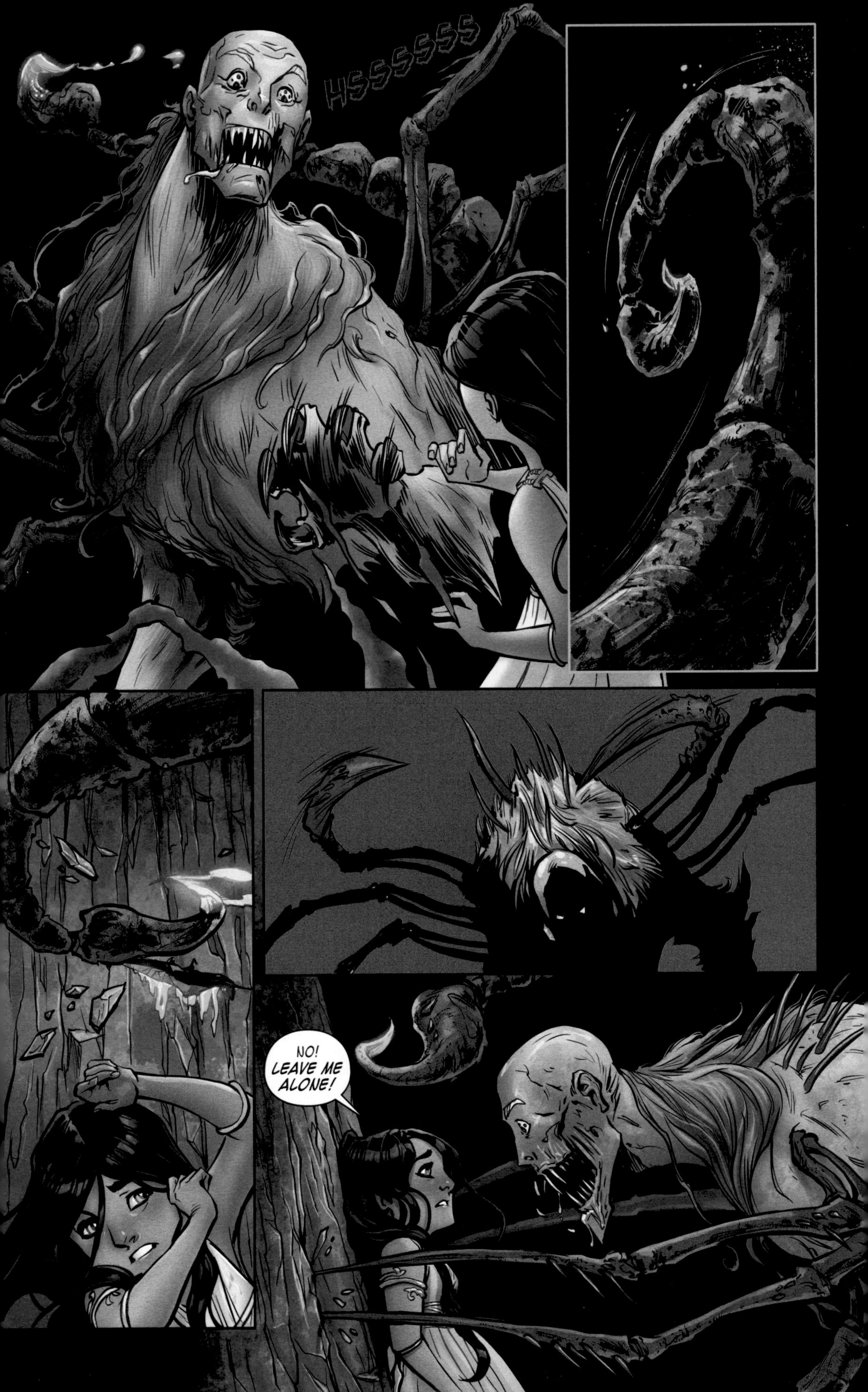
HSSSSSSS
NO! LEAVE ME ALONE!

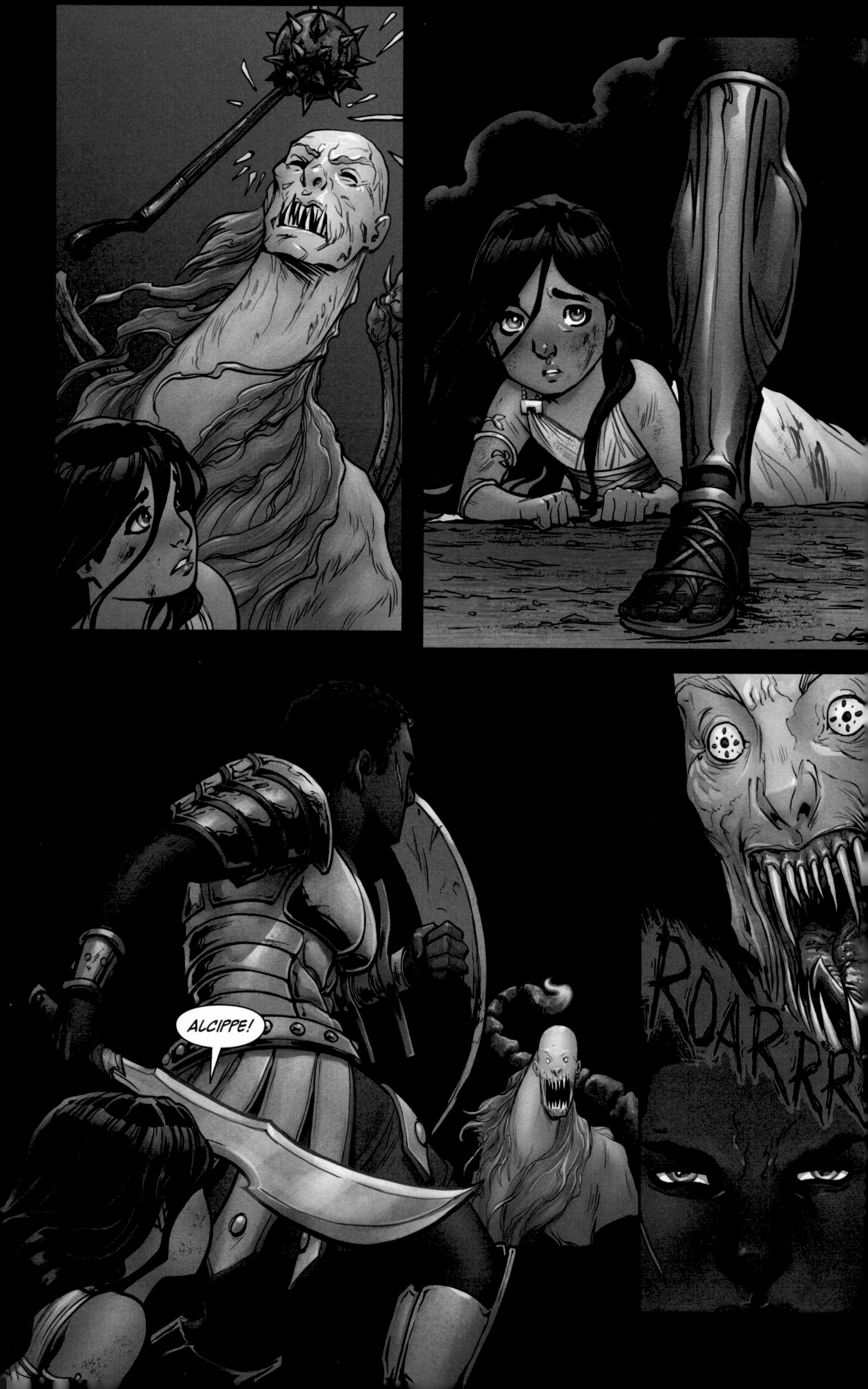
ALCIPPE!
ROARRR

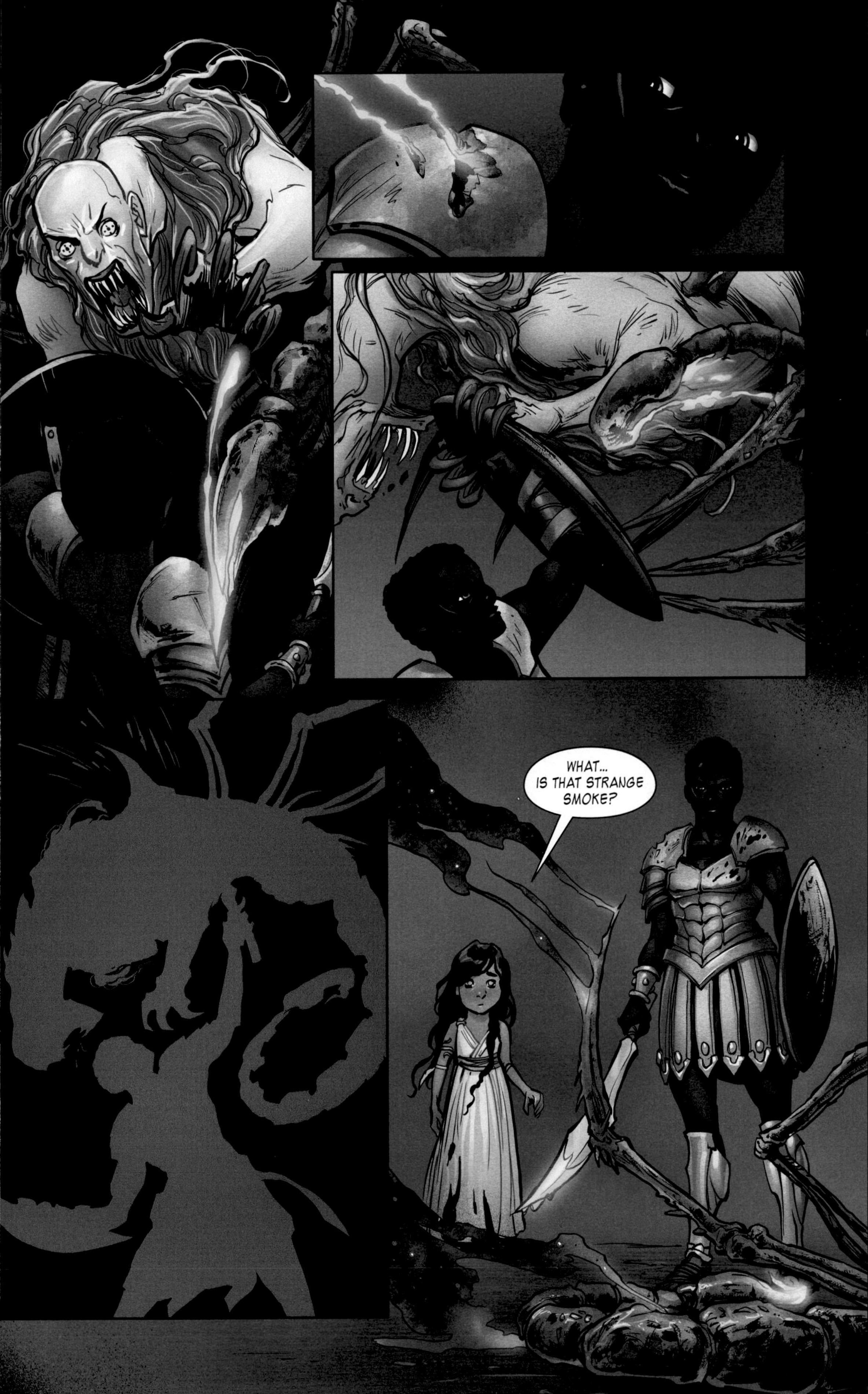
WHAT... IS THAT STRANGE SMOKE?

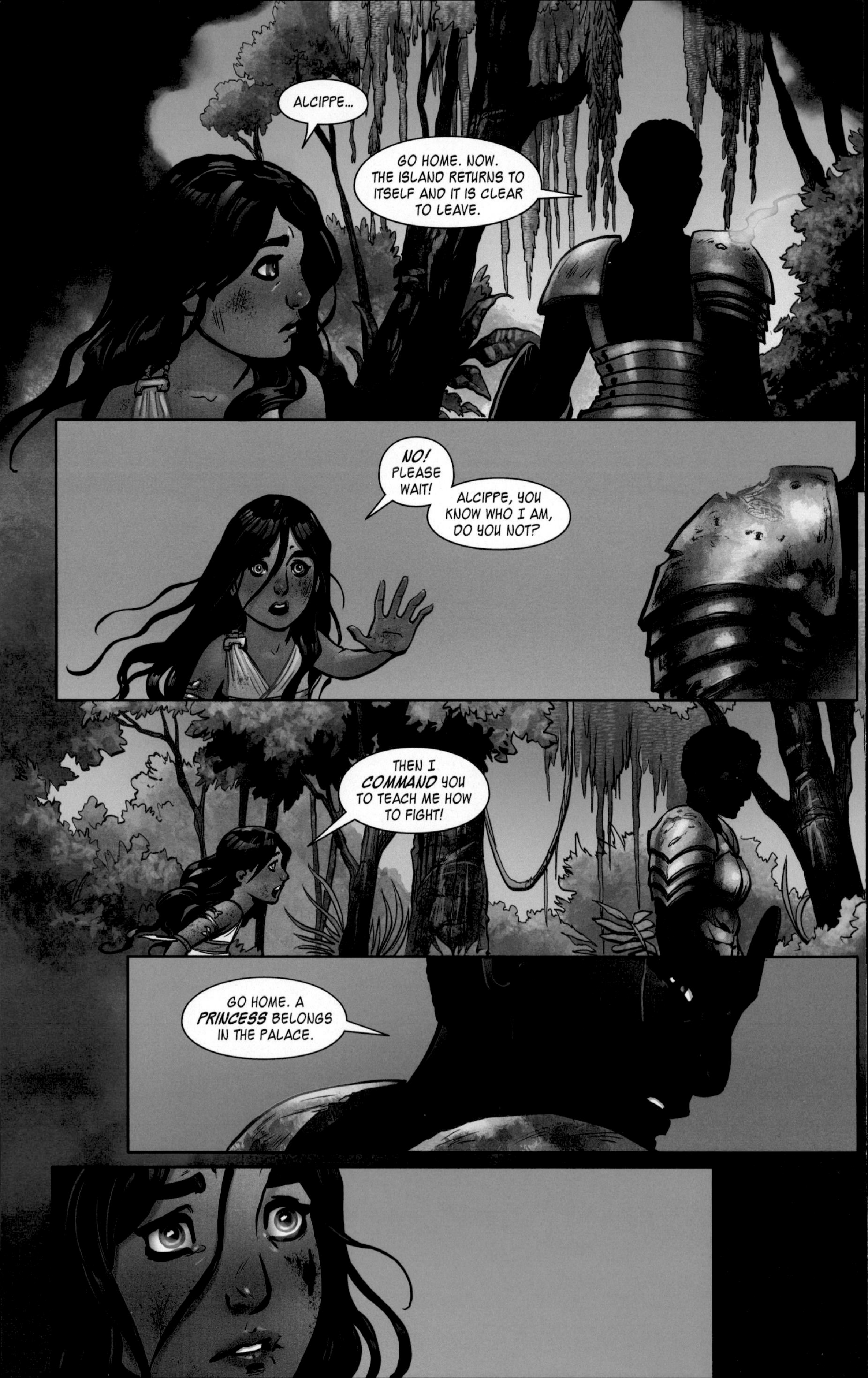
ALCIPPE...
GO HOME. NOW. THE ISLAND RETURNS TO ITSELF AND IT IS CLEAR TO LEAVE.
NO! PLEASE WAIT!
ALCIPPE, YOU KNOW WHO I AM, DO YOU NOT?
THEN I COMMAND YOU TO TEACH ME HOW TO FIGHT!
GO HOME. A PRINCESS BELONGS IN THE PALACE.

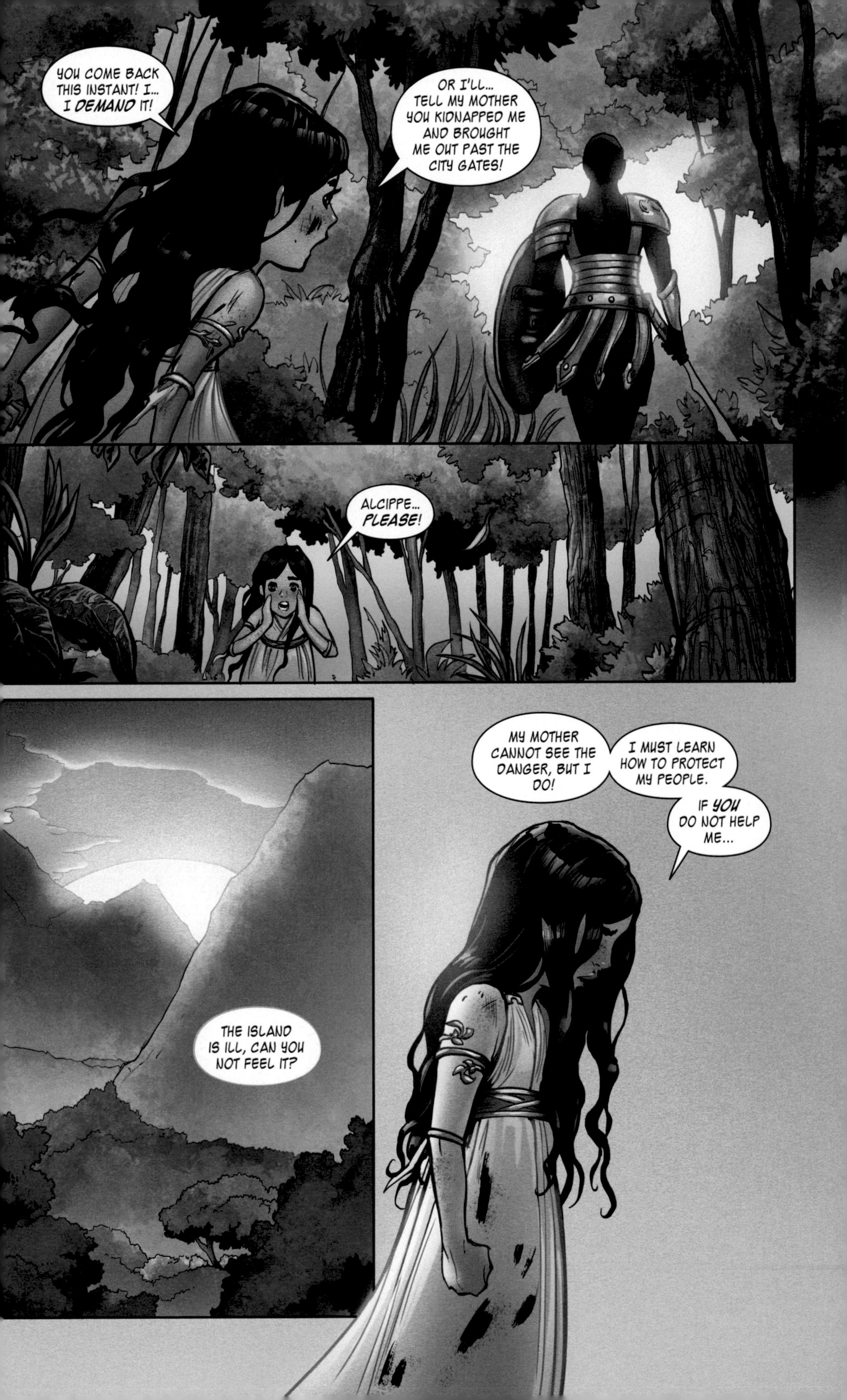
YOU COME BACK THIS INSTANT! I... I DEMAND IT!
OR I'LL... TELL MY MOTHER YOU KIDNAPPED ME AND BROUGHT ME OUT PAST THE CITY GATES!
ALCIPPE... PLEASE!
THE ISLAND IS ILL, CAN YOU NOT FEEL IT?
MY MOTHER CANNOT SEE THE DANGER, BUT I DO!
I MUST LEARN HOW TO PROTECT MY PEOPLE.
IF YOU DO NOT HELP ME...

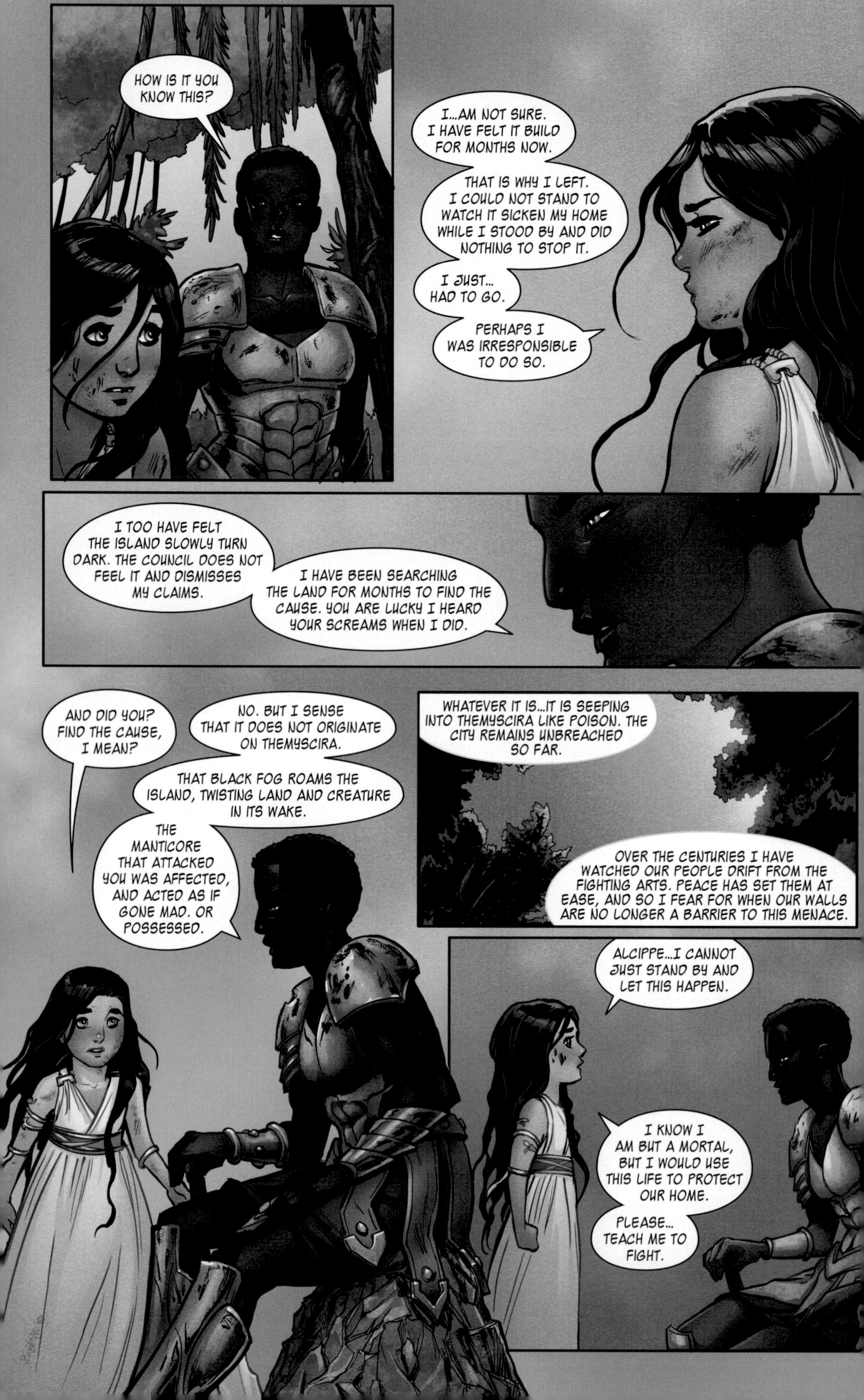

HOW IS IT YOU KNOW THIS?
I...AM NOT SURE. I HAVE FELT IT BUILD FOR MONTHS NOW.
THAT IS WHY I LEFT. I COULD NOT STAND TO WATCH IT SICKEN MY HOME WHILE I STOOD BY AND DID NOTHING TO STOP IT.
I JUST... HAD TO GO.
PERHAPS I WAS IRRESPONSIBLE TO DO SO.
I TOO HAVE FELT THE ISLAND SLOWLY TURN DARK. THE COUNCIL DOES NOT FEEL IT AND DISMISSES MY CLAIMS.
I HAVE BEEN SEARCHING THE LAND FOR MONTHS TO FIND THE CAUSE. YOU ARE LUCKY I HEARD YOUR SCREAMS WHEN I DID.
AND DID YOU? FIND THE CAUSE, I MEAN?
NO. BUT I SENSE THAT IT DOES NOT ORIGINATE ON THEMYSCIRA.
THAT BLACK FOG ROAMS THE ISLAND, TWISTING LAND AND CREATURE IN ITS WAKE.
THE MANTICORE THAT ATTACKED YOU WAS AFFECTED, AND ACTED AS IF GONE MAD. OR POSSESSED.
WHATEVER IT IS...IT IS SEEPING INTO THEMYSCIRA LIKE POISON. THE CITY REMAINS UNBREACHED SO FAR.
OVER THE CENTURIES I HAVE WATCHED OUR PEOPLE DRIFT FROM THE FIGHTING ARTS. PEACE HAS SET THEM AT EASE, AND SO I FEAR FOR WHEN OUR WALLS ARE NO LONGER A BARRIER TO THIS MENACE.
ALCIPPE...I CANNOT JUST STAND BY AND LET THIS HAPPEN.
I KNOW I AM BUT A MORTAL, BUT I WOULD USE THIS LIFE TO PROTECT OUR HOME.
PLEASE... TEACH ME TO FIGHT.

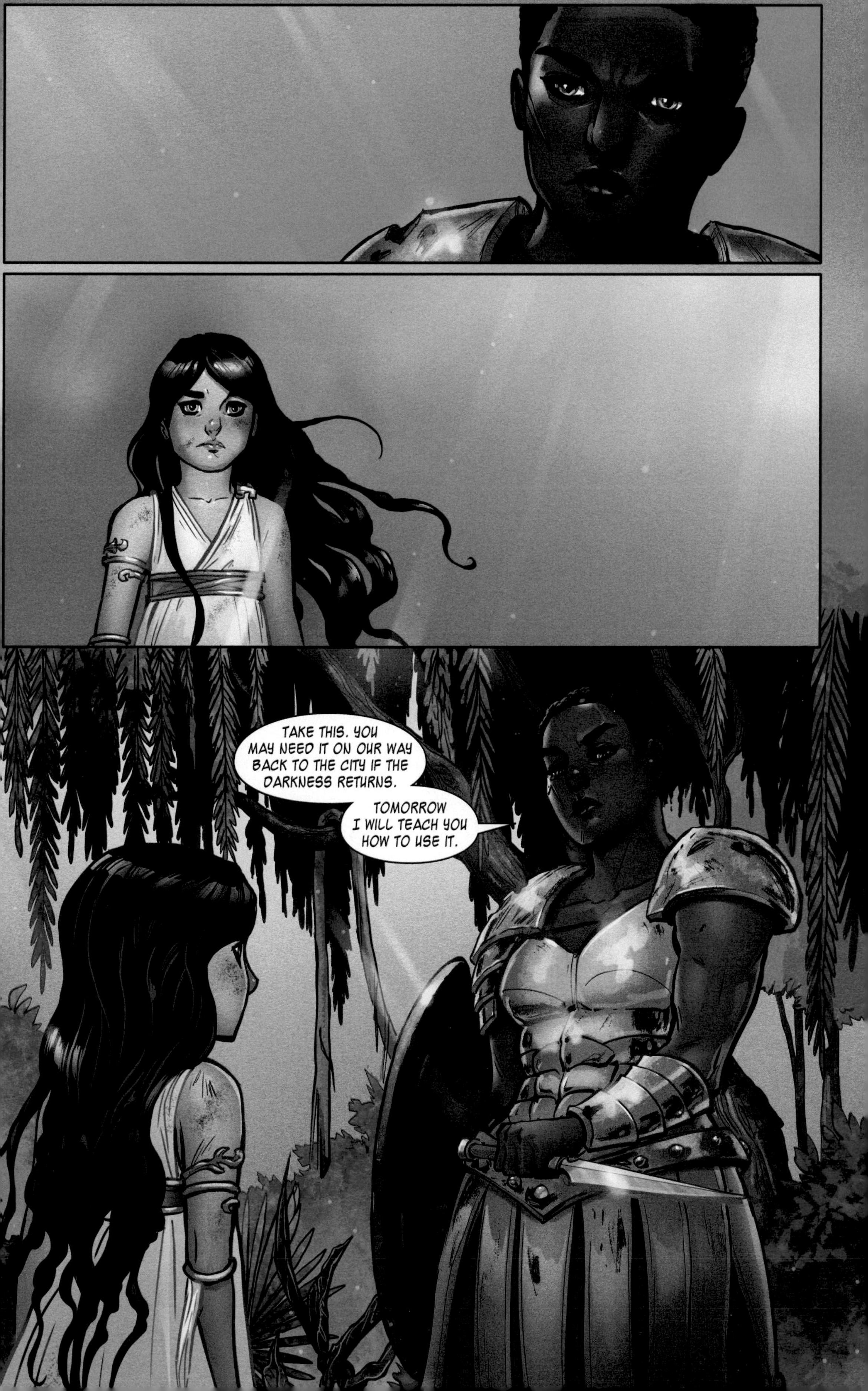
TAKE THIS. YOU MAY NEED IT ON OUR WAY BACK TO THE CITY IF THE DARKNESS RETURNS.
TOMORROW I WILL TEACH YOU HOW TO USE IT.

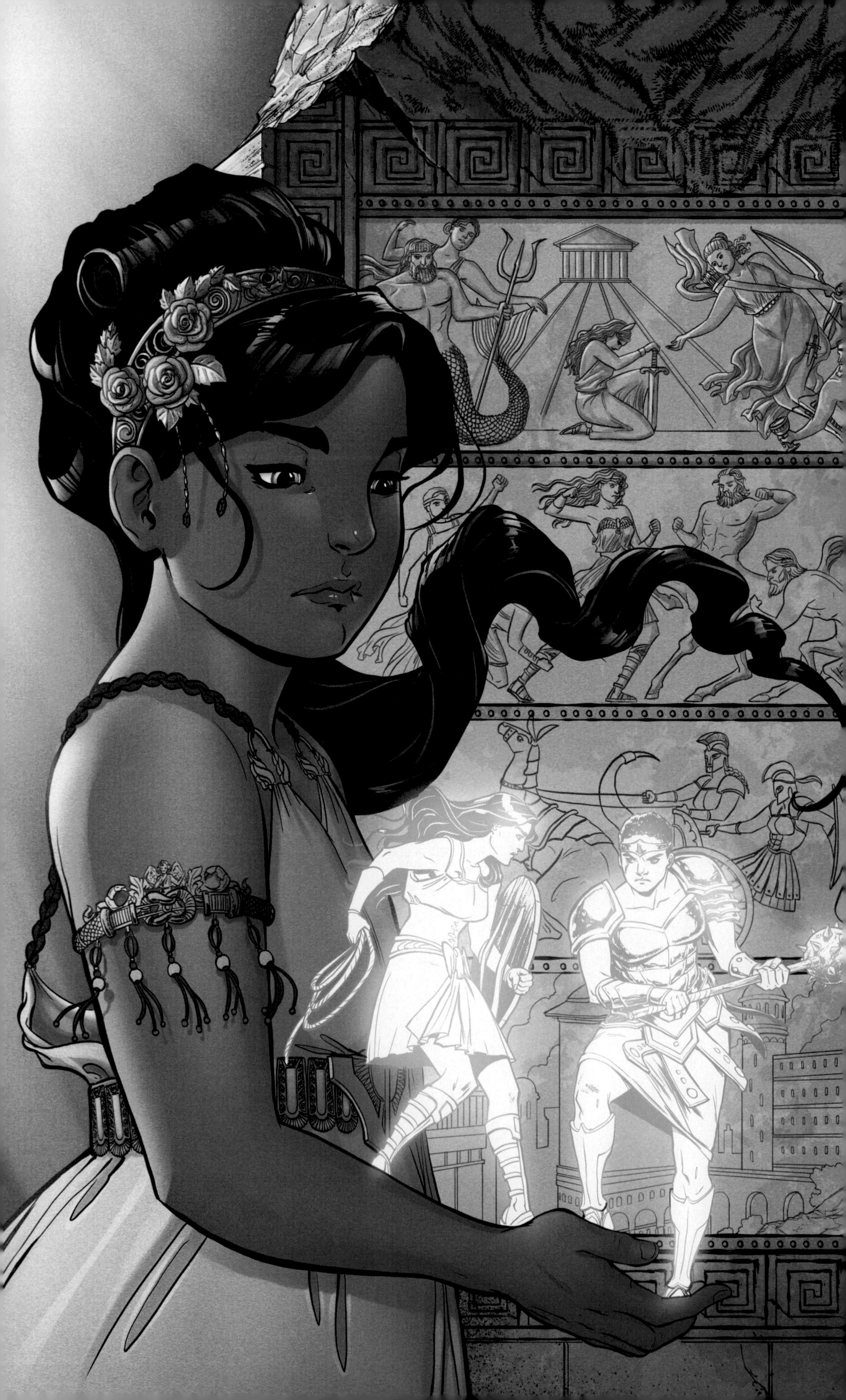

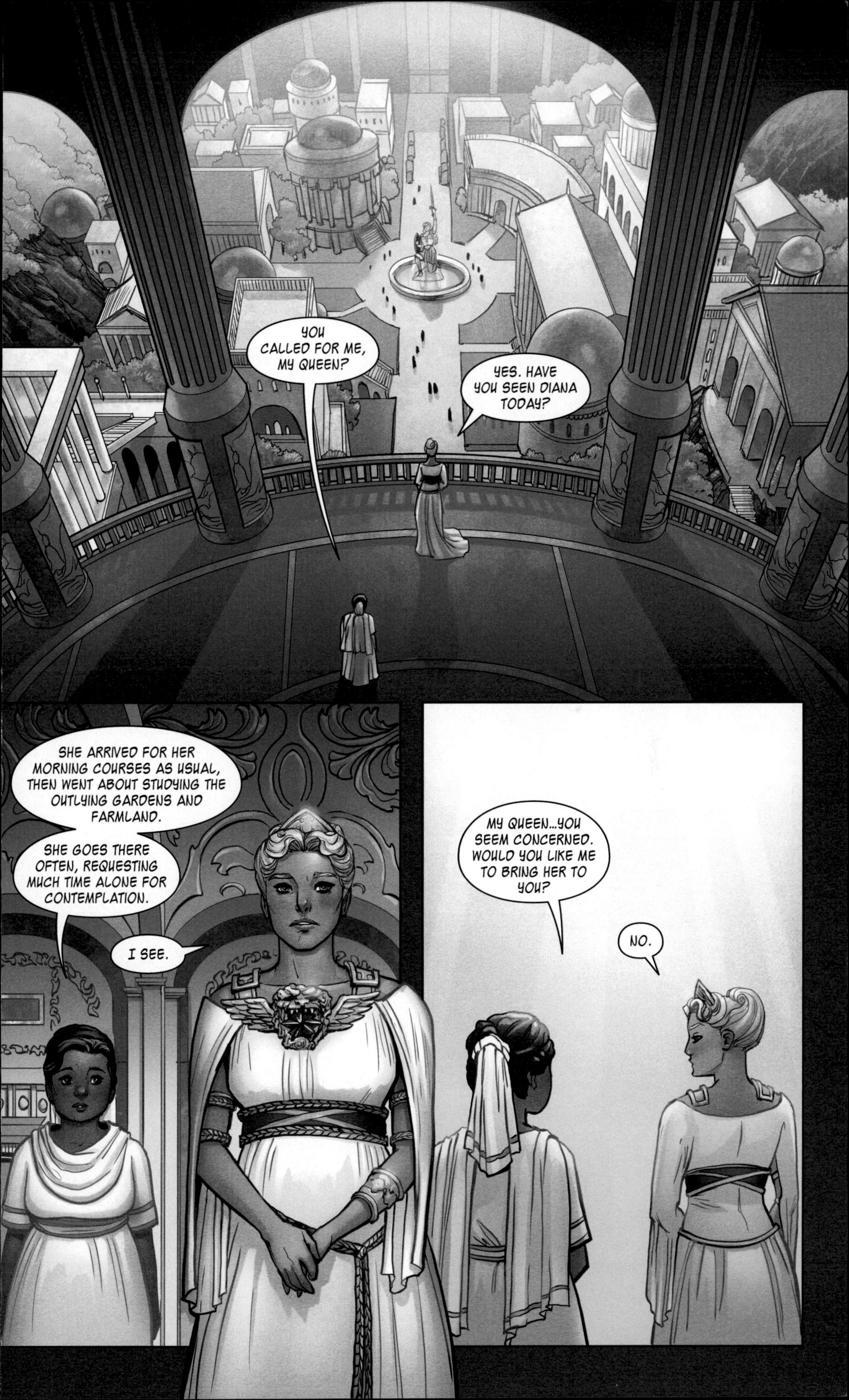
YOU CALLED FOR ME, MY QUEEN?
YES. HAVE YOU SEEN DIANA TODAY?
SHE ARRIVED FOR HER MORNING COURSES AS USUAL, THEN WENT ABOUT STUDYING THE OUTLYING GARDENS AND FARMLAND.
SHE GOES THERE OFTEN, REQUESTING MUCH TIME ALONE FOR CONTEMPLATION.
I SEE.
MY QUEEN...YOU SEEM CONCERNED. WOULD YOU LIKE ME TO BRING HER TO YOU?
NO.

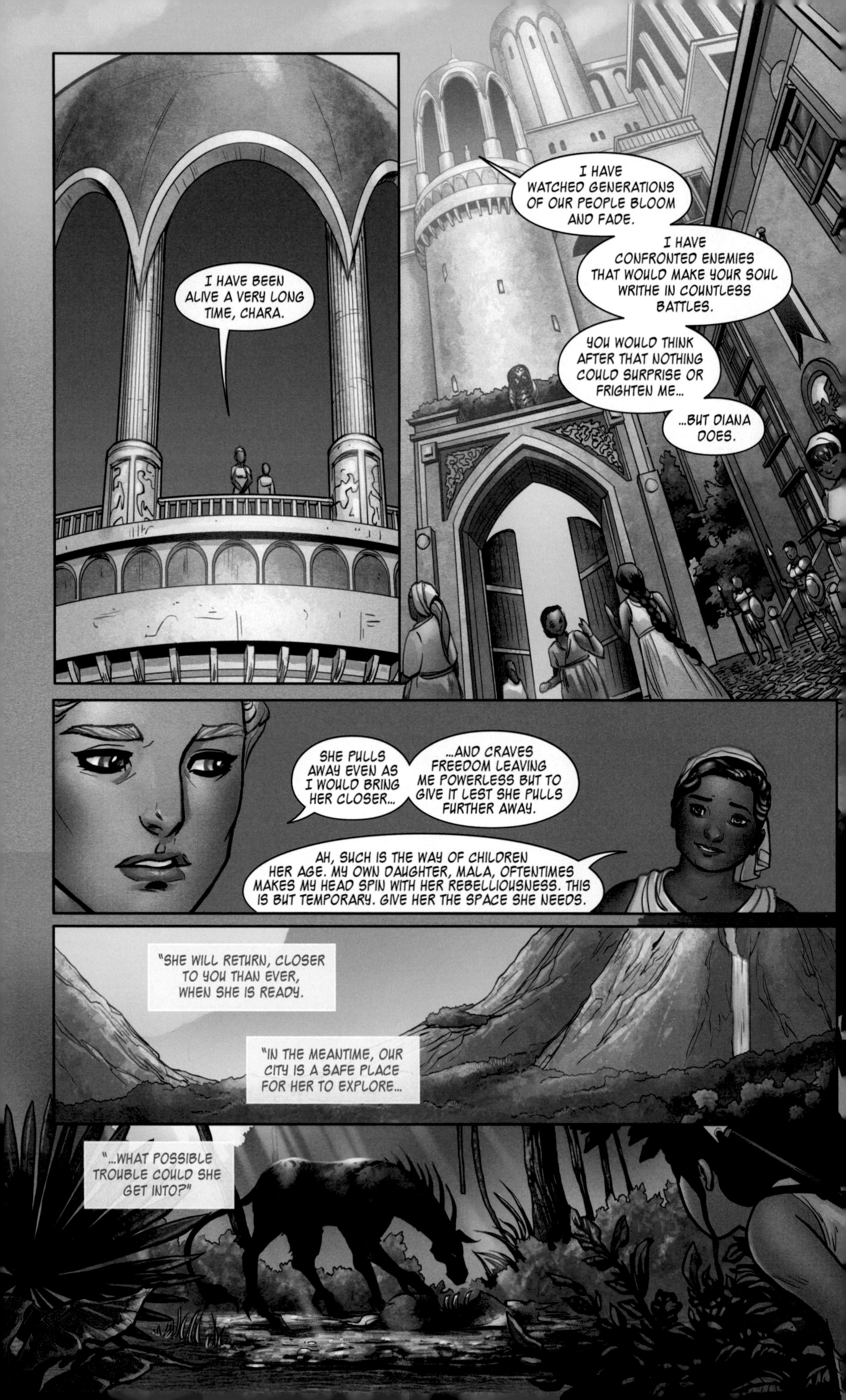
I HAVE BEEN ALIVE A VERY LONG TIME, CHARA.
I HAVE WATCHED GENERATIONS OF OUR PEOPLE BLOOM AND FADE.
I HAVE CONFRONTED ENEMIES THAT WOULD MAKE YOUR SOUL WRITHE IN COUNTLESS BATTLES.
YOU WOULD THINK AFTER THAT NOTHING COULD SURPRISE OR FRIGHTEN ME...
...BUT DIANA DOES.
SHE PULLS AWAY EVEN AS I WOULD BRING HER CLOSER...
...AND CRAVES FREEDOM LEAVING ME POWERLESS BUT TO GIVE IT LEST SHE PULLS FURTHER AWAY.
AH, SUCH IS THE WAY OF CHILDREN HER AGE. MY OWN DAUGHTER, MALA, OFTENTIMES MAKES MY HEAD SPIN WITH HER REBELLIOUSNESS. THIS IS BUT TEMPORARY. GIVE HER THE SPACE SHE NEEDS.
"SHE WILL RETURN, CLOSER TO YOU THAN EVER, WHEN SHE IS READY.
"IN THE MEANTIME, OUR CITY IS A SAFE PLACE FOR HER TO EXPLORE...
"...WHAT POSSIBLE TROUBLE COULD SHE GET INTO?"

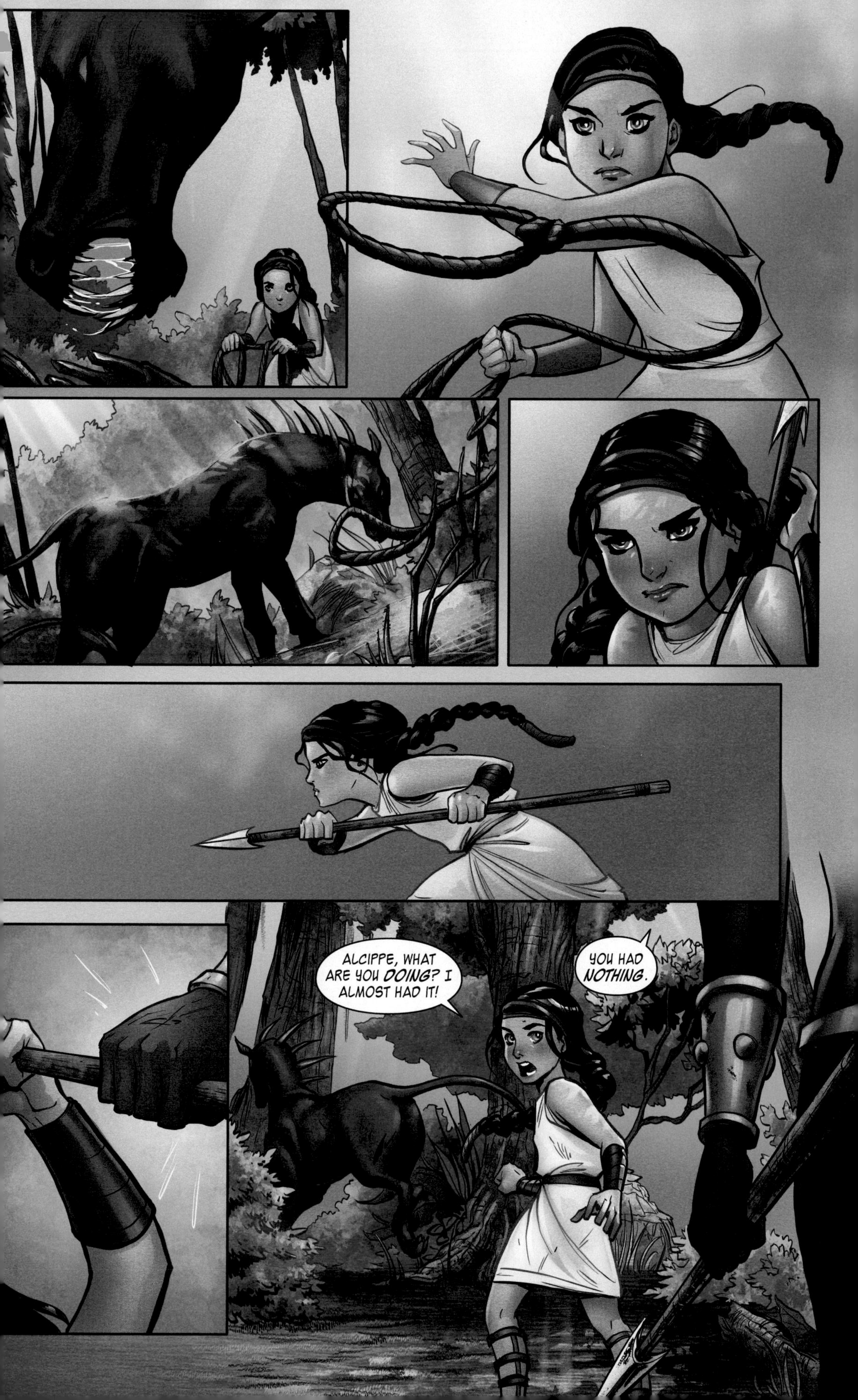
ALCIPPE, WHAT ARE YOU DOING? I ALMOST HAD IT!
YOU HAD NOTHING.

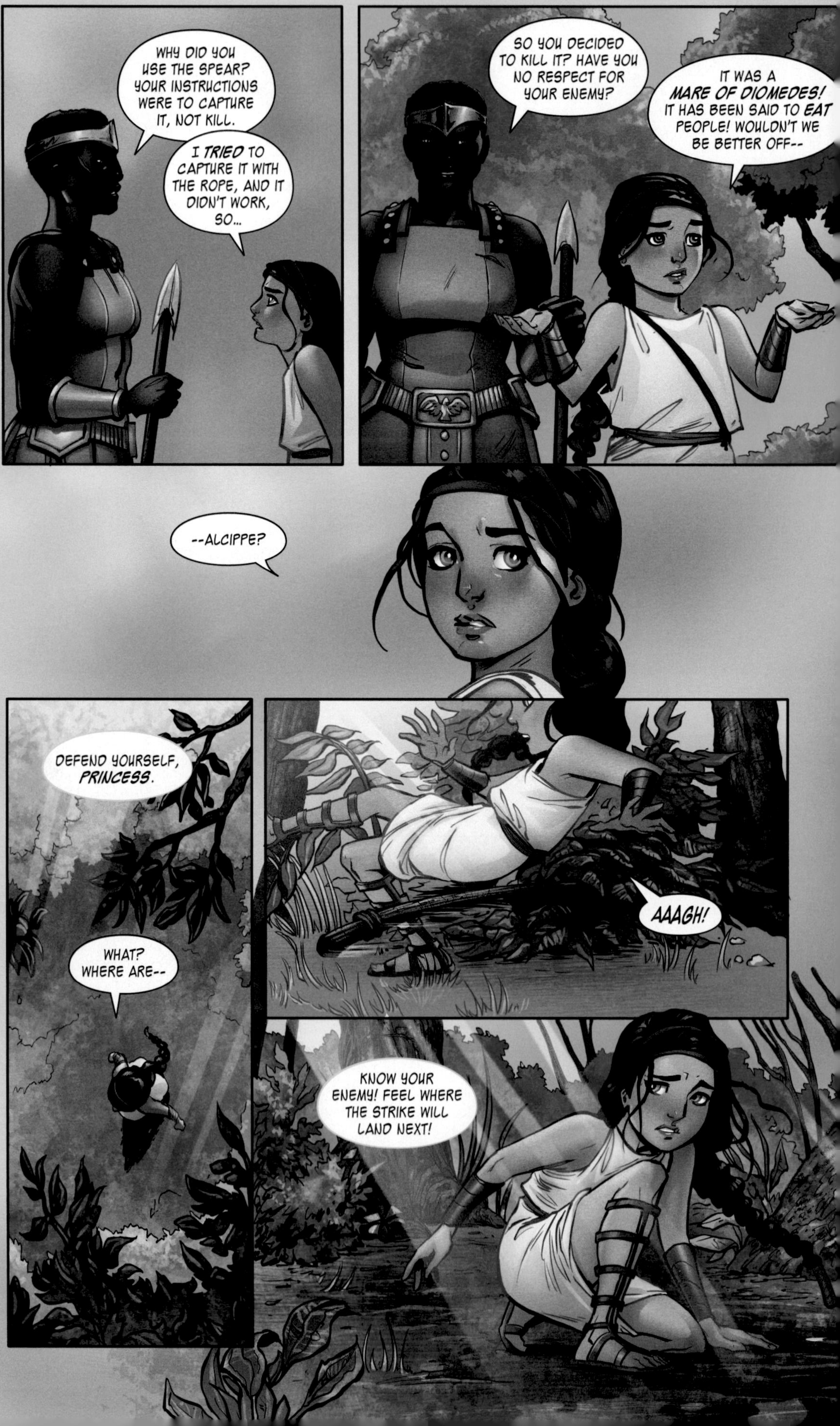
WHY DID YOU USE THE SPEAR? YOUR INSTRUCTIONS WERE TO CAPTURE IT, NOT KILL.
I TRIED TO CAPTURE IT WITH THE ROPE, AND IT DIDN'T WORK, SO...
SO YOU DECIDED TO KILL IT? HAVE YOU NO RESPECT FOR YOUR ENEMY?
IT WAS A MARE OF DIOMEDES! IT HAS BEEN SAID TO EAT PEOPLE! WOULDN'T WE BE BETTER OFF--
--ALCIPPE?
DEFEND YOURSELF, PRINCESS.
WHAT? WHERE ARE--
AAAGH!
KNOW YOUR ENEMY! FEEL WHERE THE STRIKE WILL LAND NEXT!

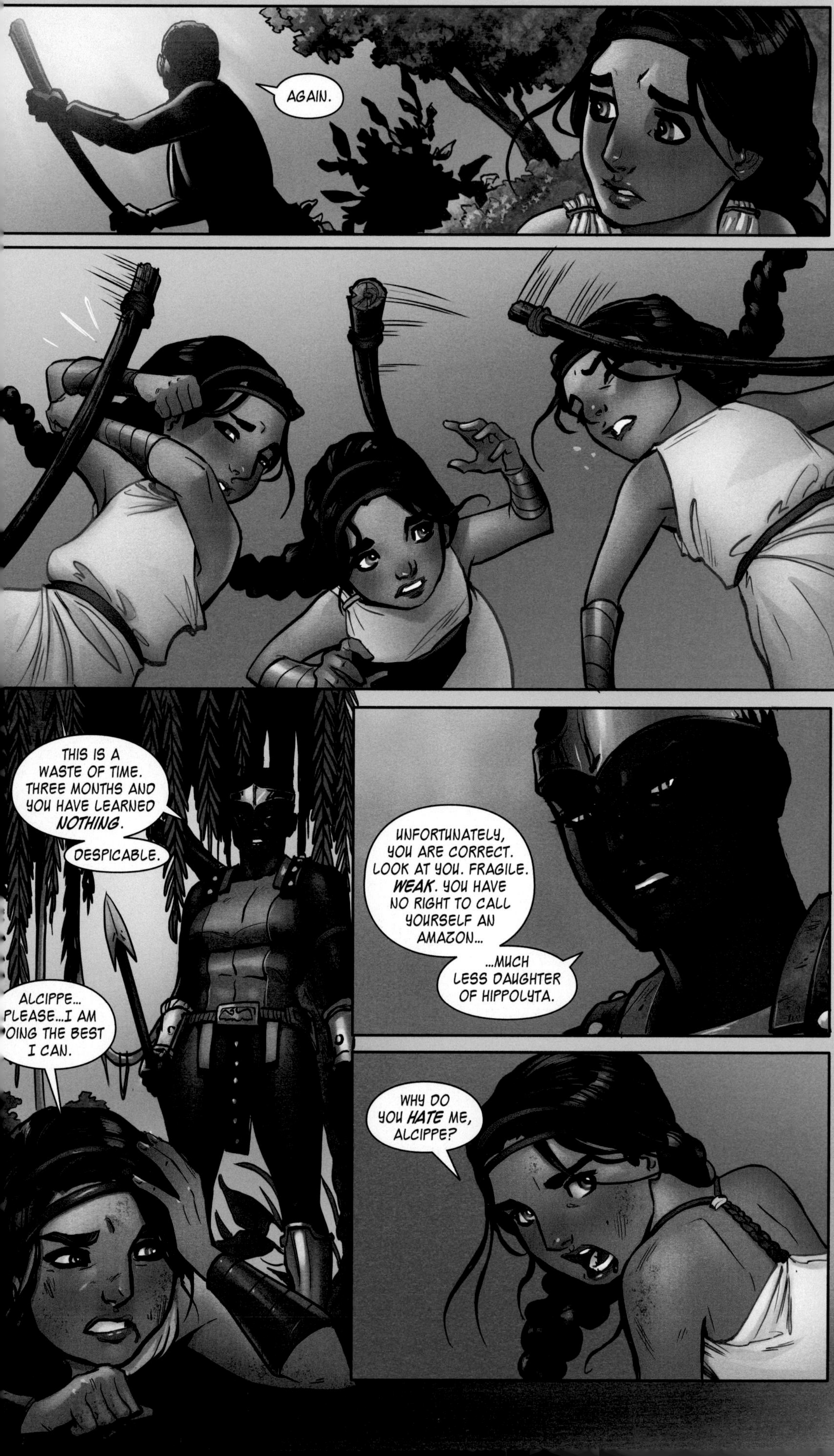

AGAIN.
THIS IS A WASTE OF TIME. THREE MONTHS AND YOU HAVE LEARNED NOTHING.
DESPICABLE.
ALCIPPE... PLEASE...I AM OING THE BEST I CAN.
UNFORTUNATELY, YOU ARE CORRECT. LOOK AT YOU. FRAGILE. WEAK. YOU HAVE NO RIGHT TO CALL YOURSELF AN AMAZON...
...MUCH LESS DAUGHTER OF HIPPOLYTA.
WHY DO YOU HATE ME, ALCIPPE?

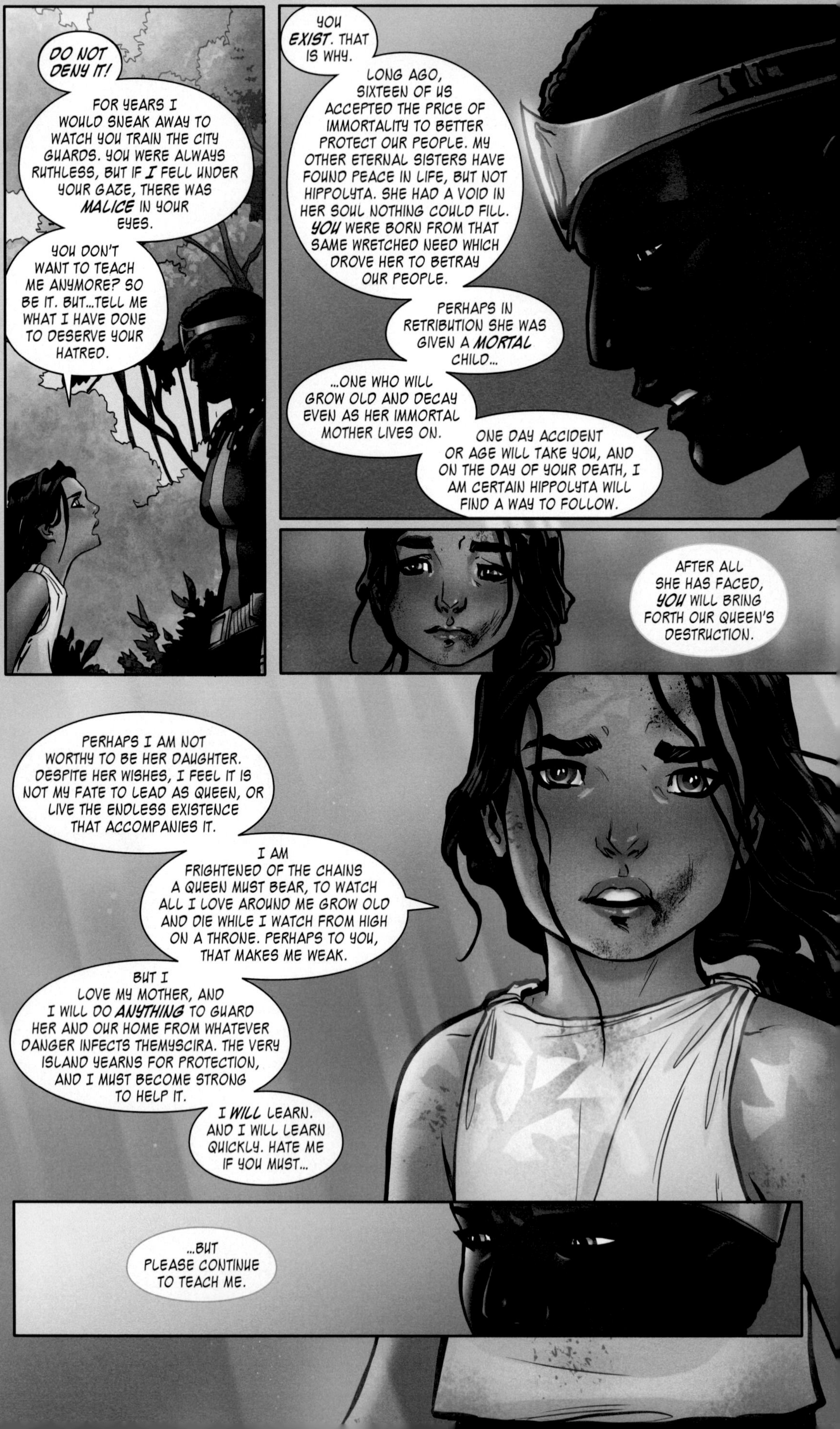
DO NOT DENY IT!
FOR YEARS I WOULD SNEAK AWAY TO WATCH YOU TRAIN THE CITY GUARDS. YOU WERE ALWAYS RUTHLESS, BUT IF I FELL UNDER YOUR GAZE, THERE WAS MALICE IN YOUR EYES.
YOU DON'T WANT TO TEACH ME ANYMORE? SO BE IT. BUT...TELL ME WHAT I HAVE DONE TO DESERVE YOUR HATRED.
YOU EXIST. THAT IS WHY.
LONG AGO, SIXTEEN OF US ACCEPTED THE PRICE OF IMMORTALITY TO BETTER PROTECT OUR PEOPLE. MY OTHER ETERNAL SISTERS HAVE FOUND PEACE IN LIFE, BUT NOT HIPPOLYTA. SHE HAD A VOID IN HER SOUL NOTHING COULD FILL. YOU WERE BORN FROM THAT SAME WRETCHED NEED WHICH DROVE HER TO BETRAY OUR PEOPLE.
PERHAPS IN RETRIBUTION SHE WAS GIVEN A MORTAL CHILD...
...ONE WHO WILL GROW OLD AND DECAY EVEN AS HER IMMORTAL MOTHER LIVES ON.
ONE DAY ACCIDENT OR AGE WILL TAKE YOU, AND ON THE DAY OF YOUR DEATH, I AM CERTAIN HIPPOLYTA WILL FIND A WAY TO FOLLOW.
AFTER ALL SHE HAS FACED, YOU WILL BRING FORTH OUR QUEEN'S DESTRUCTION.
PERHAPS I AM NOT WORTHY TO BE HER DAUGHTER. DESPITE HER WISHES, I FEEL IT IS NOT MY FATE TO LEAD AS QUEEN, OR LIVE THE ENDLESS EXISTENCE THAT ACCOMPANIES IT.
I AM FRIGHTENED OF THE CHAINS A QUEEN MUST BEAR, TO WATCH ALL I LOVE AROUND ME GROW OLD AND DIE WHILE I WATCH FROM HIGH ON A THRONE. PERHAPS TO YOU, THAT MAKES ME WEAK.
BUT I LOVE MY MOTHER, AND I WILL DO ANYTHING TO GUARD HER AND OUR HOME FROM WHATEVER DANGER INFECTS THEMYSCIRA. THE VERY ISLAND YEARNS FOR PROTECTION, AND I MUST BECOME STRONG TO HELP IT.
I WILL LEARN. AND I WILL LEARN QUICKLY. HATE ME IF YOU MUST...
...BUT PLEASE CONTINUE TO TEACH ME.

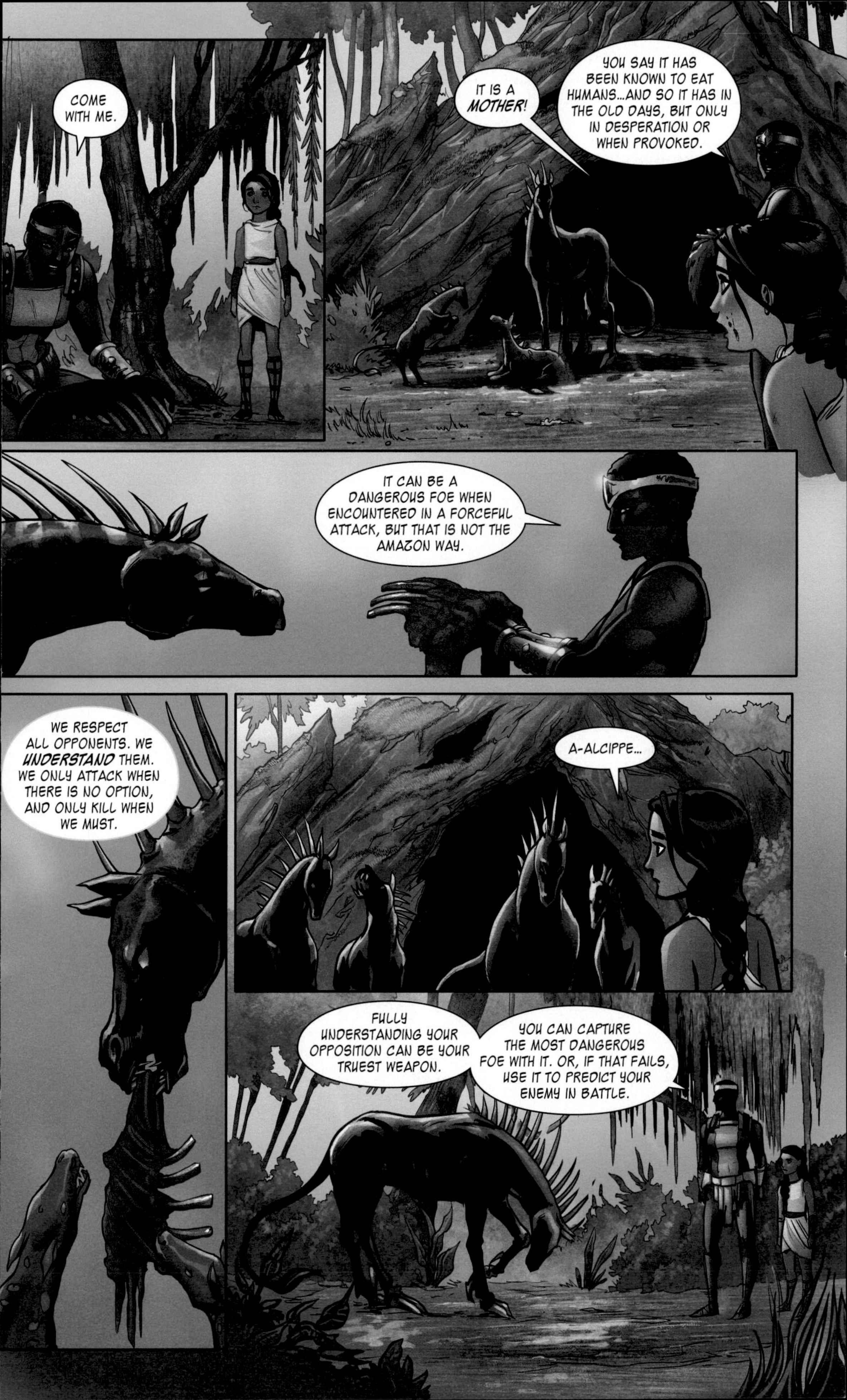
COME WITH ME.
IT IS A *MOTHER*!
YOU SAY IT HAS BEEN KNOWN TO EAT HUMANS...AND SO IT HAS IN THE OLD DAYS, BUT ONLY IN DESPERATION OR WHEN PROVOKED.
IT CAN BE A DANGEROUS FOE WHEN ENCOUNTERED IN A FORCEFUL ATTACK, BUT THAT IS NOT THE AMAZON WAY.
WE RESPECT ALL OPPONENTS. WE *UNDERSTAND* THEM. WE ONLY ATTACK WHEN THERE IS NO OPTION, AND ONLY KILL WHEN WE MUST.
A-ALCIPPE...
FULLY UNDERSTANDING YOUR OPPOSITION CAN BE YOUR TRUEST WEAPON.
YOU CAN CAPTURE THE MOST DANGEROUS FOE WITH IT. OR, IF THAT FAILS, USE IT TO PREDICT YOUR ENEMY IN BATTLE.

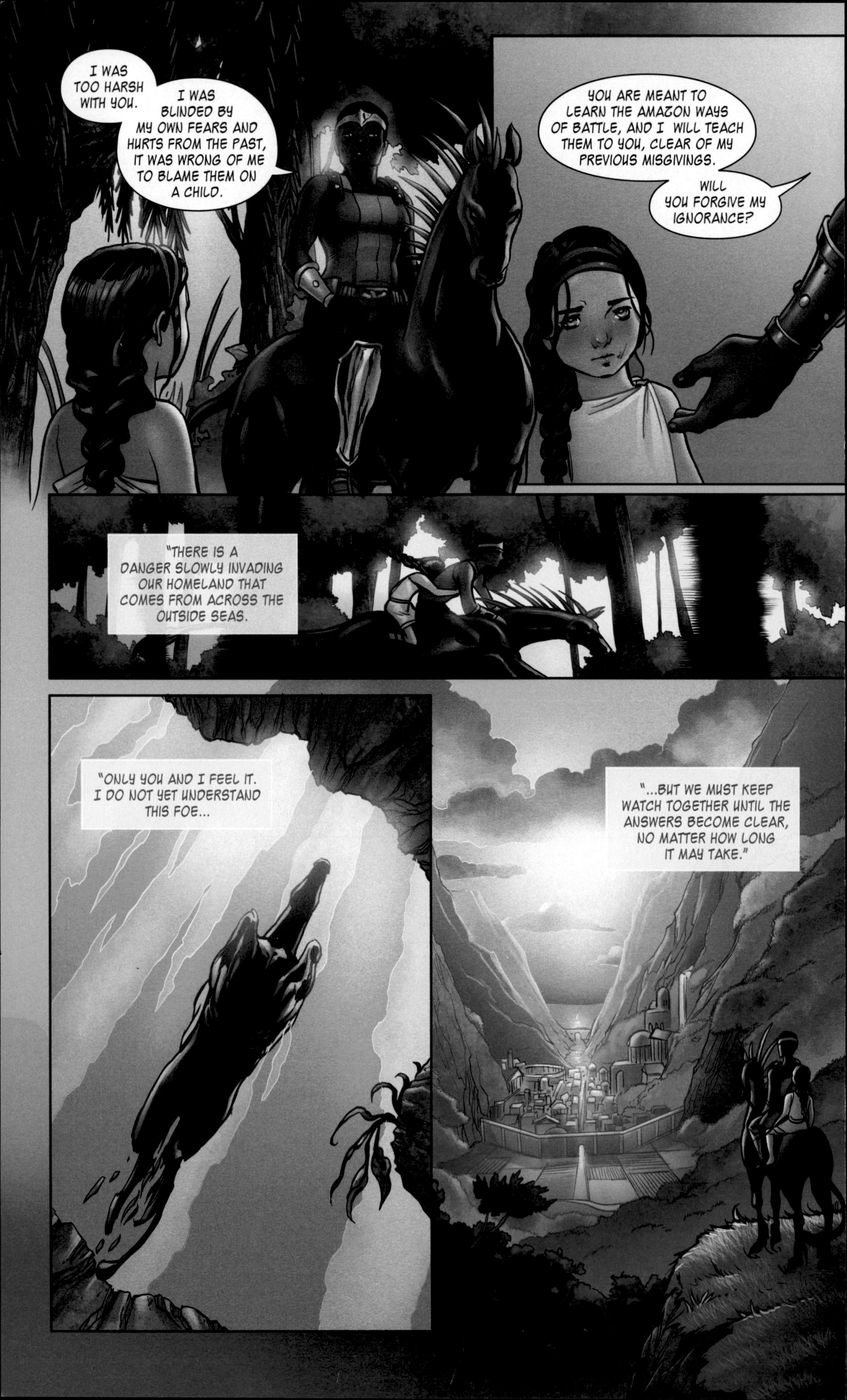
I WAS TOO HARSH WITH YOU.
I WAS BLINDED BY MY OWN FEARS AND HURTS FROM THE PAST, IT WAS WRONG OF ME TO BLAME THEM ON A CHILD.
YOU ARE MEANT TO LEARN THE AMAZON WAYS OF BATTLE, AND I WILL TEACH THEM TO YOU, CLEAR OF MY PREVIOUS MISGIVINGS.
WILL YOU FORGIVE MY IGNORANCE?
"THERE IS A DANGER SLOWLY INVADING OUR HOMELAND THAT COMES FROM ACROSS THE OUTSIDE SEAS.
"ONLY YOU AND I FEEL IT. I DO NOT YET UNDERSTAND THIS FOE...
"...BUT WE MUST KEEP WATCH TOGETHER UNTIL THE ANSWERS BECOME CLEAR, NO MATTER HOW LONG IT MAY TAKE."

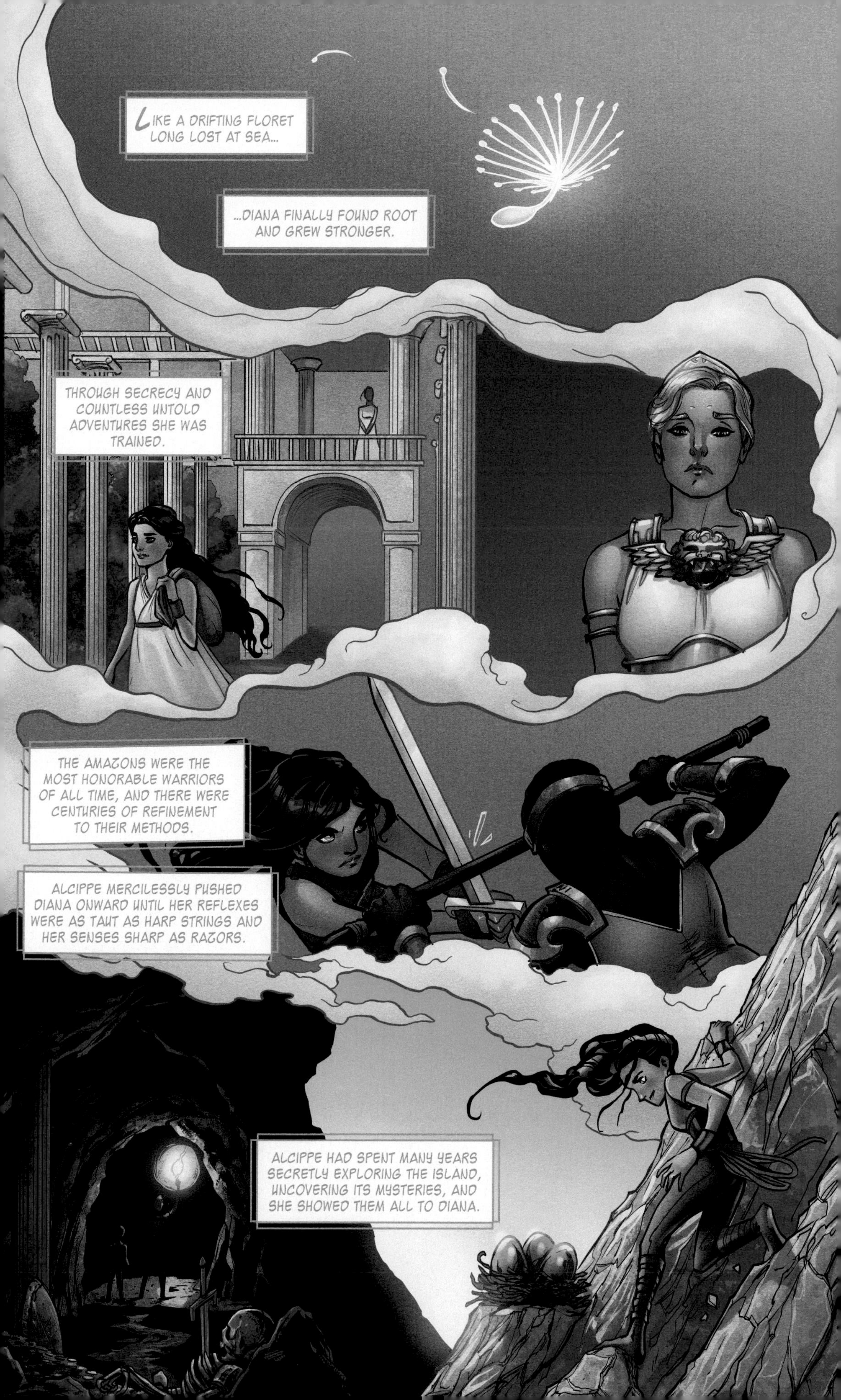
LIKE A DRIFTING FLORET LONG LOST AT SEA...
...DIANA FINALLY FOUND ROOT AND GREW STRONGER.
THROUGH SECRECY AND COUNTLESS UNTOLD ADVENTURES SHE WAS TRAINED.
THE AMAZONS WERE THE MOST HONORABLE WARRIORS OF ALL TIME, AND THERE WERE CENTURIES OF REFINEMENT TO THEIR METHODS.
ALCIPPE MERCILESSLY PUSHED DIANA ONWARD UNTIL HER REFLEXES WERE AS TAUT AS HARP STRINGS AND HER SENSES SHARP AS RAZORS.
ALCIPPE HAD SPENT MANY YEARS SECRETLY EXPLORING THE ISLAND, UNCOVERING ITS MYSTERIES, AND SHE SHOWED THEM ALL TO DIANA.

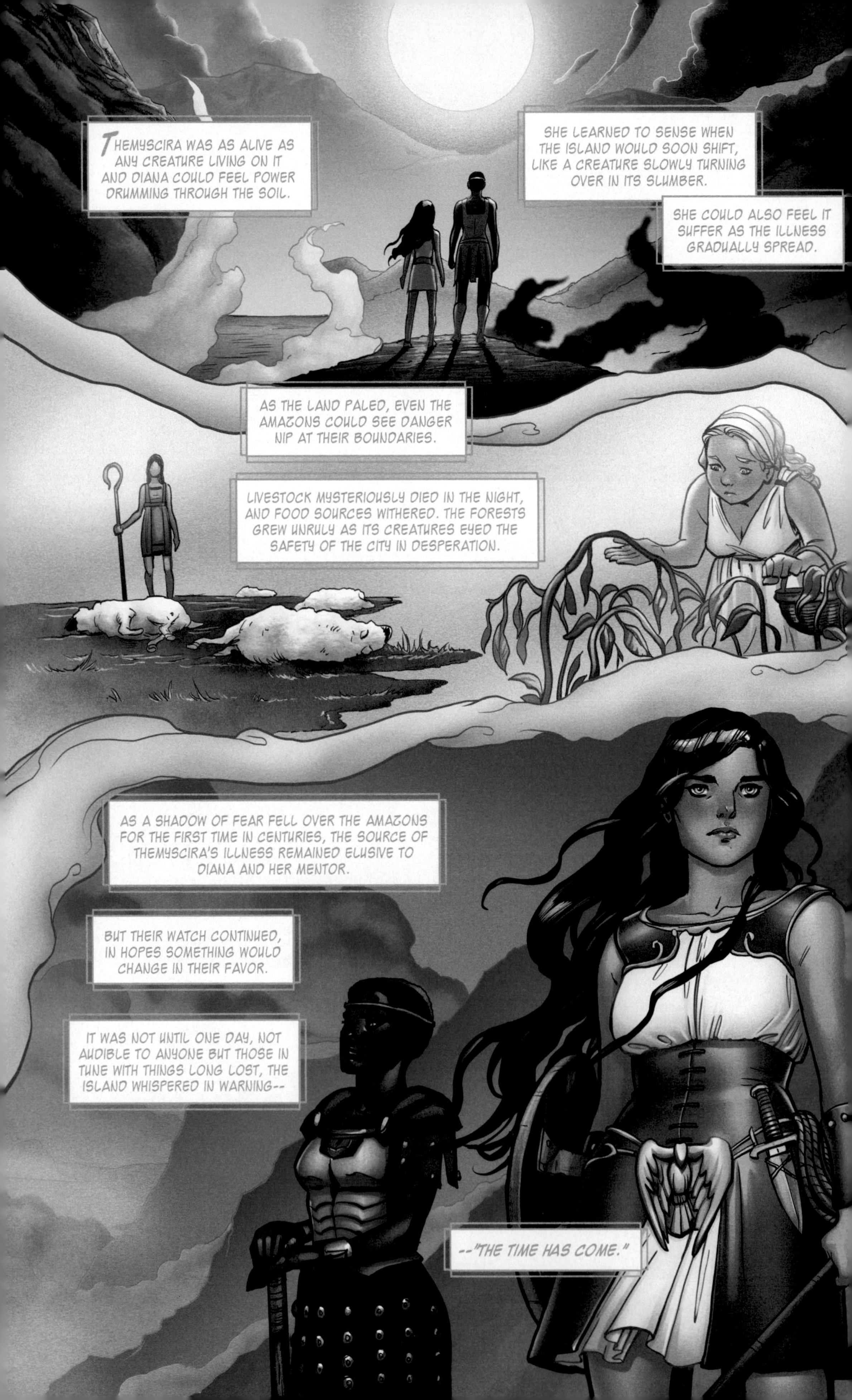
THEMYSCIRA WAS AS ALIVE AS ANY CREATURE LIVING ON IT AND DIANA COULD FEEL POWER DRUMMING THROUGH THE SOIL.
SHE LEARNED TO SENSE WHEN THE ISLAND WOULD SOON SHIFT, LIKE A CREATURE SLOWLY TURNING OVER IN ITS SLUMBER.
SHE COULD ALSO FEEL IT SUFFER AS THE ILLNESS GRADUALLY SPREAD.
AS THE LAND PALED, EVEN THE AMAZONS COULD SEE DANGER NIP AT THEIR BOUNDARIES.
LIVESTOCK MYSTERIOUSLY DIED IN THE NIGHT, AND FOOD SOURCES WITHERED. THE FORESTS GREW UNRULY AS ITS CREATURES EYED THE SAFETY OF THE CITY IN DESPERATION.
AS A SHADOW OF FEAR FELL OVER THE AMAZONS FOR THE FIRST TIME IN CENTURIES, THE SOURCE OF THEMYSCIRA'S ILLNESS REMAINED ELUSIVE TO DIANA AND HER MENTOR.
BUT THEIR WATCH CONTINUED, IN HOPES SOMETHING WOULD CHANGE IN THEIR FAVOR.
IT WAS NOT UNTIL ONE DAY, NOT AUDIBLE TO ANYONE BUT THOSE IN TUNE WITH THINGS LONG LOST, THE ISLAND WHISPERED IN WARNING--
--"THE TIME HAS COME."

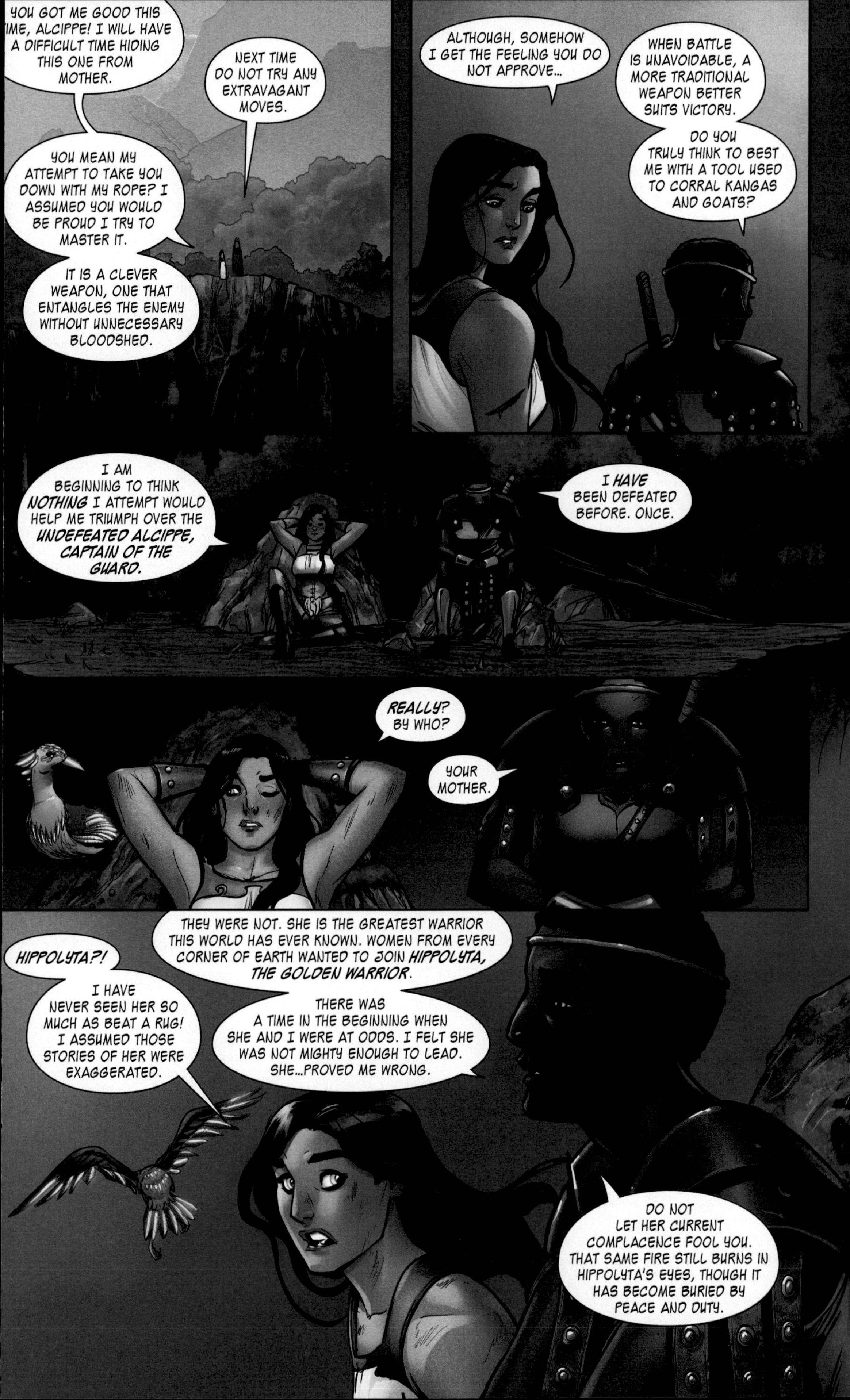
YOU GOT ME GOOD THIS TIME, ALCIPPE! I WILL HAVE A DIFFICULT TIME HIDING THIS ONE FROM MOTHER.
NEXT TIME DO NOT TRY ANY EXTRAVAGANT MOVES.
YOU MEAN MY ATTEMPT TO TAKE YOU DOWN WITH MY ROPE? I ASSUMED YOU WOULD BE PROUD I TRY TO MASTER IT.
IT IS A CLEVER WEAPON, ONE THAT ENTANGLES THE ENEMY WITHOUT UNNECESSARY BLOODSHED.
ALTHOUGH, SOMEHOW I GET THE FEELING YOU DO NOT APPROVE...
WHEN BATTLE IS UNAVOIDABLE, A MORE TRADITIONAL WEAPON BETTER SUITS VICTORY.
DO YOU TRULY THINK TO BEST ME WITH A TOOL USED TO CORRAL KANGAS AND GOATS?
I AM BEGINNING TO THINK *NOTHING* I ATTEMPT WOULD HELP ME TRIUMPH OVER THE *UNDEFEATED ALCIPPE, CAPTAIN OF THE GUARD.*
I *HAVE* BEEN DEFEATED BEFORE. ONCE.
REALLY? BY WHO?
YOUR MOTHER.
HIPPOLYTA?!
I HAVE NEVER SEEN HER SO MUCH AS BEAT A RUG! I ASSUMED THOSE STORIES OF HER WERE EXAGGERATED.
THEY WERE NOT. SHE IS THE GREATEST WARRIOR THIS WORLD HAS EVER KNOWN. WOMEN FROM EVERY CORNER OF EARTH WANTED TO JOIN *HIPPOLYTA, THE GOLDEN WARRIOR*.
THERE WAS A TIME IN THE BEGINNING WHEN SHE AND I WERE AT ODDS. I FELT SHE WAS NOT MIGHTY ENOUGH TO LEAD. SHE...PROVED ME WRONG.
DO NOT LET HER CURRENT COMPLACENCE FOOL YOU. THAT SAME FIRE STILL BURNS IN HIPPOLYTA'S EYES, THOUGH IT HAS BECOME BURIED BY PEACE AND DUTY.

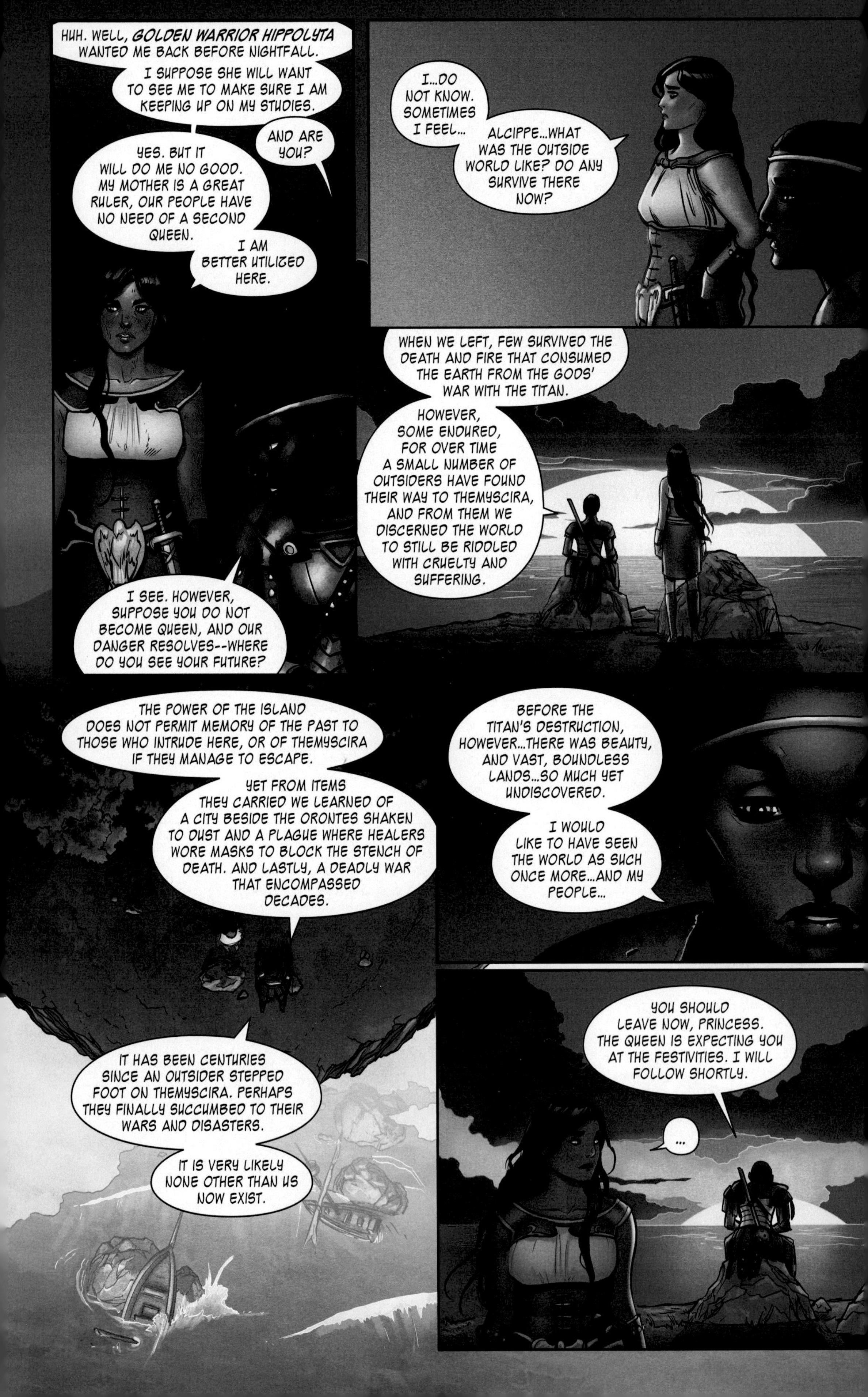
HUH. WELL, GOLDEN WARRIOR HIPPOLYTA WANTED ME BACK BEFORE NIGHTFALL.
I SUPPOSE SHE WILL WANT TO SEE ME TO MAKE SURE I AM KEEPING UP ON MY STUDIES.
AND ARE YOU?
YES. BUT IT WILL DO ME NO GOOD. MY MOTHER IS A GREAT RULER, OUR PEOPLE HAVE NO NEED OF A SECOND QUEEN.
I AM BETTER UTILIZED HERE.
I SEE. HOWEVER, SUPPOSE YOU DO NOT BECOME QUEEN, AND OUR DANGER RESOLVES--WHERE DO YOU SEE YOUR FUTURE?
I...DO NOT KNOW. SOMETIMES I FEEL...
ALCIPPE...WHAT WAS THE OUTSIDE WORLD LIKE? DO ANY SURVIVE THERE NOW?
WHEN WE LEFT, FEW SURVIVED THE DEATH AND FIRE THAT CONSUMED THE EARTH FROM THE GODS' WAR WITH THE TITAN.
HOWEVER, SOME ENDURED, FOR OVER TIME A SMALL NUMBER OF OUTSIDERS HAVE FOUND THEIR WAY TO THEMYSCIRA, AND FROM THEM WE DISCERNED THE WORLD TO STILL BE RIDDLED WITH CRUELTY AND SUFFERING.
THE POWER OF THE ISLAND DOES NOT PERMIT MEMORY OF THE PAST TO THOSE WHO INTRUDE HERE, OR OF THEMYSCIRA IF THEY MANAGE TO ESCAPE.
YET FROM ITEMS THEY CARRIED WE LEARNED OF A CITY BESIDE THE ORONTES SHAKEN TO DUST AND A PLAGUE WHERE HEALERS WORE MASKS TO BLOCK THE STENCH OF DEATH. AND LASTLY, A DEADLY WAR THAT ENCOMPASSED DECADES.
IT HAS BEEN CENTURIES SINCE AN OUTSIDER STEPPED FOOT ON THEMYSCIRA. PERHAPS THEY FINALLY SUCCUMBED TO THEIR WARS AND DISASTERS.
IT IS VERY LIKELY NONE OTHER THAN US NOW EXIST.
BEFORE THE TITAN'S DESTRUCTION, HOWEVER...THERE WAS BEAUTY, AND VAST, BOUNDLESS LANDS...SO MUCH YET UNDISCOVERED.
I WOULD LIKE TO HAVE SEEN THE WORLD AS SUCH ONCE MORE...AND MY PEOPLE...
YOU SHOULD LEAVE NOW, PRINCESS. THE QUEEN IS EXPECTING YOU AT THE FESTIVITIES. I WILL FOLLOW SHORTLY.
...

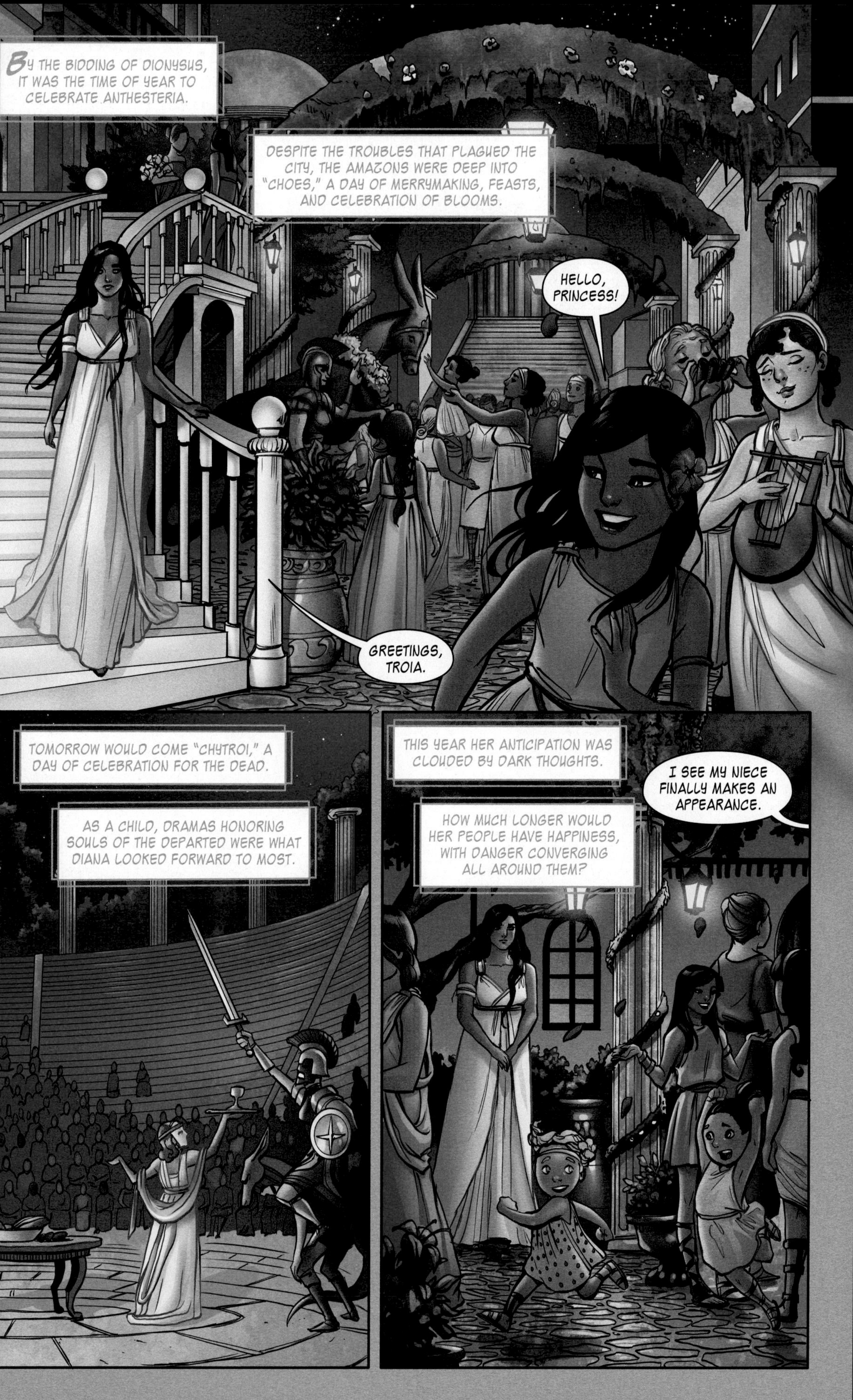
BY THE BIDDING OF DIONYSUS, IT WAS THE TIME OF YEAR TO CELEBRATE ANTHESTERIA.
DESPITE THE TROUBLES THAT PLAGUED THE CITY, THE AMAZONS WERE DEEP INTO "CHOES," A DAY OF MERRYMAKING, FEASTS, AND CELEBRATION OF BLOOMS.
HELLO, PRINCESS!
GREETINGS, TROIA.
TOMORROW WOULD COME "CHYTROI," A DAY OF CELEBRATION FOR THE DEAD.
AS A CHILD, DRAMAS HONORING SOULS OF THE DEPARTED WERE WHAT DIANA LOOKED FORWARD TO MOST.
THIS YEAR HER ANTICIPATION WAS CLOUDED BY DARK THOUGHTS.
HOW MUCH LONGER WOULD HER PEOPLE HAVE HAPPINESS, WITH DANGER CONVERGING ALL AROUND THEM?
I SEE MY NIECE FINALLY MAKES AN APPEARANCE.

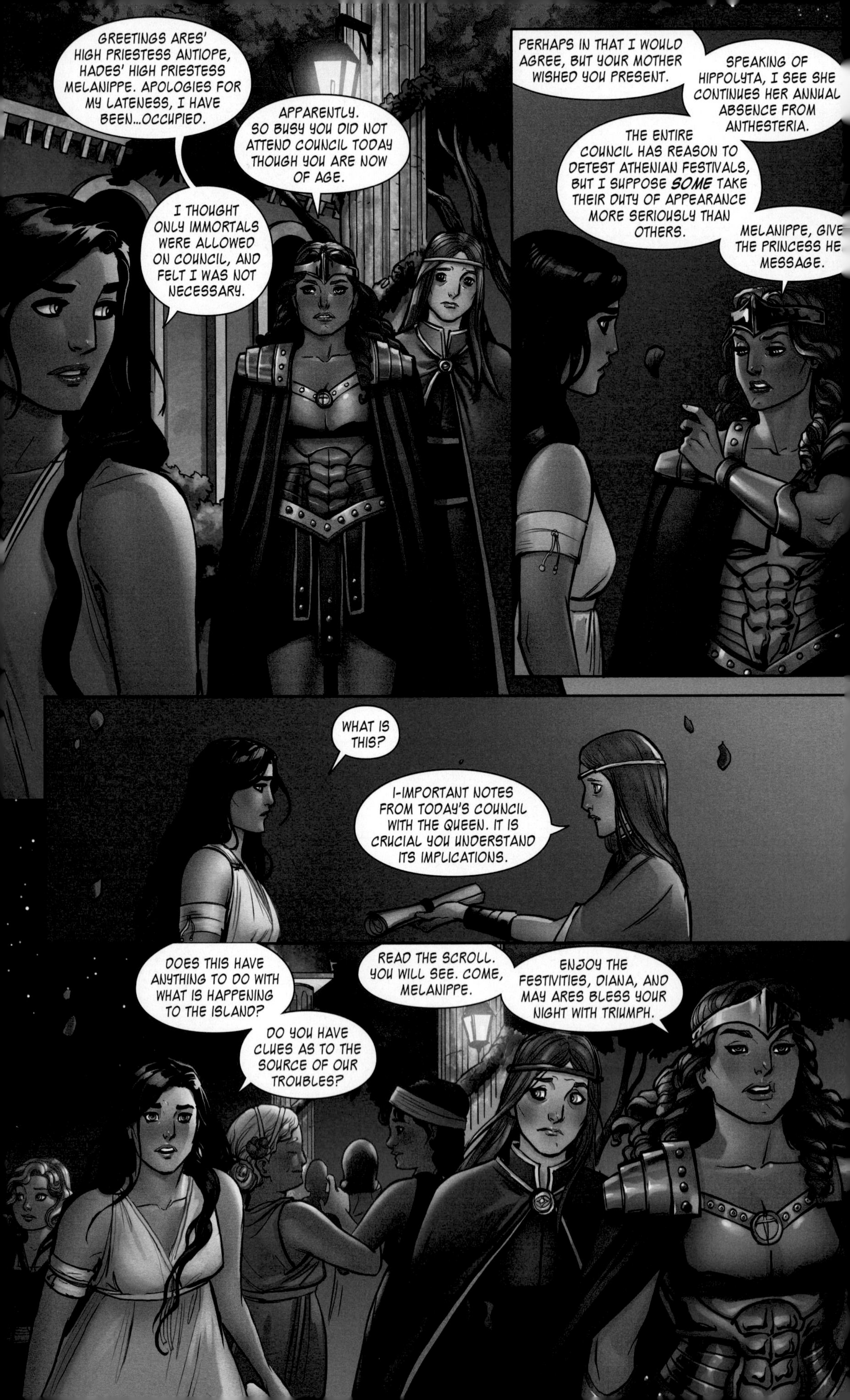
GREETINGS ARES' HIGH PRIESTESS ANTIOPE, HADES' HIGH PRIESTESS MELANIPPE. APOLOGIES FOR MY LATENESS, I HAVE BEEN...OCCUPIED.
APPARENTLY. SO BUSY YOU DID NOT ATTEND COUNCIL TODAY THOUGH YOU ARE NOW OF AGE.
I THOUGHT ONLY IMMORTALS WERE ALLOWED ON COUNCIL, AND FELT I WAS NOT NECESSARY.
PERHAPS IN THAT I WOULD AGREE, BUT YOUR MOTHER WISHED YOU PRESENT.
SPEAKING OF HIPPOLYTA, I SEE SHE CONTINUES HER ANNUAL ABSENCE FROM ANTHESTERIA.
THE ENTIRE COUNCIL HAS REASON TO DETEST ATHENIAN FESTIVALS, BUT I SUPPOSE SOME TAKE THEIR DUTY OF APPEARANCE MORE SERIOUSLY THAN OTHERS.
MELANIPPE, GIVE THE PRINCESS HE MESSAGE.
WHAT IS THIS?
I-IMPORTANT NOTES FROM TODAY'S COUNCIL WITH THE QUEEN. IT IS CRUCIAL YOU UNDERSTAND ITS IMPLICATIONS.
DOES THIS HAVE ANYTHING TO DO WITH WHAT IS HAPPENING TO THE ISLAND?
DO YOU HAVE CLUES AS TO THE SOURCE OF OUR TROUBLES?
READ THE SCROLL. YOU WILL SEE. COME, MELANIPPE.
ENJOY THE FESTIVITIES, DIANA, AND MAY ARES BLESS YOUR NIGHT WITH TRIUMPH.

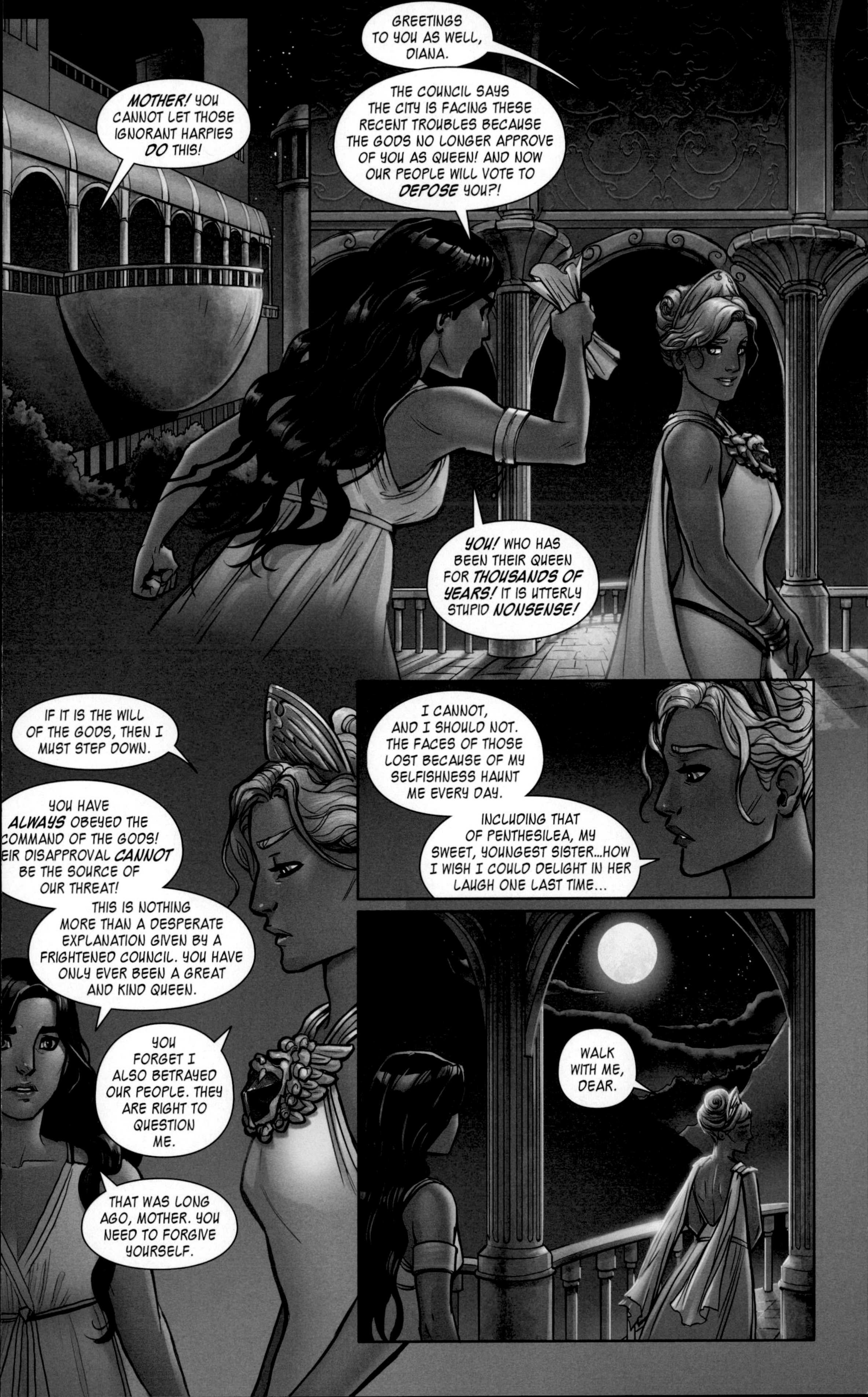

MOTHER! YOU CANNOT LET THOSE IGNORANT HARPIES DO THIS!
GREETINGS TO YOU AS WELL, DIANA.
THE COUNCIL SAYS THE CITY IS FACING THESE RECENT TROUBLES BECAUSE THE GODS NO LONGER APPROVE OF YOU AS QUEEN! AND NOW OUR PEOPLE WILL VOTE TO DEPOSE YOU?!
YOU! WHO HAS BEEN THEIR QUEEN FOR THOUSANDS OF YEARS! IT IS UTTERLY STUPID NONSENSE!
IF IT IS THE WILL OF THE GODS, THEN I MUST STEP DOWN.
YOU HAVE ALWAYS OBEYED THE COMMAND OF THE GODS! EIR DISAPPROVAL CANNOT BE THE SOURCE OF OUR THREAT!
THIS IS NOTHING MORE THAN A DESPERATE EXPLANATION GIVEN BY A FRIGHTENED COUNCIL. YOU HAVE ONLY EVER BEEN A GREAT AND KIND QUEEN.
YOU FORGET I ALSO BETRAYED OUR PEOPLE. THEY ARE RIGHT TO QUESTION ME.
THAT WAS LONG AGO, MOTHER. YOU NEED TO FORGIVE YOURSELF.
I CANNOT, AND I SHOULD NOT. THE FACES OF THOSE LOST BECAUSE OF MY SELFISHNESS HAUNT ME EVERY DAY.
INCLUDING THAT OF PENTHESILEA, MY SWEET, YOUNGEST SISTER...HOW I WISH I COULD DELIGHT IN HER LAUGH ONE LAST TIME...
WALK WITH ME, DEAR.

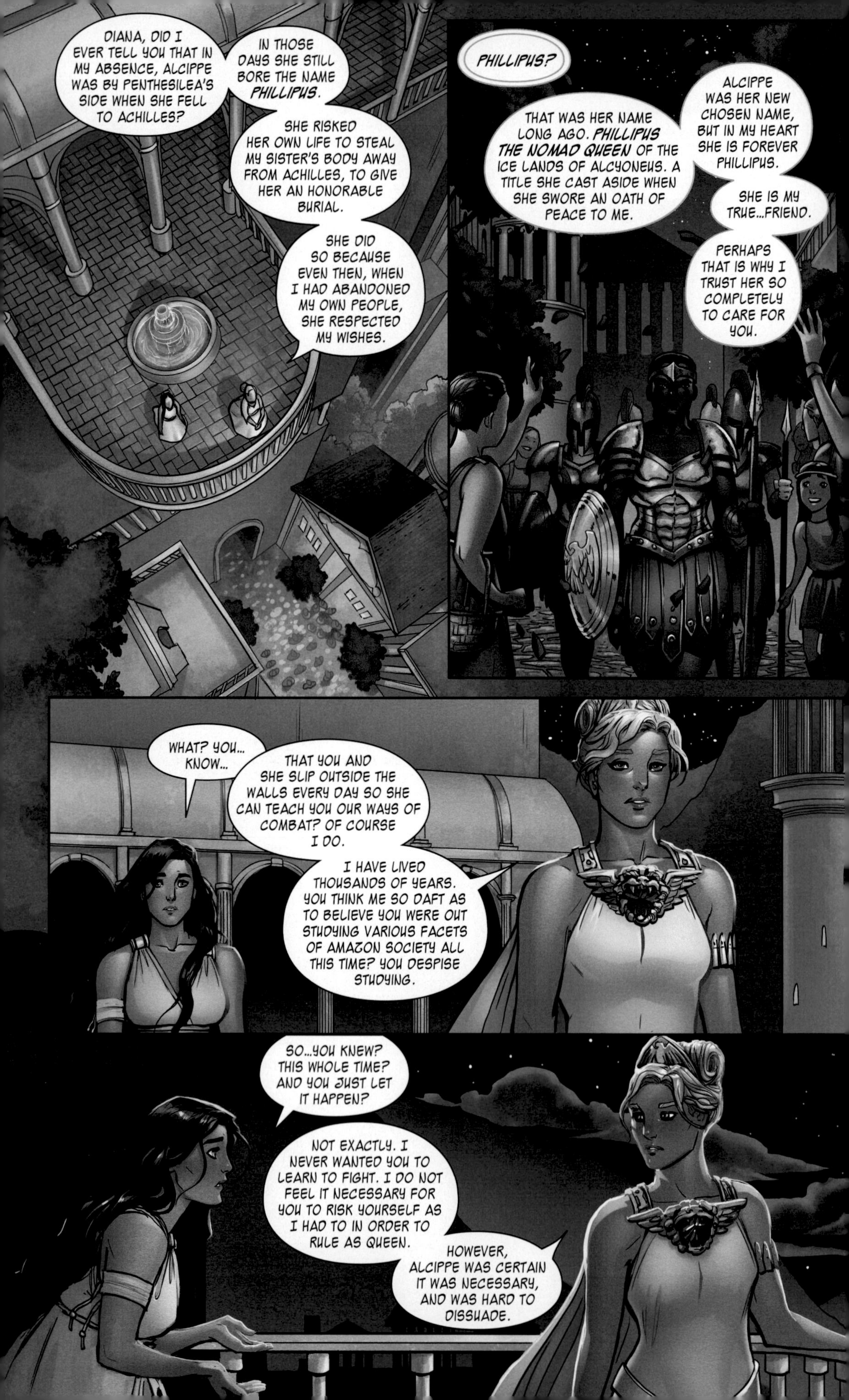

DIANA, DID I EVER TELL YOU THAT IN MY ABSENCE, ALCIPPE WAS BY PENTHESILEA'S SIDE WHEN SHE FELL TO ACHILLES?
IN THOSE DAYS SHE STILL BORE THE NAME *PHILLIPUS*.
SHE RISKED HER OWN LIFE TO STEAL MY SISTER'S BODY AWAY FROM ACHILLES, TO GIVE HER AN HONORABLE BURIAL.
SHE DID SO BECAUSE EVEN THEN, WHEN I HAD ABANDONED MY OWN PEOPLE, SHE RESPECTED MY WISHES.
PHILLIPUS?
THAT WAS HER NAME LONG AGO. ***PHILLIPUS THE NOMAD QUEEN*** OF THE ICE LANDS OF ALCYONEUS. A TITLE SHE CAST ASIDE WHEN SHE SWORE AN OATH OF PEACE TO ME.
ALCIPPE WAS HER NEW CHOSEN NAME, BUT IN MY HEART SHE IS FOREVER PHILLIPUS.
SHE IS MY TRUE...FRIEND.
PERHAPS THAT IS WHY I TRUST HER SO COMPLETELY TO CARE FOR YOU.
WHAT? YOU... KNOW...
THAT YOU AND SHE SLIP OUTSIDE THE WALLS EVERY DAY SO SHE CAN TEACH YOU OUR WAYS OF COMBAT? OF COURSE I DO.
I HAVE LIVED THOUSANDS OF YEARS. YOU THINK ME SO DAFT AS TO BELIEVE YOU WERE OUT STUDYING VARIOUS FACETS OF AMAZON SOCIETY ALL THIS TIME? YOU DESPISE STUDYING.
SO...YOU KNEW? THIS WHOLE TIME? AND YOU JUST LET IT HAPPEN?
NOT EXACTLY. I NEVER WANTED YOU TO LEARN TO FIGHT. I DO NOT FEEL IT NECESSARY FOR YOU TO RISK YOURSELF AS I HAD TO IN ORDER TO RULE AS QUEEN.
HOWEVER, ALCIPPE WAS CERTAIN IT WAS NECESSARY, AND WAS HARD TO DISSUADE.

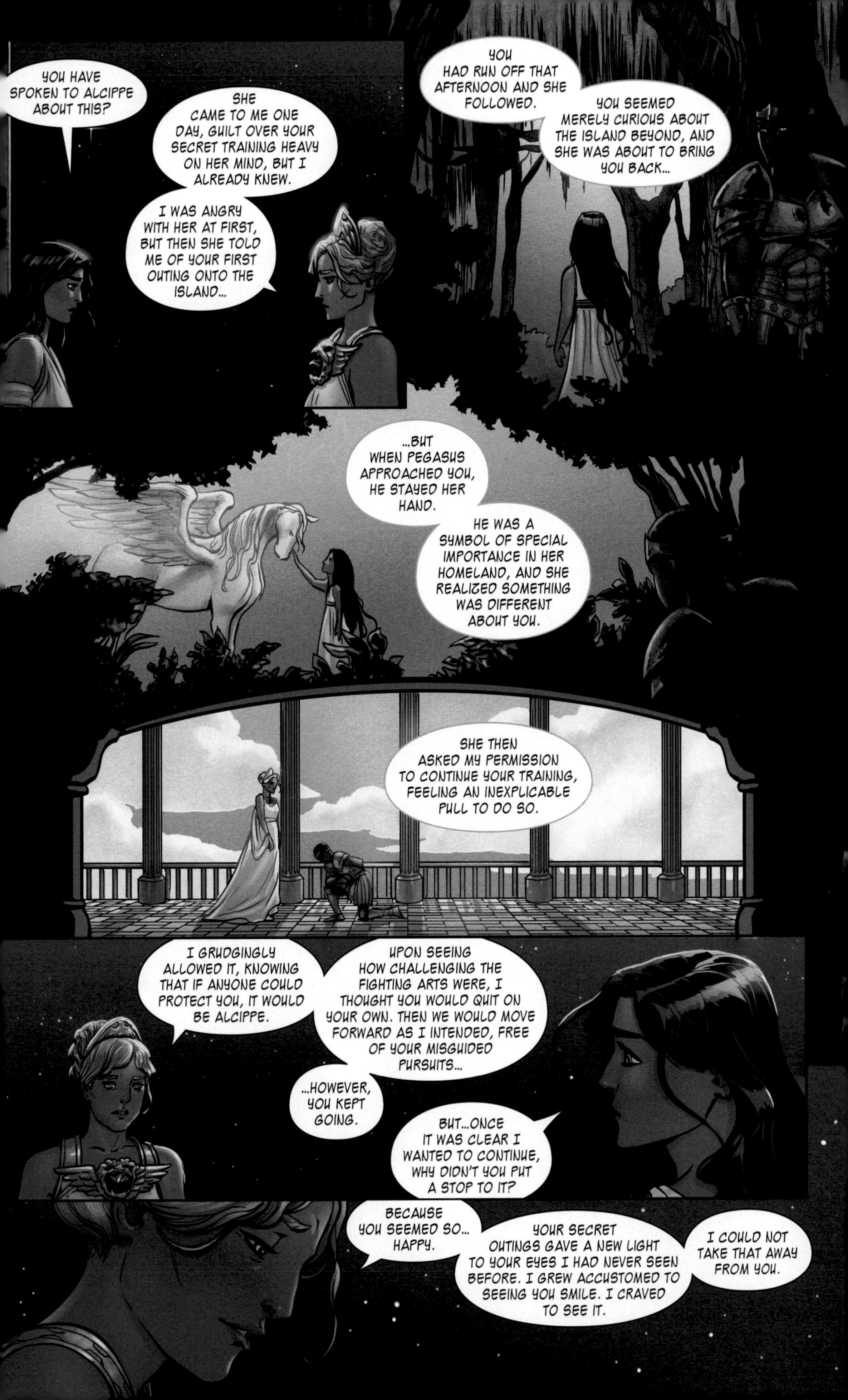
YOU HAVE SPOKEN TO ALCIPPE ABOUT THIS?
SHE CAME TO ME ONE DAY, GUILT OVER YOUR SECRET TRAINING HEAVY ON HER MIND, BUT I ALREADY KNEW.
I WAS ANGRY WITH HER AT FIRST, BUT THEN SHE TOLD ME OF YOUR FIRST OUTING ONTO THE ISLAND...
YOU HAD RUN OFF THAT AFTERNOON AND SHE FOLLOWED.
YOU SEEMED MERELY CURIOUS ABOUT THE ISLAND BEYOND, AND SHE WAS ABOUT TO BRING YOU BACK...
...BUT WHEN PEGASUS APPROACHED YOU, HE STAYED HER HAND.
HE WAS A SYMBOL OF SPECIAL IMPORTANCE IN HER HOMELAND, AND SHE REALIZED SOMETHING WAS DIFFERENT ABOUT YOU.
SHE THEN ASKED MY PERMISSION TO CONTINUE YOUR TRAINING, FEELING AN INEXPLICABLE PULL TO DO SO.
I GRUDGINGLY ALLOWED IT, KNOWING THAT IF ANYONE COULD PROTECT YOU, IT WOULD BE ALCIPPE.
UPON SEEING HOW CHALLENGING THE FIGHTING ARTS WERE, I THOUGHT YOU WOULD QUIT ON YOUR OWN. THEN WE WOULD MOVE FORWARD AS I INTENDED, FREE OF YOUR MISGUIDED PURSUITS...
...HOWEVER, YOU KEPT GOING.
BUT...ONCE IT WAS CLEAR I WANTED TO CONTINUE, WHY DIDN'T YOU PUT A STOP TO IT?
BECAUSE YOU SEEMED SO... HAPPY.
YOUR SECRET OUTINGS GAVE A NEW LIGHT TO YOUR EYES I HAD NEVER SEEN BEFORE. I GREW ACCUSTOMED TO SEEING YOU SMILE. I CRAVED TO SEE IT.
I COULD NOT TAKE THAT AWAY FROM YOU.

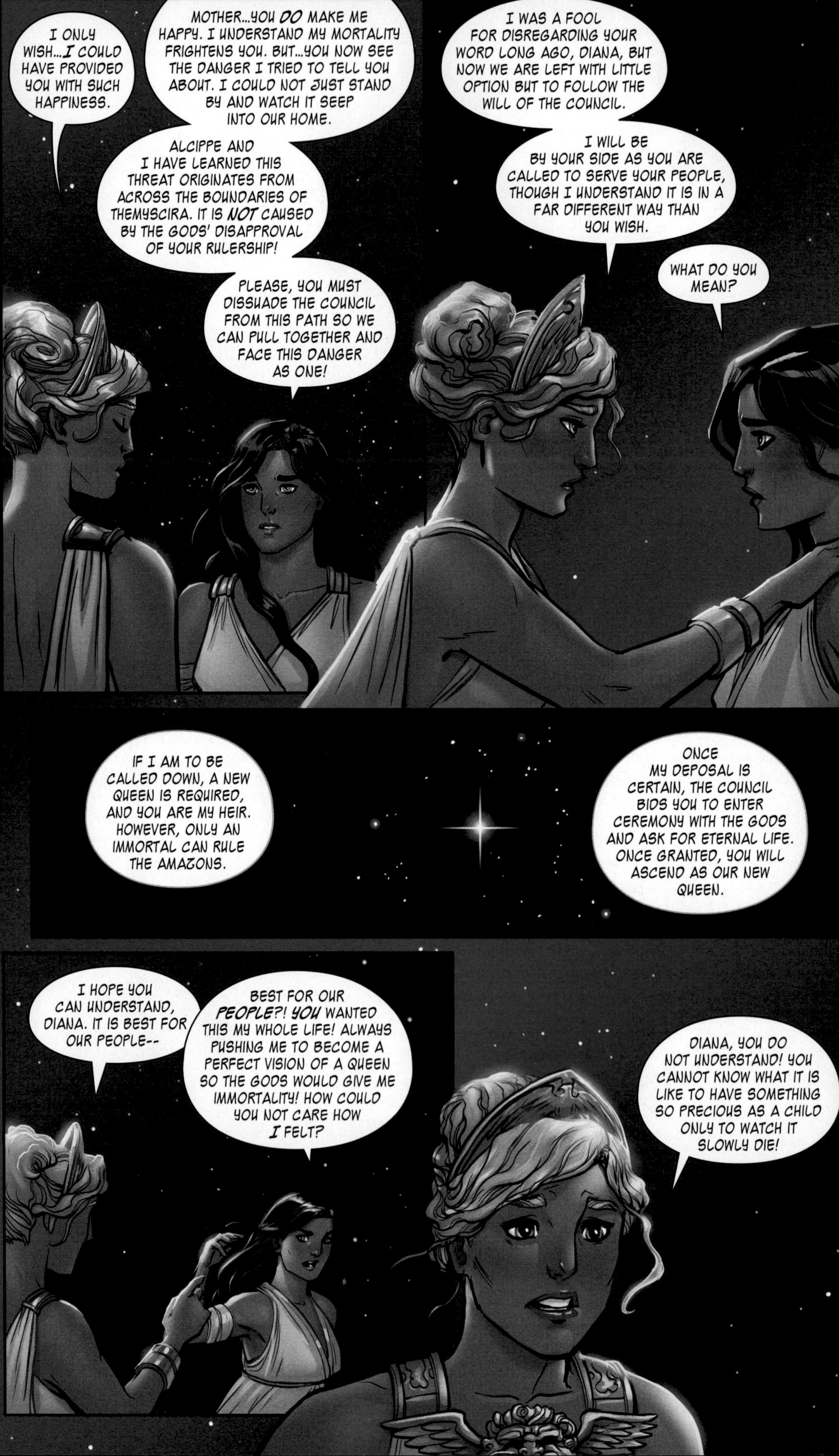

I ONLY WISH...I COULD HAVE PROVIDED YOU WITH SUCH HAPPINESS.
MOTHER...YOU DO MAKE ME HAPPY. I UNDERSTAND MY MORTALITY FRIGHTENS YOU. BUT...YOU NOW SEE THE DANGER I TRIED TO TELL YOU ABOUT. I COULD NOT JUST STAND BY AND WATCH IT SEEP INTO OUR HOME.
ALCIPPE AND I HAVE LEARNED THIS THREAT ORIGINATES FROM ACROSS THE BOUNDARIES OF THEMYSCIRA. IT IS NOT CAUSED BY THE GODS' DISAPPROVAL OF YOUR RULERSHIP!
PLEASE, YOU MUST DISSUADE THE COUNCIL FROM THIS PATH SO WE CAN PULL TOGETHER AND FACE THIS DANGER AS ONE!
I WAS A FOOL FOR DISREGARDING YOUR WORD LONG AGO, DIANA, BUT NOW WE ARE LEFT WITH LITTLE OPTION BUT TO FOLLOW THE WILL OF THE COUNCIL.
I WILL BE BY YOUR SIDE AS YOU ARE CALLED TO SERVE YOUR PEOPLE, THOUGH I UNDERSTAND IT IS IN A FAR DIFFERENT WAY THAN YOU WISH.
WHAT DO YOU MEAN?
IF I AM TO BE CALLED DOWN, A NEW QUEEN IS REQUIRED, AND YOU ARE MY HEIR. HOWEVER, ONLY AN IMMORTAL CAN RULE THE AMAZONS.
ONCE MY DEPOSAL IS CERTAIN, THE COUNCIL BIDS YOU TO ENTER CEREMONY WITH THE GODS AND ASK FOR ETERNAL LIFE. ONCE GRANTED, YOU WILL ASCEND AS OUR NEW QUEEN.
I HOPE YOU CAN UNDERSTAND, DIANA. IT IS BEST FOR OUR PEOPLE--
BEST FOR OUR PEOPLE?! YOU WANTED THIS MY WHOLE LIFE! ALWAYS PUSHING ME TO BECOME A PERFECT VISION OF A QUEEN SO THE GODS WOULD GIVE ME IMMORTALITY! HOW COULD YOU NOT CARE HOW I FELT?
DIANA, YOU DO NOT UNDERSTAND! YOU CANNOT KNOW WHAT IT IS LIKE TO HAVE SOMETHING SO PRECIOUS AS A CHILD ONLY TO WATCH IT SLOWLY DIE!

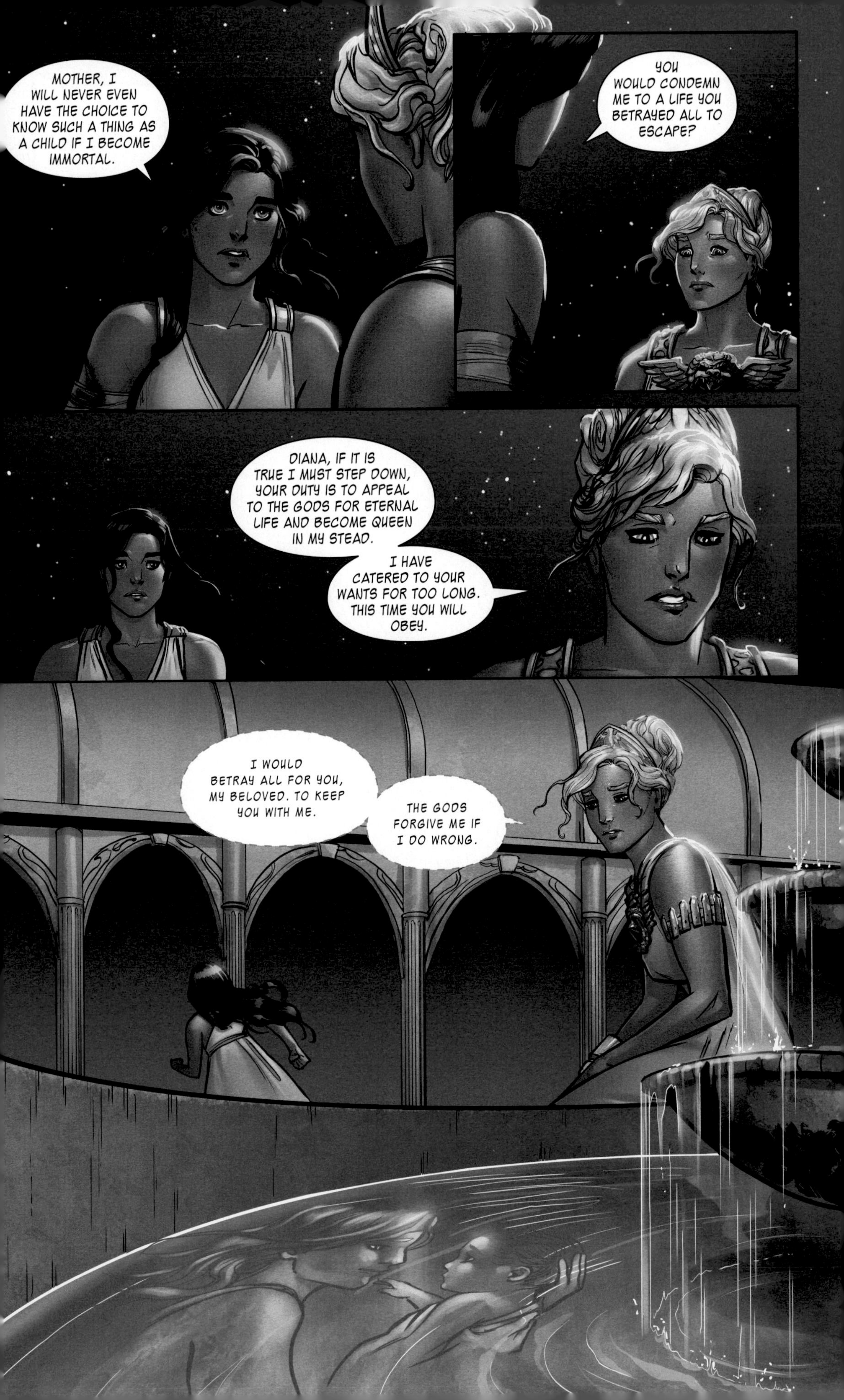
MOTHER, I WILL NEVER EVEN HAVE THE CHOICE TO KNOW SUCH A THING AS A CHILD IF I BECOME IMMORTAL.
YOU WOULD CONDEMN ME TO A LIFE YOU BETRAYED ALL TO ESCAPE?
DIANA, IF IT IS TRUE I MUST STEP DOWN, YOUR DUTY IS TO APPEAL TO THE GODS FOR ETERNAL LIFE AND BECOME QUEEN IN MY STEAD.
I HAVE CATERED TO YOUR WANTS FOR TOO LONG. THIS TIME YOU WILL OBEY.
I WOULD BETRAY ALL FOR YOU, MY BELOVED. TO KEEP YOU WITH ME.
THE GODS FORGIVE ME IF I DO WRONG.

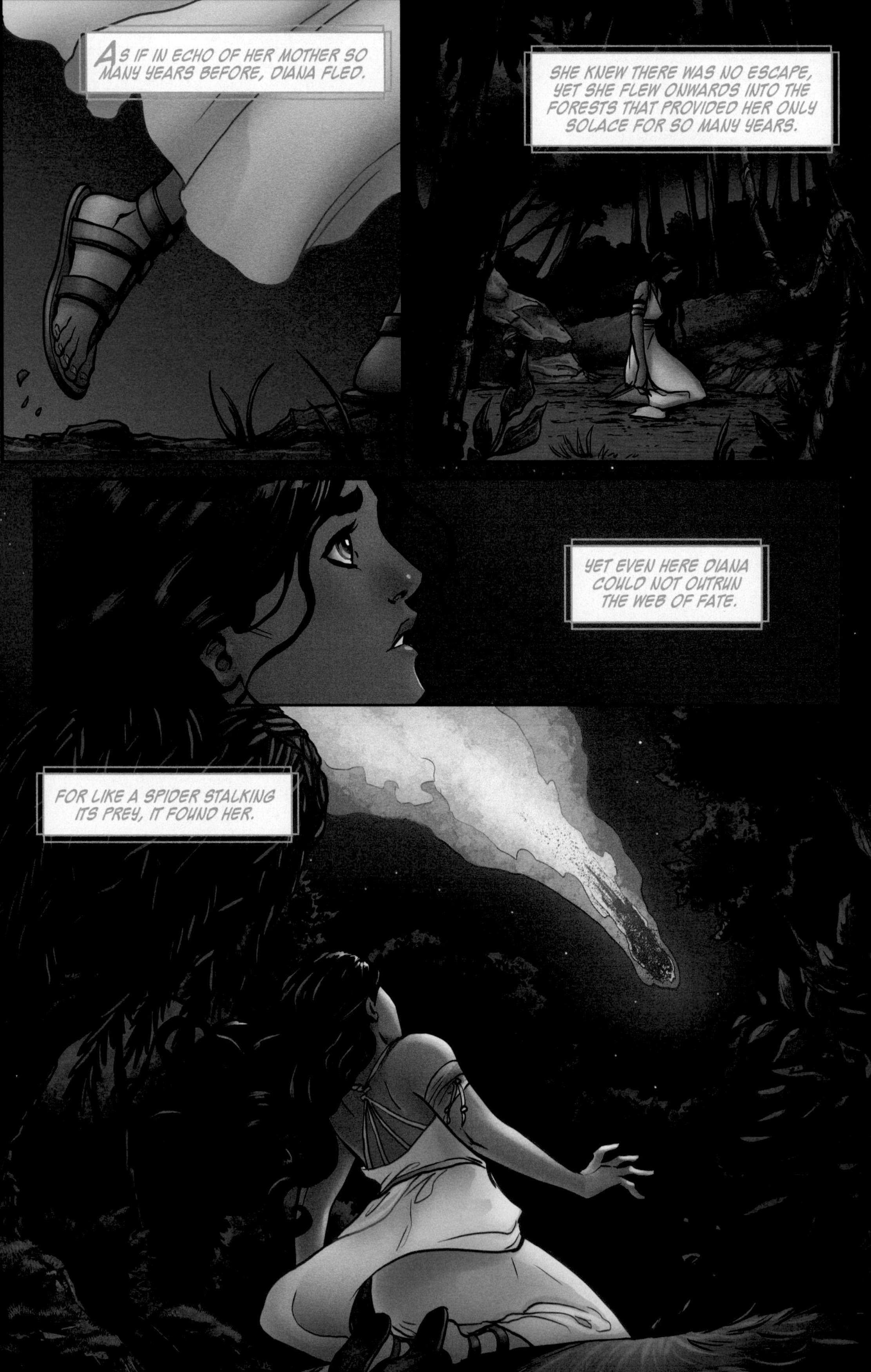
AS IF IN ECHO OF HER MOTHER SO MANY YEARS BEFORE, DIANA FLED.
SHE KNEW THERE WAS NO ESCAPE, YET SHE FLEW ONWARDS INTO THE FORESTS THAT PROVIDED HER ONLY SOLACE FOR SO MANY YEARS.
YET EVEN HERE DIANA COULD NOT OUTRUN THE WEB OF FATE.
FOR LIKE A SPIDER STALKING ITS PREY, IT FOUND HER.

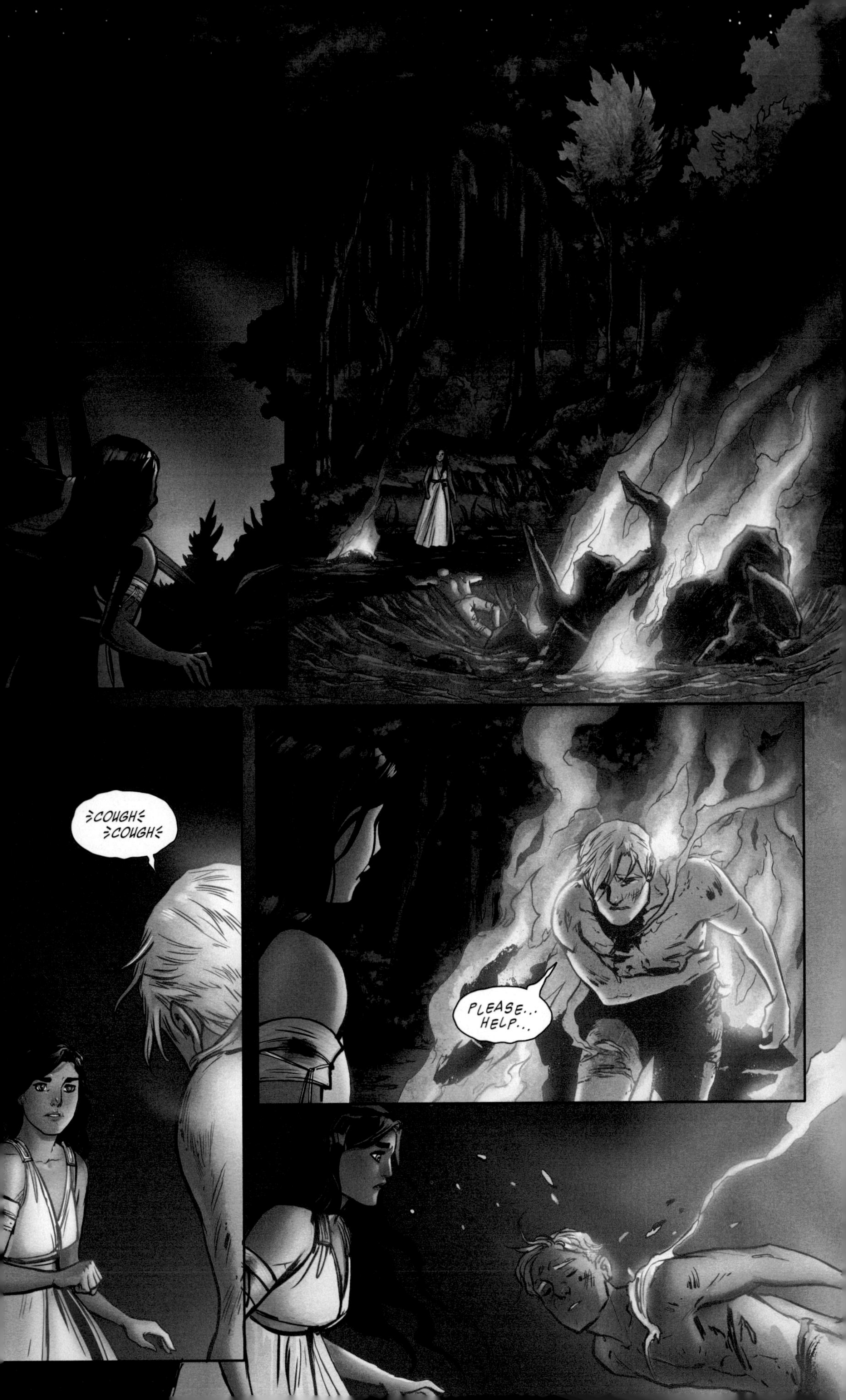
COUGH COUGH
PLEASE... HELP...

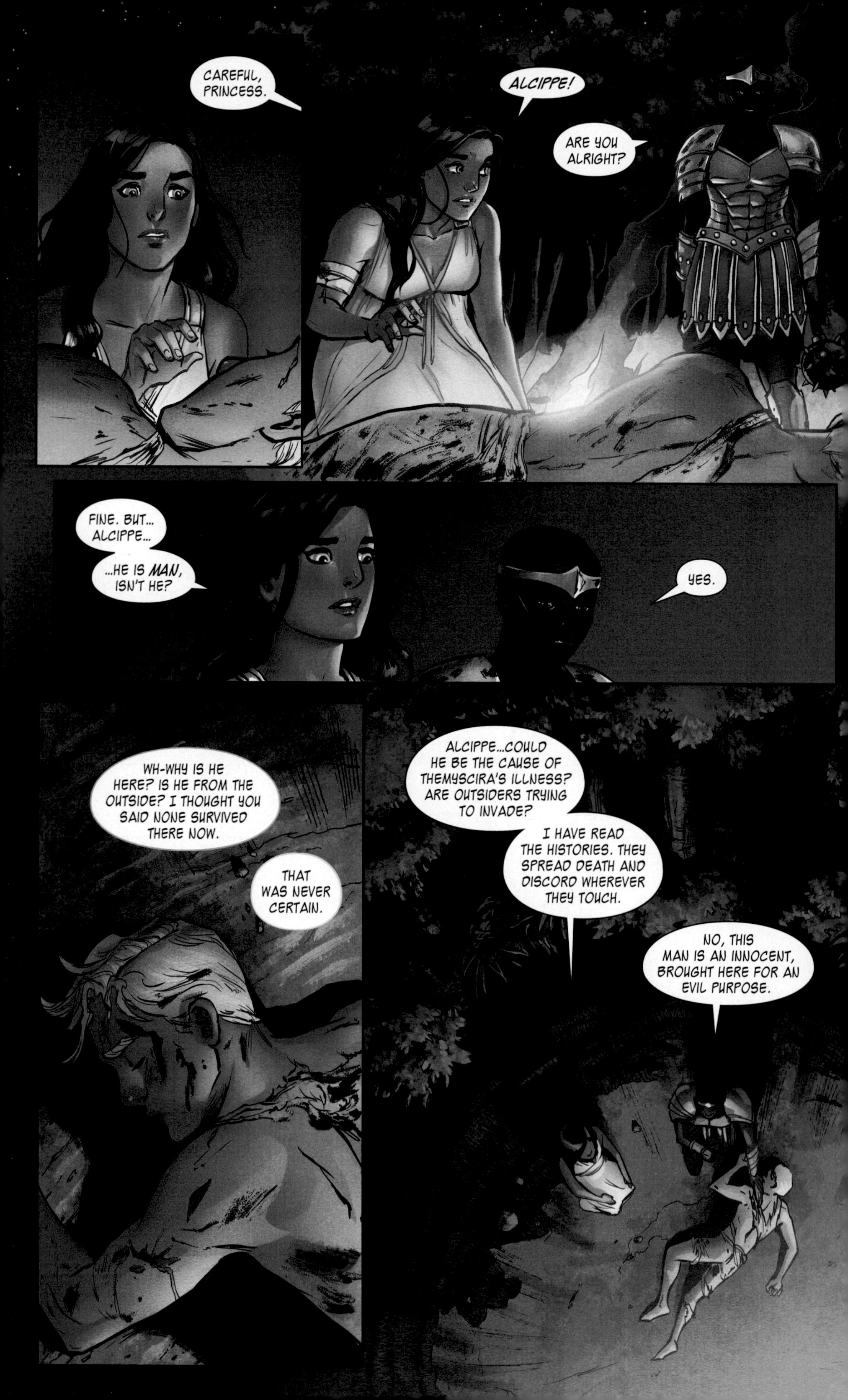
CAREFUL, PRINCESS.
ALCIPPE!
ARE YOU ALRIGHT?
FINE. BUT... ALCIPPE...
...HE IS *MAN*, ISN'T HE?
YES.
WH-WHY IS HE HERE? IS HE FROM THE OUTSIDE? I THOUGHT YOU SAID NONE SURVIVED THERE NOW.
THAT WAS NEVER CERTAIN.
ALCIPPE...COULD HE BE THE CAUSE OF THEMYSCIRA'S ILLNESS? ARE OUTSIDERS TRYING TO INVADE?
I HAVE READ THE HISTORIES. THEY SPREAD DEATH AND DISCORD WHEREVER THEY TOUCH.
NO, THIS MAN IS AN INNOCENT, BROUGHT HERE FOR AN EVIL PURPOSE.

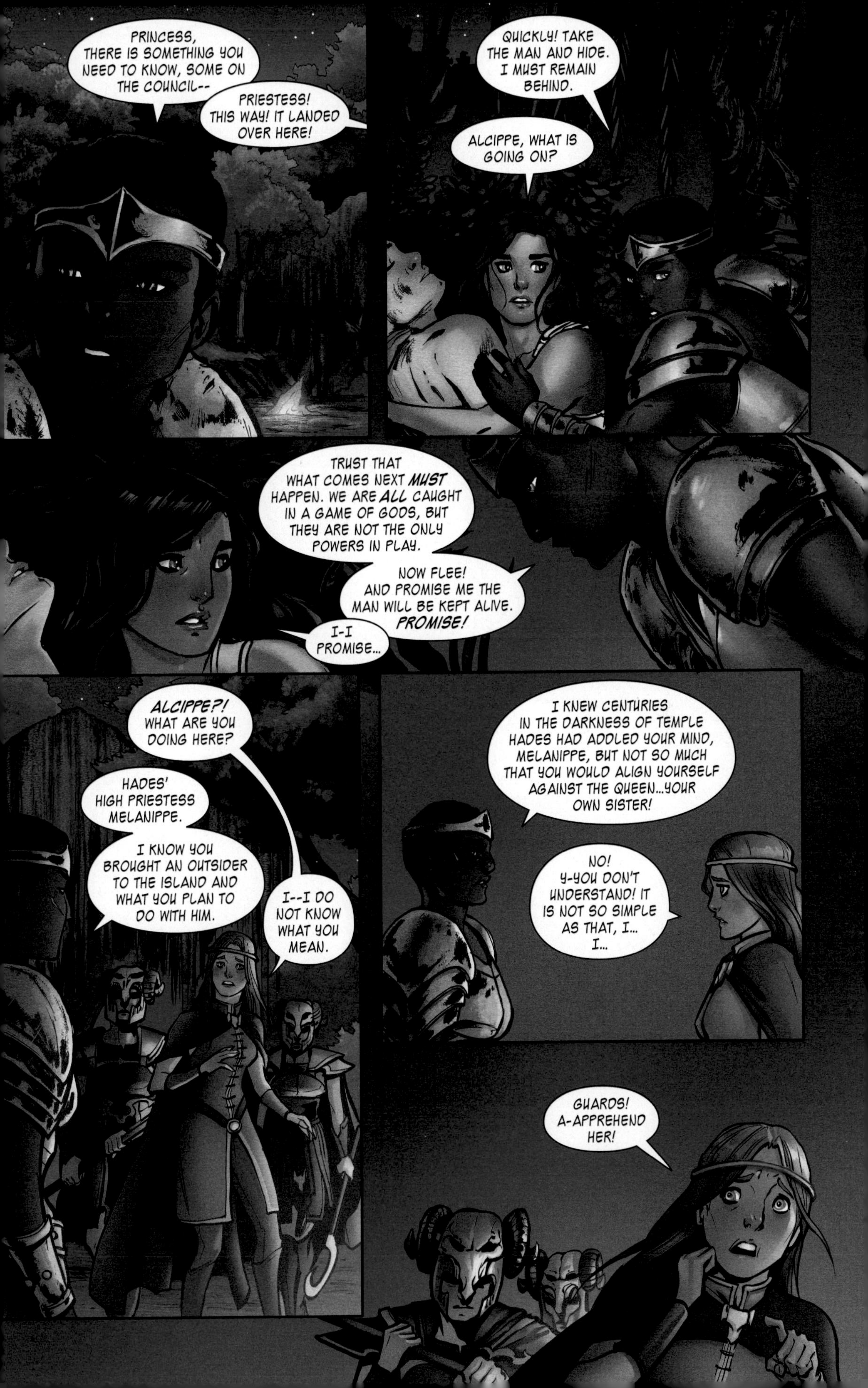
PRINCESS, THERE IS SOMETHING YOU NEED TO KNOW, SOME ON THE COUNCIL--
PRIESTESS! THIS WAY! IT LANDED OVER HERE!
QUICKLY! TAKE THE MAN AND HIDE. I MUST REMAIN BEHIND.
ALCIPPE, WHAT IS GOING ON?
TRUST THAT WHAT COMES NEXT MUST HAPPEN. WE ARE ALL CAUGHT IN A GAME OF GODS, BUT THEY ARE NOT THE ONLY POWERS IN PLAY.
NOW FLEE! AND PROMISE ME THE MAN WILL BE KEPT ALIVE. PROMISE!
I-I PROMISE...
ALCIPPE?! WHAT ARE YOU DOING HERE?
HADES' HIGH PRIESTESS MELANIPPE.
I KNOW YOU BROUGHT AN OUTSIDER TO THE ISLAND AND WHAT YOU PLAN TO DO WITH HIM.
I--I DO NOT KNOW WHAT YOU MEAN.
I KNEW CENTURIES IN THE DARKNESS OF TEMPLE HADES HAD ADDLED YOUR MIND, MELANIPPE, BUT NOT SO MUCH THAT YOU WOULD ALIGN YOURSELF AGAINST THE QUEEN...YOUR OWN SISTER!
NO! Y-YOU DON'T UNDERSTAND! IT IS NOT SO SIMPLE AS THAT, I... I...
GUARDS! A-APPREHEND HER!

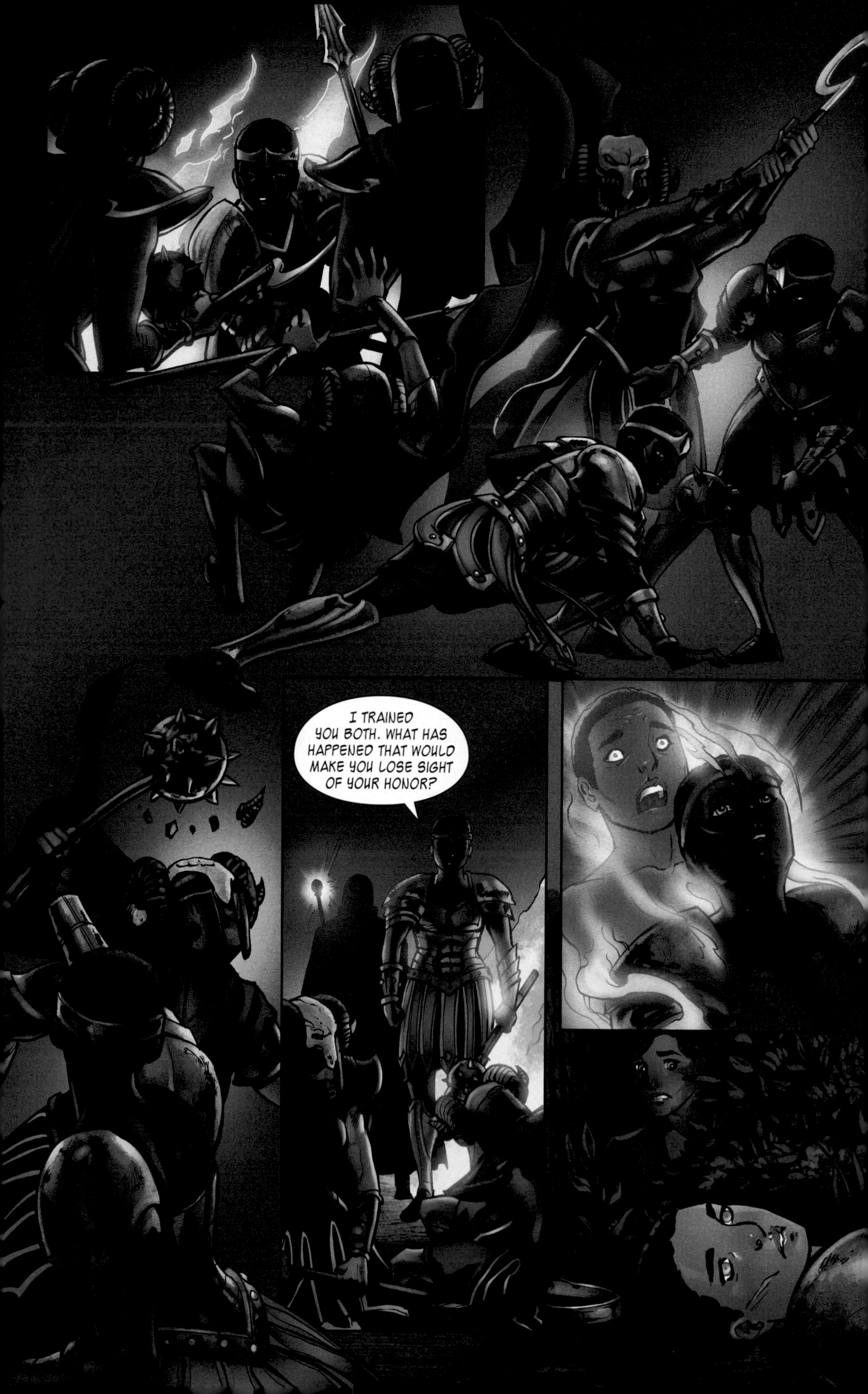
I TRAINED YOU BOTH. WHAT HAS HAPPENED THAT WOULD MAKE YOU LOSE SIGHT OF YOUR HONOR?

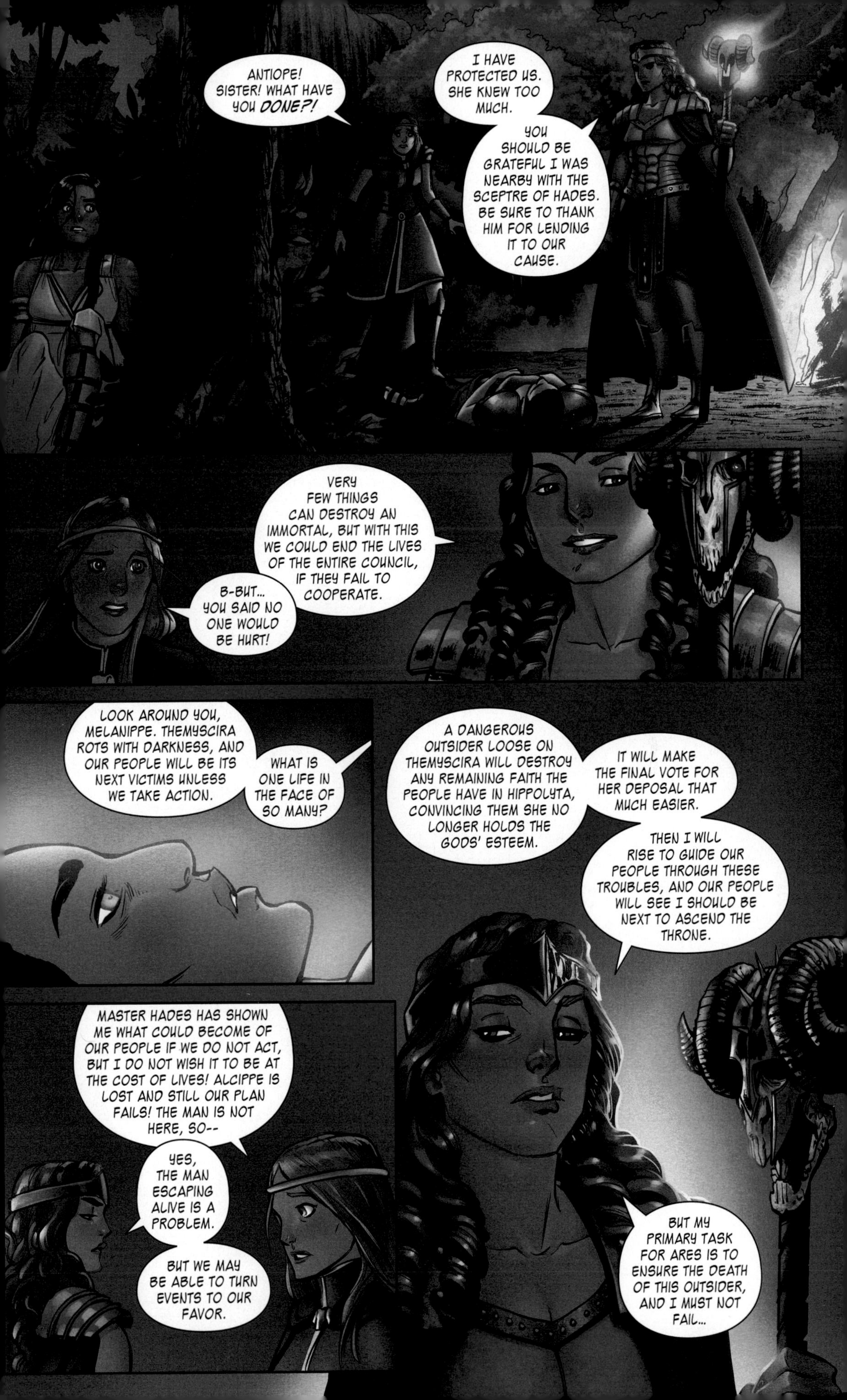

ANTIOPE! SISTER! WHAT HAVE YOU *DONE?!*
I HAVE PROTECTED US. SHE KNEW TOO MUCH.
YOU SHOULD BE GRATEFUL I WAS NEARBY WITH THE SCEPTRE OF HADES. BE SURE TO THANK HIM FOR LENDING IT TO OUR CAUSE.
VERY FEW THINGS CAN DESTROY AN IMMORTAL, BUT WITH THIS WE COULD END THE LIVES OF THE ENTIRE COUNCIL, IF THEY FAIL TO COOPERATE.
B-BUT... YOU SAID NO ONE WOULD BE HURT!
LOOK AROUND YOU, MELANIPPE. THEMYSCIRA ROTS WITH DARKNESS, AND OUR PEOPLE WILL BE ITS NEXT VICTIMS UNLESS WE TAKE ACTION.
WHAT IS ONE LIFE IN THE FACE OF SO MANY?
A DANGEROUS OUTSIDER LOOSE ON THEMYSCIRA WILL DESTROY ANY REMAINING FAITH THE PEOPLE HAVE IN HIPPOLYTA, CONVINCING THEM SHE NO LONGER HOLDS THE GODS' ESTEEM.
IT WILL MAKE THE FINAL VOTE FOR HER DEPOSAL THAT MUCH EASIER.
THEN I WILL RISE TO GUIDE OUR PEOPLE THROUGH THESE TROUBLES, AND OUR PEOPLE WILL SEE I SHOULD BE NEXT TO ASCEND THE THRONE.
MASTER HADES HAS SHOWN ME WHAT COULD BECOME OF OUR PEOPLE IF WE DO NOT ACT, BUT I DO NOT WISH IT TO BE AT THE COST OF LIVES! ALCIPPE IS LOST AND STILL OUR PLAN FAILS! THE MAN IS NOT HERE, SO--
YES, THE MAN ESCAPING ALIVE IS A PROBLEM.
BUT WE MAY BE ABLE TO TURN EVENTS TO OUR FAVOR.
BUT MY PRIMARY TASK FOR ARES IS TO ENSURE THE DEATH OF THIS OUTSIDER, AND I MUST NOT FAIL...

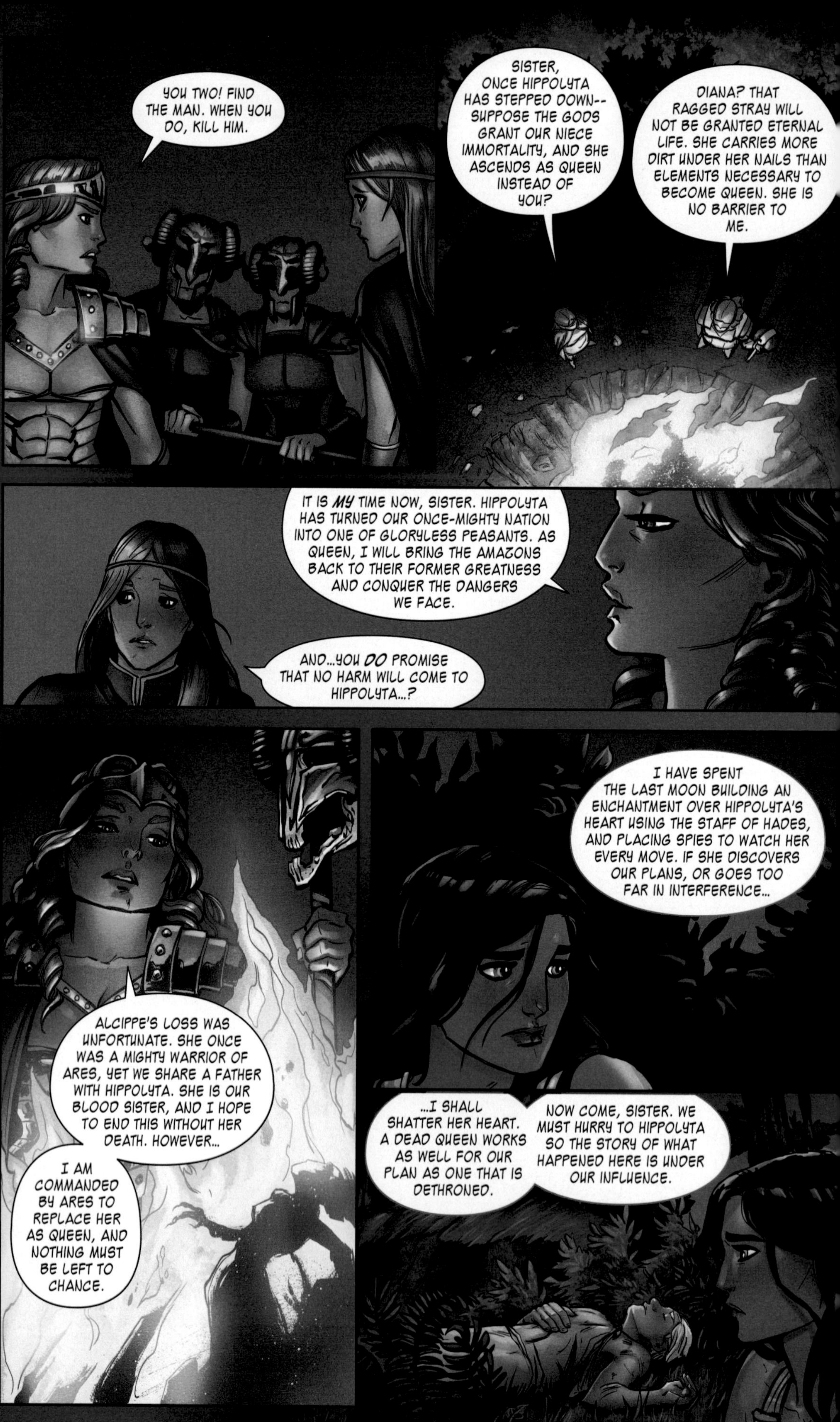
YOU TWO! FIND THE MAN. WHEN YOU DO, KILL HIM.
SISTER, ONCE HIPPOLYTA HAS STEPPED DOWN-- SUPPOSE THE GODS GRANT OUR NIECE IMMORTALITY, AND SHE ASCENDS AS QUEEN INSTEAD OF YOU?
DIANA? THAT RAGGED STRAY WILL NOT BE GRANTED ETERNAL LIFE. SHE CARRIES MORE DIRT UNDER HER NAILS THAN ELEMENTS NECESSARY TO BECOME QUEEN. SHE IS NO BARRIER TO ME.
IT IS *MY* TIME NOW, SISTER. HIPPOLYTA HAS TURNED OUR ONCE-MIGHTY NATION INTO ONE OF GLORYLESS PEASANTS. AS QUEEN, I WILL BRING THE AMAZONS BACK TO THEIR FORMER GREATNESS AND CONQUER THE DANGERS WE FACE.
AND...YOU *DO* PROMISE THAT NO HARM WILL COME TO HIPPOLYTA...?
ALCIPPE'S LOSS WAS UNFORTUNATE. SHE ONCE WAS A MIGHTY WARRIOR OF ARES, YET WE SHARE A FATHER WITH HIPPOLYTA. SHE IS OUR BLOOD SISTER, AND I HOPE TO END THIS WITHOUT HER DEATH. HOWEVER...
I AM COMMANDED BY ARES TO REPLACE HER AS QUEEN, AND NOTHING MUST BE LEFT TO CHANCE.
I HAVE SPENT THE LAST MOON BUILDING AN ENCHANTMENT OVER HIPPOLYTA'S HEART USING THE STAFF OF HADES, AND PLACING SPIES TO WATCH HER EVERY MOVE. IF SHE DISCOVERS OUR PLANS, OR GOES TOO FAR IN INTERFERENCE...
...I SHALL SHATTER HER HEART. A DEAD QUEEN WORKS AS WELL FOR OUR PLAN AS ONE THAT IS DETHRONED.
NOW COME, SISTER. WE MUST HURRY TO HIPPOLYTA SO THE STORY OF WHAT HAPPENED HERE IS UNDER OUR INFLUENCE.

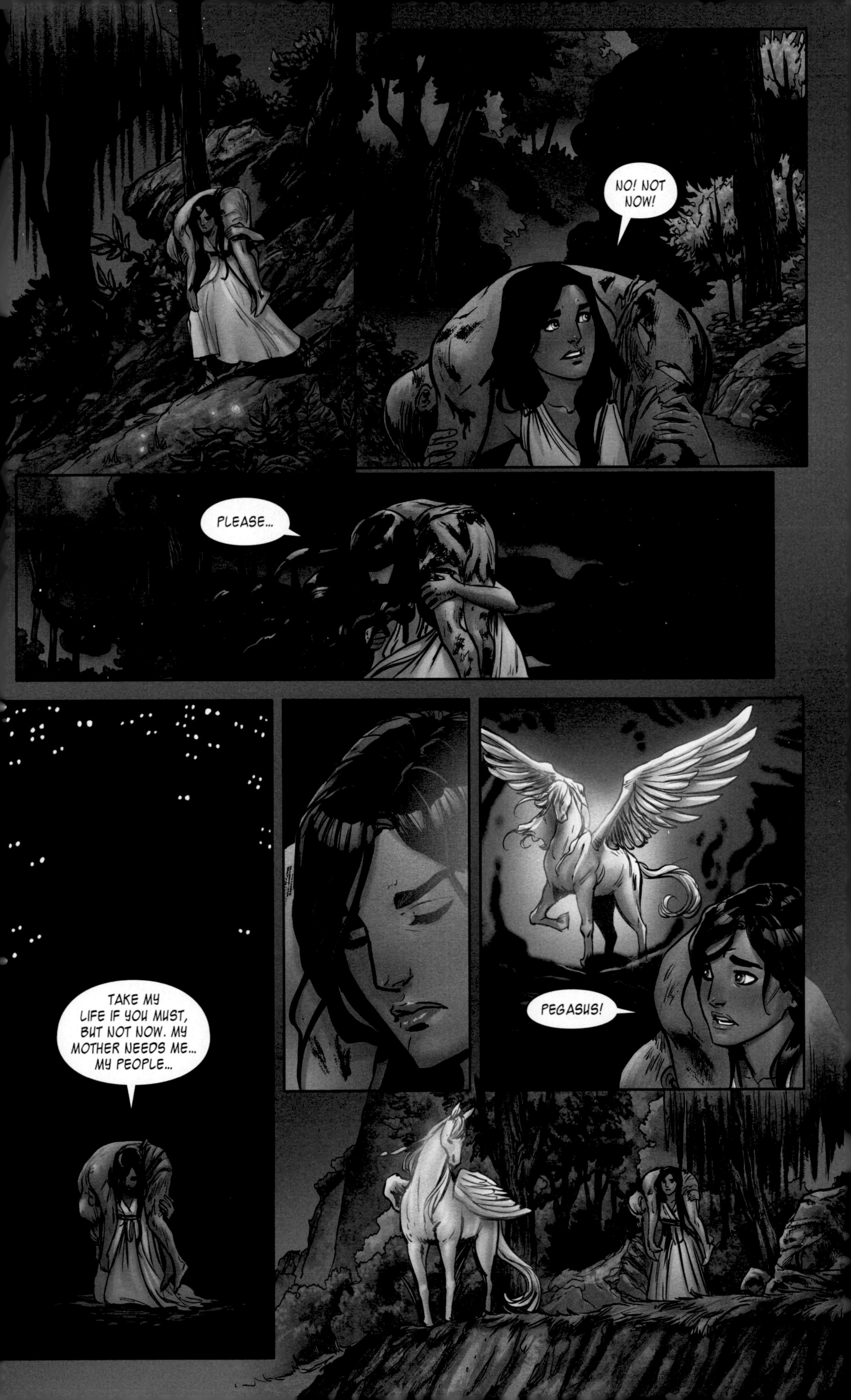
NO! NOT NOW!
PLEASE...
TAKE MY LIFE IF YOU MUST, BUT NOT NOW. MY MOTHER NEEDS ME... MY PEOPLE...
PEGASUS!

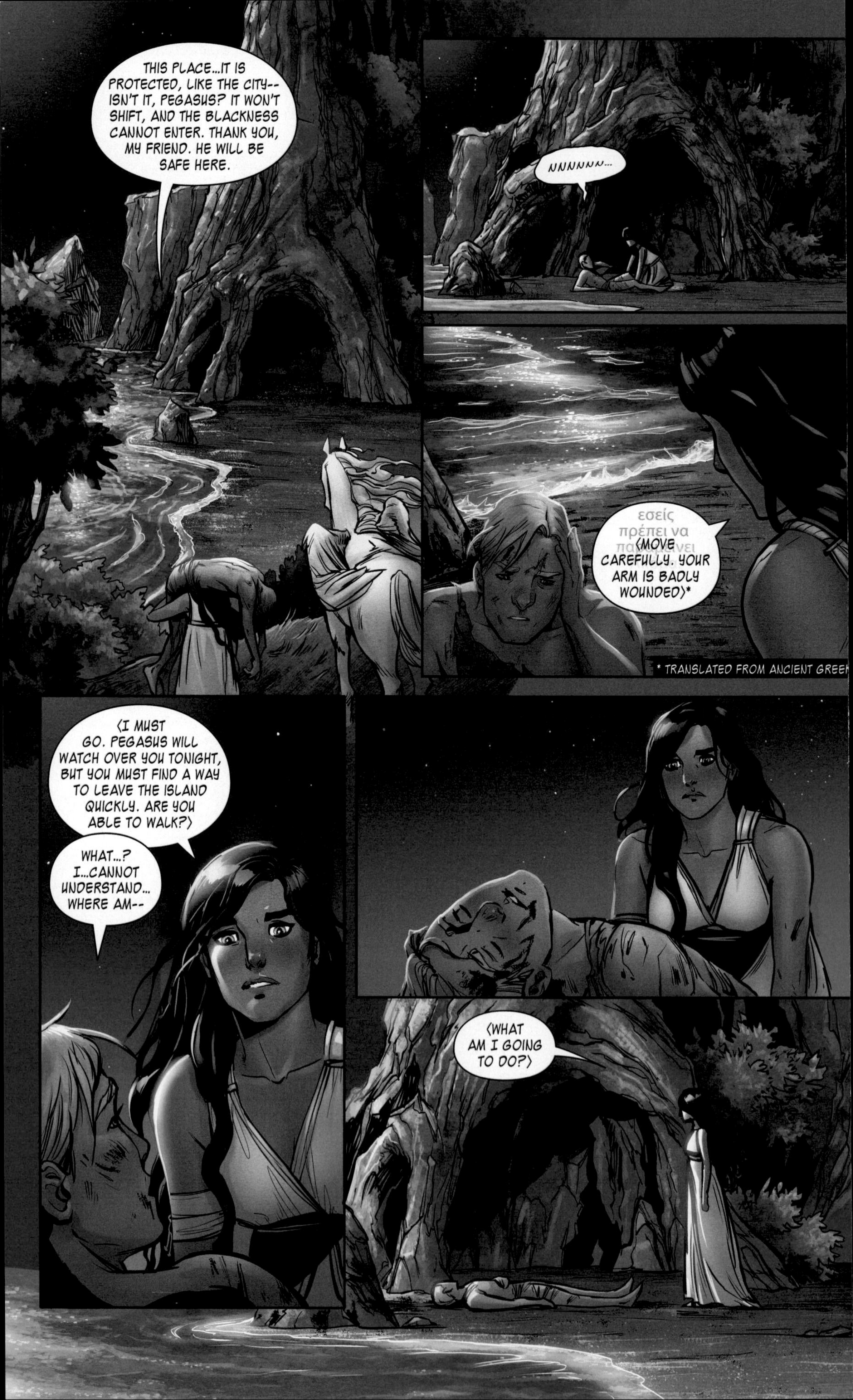
THIS PLACE...IT IS PROTECTED, LIKE THE CITY--ISN'T IT, PEGASUS? IT WON'T SHIFT, AND THE BLACKNESS CANNOT ENTER. THANK YOU, MY FRIEND. HE WILL BE SAFE HERE.
NNNNNN...
εσείς
πρέπει να
‹MOVE CAREFULLY. YOUR ARM IS BADLY WOUNDED›*
* TRANSLATED FROM ANCIENT GREEK
‹I MUST GO. PEGASUS WILL WATCH OVER YOU TONIGHT, BUT YOU MUST FIND A WAY TO LEAVE THE ISLAND QUICKLY. ARE YOU ABLE TO WALK?›
WHAT...? I...CANNOT UNDERSTAND... WHERE AM--
‹WHAT AM I GOING TO DO?›

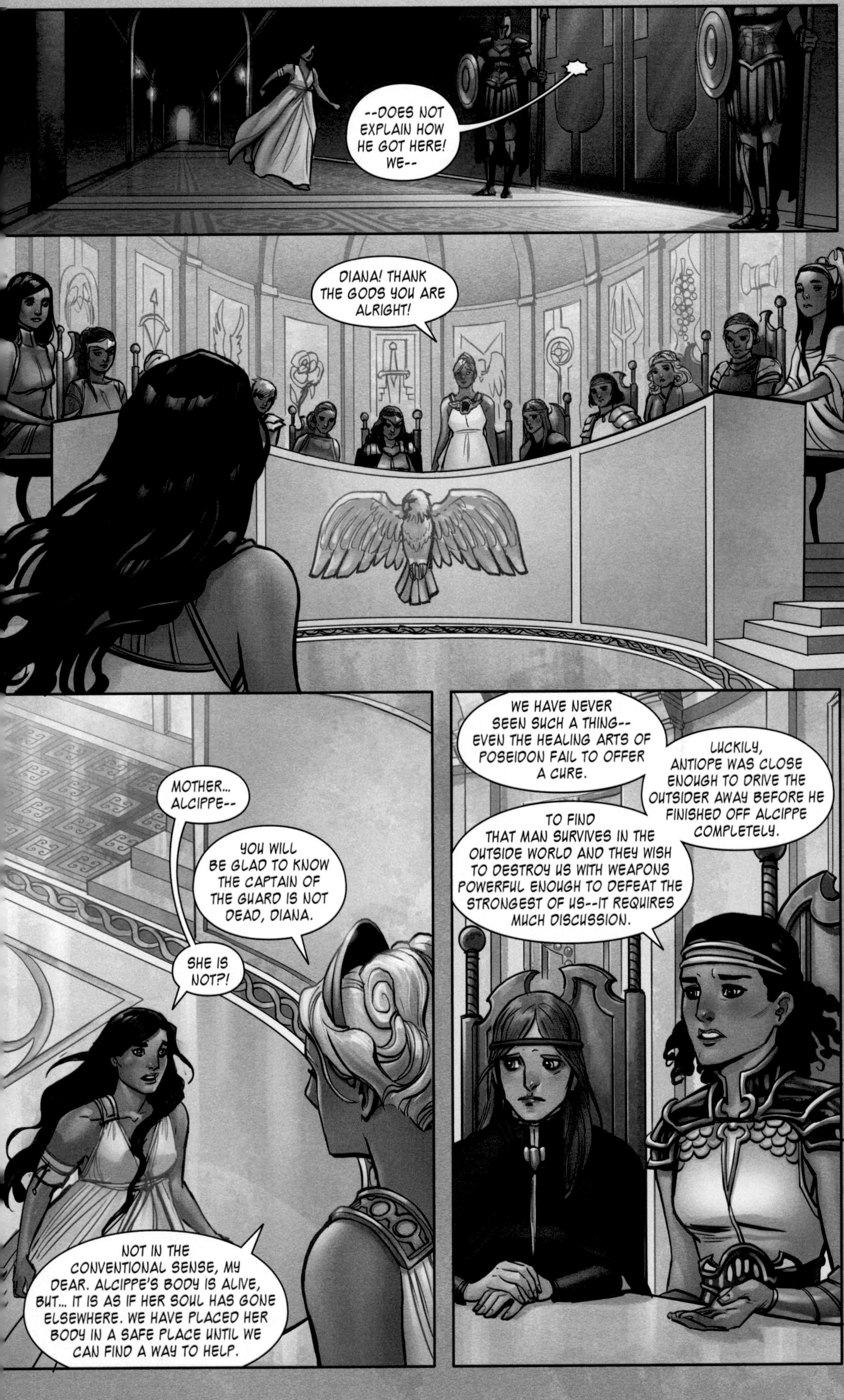
--DOES NOT EXPLAIN HOW HE GOT HERE! WE--
DIANA! THANK THE GODS YOU ARE ALRIGHT!
MOTHER... ALCIPPE--
YOU WILL BE GLAD TO KNOW THE CAPTAIN OF THE GUARD IS NOT DEAD, DIANA.
SHE IS NOT?!
NOT IN THE CONVENTIONAL SENSE, MY DEAR. ALCIPPE'S BODY IS ALIVE, BUT... IT IS AS IF HER SOUL HAS GONE ELSEWHERE. WE HAVE PLACED HER BODY IN A SAFE PLACE UNTIL WE CAN FIND A WAY TO HELP.
WE HAVE NEVER SEEN SUCH A THING-- EVEN THE HEALING ARTS OF POSEIDON FAIL TO OFFER A CURE.
LUCKILY, ANTIOPE WAS CLOSE ENOUGH TO DRIVE THE OUTSIDER AWAY BEFORE HE FINISHED OFF ALCIPPE COMPLETELY.
TO FIND THAT MAN SURVIVES IN THE OUTSIDE WORLD AND THEY WISH TO DESTROY US WITH WEAPONS POWERFUL ENOUGH TO DEFEAT THE STRONGEST OF US--IT REQUIRES MUCH DISCUSSION.

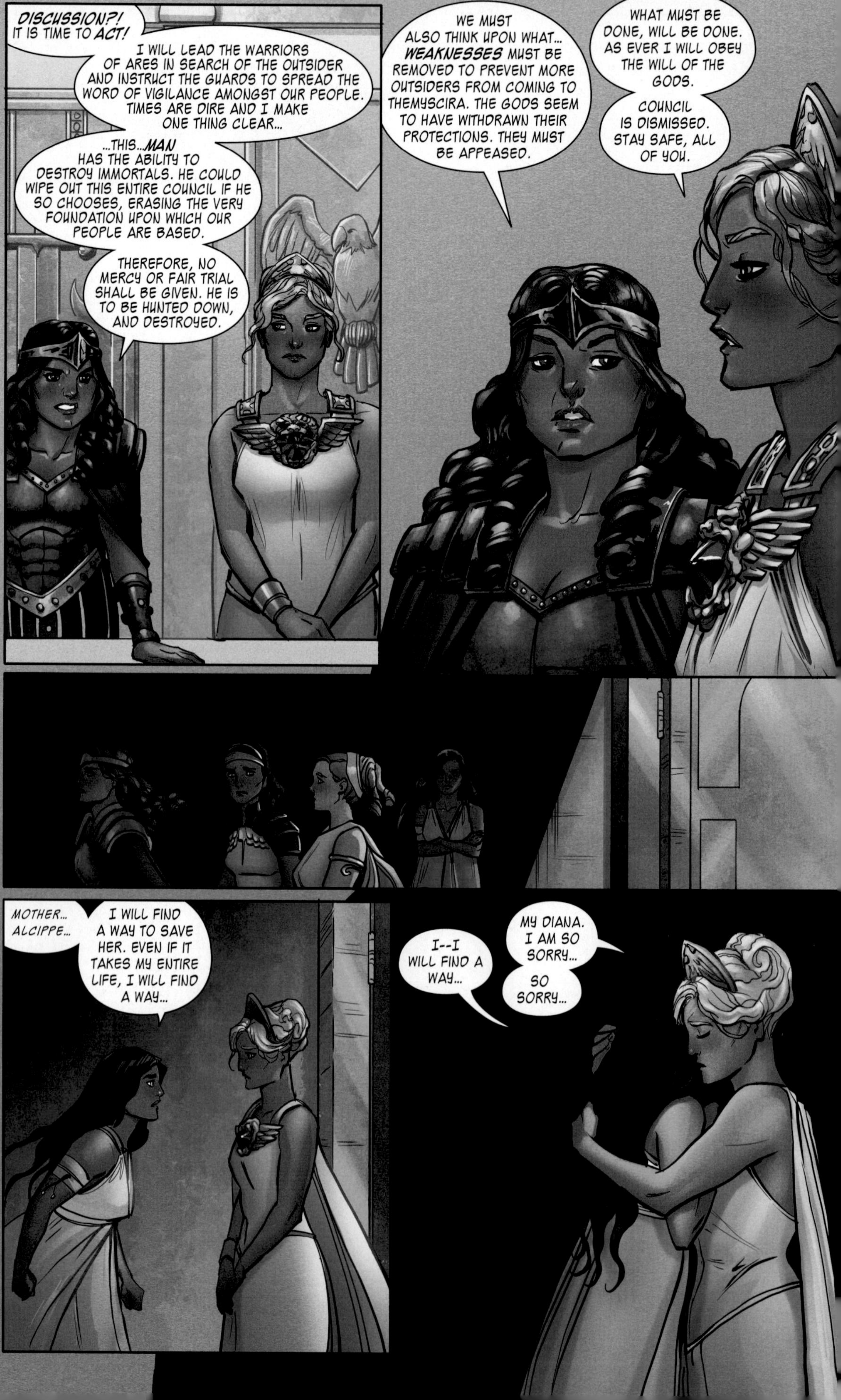
DISCUSSION?! IT IS TIME TO ACT!
I WILL LEAD THE WARRIORS OF ARES IN SEARCH OF THE OUTSIDER AND INSTRUCT THE GUARDS TO SPREAD THE WORD OF VIGILANCE AMONGST OUR PEOPLE. TIMES ARE DIRE AND I MAKE ONE THING CLEAR...
...THIS...MAN HAS THE ABILITY TO DESTROY IMMORTALS. HE COULD WIPE OUT THIS ENTIRE COUNCIL IF HE SO CHOOSES, ERASING THE VERY FOUNDATION UPON WHICH OUR PEOPLE ARE BASED.
THEREFORE, NO MERCY OR FAIR TRIAL SHALL BE GIVEN. HE IS TO BE HUNTED DOWN, AND DESTROYED.
WE MUST ALSO THINK UPON WHAT... WEAKNESSES MUST BE REMOVED TO PREVENT MORE OUTSIDERS FROM COMING TO THEMYSCIRA. THE GODS SEEM TO HAVE WITHDRAWN THEIR PROTECTIONS. THEY MUST BE APPEASED.
WHAT MUST BE DONE, WILL BE DONE. AS EVER I WILL OBEY THE WILL OF THE GODS.
COUNCIL IS DISMISSED. STAY SAFE, ALL OF YOU.
MOTHER... ALCIPPE...
I WILL FIND A WAY TO SAVE HER. EVEN IF IT TAKES MY ENTIRE LIFE, I WILL FIND A WAY...
I--I WILL FIND A WAY...
MY DIANA. I AM SO SORRY...
SO SORRY...

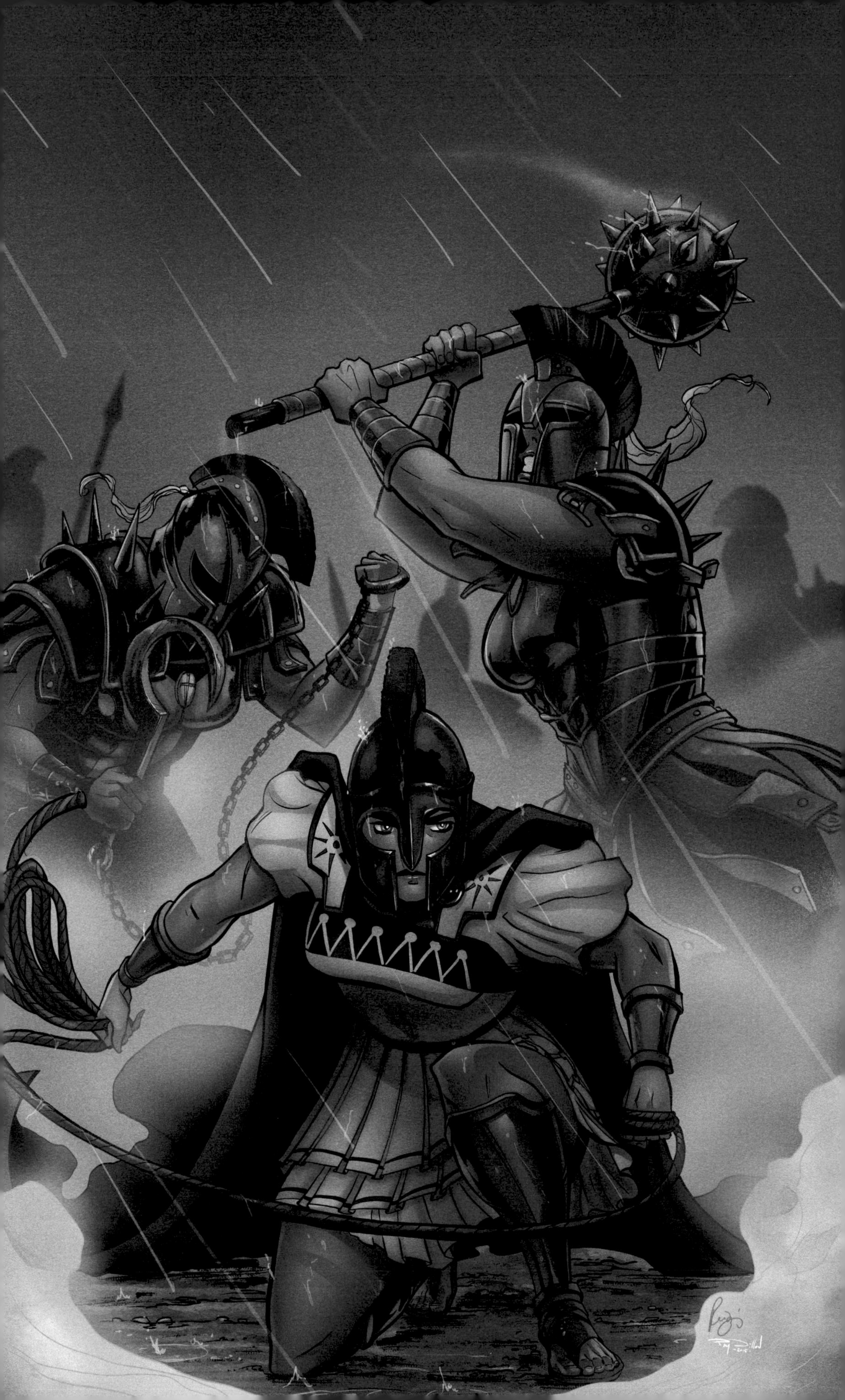

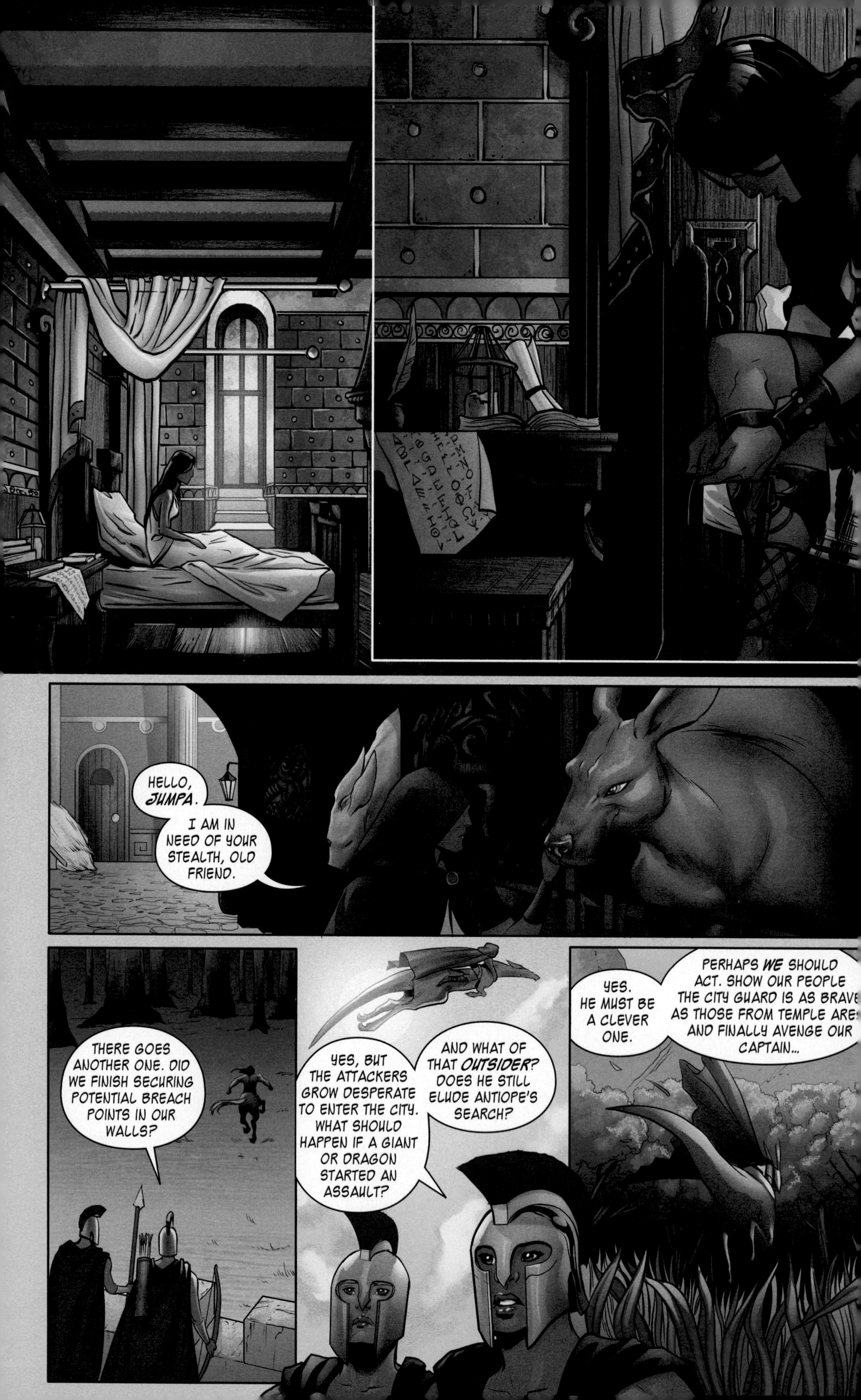
HELLO, JUMPA.
I AM IN NEED OF YOUR STEALTH, OLD FRIEND.
THERE GOES ANOTHER ONE. DID WE FINISH SECURING POTENTIAL BREACH POINTS IN OUR WALLS?
YES, BUT THE ATTACKERS GROW DESPERATE TO ENTER THE CITY. WHAT SHOULD HAPPEN IF A GIANT OR DRAGON STARTED AN ASSAULT?
AND WHAT OF THAT OUTSIDER? DOES HE STILL ELUDE ANTIOPE'S SEARCH?
YES. HE MUST BE A CLEVER ONE.
PERHAPS WE SHOULD ACT. SHOW OUR PEOPLE THE CITY GUARD IS AS BRAVE AS THOSE FROM TEMPLE ARES AND FINALLY AVENGE OUR CAPTAIN...

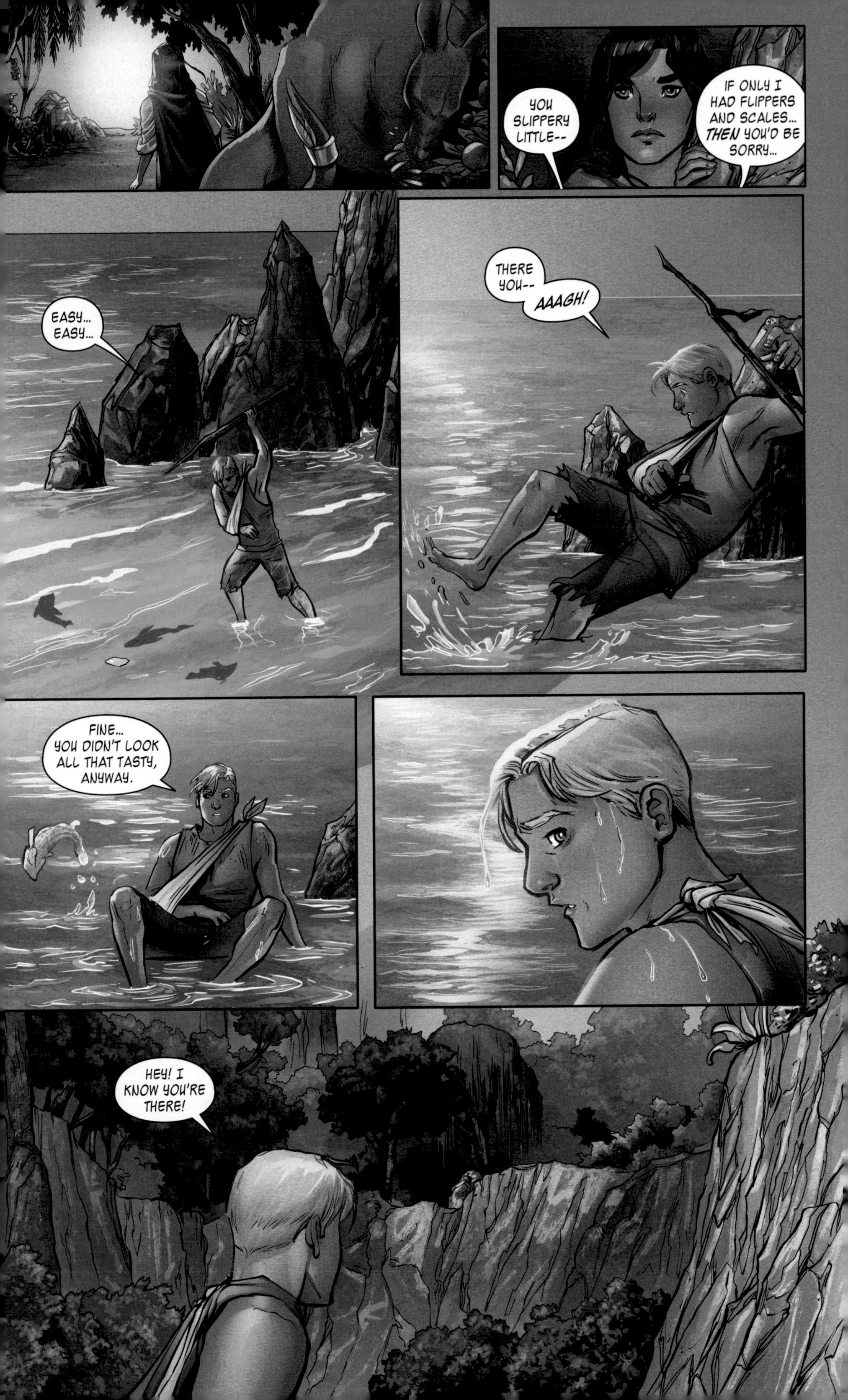
YOU SLIPPERY LITTLE--
IF ONLY I HAD FLIPPERS AND SCALES... **THEN** YOU'D BE SORRY...
EASY... EASY...
THERE YOU-- **AAAGH!**
FINE... YOU DIDN'T LOOK ALL THAT TASTY, ANYWAY.
HEY! I KNOW YOU'RE THERE!

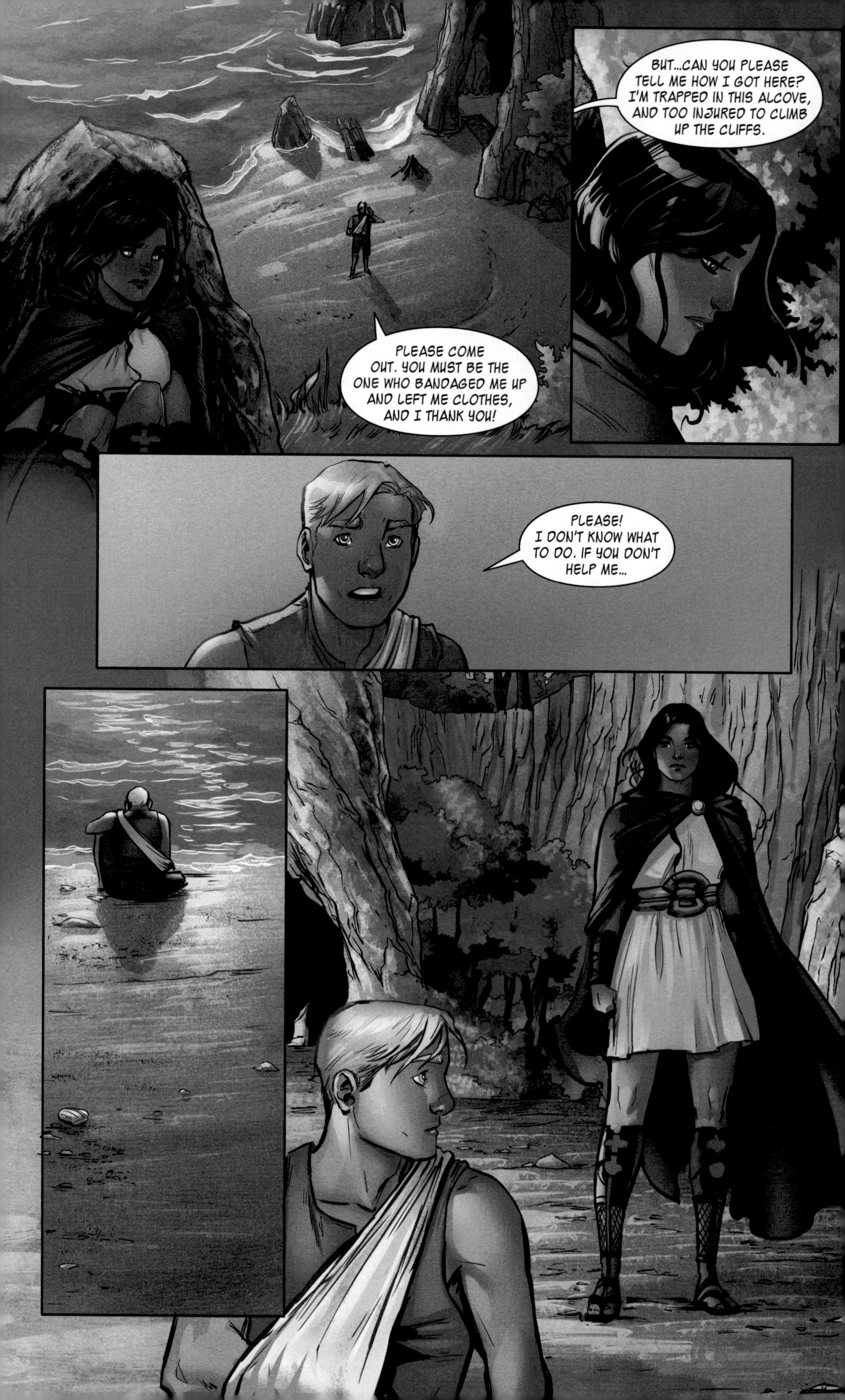
PLEASE COME OUT. YOU MUST BE THE ONE WHO BANDAGED ME UP AND LEFT ME CLOTHES, AND I THANK YOU!
BUT...CAN YOU PLEASE TELL ME HOW I GOT HERE? I'M TRAPPED IN THIS ALCOVE, AND TOO INJURED TO CLIMB UP THE CLIFFS.
PLEASE! I DON'T KNOW WHAT TO DO. IF YOU DON'T HELP ME...

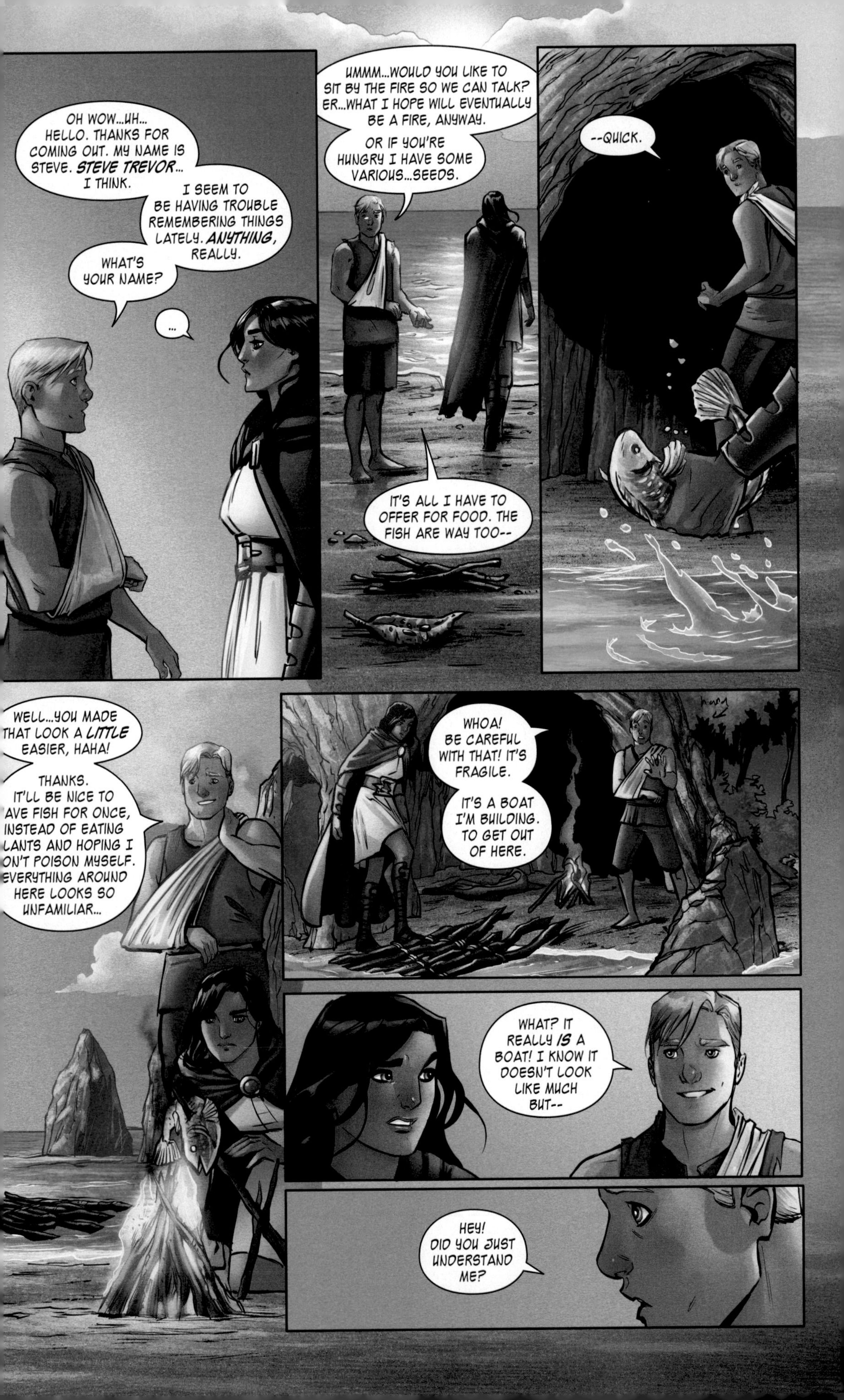

OH WOW...UH... HELLO. THANKS FOR COMING OUT. MY NAME IS STEVE. STEVE TREVOR... I THINK.
I SEEM TO BE HAVING TROUBLE REMEMBERING THINGS LATELY. ANYTHING, REALLY.
WHAT'S YOUR NAME?
...
UMMM...WOULD YOU LIKE TO SIT BY THE FIRE SO WE CAN TALK? ER...WHAT I HOPE WILL EVENTUALLY BE A FIRE, ANYWAY.
OR IF YOU'RE HUNGRY I HAVE SOME VARIOUS...SEEDS.
IT'S ALL I HAVE TO OFFER FOR FOOD. THE FISH ARE WAY TOO--
--QUICK.
WELL...YOU MADE THAT LOOK A LITTLE EASIER, HAHA!
THANKS. IT'LL BE NICE TO 'AVE FISH FOR ONCE, INSTEAD OF EATING LANTS AND HOPING I ON'T POISON MYSELF. EVERYTHING AROUND HERE LOOKS SO UNFAMILIAR...
WHOA! BE CAREFUL WITH THAT! IT'S FRAGILE.
IT'S A BOAT I'M BUILDING. TO GET OUT OF HERE.
WHAT? IT REALLY IS A BOAT! I KNOW IT DOESN'T LOOK LIKE MUCH BUT--
HEY! DID YOU JUST UNDERSTAND ME?

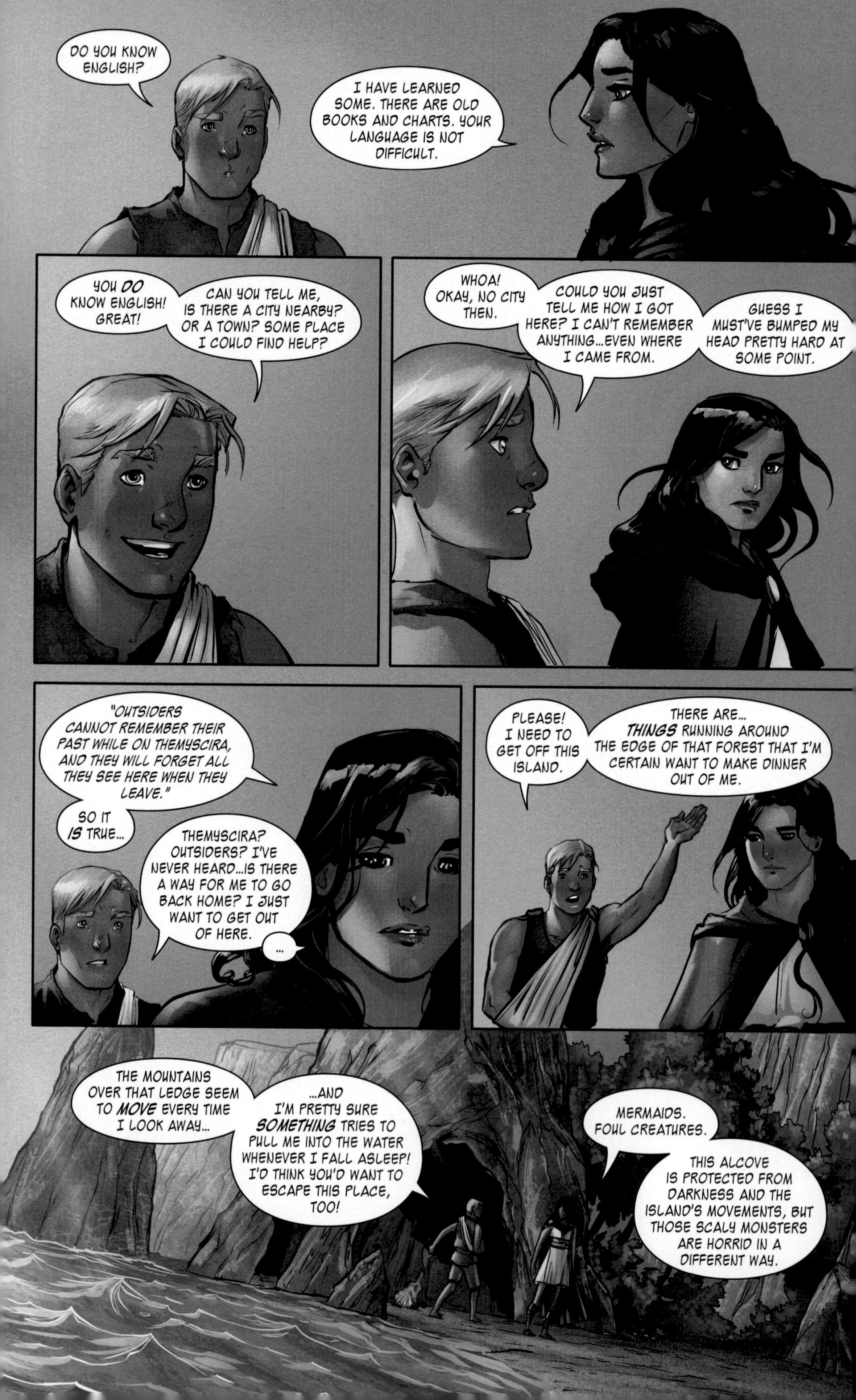
DO YOU KNOW ENGLISH?
I HAVE LEARNED SOME. THERE ARE OLD BOOKS AND CHARTS. YOUR LANGUAGE IS NOT DIFFICULT.
YOU *DO* KNOW ENGLISH! GREAT!
CAN YOU TELL ME, IS THERE A CITY NEARBY? OR A TOWN? SOME PLACE I COULD FIND HELP?
WHOA! OKAY, NO CITY THEN.
COULD YOU JUST TELL ME HOW I GOT HERE? I CAN'T REMEMBER ANYTHING...EVEN WHERE I CAME FROM.
GUESS I MUST'VE BUMPED MY HEAD PRETTY HARD AT SOME POINT.
"OUTSIDERS CANNOT REMEMBER THEIR PAST WHILE ON THEMYSCIRA, AND THEY WILL FORGET ALL THEY SEE HERE WHEN THEY LEAVE."
SO IT *IS* TRUE...
THEMYSCIRA? OUTSIDERS? I'VE NEVER HEARD...IS THERE A WAY FOR ME TO GO BACK HOME? I JUST WANT TO GET OUT OF HERE.
...
PLEASE! I NEED TO GET OFF THIS ISLAND.
THERE ARE... *THINGS* RUNNING AROUND THE EDGE OF THAT FOREST THAT I'M CERTAIN WANT TO MAKE DINNER OUT OF ME.
THE MOUNTAINS OVER THAT LEDGE SEEM TO *MOVE* EVERY TIME I LOOK AWAY...
...AND I'M PRETTY SURE *SOMETHING* TRIES TO PULL ME INTO THE WATER WHENEVER I FALL ASLEEP! I'D THINK YOU'D WANT TO ESCAPE THIS PLACE, TOO!
MERMAIDS. FOUL CREATURES.
THIS ALCOVE IS PROTECTED FROM DARKNESS AND THE ISLAND'S MOVEMENTS, BUT THOSE SCALY MONSTERS ARE HORRID IN A DIFFERENT WAY.

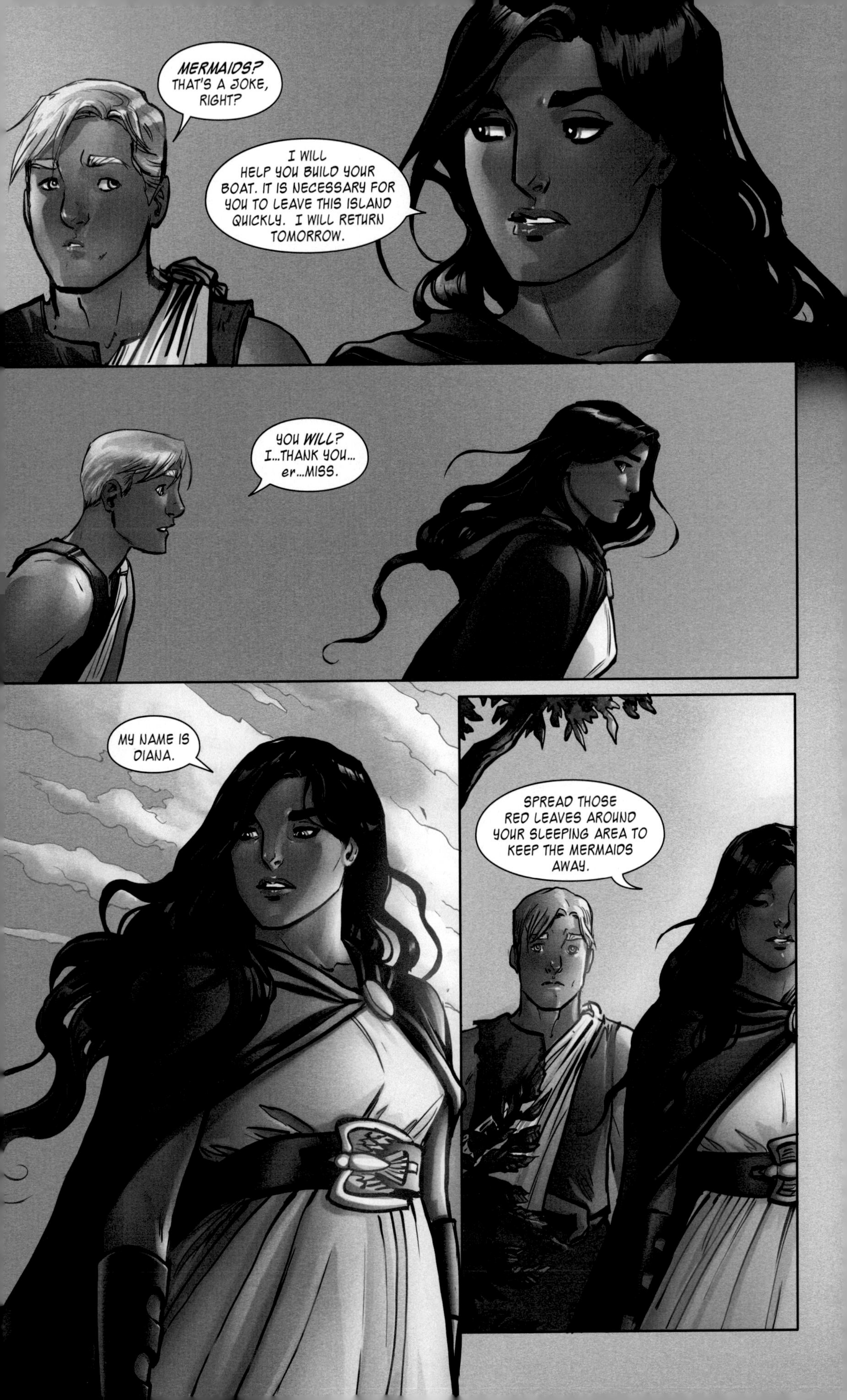
MERMAIDS? THAT'S A JOKE, RIGHT?
I WILL HELP YOU BUILD YOUR BOAT. IT IS NECESSARY FOR YOU TO LEAVE THIS ISLAND QUICKLY. I WILL RETURN TOMORROW.
YOU WILL? I...THANK YOU... er...MISS.
MY NAME IS DIANA.
SPREAD THOSE RED LEAVES AROUND YOUR SLEEPING AREA TO KEEP THE MERMAIDS AWAY.

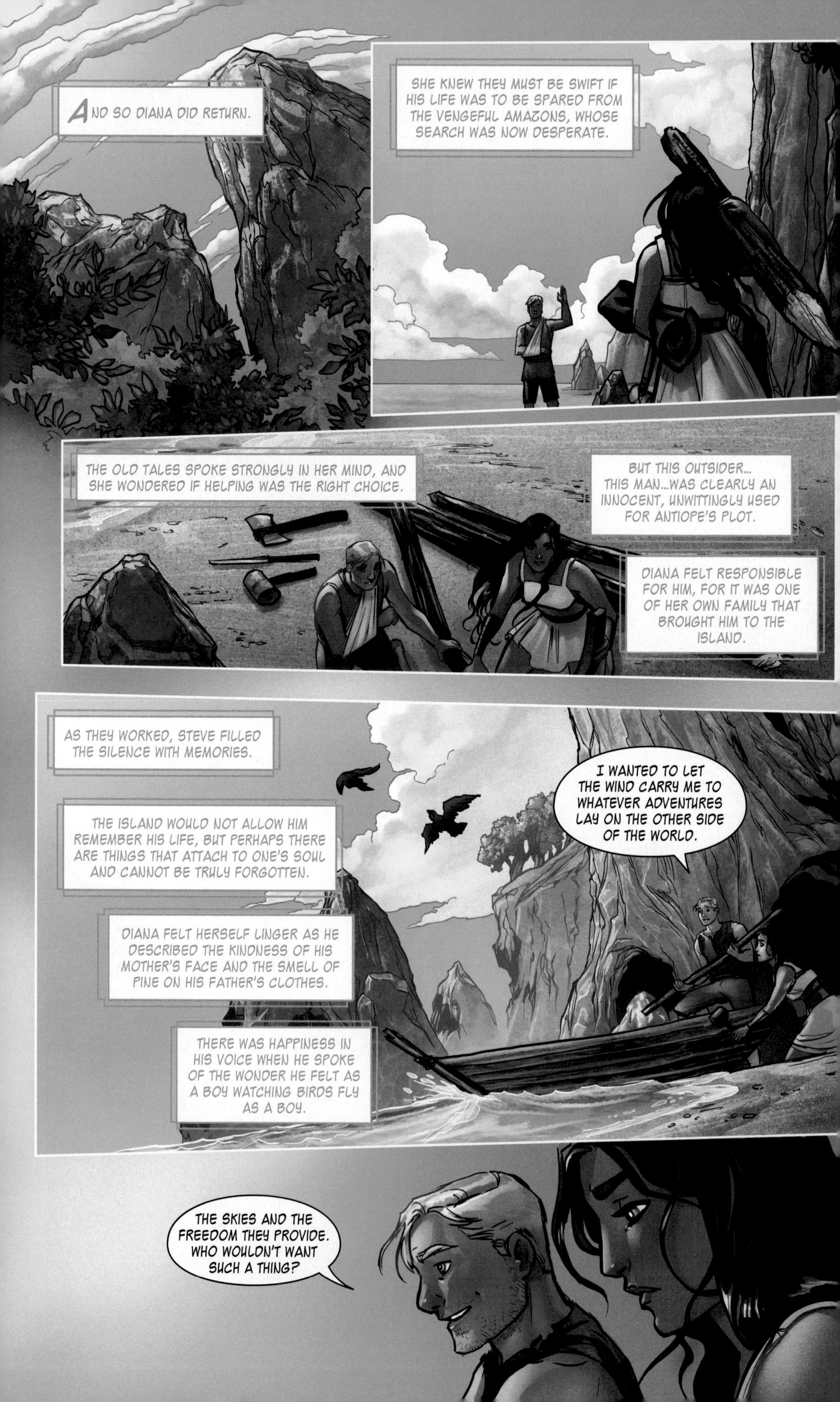
AND SO DIANA DID RETURN.
SHE KNEW THEY MUST BE SWIFT IF HIS LIFE WAS TO BE SPARED FROM THE VENGEFUL AMAZONS, WHOSE SEARCH WAS NOW DESPERATE.
THE OLD TALES SPOKE STRONGLY IN HER MIND, AND SHE WONDERED IF HELPING WAS THE RIGHT CHOICE.
BUT THIS OUTSIDER... THIS MAN...WAS CLEARLY AN INNOCENT, UNWITTINGLY USED FOR ANTIOPE'S PLOT.
DIANA FELT RESPONSIBLE FOR HIM, FOR IT WAS ONE OF HER OWN FAMILY THAT BROUGHT HIM TO THE ISLAND.
AS THEY WORKED, STEVE FILLED THE SILENCE WITH MEMORIES.
THE ISLAND WOULD NOT ALLOW HIM REMEMBER HIS LIFE, BUT PERHAPS THERE ARE THINGS THAT ATTACH TO ONE'S SOUL AND CANNOT BE TRULY FORGOTTEN.
DIANA FELT HERSELF LINGER AS HE DESCRIBED THE KINDNESS OF HIS MOTHER'S FACE AND THE SMELL OF PINE ON HIS FATHER'S CLOTHES.
THERE WAS HAPPINESS IN HIS VOICE WHEN HE SPOKE OF THE WONDER HE FELT AS A BOY WATCHING BIRDS FLY AS A BOY.
I WANTED TO LET THE WIND CARRY ME TO WHATEVER ADVENTURES LAY ON THE OTHER SIDE OF THE WORLD.
THE SKIES AND THE FREEDOM THEY PROVIDE. WHO WOULDN'T WANT SUCH A THING?

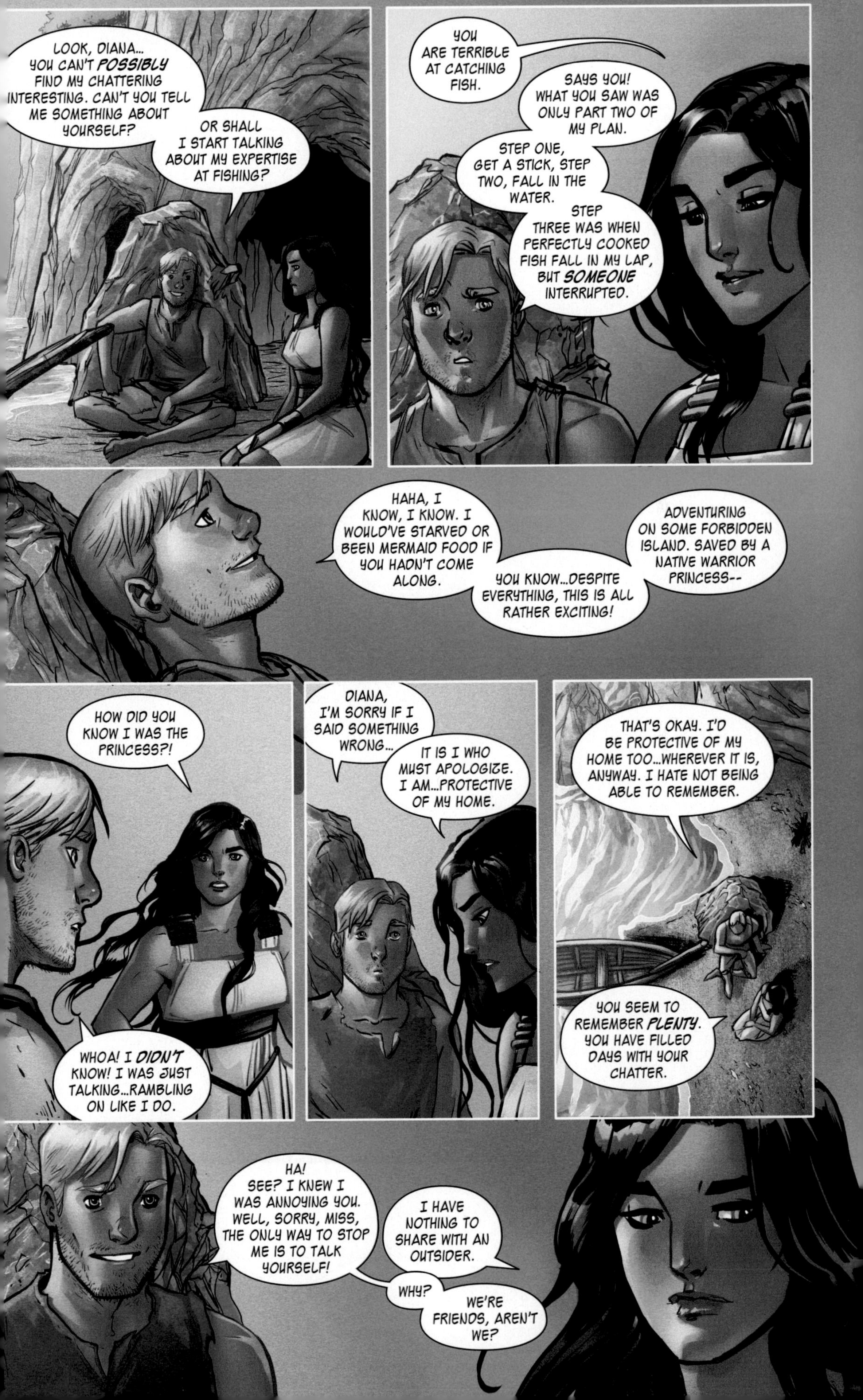
LOOK, DIANA... YOU CAN'T POSSIBLY FIND MY CHATTERING INTERESTING. CAN'T YOU TELL ME SOMETHING ABOUT YOURSELF?
OR SHALL I START TALKING ABOUT MY EXPERTISE AT FISHING?
YOU ARE TERRIBLE AT CATCHING FISH.
SAYS YOU! WHAT YOU SAW WAS ONLY PART TWO OF MY PLAN.
STEP ONE, GET A STICK, STEP TWO, FALL IN THE WATER.
STEP THREE WAS WHEN PERFECTLY COOKED FISH FALL IN MY LAP, BUT SOMEONE INTERRUPTED.
HAHA, I KNOW, I KNOW. I WOULD'VE STARVED OR BEEN MERMAID FOOD IF YOU HADN'T COME ALONG.
YOU KNOW...DESPITE EVERYTHING, THIS IS ALL RATHER EXCITING!
ADVENTURING ON SOME FORBIDDEN ISLAND. SAVED BY A NATIVE WARRIOR PRINCESS--
HOW DID YOU KNOW I WAS THE PRINCESS?!
WHOA! I DIDN'T KNOW! I WAS JUST TALKING...RAMBLING ON LIKE I DO.
DIANA, I'M SORRY IF I SAID SOMETHING WRONG...
IT IS I WHO MUST APOLOGIZE. I AM...PROTECTIVE OF MY HOME.
THAT'S OKAY. I'D BE PROTECTIVE OF MY HOME TOO...WHEREVER IT IS, ANYWAY. I HATE NOT BEING ABLE TO REMEMBER.
YOU SEEM TO REMEMBER PLENTY. YOU HAVE FILLED DAYS WITH YOUR CHATTER.
HA! SEE? I KNEW I WAS ANNOYING YOU. WELL, SORRY, MISS, THE ONLY WAY TO STOP ME IS TO TALK YOURSELF!
I HAVE NOTHING TO SHARE WITH AN OUTSIDER.
WHY?
WE'RE FRIENDS, AREN'T WE?

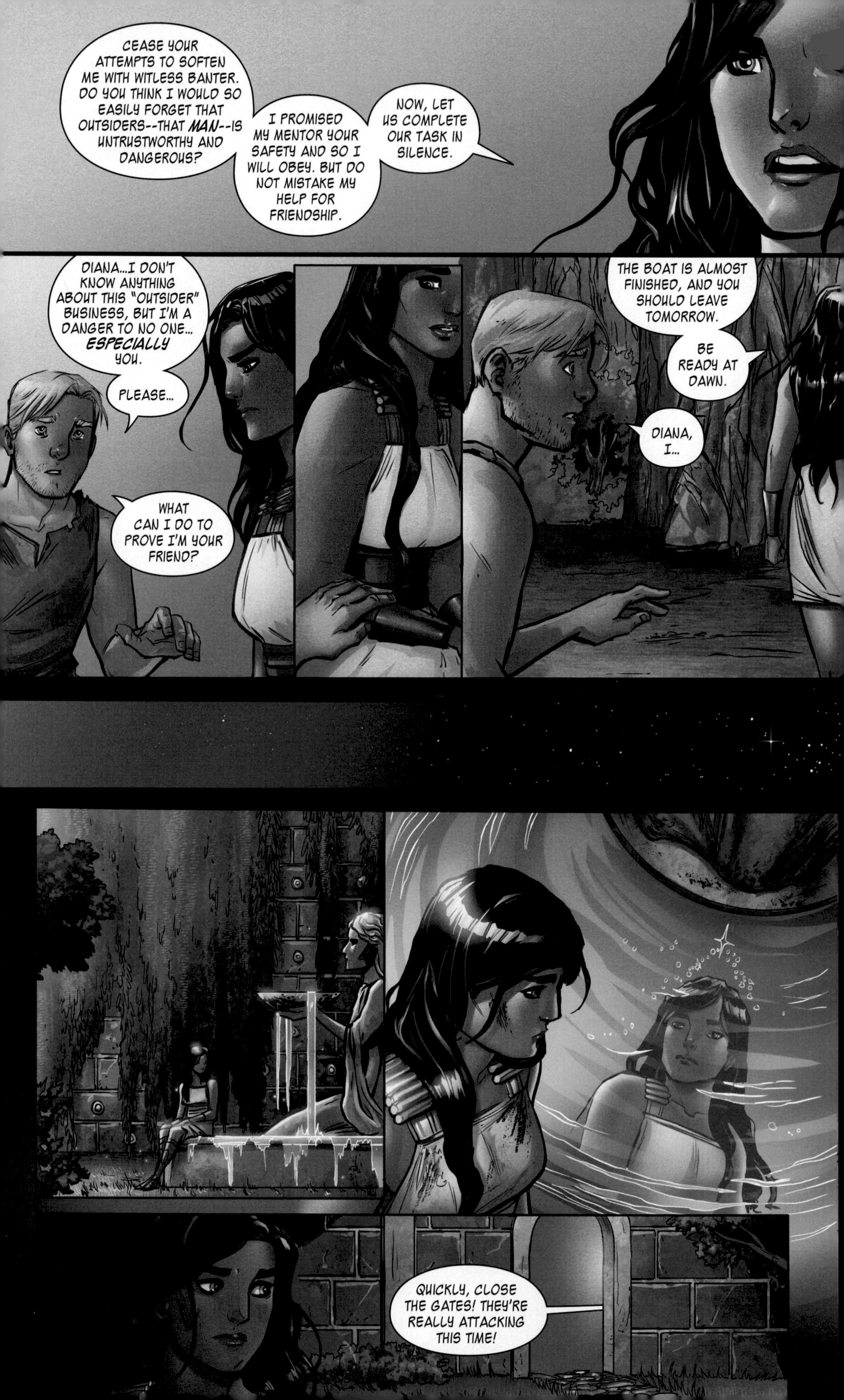
CEASE YOUR ATTEMPTS TO SOFTEN ME WITH WITLESS BANTER. DO YOU THINK I WOULD SO EASILY FORGET THAT OUTSIDERS--THAT MAN--IS UNTRUSTWORTHY AND DANGEROUS?
I PROMISED MY MENTOR YOUR SAFETY AND SO I WILL OBEY. BUT DO NOT MISTAKE MY HELP FOR FRIENDSHIP.
NOW, LET US COMPLETE OUR TASK IN SILENCE.
DIANA...I DON'T KNOW ANYTHING ABOUT THIS "OUTSIDER" BUSINESS, BUT I'M A DANGER TO NO ONE... ESPECIALLY YOU.
PLEASE...
WHAT CAN I DO TO PROVE I'M YOUR FRIEND?
THE BOAT IS ALMOST FINISHED, AND YOU SHOULD LEAVE TOMORROW.
BE READY AT DAWN.
DIANA, I...
QUICKLY, CLOSE THE GATES! THEY'RE REALLY ATTACKING THIS TIME!

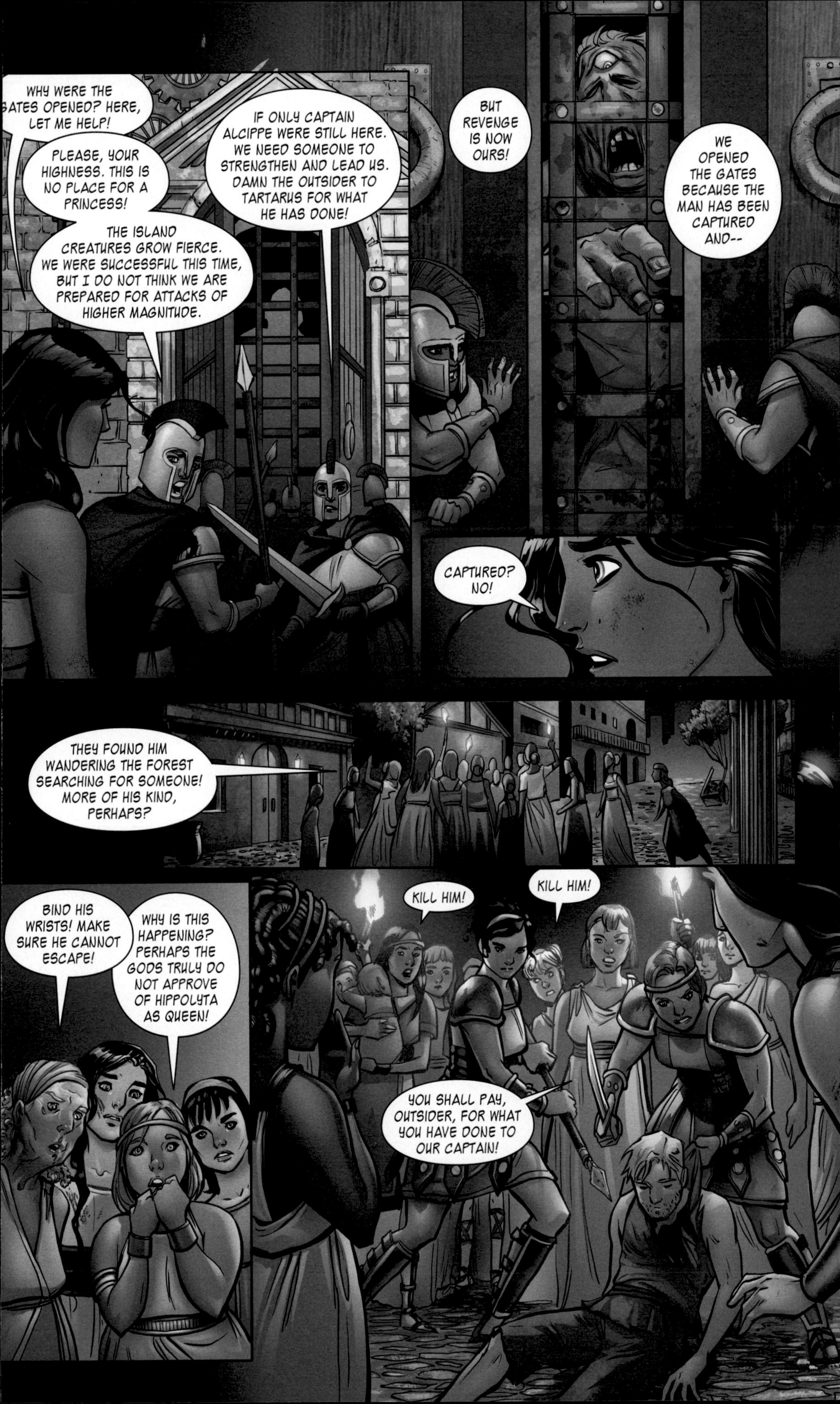
WHY WERE THE GATES OPENED? HERE, LET ME HELP!
PLEASE, YOUR HIGHNESS. THIS IS NO PLACE FOR A PRINCESS!
THE ISLAND CREATURES GROW FIERCE. WE WERE SUCCESSFUL THIS TIME, BUT I DO NOT THINK WE ARE PREPARED FOR ATTACKS OF HIGHER MAGNITUDE.
IF ONLY CAPTAIN ALCIPPE WERE STILL HERE. WE NEED SOMEONE TO STRENGTHEN AND LEAD US. DAMN THE OUTSIDER TO TARTARUS FOR WHAT HE HAS DONE!
BUT REVENGE IS NOW OURS!
WE OPENED THE GATES BECAUSE THE MAN HAS BEEN CAPTURED AND--
CAPTURED? NO!
THEY FOUND HIM WANDERING THE FOREST SEARCHING FOR SOMEONE! MORE OF HIS KIND, PERHAPS?
BIND HIS WRISTS! MAKE SURE HE CANNOT ESCAPE!
WHY IS THIS HAPPENING? PERHAPS THE GODS TRULY DO NOT APPROVE OF HIPPOLYTA AS QUEEN!
KILL HIM!
KILL HIM!
YOU SHALL PAY, OUTSIDER, FOR WHAT YOU HAVE DONE TO OUR CAPTAIN!

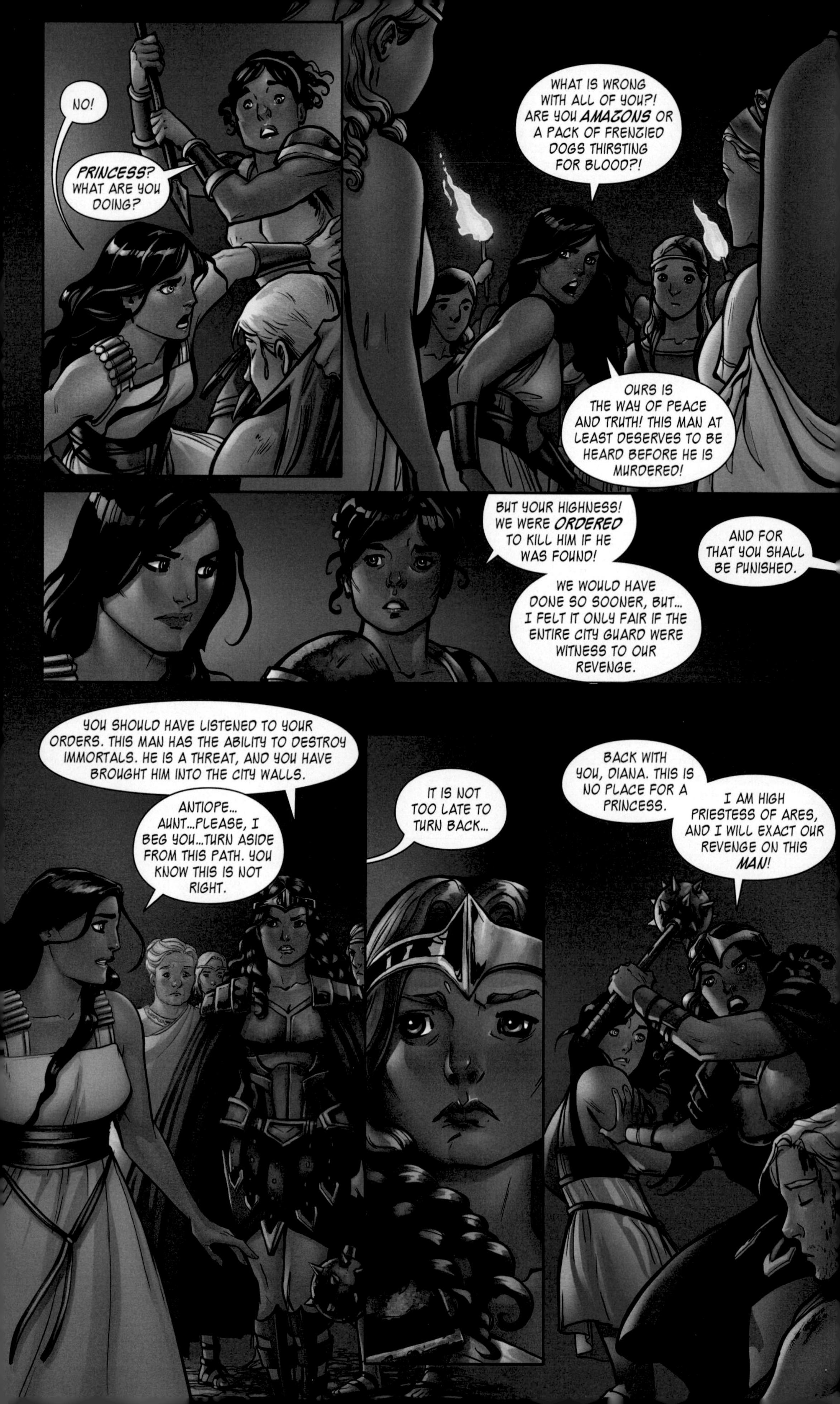

NO!
PRINCESS? WHAT ARE YOU DOING?
WHAT IS WRONG WITH ALL OF YOU?! ARE YOU AMAZONS OR A PACK OF FRENZIED DOGS THIRSTING FOR BLOOD?!
OURS IS THE WAY OF PEACE AND TRUTH! THIS MAN AT LEAST DESERVES TO BE HEARD BEFORE HE IS MURDERED!
BUT YOUR HIGHNESS! WE WERE ORDERED TO KILL HIM IF HE WAS FOUND!
WE WOULD HAVE DONE SO SOONER, BUT... I FELT IT ONLY FAIR IF THE ENTIRE CITY GUARD WERE WITNESS TO OUR REVENGE.
AND FOR THAT YOU SHALL BE PUNISHED.
YOU SHOULD HAVE LISTENED TO YOUR ORDERS. THIS MAN HAS THE ABILITY TO DESTROY IMMORTALS. HE IS A THREAT, AND YOU HAVE BROUGHT HIM INTO THE CITY WALLS.
ANTIOPE... AUNT...PLEASE, I BEG YOU...TURN ASIDE FROM THIS PATH. YOU KNOW THIS IS NOT RIGHT.
IT IS NOT TOO LATE TO TURN BACK...
BACK WITH YOU, DIANA. THIS IS NO PLACE FOR A PRINCESS.
I AM HIGH PRIESTESS OF ARES, AND I WILL EXACT OUR REVENGE ON THIS MAN!

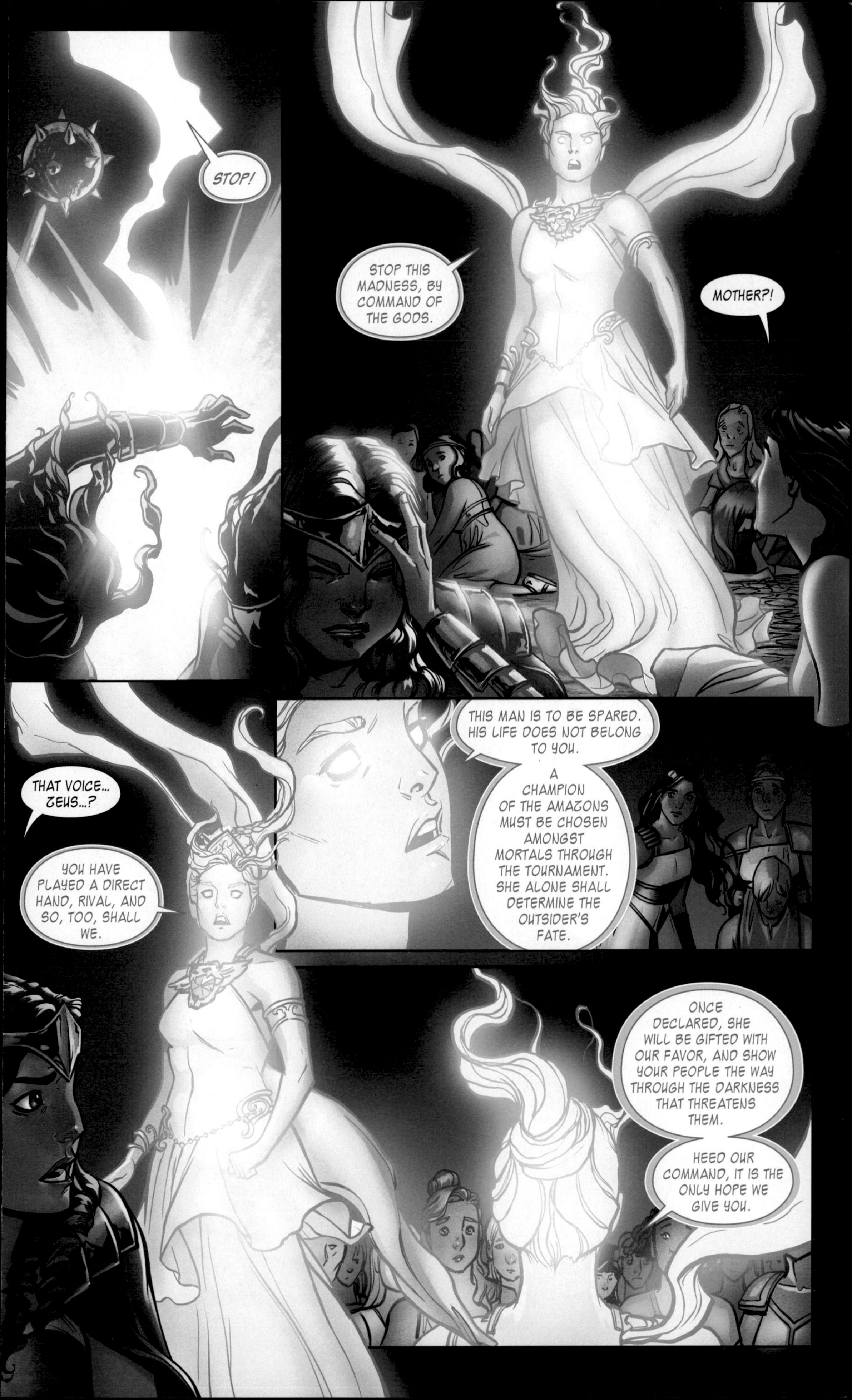
STOP!
STOP THIS MADNESS, BY COMMAND OF THE GODS.
MOTHER?!
THAT VOICE... ZEUS...?
YOU HAVE PLAYED A DIRECT HAND, RIVAL, AND SO, TOO, SHALL WE.
THIS MAN IS TO BE SPARED. HIS LIFE DOES NOT BELONG TO YOU.
A CHAMPION OF THE AMAZONS MUST BE CHOSEN AMONGST MORTALS THROUGH THE TOURNAMENT. SHE ALONE SHALL DETERMINE THE OUTSIDER'S FATE.
ONCE DECLARED, SHE WILL BE GIFTED WITH OUR FAVOR, AND SHOW YOUR PEOPLE THE WAY THROUGH THE DARKNESS THAT THREATENS THEM.
HEED OUR COMMAND, IT IS THE ONLY HOPE WE GIVE YOU.

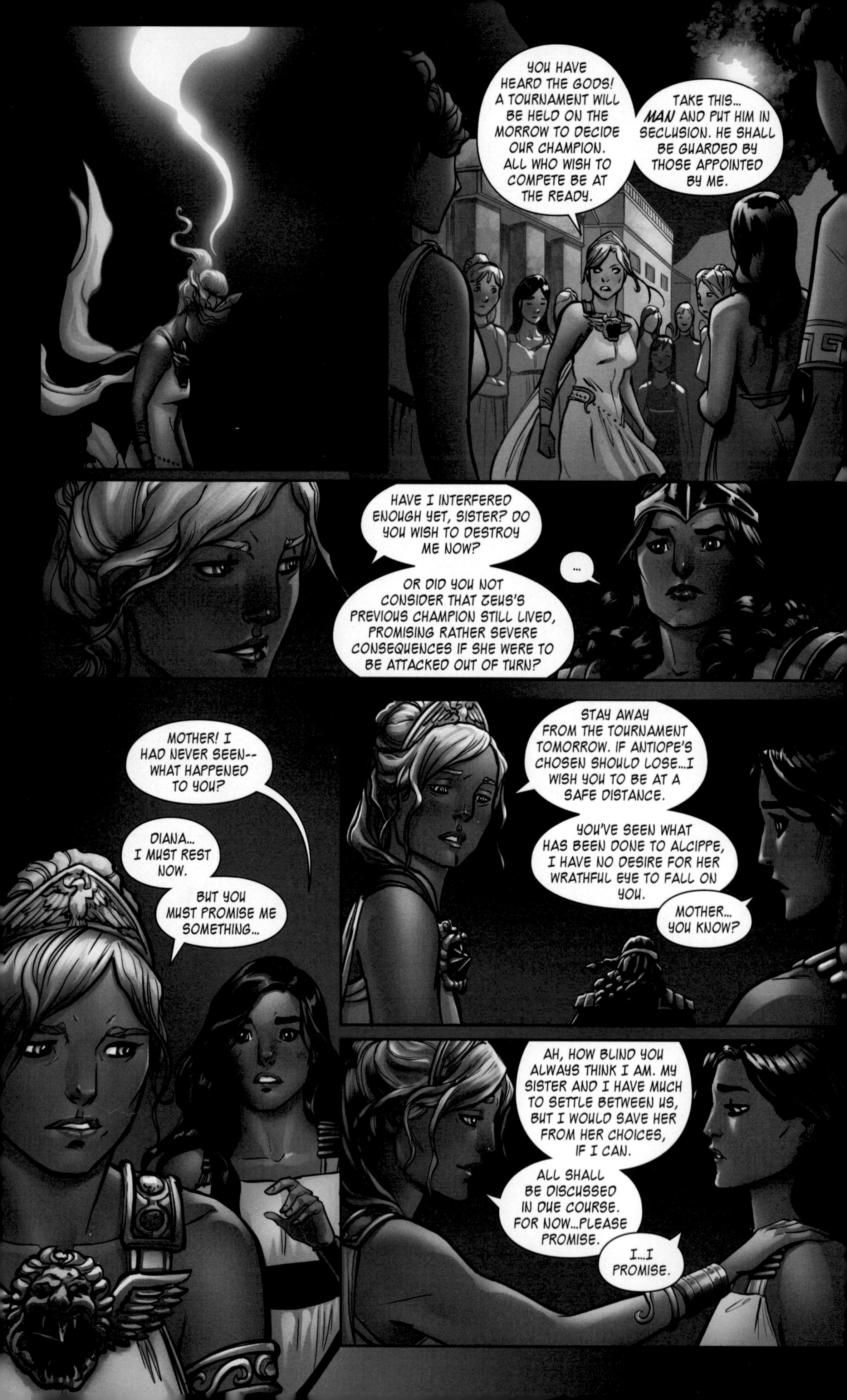
YOU HAVE HEARD THE GODS! A TOURNAMENT WILL BE HELD ON THE MORROW TO DECIDE OUR CHAMPION. ALL WHO WISH TO COMPETE BE AT THE READY.
TAKE THIS... MAN AND PUT HIM IN SECLUSION. HE SHALL BE GUARDED BY THOSE APPOINTED BY ME.
HAVE I INTERFERED ENOUGH YET, SISTER? DO YOU WISH TO DESTROY ME NOW?
...
OR DID YOU NOT CONSIDER THAT ZEUS'S PREVIOUS CHAMPION STILL LIVED, PROMISING RATHER SEVERE CONSEQUENCES IF SHE WERE TO BE ATTACKED OUT OF TURN?
MOTHER! I HAD NEVER SEEN-- WHAT HAPPENED TO YOU?
DIANA... I MUST REST NOW.
BUT YOU MUST PROMISE ME SOMETHING...
STAY AWAY FROM THE TOURNAMENT TOMORROW. IF ANTIOPE'S CHOSEN SHOULD LOSE...I WISH YOU TO BE AT A SAFE DISTANCE.
YOU'VE SEEN WHAT HAS BEEN DONE TO ALCIPPE, I HAVE NO DESIRE FOR HER WRATHFUL EYE TO FALL ON YOU.
MOTHER... YOU KNOW?
AH, HOW BLIND YOU ALWAYS THINK I AM. MY SISTER AND I HAVE MUCH TO SETTLE BETWEEN US, BUT I WOULD SAVE HER FROM HER CHOICES, IF I CAN.
ALL SHALL BE DISCUSSED IN DUE COURSE. FOR NOW...PLEASE PROMISE.
I...I PROMISE.

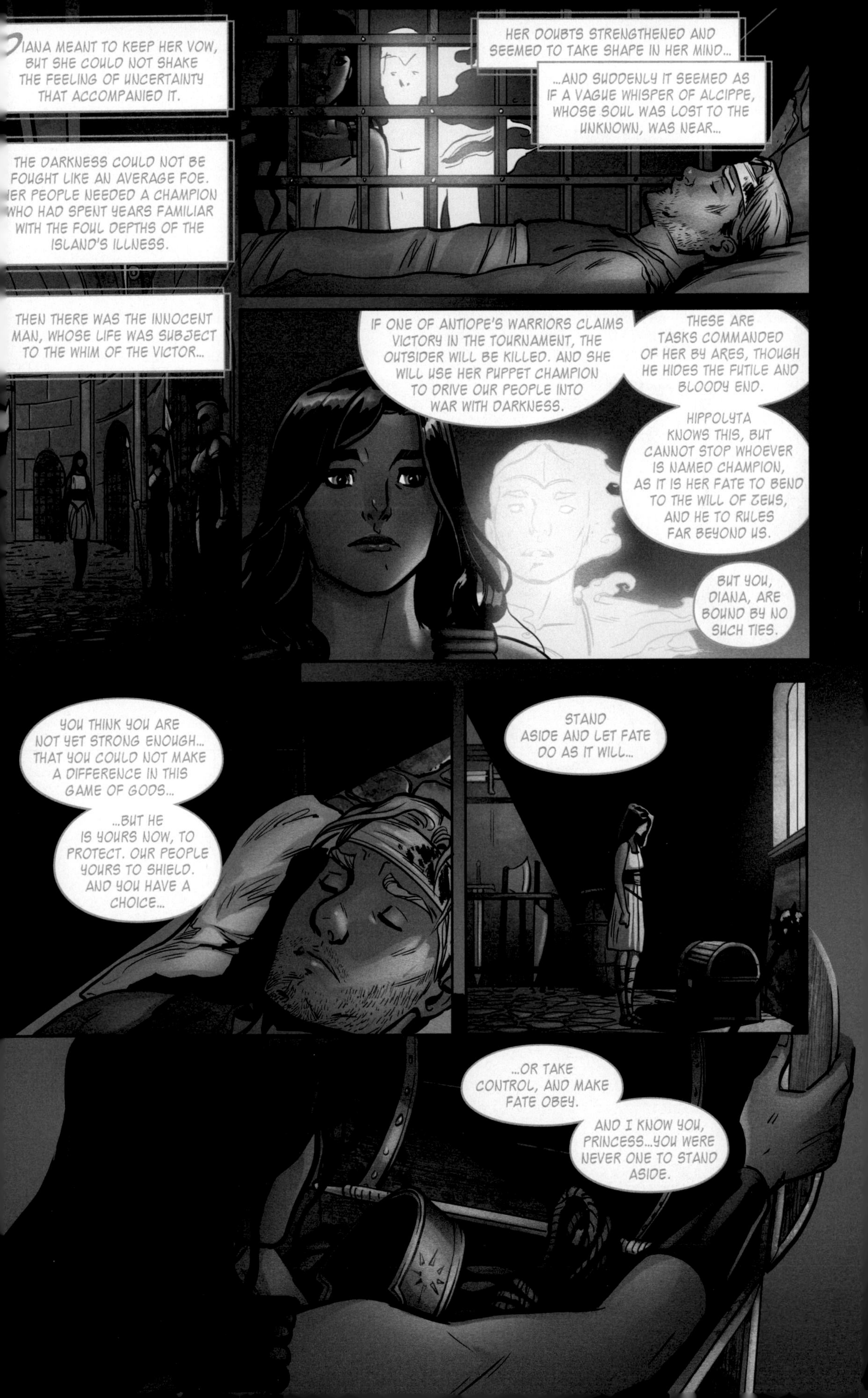
DIANA MEANT TO KEEP HER VOW, BUT SHE COULD NOT SHAKE THE FEELING OF UNCERTAINTY THAT ACCOMPANIED IT.
HER DOUBTS STRENGTHENED AND SEEMED TO TAKE SHAPE IN HER MIND...
...AND SUDDENLY IT SEEMED AS IF A VAGUE WHISPER OF ALCIPPE, WHOSE SOUL WAS LOST TO THE UNKNOWN, WAS NEAR...
THE DARKNESS COULD NOT BE FOUGHT LIKE AN AVERAGE FOE. HER PEOPLE NEEDED A CHAMPION WHO HAD SPENT YEARS FAMILIAR WITH THE FOUL DEPTHS OF THE ISLAND'S ILLNESS.
THEN THERE WAS THE INNOCENT MAN, WHOSE LIFE WAS SUBJECT TO THE WHIM OF THE VICTOR...
IF ONE OF ANTIOPE'S WARRIORS CLAIMS VICTORY IN THE TOURNAMENT, THE OUTSIDER WILL BE KILLED. AND SHE WILL USE HER PUPPET CHAMPION TO DRIVE OUR PEOPLE INTO WAR WITH DARKNESS.
THESE ARE TASKS COMMANDED OF HER BY ARES, THOUGH HE HIDES THE FUTILE AND BLOODY END.
HIPPOLYTA KNOWS THIS, BUT CANNOT STOP WHOEVER IS NAMED CHAMPION, AS IT IS HER FATE TO BEND TO THE WILL OF ZEUS, AND HE TO RULES FAR BEYOND US.
BUT YOU, DIANA, ARE BOUND BY NO SUCH TIES.
YOU THINK YOU ARE NOT YET STRONG ENOUGH... THAT YOU COULD NOT MAKE A DIFFERENCE IN THIS GAME OF GODS...
...BUT HE IS YOURS NOW, TO PROTECT. OUR PEOPLE YOURS TO SHIELD. AND YOU HAVE A CHOICE...
STAND ASIDE AND LET FATE DO AS IT WILL...
...OR TAKE CONTROL, AND MAKE FATE OBEY.
AND I KNOW YOU, PRINCESS...YOU WERE NEVER ONE TO STAND ASIDE.

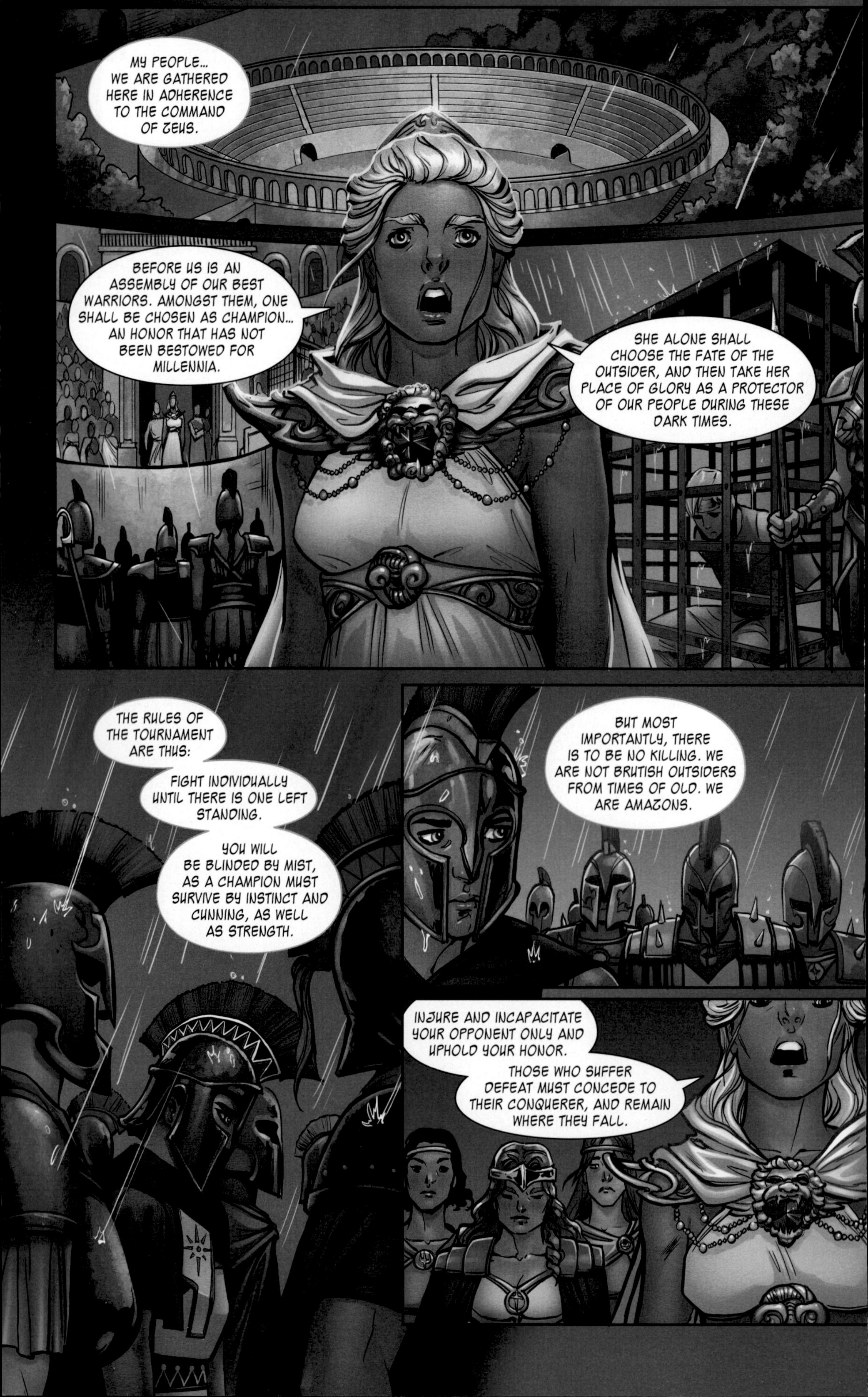
MY PEOPLE... WE ARE GATHERED HERE IN ADHERENCE TO THE COMMAND OF ZEUS.
BEFORE US IS AN ASSEMBLY OF OUR BEST WARRIORS. AMONGST THEM, ONE SHALL BE CHOSEN AS CHAMPION... AN HONOR THAT HAS NOT BEEN BESTOWED FOR MILLENNIA.
SHE ALONE SHALL CHOOSE THE FATE OF THE OUTSIDER, AND THEN TAKE HER PLACE OF GLORY AS A PROTECTOR OF OUR PEOPLE DURING THESE DARK TIMES.
THE RULES OF THE TOURNAMENT ARE THUS:
FIGHT INDIVIDUALLY UNTIL THERE IS ONE LEFT STANDING.
YOU WILL BE BLINDED BY MIST, AS A CHAMPION MUST SURVIVE BY INSTINCT AND CUNNING, AS WELL AS STRENGTH.
BUT MOST IMPORTANTLY, THERE IS TO BE NO KILLING. WE ARE NOT BRUTISH OUTSIDERS FROM TIMES OF OLD. WE ARE AMAZONS.
INJURE AND INCAPACITATE YOUR OPPONENT ONLY AND UPHOLD YOUR HONOR.
THOSE WHO SUFFER DEFEAT MUST CONCEDE TO THEIR CONQUERER, AND REMAIN WHERE THEY FALL.

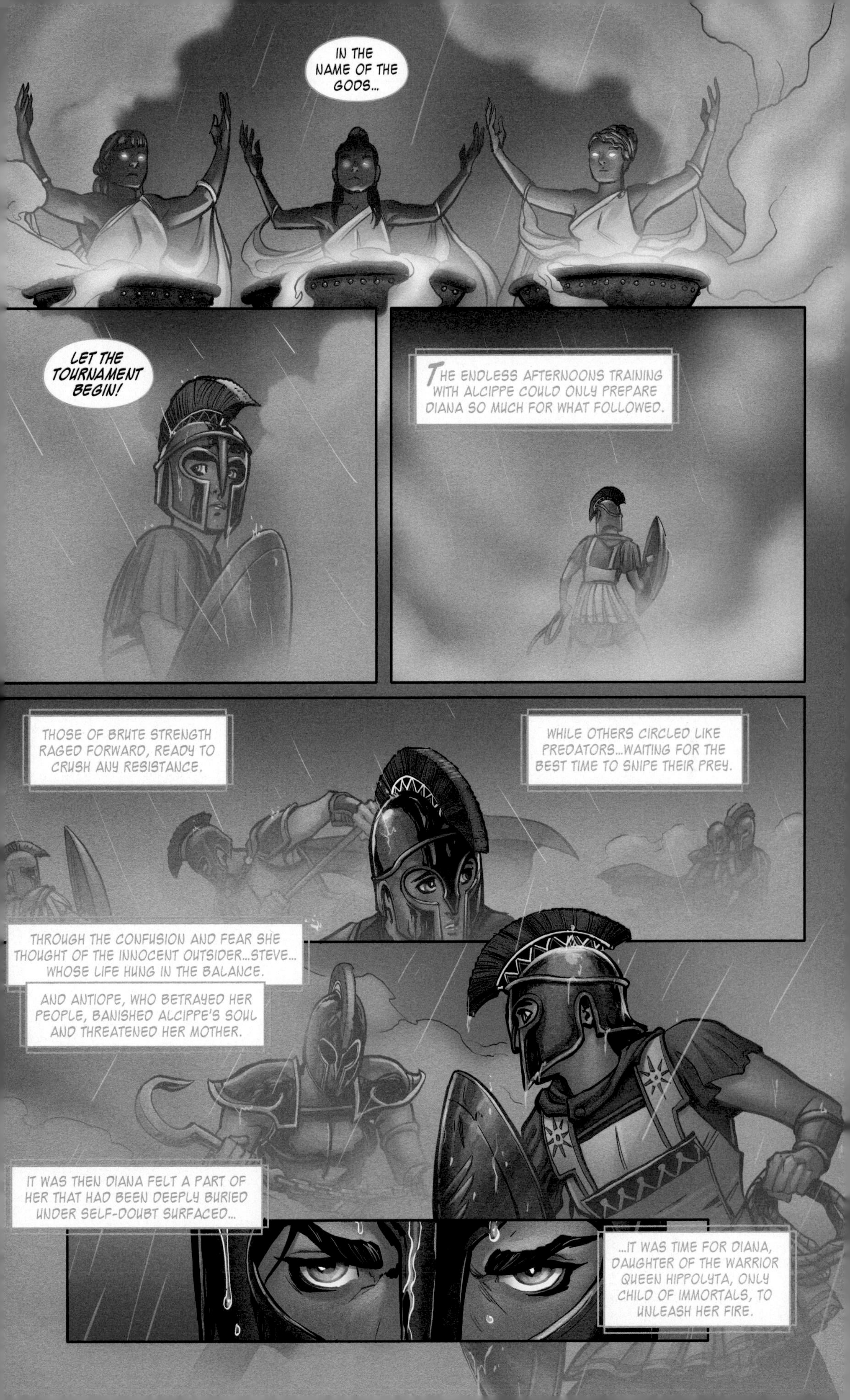
IN THE NAME OF THE GODS...
LET THE TOURNAMENT BEGIN!
THE ENDLESS AFTERNOONS TRAINING WITH ALCIPPE COULD ONLY PREPARE DIANA SO MUCH FOR WHAT FOLLOWED.
THOSE OF BRUTE STRENGTH RAGED FORWARD, READY TO CRUSH ANY RESISTANCE.
WHILE OTHERS CIRCLED LIKE PREDATORS...WAITING FOR THE BEST TIME TO SNIPE THEIR PREY.
THROUGH THE CONFUSION AND FEAR SHE THOUGHT OF THE INNOCENT OUTSIDER...STEVE... WHOSE LIFE HUNG IN THE BALANCE.
AND ANTIOPE, WHO BETRAYED HER PEOPLE, BANISHED ALCIPPE'S SOUL AND THREATENED HER MOTHER.
IT WAS THEN DIANA FELT A PART OF HER THAT HAD BEEN DEEPLY BURIED UNDER SELF-DOUBT SURFACED...
...IT WAS TIME FOR DIANA, DAUGHTER OF THE WARRIOR QUEEN HIPPOLYTA, ONLY CHILD OF IMMORTALS, TO UNLEASH HER FIRE.

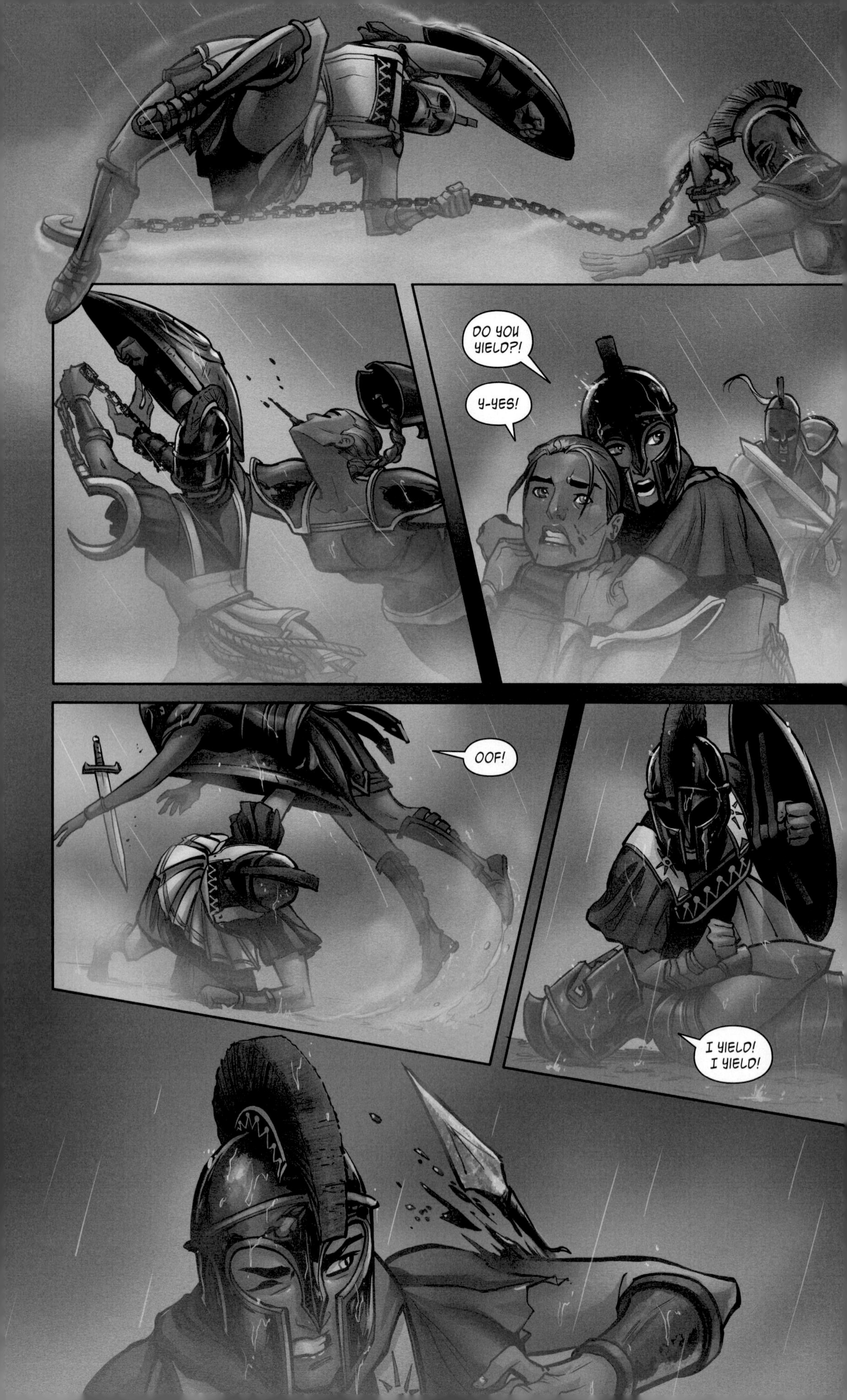
DO YOU YIELD?!
Y-YES!
OOF!
I YIELD! I YIELD!

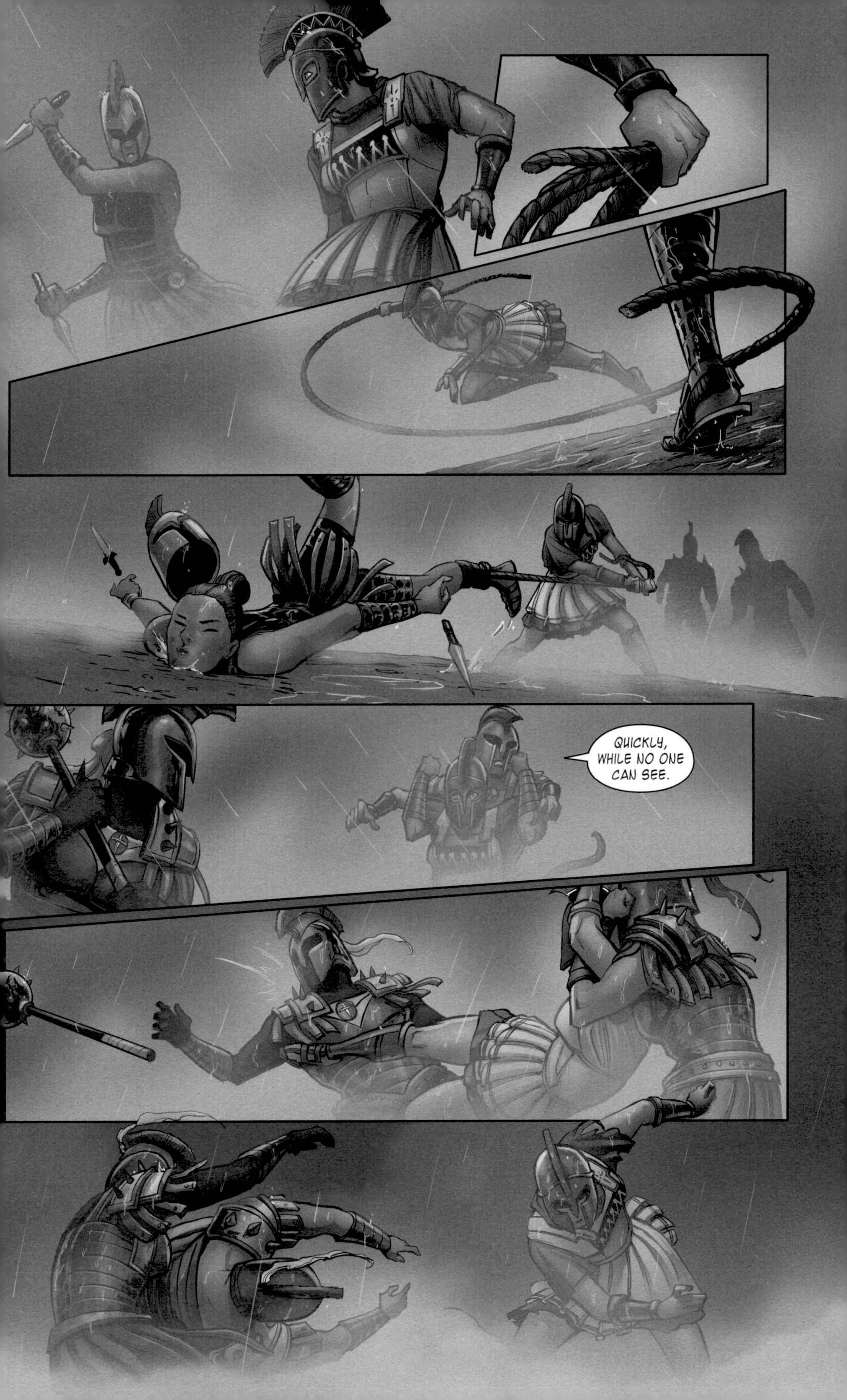
QUICKLY, WHILE NO ONE CAN SEE.

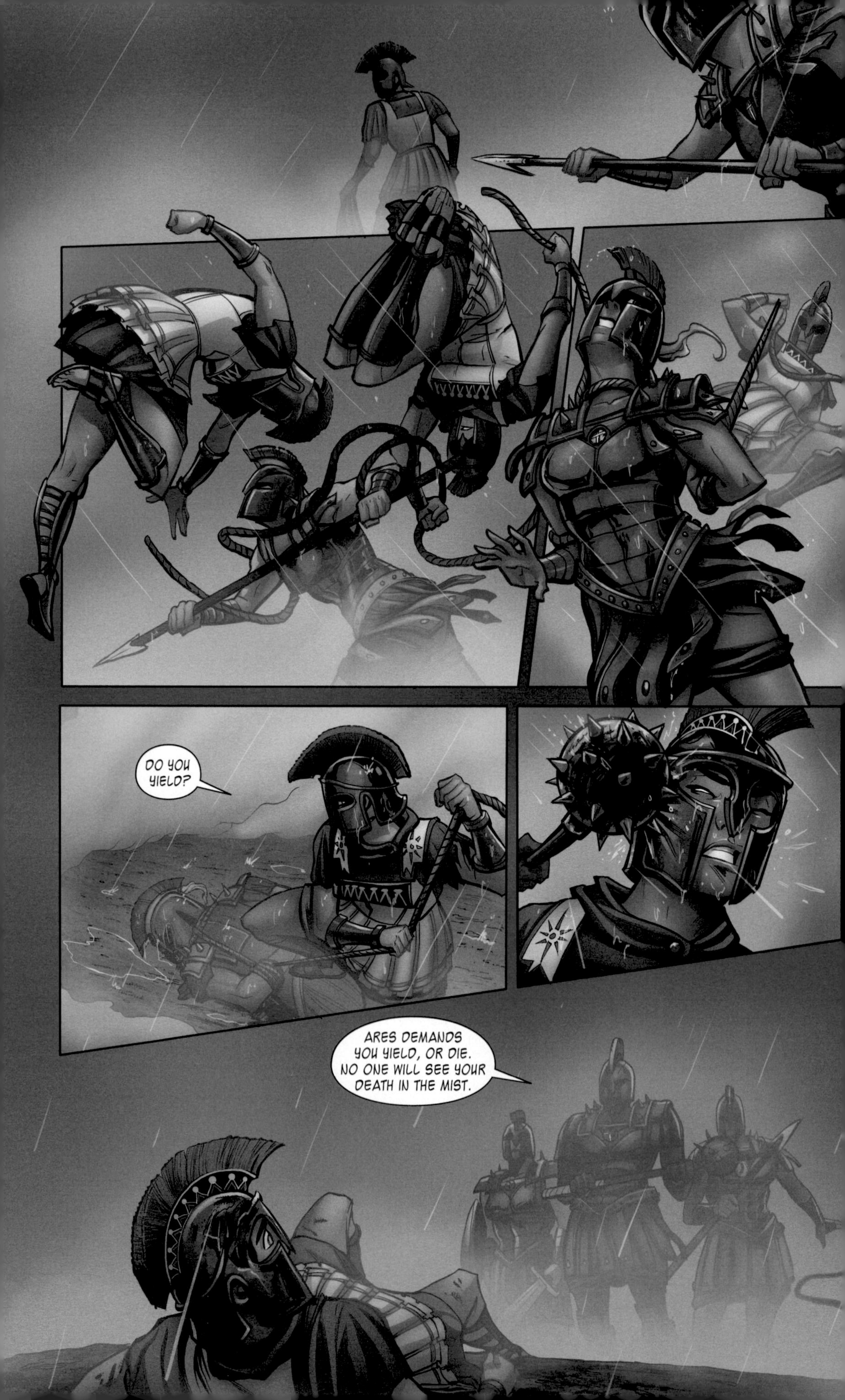
DO YOU YIELD?
ARES DEMANDS YOU YIELD, OR DIE. NO ONE WILL SEE YOUR DEATH IN THE MIST.

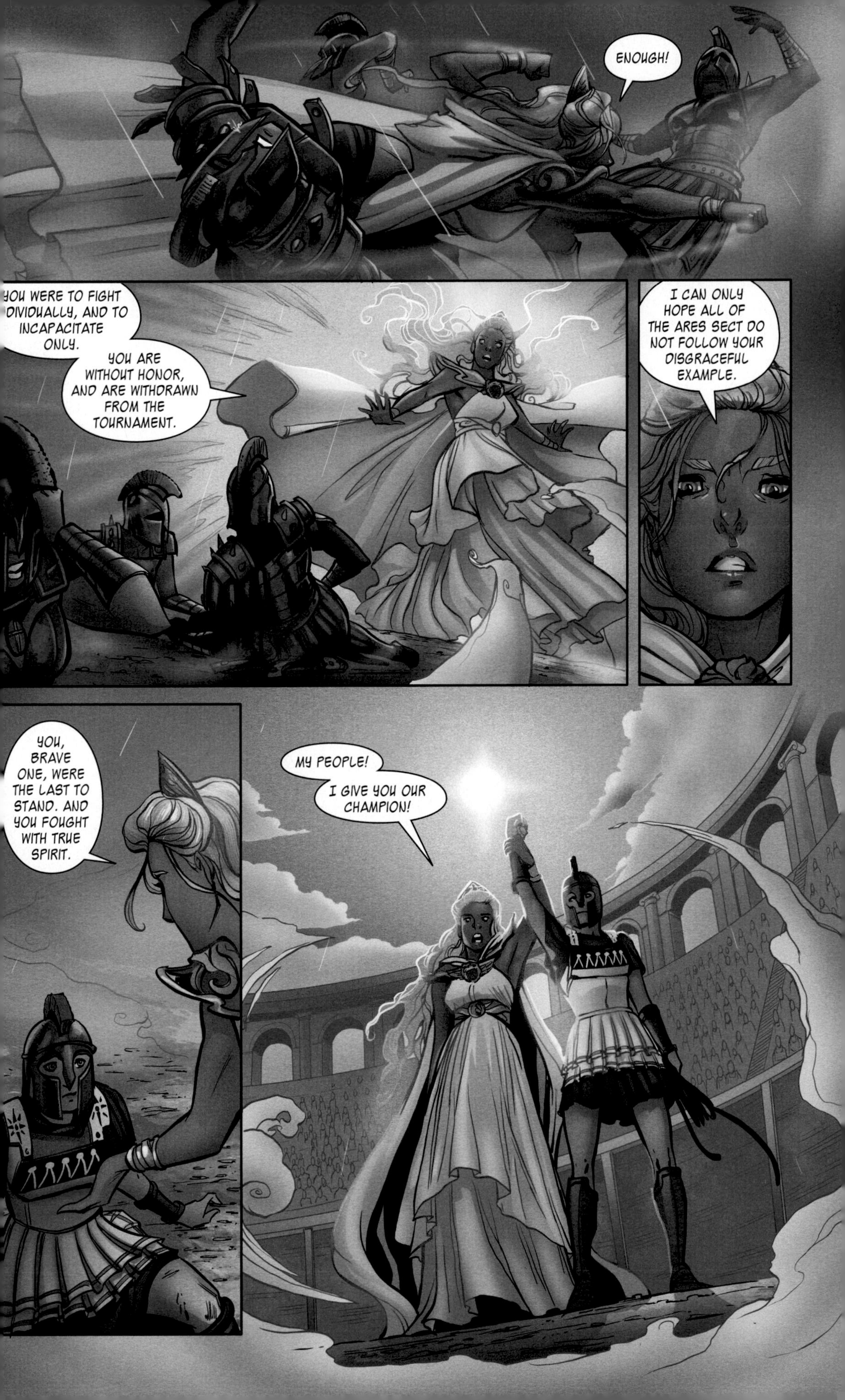
ENOUGH!
YOU WERE TO FIGHT
DIVIDUALLY, AND TO INCAPACITATE ONLY.
YOU ARE WITHOUT HONOR, AND ARE WITHDRAWN FROM THE TOURNAMENT.
I CAN ONLY HOPE ALL OF THE ARES SECT DO NOT FOLLOW YOUR DISGRACEFUL EXAMPLE.
YOU, BRAVE ONE, WERE THE LAST TO STAND. AND YOU FOUGHT WITH TRUE SPIRIT.
MY PEOPLE!
I GIVE YOU OUR CHAMPION!

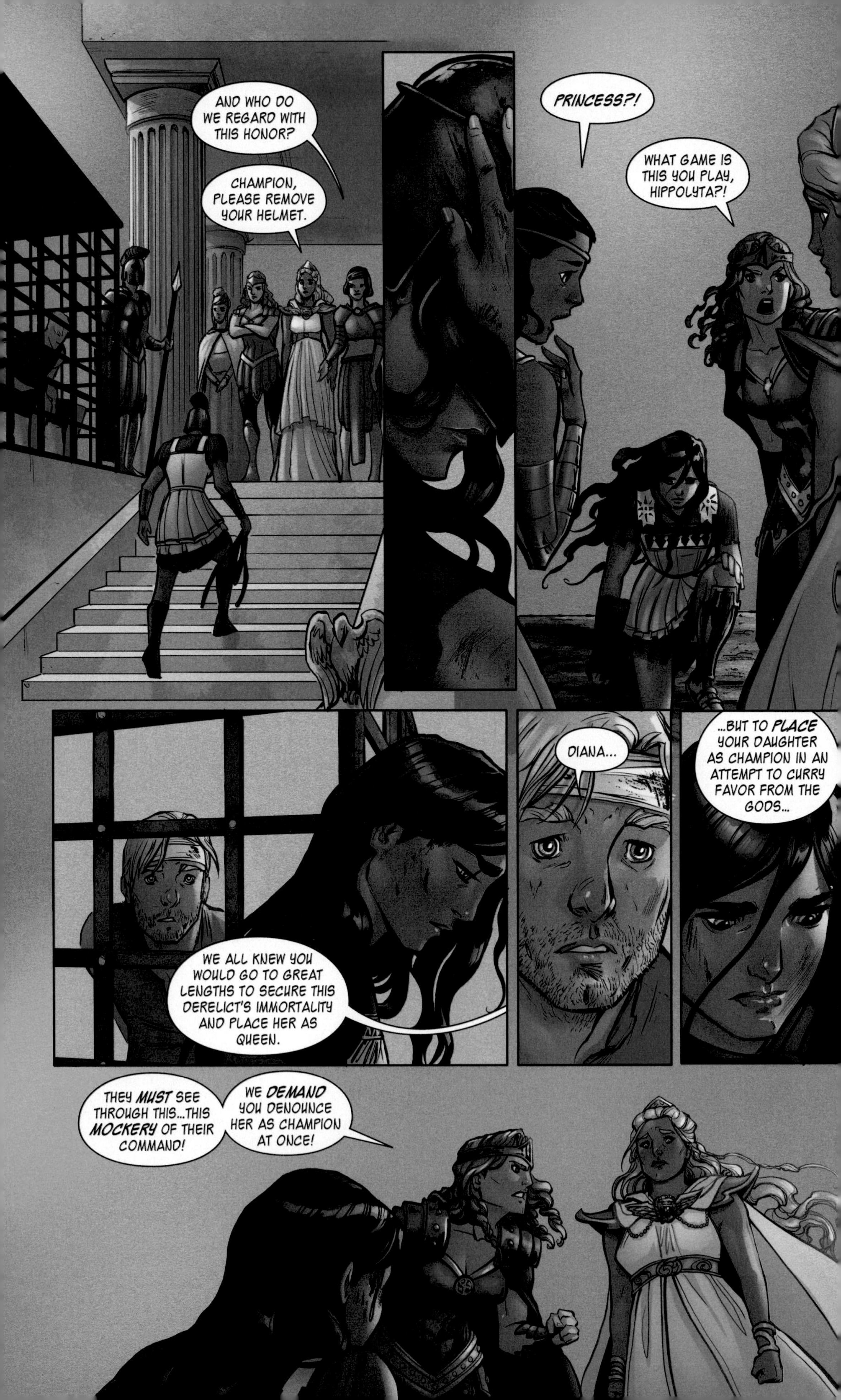
AND WHO DO WE REGARD WITH THIS HONOR?
CHAMPION, PLEASE REMOVE YOUR HELMET.
PRINCESS?!
WHAT GAME IS THIS YOU PLAY, HIPPOLYTA?!
WE ALL KNEW YOU WOULD GO TO GREAT LENGTHS TO SECURE THIS DERELICT'S IMMORTALITY AND PLACE HER AS QUEEN.
DIANA...
...BUT TO PLACE YOUR DAUGHTER AS CHAMPION IN AN ATTEMPT TO CURRY FAVOR FROM THE GODS...
THEY MUST SEE THROUGH THIS...THIS MOCKERY OF THEIR COMMAND!
WE DEMAND YOU DENOUNCE HER AS CHAMPION AT ONCE!

YOU DO NOT SPEAK FOR ALL OF US, ANTIOPE.

TO ACCUSE THE QUEEN OF SUCH A THING, IT IS ABSURD.

IT IS ABSURD TO IGNORE SUCH BLASPHEMY! NOT ONLY DOES SHE RAISE HER OWN DAUGHTER UNFAIRLY ABOVE THOSE MORE WORTHY...

...SHE ALSO SETS UP THIS TOURNAMENT TO SAVE THE LIFE OF THE OUTSIDER MAN WHO DESTROYED THE CAPTAIN OF THE GUARD!

MAY OUR PEOPLE SEE THE TREACHERY OF THE QUEEN!

SILENCE!

THE LIFE OF A CHAMPION IS DANGEROUS AND RIDDLED WITH TRIAL.

I WISH HER TO REMAIN BY MY SIDE, SAFE AND WHOLE, READYING HERSELF TO BECOME IMMORTAL BY THE GRACE OF THE GODS...

...BUT THOSE ARE HOPES OF A MOTHER.

I AM HIPPOLYTA, IMMORTAL QUEEN OF THE AMAZONS.

AND I DECLARE THIS WOMAN TO BE CHAMPION.

SHE SHALL HENCEFORTH PROTECT OUR PEOPLE, LEAD THE OPPOSITION AGAINST THE DARKNESS WE FACE, AND FIGHT FOR PEACE UNTIL DEATH TAKES HER.

CHAMPION, YOUR FIRST TASK IS TO DETERMINE THE FATE OF THE OUTSIDER. WHAT SAY YOU?

I WISH TO DELIVER HIM TO THE BOUNDARIES AT SEA, MY QUEEN. I WILL SEND HIM OVER AND RETURN TO THE DUTIES THAT AWAIT ME.

THEN SO SHALL IT BE.

AFTER THE PROCLAMATION, ONLY TWO NOTICED HIPPOLYTA WILT...AS IF CRUSHED BY SOME TERRIBLE WEIGHT.

DIANA, WHO SUDDENLY FELT VERY AFRAID FOR HER MOTHER...

AND ANTIOPE...WHO LIKE A SNAKE SENSING WEAKNESS, TIGHTENED HER COIL IN PREPARATION TO STRIKE.

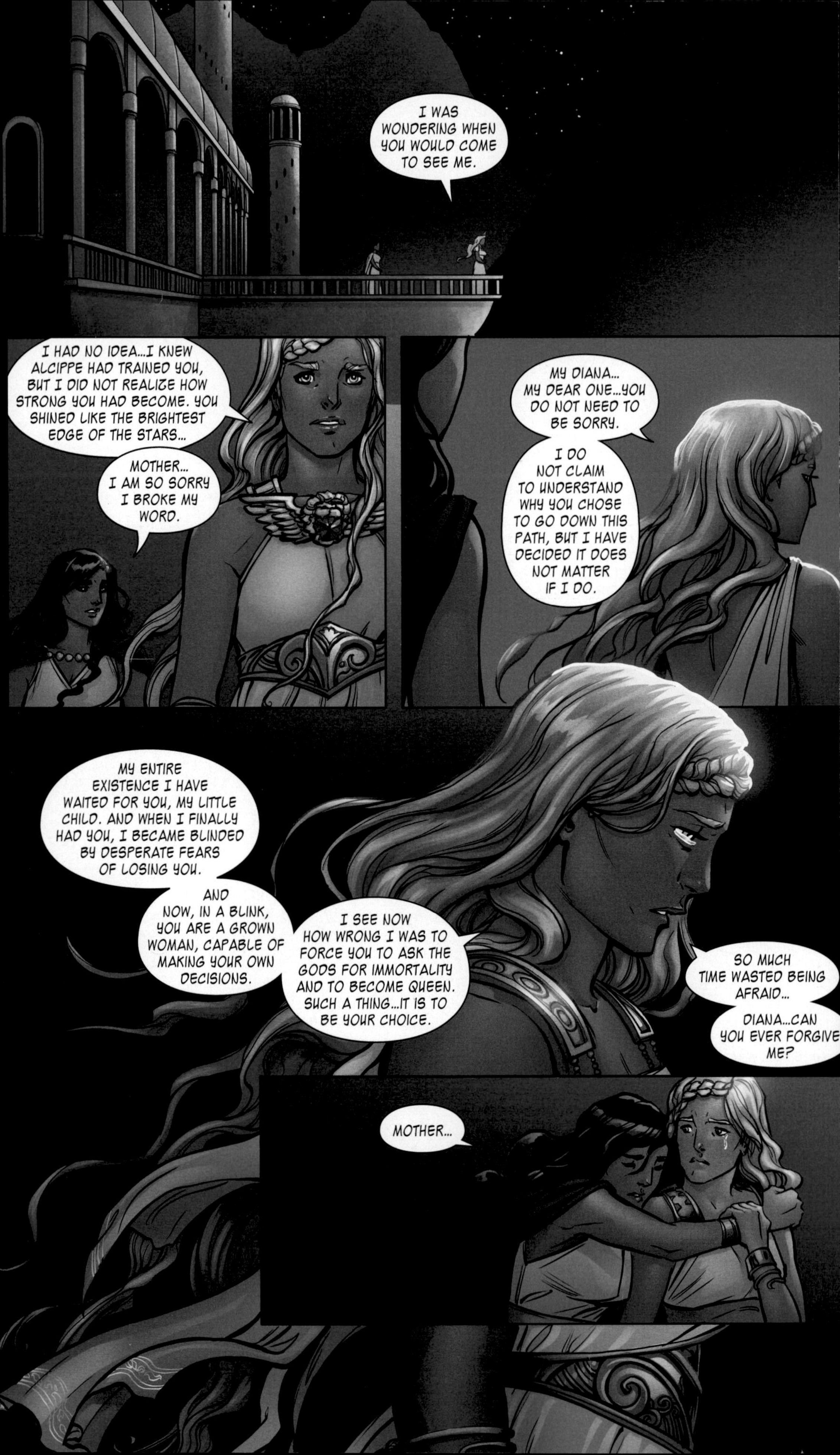
I WAS WONDERING WHEN YOU WOULD COME TO SEE ME.
I HAD NO IDEA...I KNEW ALCIPPE HAD TRAINED YOU, BUT I DID NOT REALIZE HOW STRONG YOU HAD BECOME. YOU SHINED LIKE THE BRIGHTEST EDGE OF THE STARS...
MOTHER... I AM SO SORRY I BROKE MY WORD.
MY DIANA... MY DEAR ONE...YOU DO NOT NEED TO BE SORRY.
I DO NOT CLAIM TO UNDERSTAND WHY YOU CHOSE TO GO DOWN THIS PATH, BUT I HAVE DECIDED IT DOES NOT MATTER IF I DO.
MY ENTIRE EXISTENCE I HAVE WAITED FOR YOU, MY LITTLE CHILD. AND WHEN I FINALLY HAD YOU, I BECAME BLINDED BY DESPERATE FEARS OF LOSING YOU.
AND NOW, IN A BLINK, YOU ARE A GROWN WOMAN, CAPABLE OF MAKING YOUR OWN DECISIONS.
I SEE NOW HOW WRONG I WAS TO FORCE YOU TO ASK THE GODS FOR IMMORTALITY AND TO BECOME QUEEN. SUCH A THING...IT IS TO BE YOUR CHOICE.
SO MUCH TIME WASTED BEING AFRAID...
DIANA...CAN YOU EVER FORGIVE ME?
MOTHER...

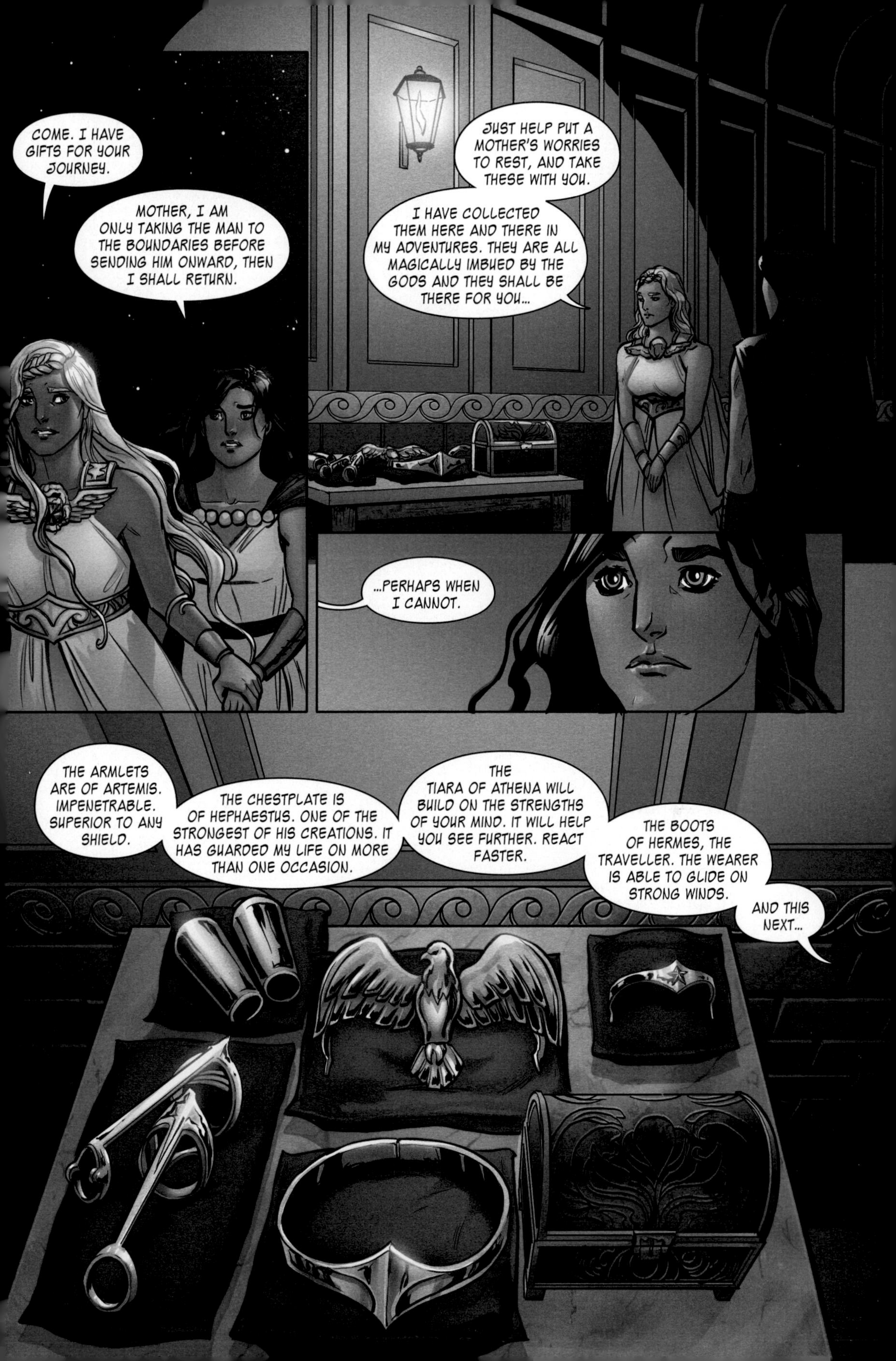
COME. I HAVE GIFTS FOR YOUR JOURNEY.
MOTHER, I AM ONLY TAKING THE MAN TO THE BOUNDARIES BEFORE SENDING HIM ONWARD, THEN I SHALL RETURN.
JUST HELP PUT A MOTHER'S WORRIES TO REST, AND TAKE THESE WITH YOU.
I HAVE COLLECTED THEM HERE AND THERE IN MY ADVENTURES. THEY ARE ALL MAGICALLY IMBUED BY THE GODS AND THEY SHALL BE THERE FOR YOU...
...PERHAPS WHEN I CANNOT.
THE ARMLETS ARE OF ARTEMIS. IMPENETRABLE. SUPERIOR TO ANY SHIELD.
THE CHESTPLATE IS OF HEPHAESTUS. ONE OF THE STRONGEST OF HIS CREATIONS. IT HAS GUARDED MY LIFE ON MORE THAN ONE OCCASION.
THE TIARA OF ATHENA WILL BUILD ON THE STRENGTHS OF YOUR MIND. IT WILL HELP YOU SEE FURTHER. REACT FASTER.
THE BOOTS OF HERMES, THE TRAVELLER. THE WEARER IS ABLE TO GLIDE ON STRONG WINDS.
AND THIS NEXT...

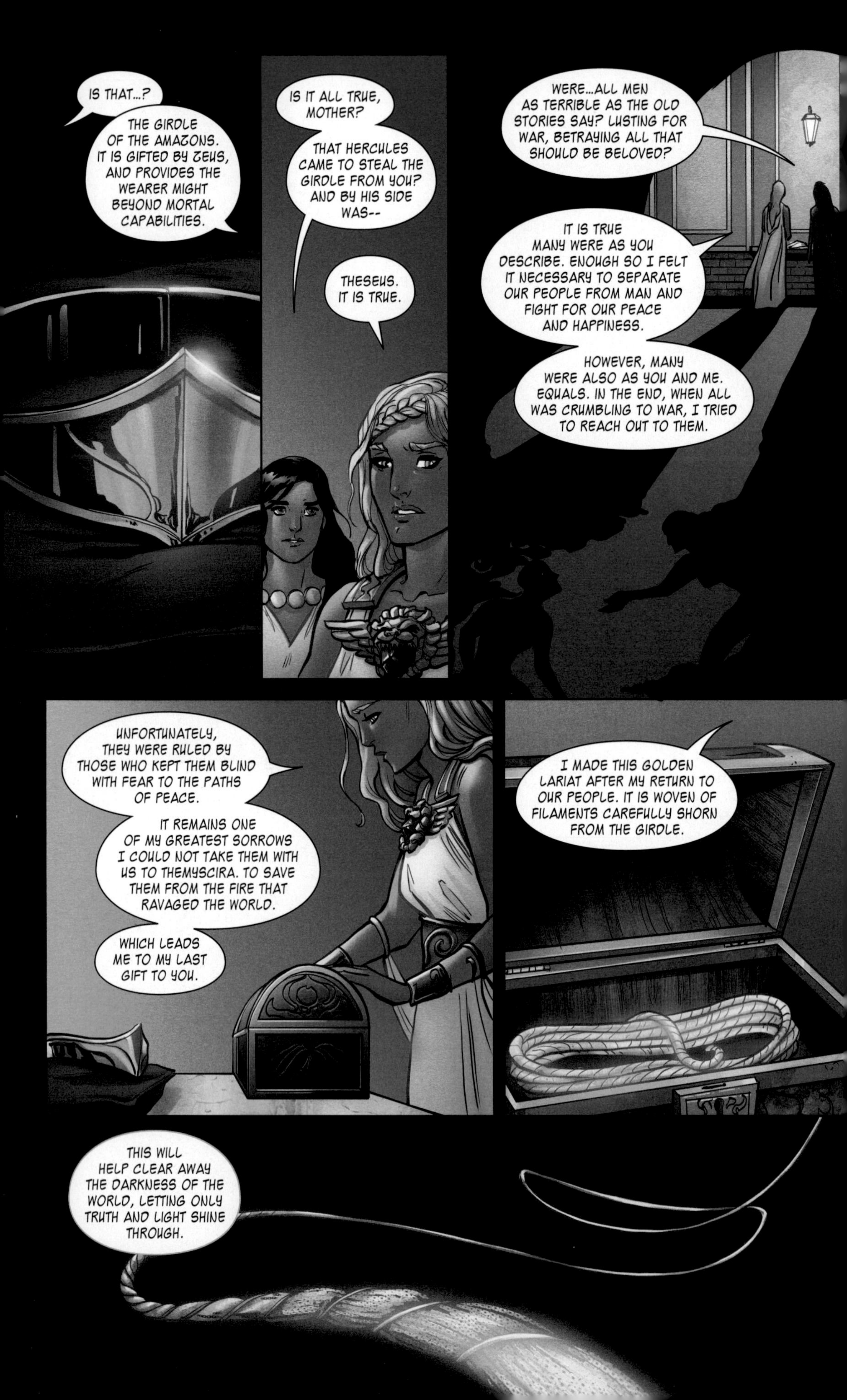
IS THAT...?
THE GIRDLE OF THE AMAZONS. IT IS GIFTED BY ZEUS, AND PROVIDES THE WEARER MIGHT BEYOND MORTAL CAPABILITIES.
IS IT ALL TRUE, MOTHER?
THAT HERCULES CAME TO STEAL THE GIRDLE FROM YOU? AND BY HIS SIDE WAS--
THESEUS. IT IS TRUE.
WERE...ALL MEN AS TERRIBLE AS THE OLD STORIES SAY? LUSTING FOR WAR, BETRAYING ALL THAT SHOULD BE BELOVED?
IT IS TRUE MANY WERE AS YOU DESCRIBE. ENOUGH SO I FELT IT NECESSARY TO SEPARATE OUR PEOPLE FROM MAN AND FIGHT FOR OUR PEACE AND HAPPINESS.
HOWEVER, MANY WERE ALSO AS YOU AND ME. EQUALS. IN THE END, WHEN ALL WAS CRUMBLING TO WAR, I TRIED TO REACH OUT TO THEM.
UNFORTUNATELY, THEY WERE RULED BY THOSE WHO KEPT THEM BLIND WITH FEAR TO THE PATHS OF PEACE.
IT REMAINS ONE OF MY GREATEST SORROWS I COULD NOT TAKE THEM WITH US TO THEMYSCIRA. TO SAVE THEM FROM THE FIRE THAT RAVAGED THE WORLD.
WHICH LEADS ME TO MY LAST GIFT TO YOU.
I MADE THIS GOLDEN LARIAT AFTER MY RETURN TO OUR PEOPLE. IT IS WOVEN OF FILAMENTS CAREFULLY SHORN FROM THE GIRDLE.
THIS WILL HELP CLEAR AWAY THE DARKNESS OF THE WORLD, LETTING ONLY TRUTH AND LIGHT SHINE THROUGH.

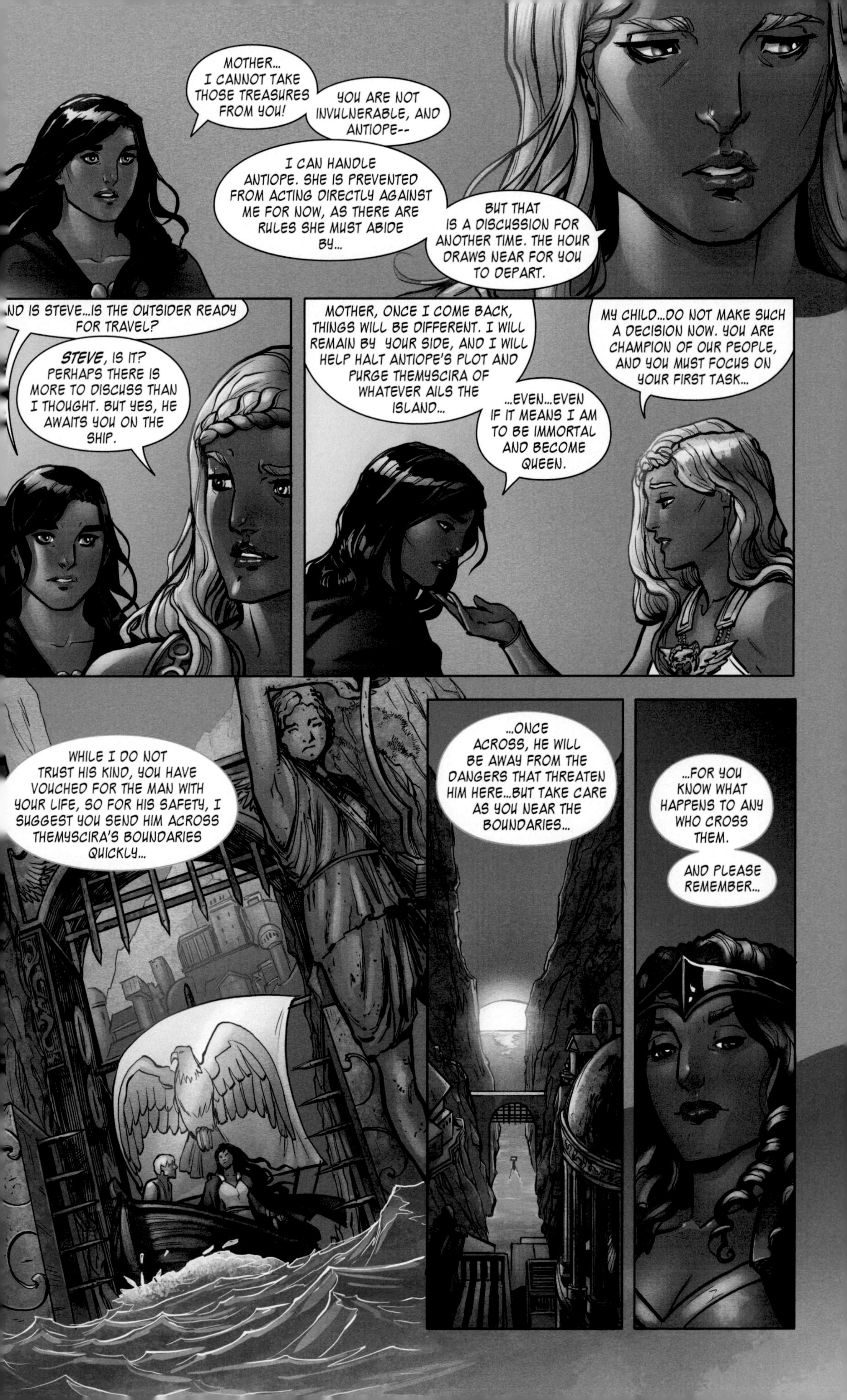
MOTHER... I CANNOT TAKE THOSE TREASURES FROM YOU!
YOU ARE NOT INVULNERABLE, AND ANTIOPE--
I CAN HANDLE ANTIOPE. SHE IS PREVENTED FROM ACTING DIRECTLY AGAINST ME FOR NOW, AS THERE ARE RULES SHE MUST ABIDE BY...
BUT THAT IS A DISCUSSION FOR ANOTHER TIME. THE HOUR DRAWS NEAR FOR YOU TO DEPART.
ND IS STEVE...IS THE OUTSIDER READY FOR TRAVEL?
STEVE, IS IT? PERHAPS THERE IS MORE TO DISCUSS THAN I THOUGHT. BUT YES, HE AWAITS YOU ON THE SHIP.
MOTHER, ONCE I COME BACK, THINGS WILL BE DIFFERENT. I WILL REMAIN BY YOUR SIDE, AND I WILL HELP HALT ANTIOPE'S PLOT AND PURGE THEMYSCIRA OF WHATEVER AILS THE ISLAND...
...EVEN...EVEN IF IT MEANS I AM TO BE IMMORTAL AND BECOME QUEEN.
MY CHILD...DO NOT MAKE SUCH A DECISION NOW. YOU ARE CHAMPION OF OUR PEOPLE, AND YOU MUST FOCUS ON YOUR FIRST TASK...
WHILE I DO NOT TRUST HIS KIND, YOU HAVE VOUCHED FOR THE MAN WITH YOUR LIFE, SO FOR HIS SAFETY, I SUGGEST YOU SEND HIM ACROSS THEMYSCIRA'S BOUNDARIES QUICKLY...
...ONCE ACROSS, HE WILL BE AWAY FROM THE DANGERS THAT THREATEN HIM HERE...BUT TAKE CARE AS YOU NEAR THE BOUNDARIES...
...FOR YOU KNOW WHAT HAPPENS TO ANY WHO CROSS THEM.
AND PLEASE REMEMBER...

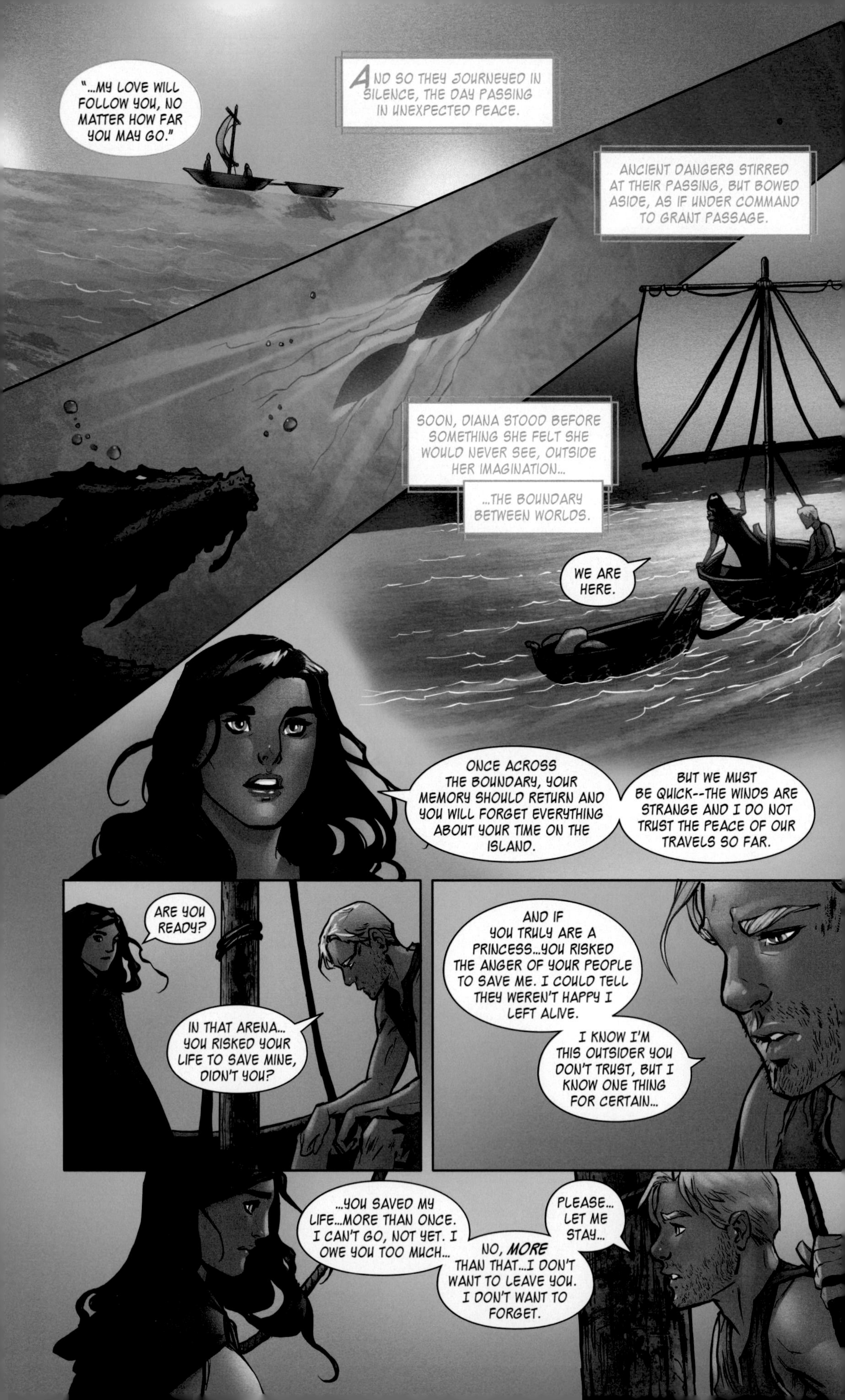
"...MY LOVE WILL FOLLOW YOU, NO MATTER HOW FAR YOU MAY GO."
AND SO THEY JOURNEYED IN SILENCE, THE DAY PASSING IN UNEXPECTED PEACE.
ANCIENT DANGERS STIRRED AT THEIR PASSING, BUT BOWED ASIDE, AS IF UNDER COMMAND TO GRANT PASSAGE.
SOON, DIANA STOOD BEFORE SOMETHING SHE FELT SHE WOULD NEVER SEE, OUTSIDE HER IMAGINATION...
...THE BOUNDARY BETWEEN WORLDS.
WE ARE HERE.
ONCE ACROSS THE BOUNDARY, YOUR MEMORY SHOULD RETURN AND YOU WILL FORGET EVERYTHING ABOUT YOUR TIME ON THE ISLAND.
BUT WE MUST BE QUICK--THE WINDS ARE STRANGE AND I DO NOT TRUST THE PEACE OF OUR TRAVELS SO FAR.
ARE YOU READY?
IN THAT ARENA... YOU RISKED YOUR LIFE TO SAVE MINE, DIDN'T YOU?
AND IF YOU TRULY ARE A PRINCESS...YOU RISKED THE ANGER OF YOUR PEOPLE TO SAVE ME. I COULD TELL THEY WEREN'T HAPPY I LEFT ALIVE.
I KNOW I'M THIS OUTSIDER YOU DON'T TRUST, BUT I KNOW ONE THING FOR CERTAIN...
...YOU SAVED MY LIFE...MORE THAN ONCE. I CAN'T GO, NOT YET. I OWE YOU TOO MUCH...
NO, *MORE* THAN THAT...I DON'T WANT TO LEAVE YOU. I DON'T WANT TO FORGET.
PLEASE... LET ME STAY...

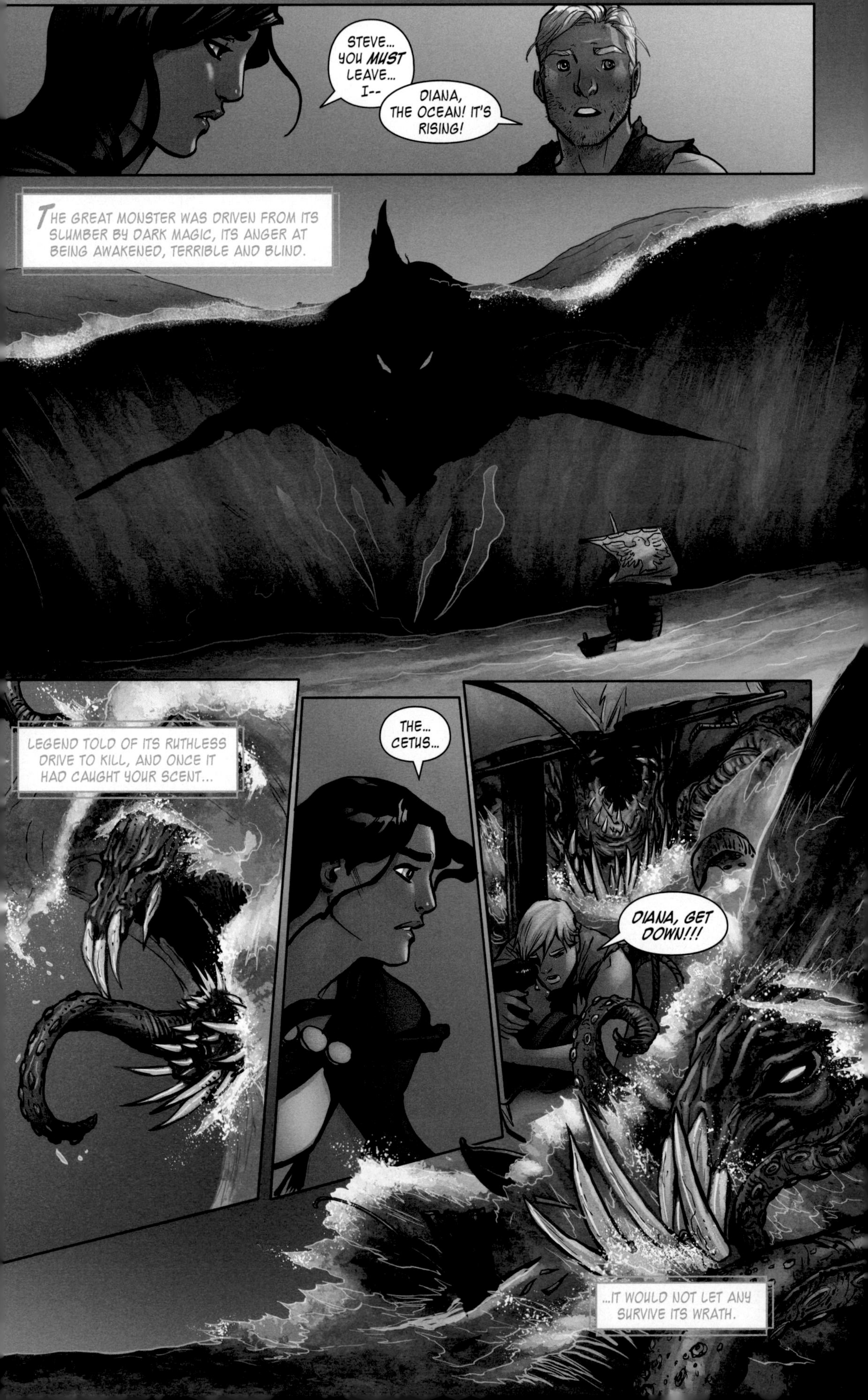
STEVE... YOU *MUST* LEAVE... I--
DIANA, THE OCEAN! IT'S RISING!
THE GREAT MONSTER WAS DRIVEN FROM ITS SLUMBER BY DARK MAGIC, ITS ANGER AT BEING AWAKENED, TERRIBLE AND BLIND.
LEGEND TOLD OF ITS RUTHLESS DRIVE TO KILL, AND ONCE IT HAD CAUGHT YOUR SCENT...
THE... CETUS...
DIANA, GET DOWN!!!
...IT WOULD NOT LET ANY SURVIVE ITS WRATH.

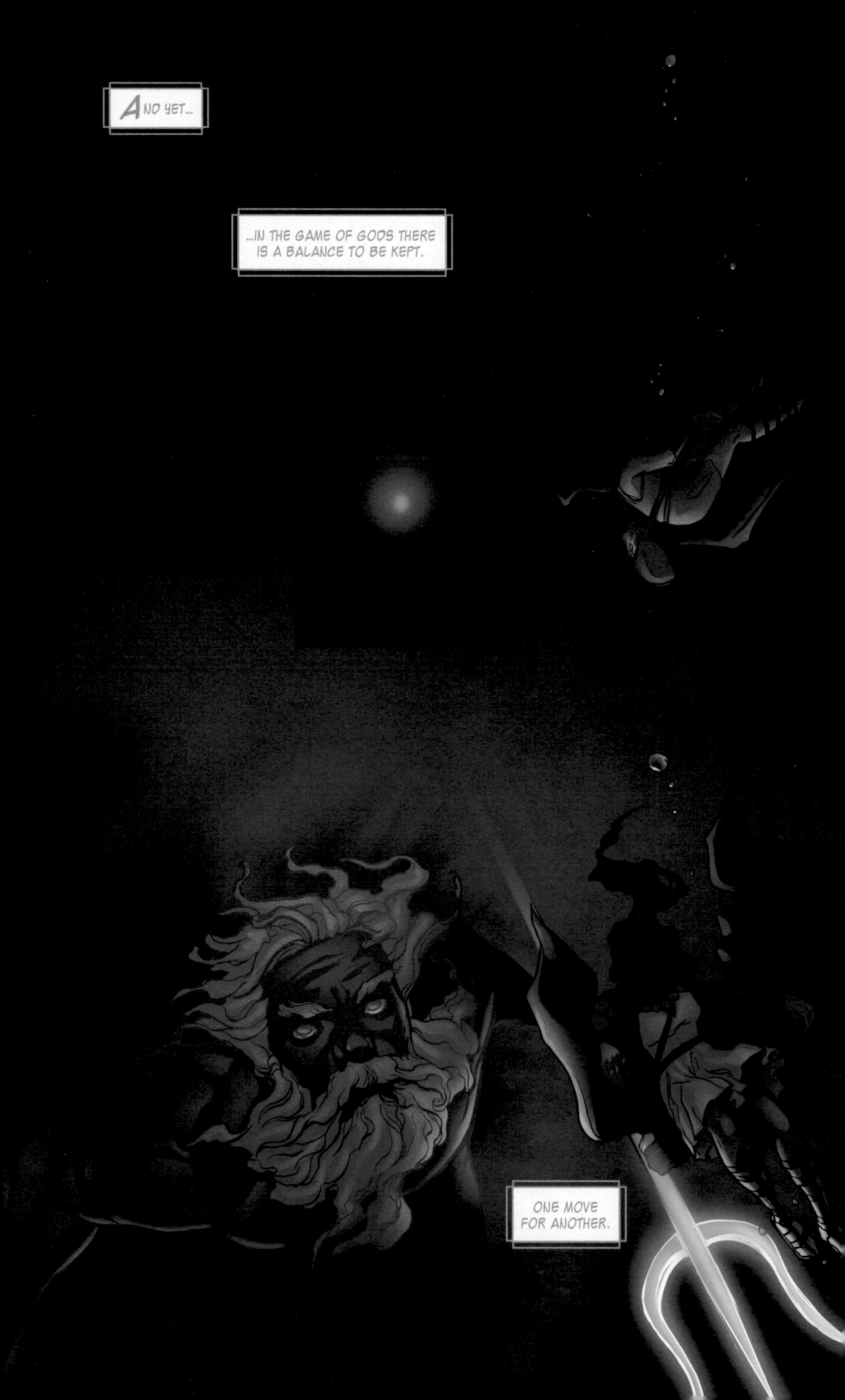
AND YET...
...IN THE GAME OF GODS THERE IS A BALANCE TO BE KEPT.
ONE MOVE FOR ANOTHER.

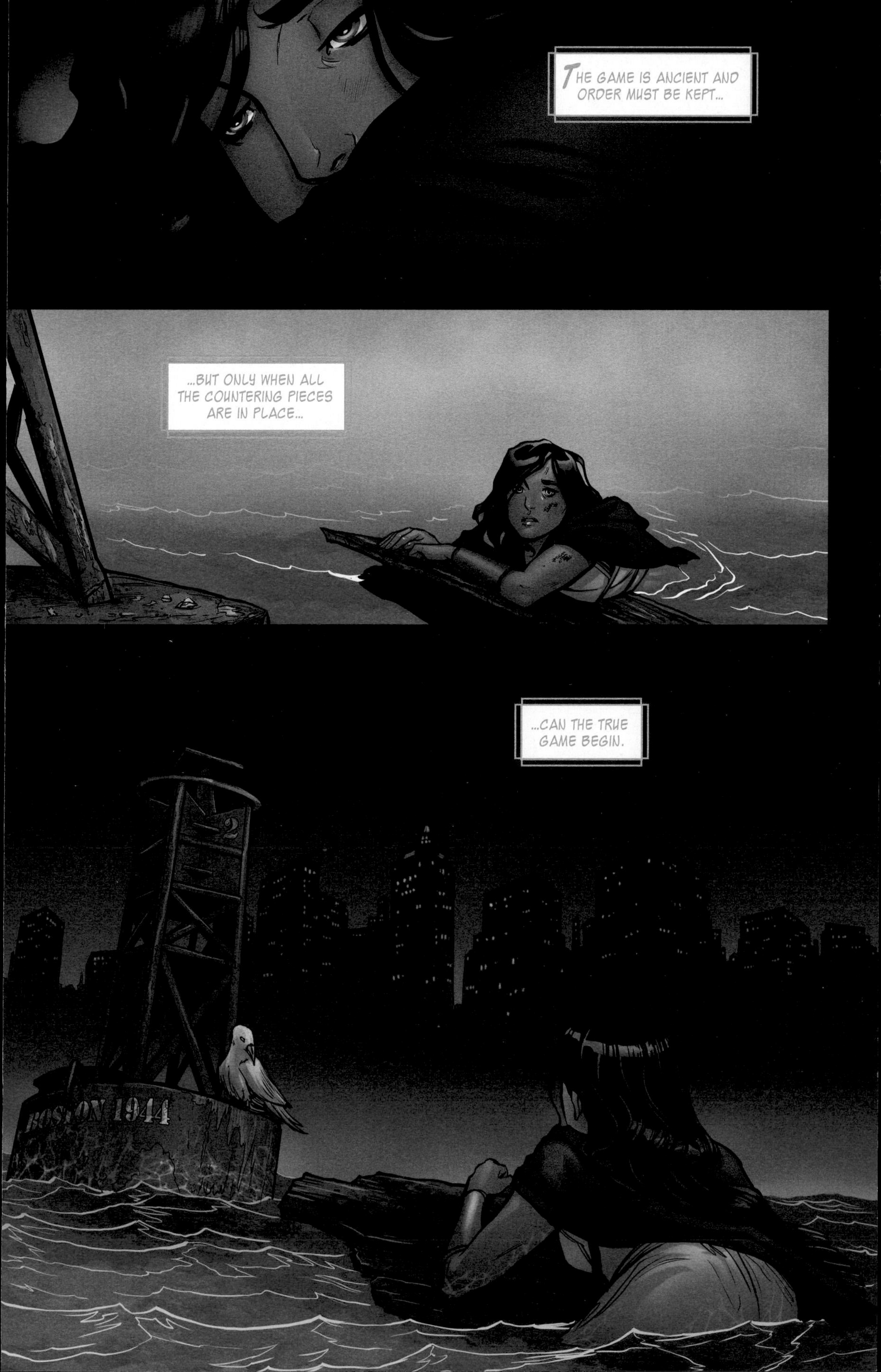
THE GAME IS ANCIENT AND ORDER MUST BE KEPT...
...BUT ONLY WHEN ALL THE COUNTERING PIECES ARE IN PLACE...
...CAN THE TRUE GAME BEGIN.
2
BOSTON 1944

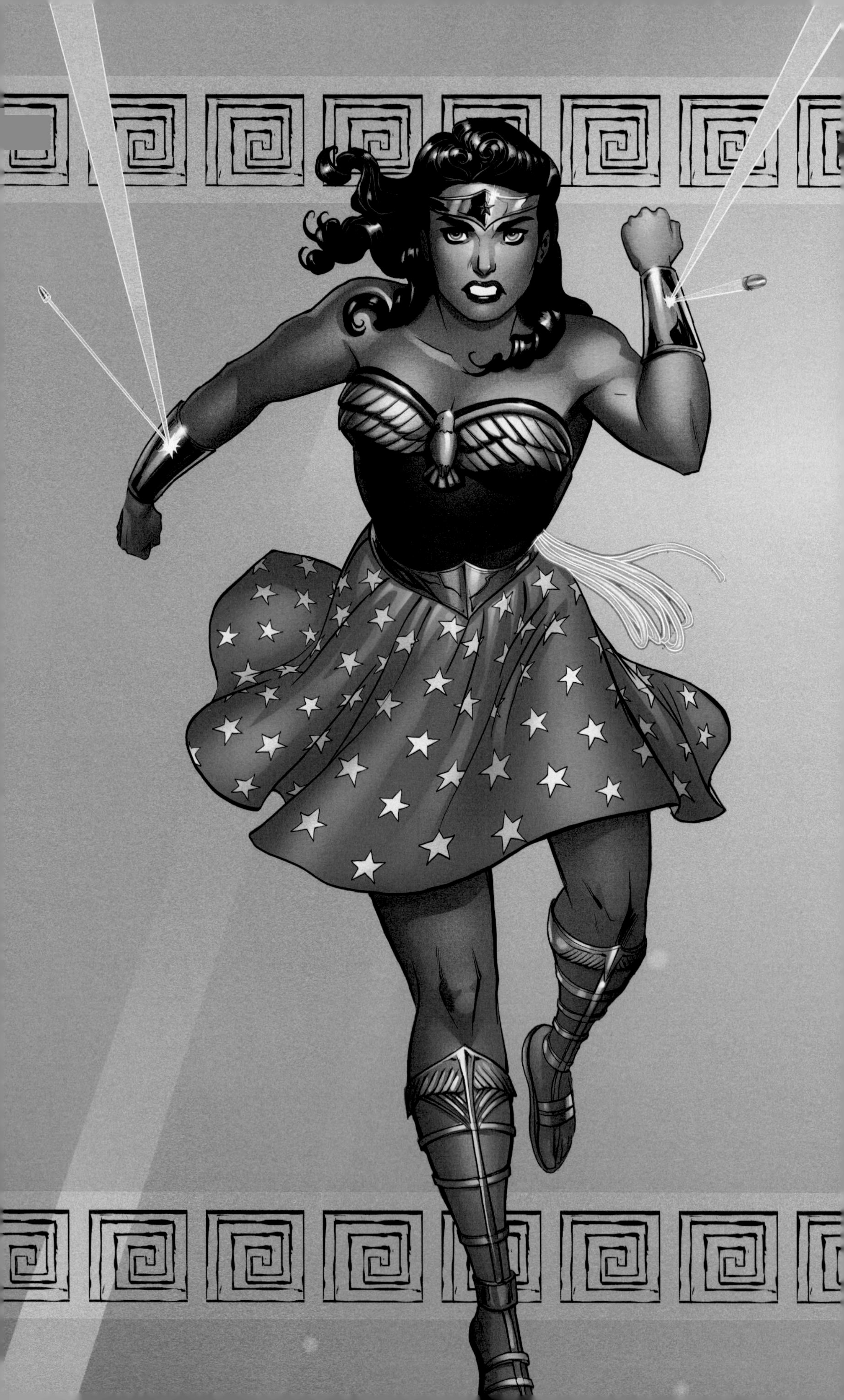

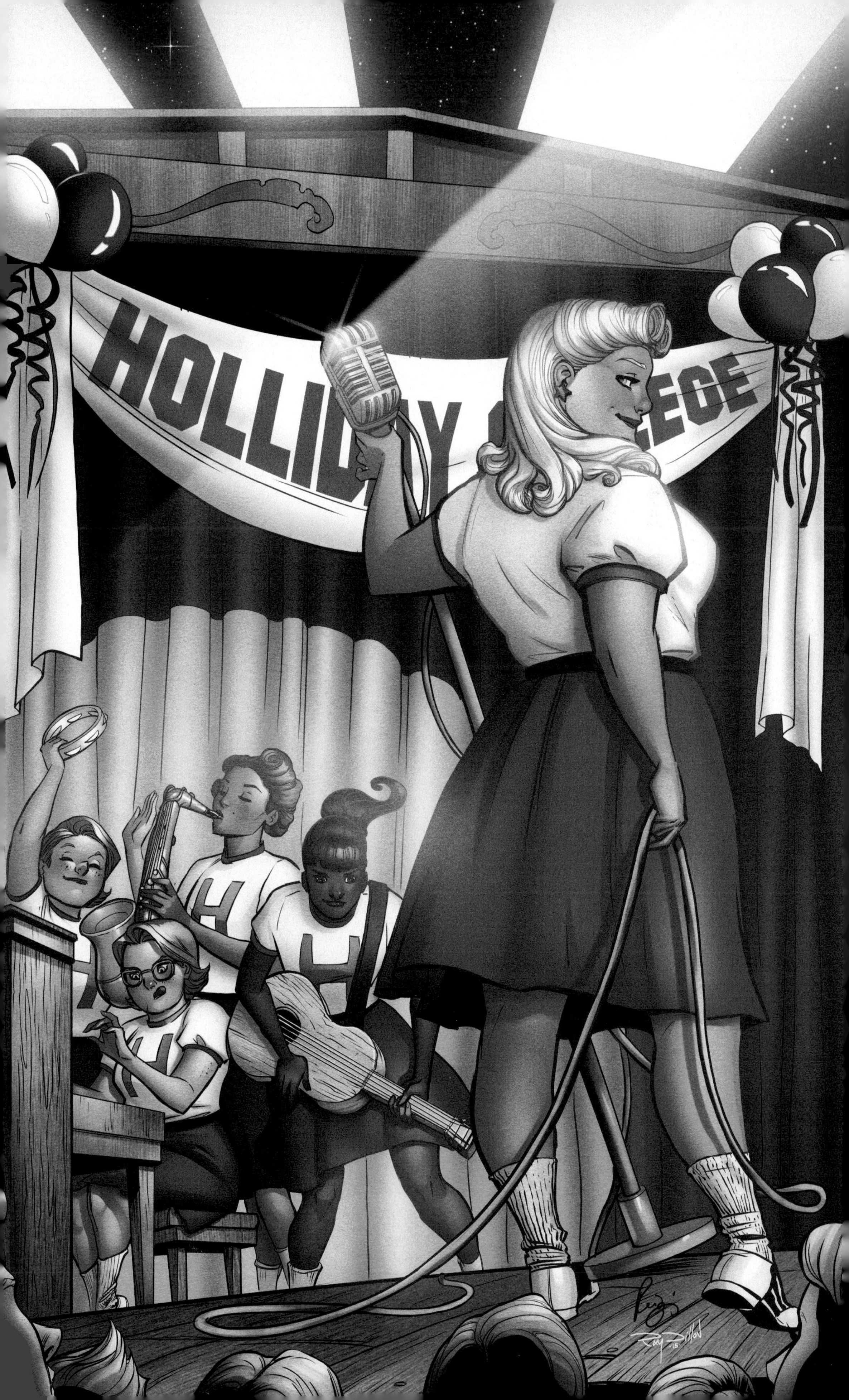

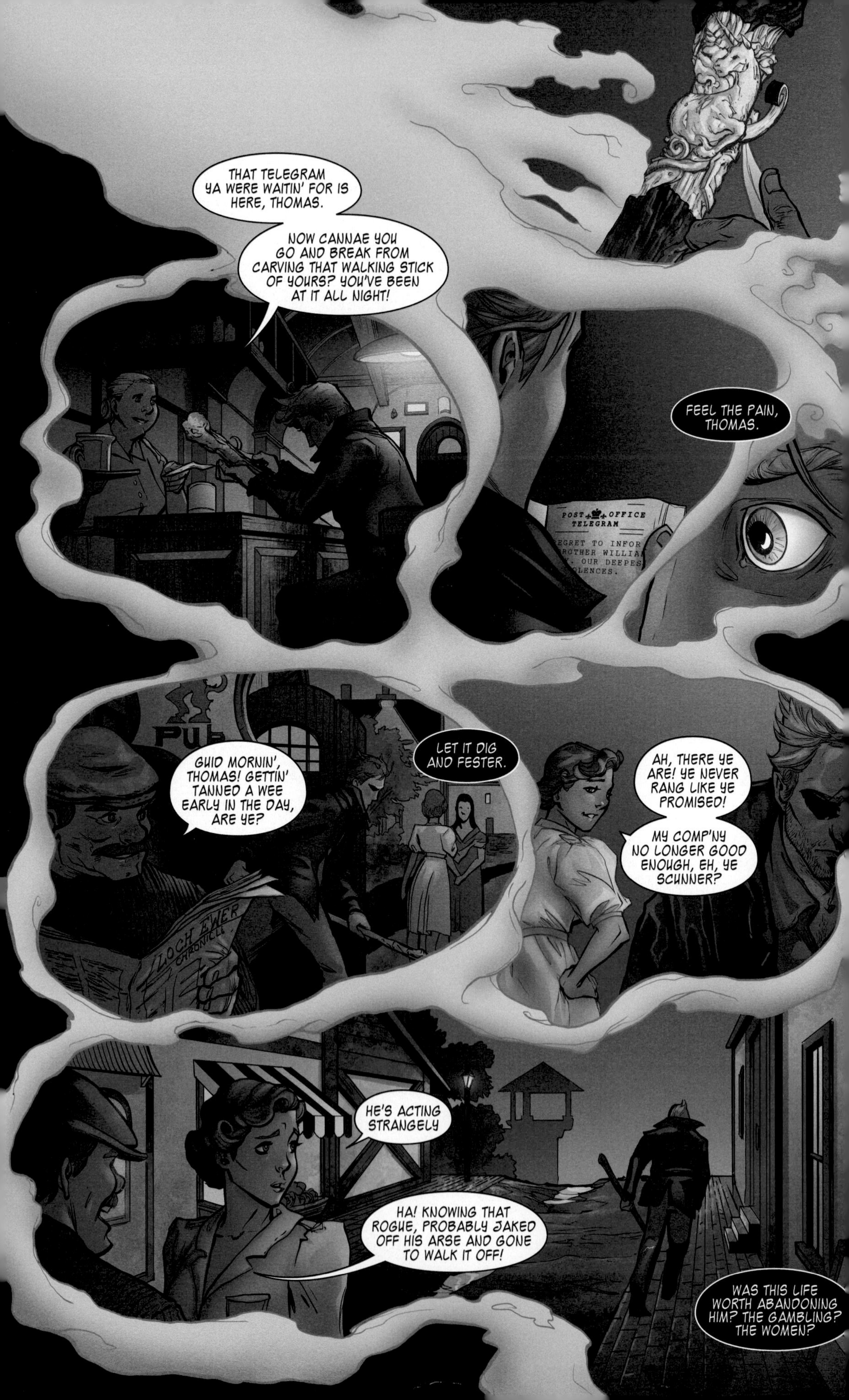
THAT TELEGRAM YA WERE WAITIN' FOR IS HERE, THOMAS.
NOW CANNAE YOU GO AND BREAK FROM CARVING THAT WALKING STICK OF YOURS? YOU'VE BEEN AT IT ALL NIGHT!
FEEL THE PAIN, THOMAS.
POST OFFICE
TELEGRAM
EGRET TO INFOR
ROTHER WILLIA
Y. OUR DEEPES
OLENCES.
PUB
GUID MORNIN', THOMAS! GETTIN' TANNED A WEE EARLY IN THE DAY, ARE YE?
LOCH EWER
LET IT DIG AND FESTER.
AH, THERE YE ARE! YE NEVER RANG LIKE YE PROMISED!
MY COMP'NY NO LONGER GOOD ENOUGH, EH, YE SCUNNER?
HE'S ACTING STRANGELY
HA! KNOWING THAT ROGUE, PROBABLY JAKED OFF HIS ARSE AND GONE TO WALK IT OFF!
WAS THIS LIFE WORTH ABANDONING HIM? THE GAMBLING? THE WOMEN?

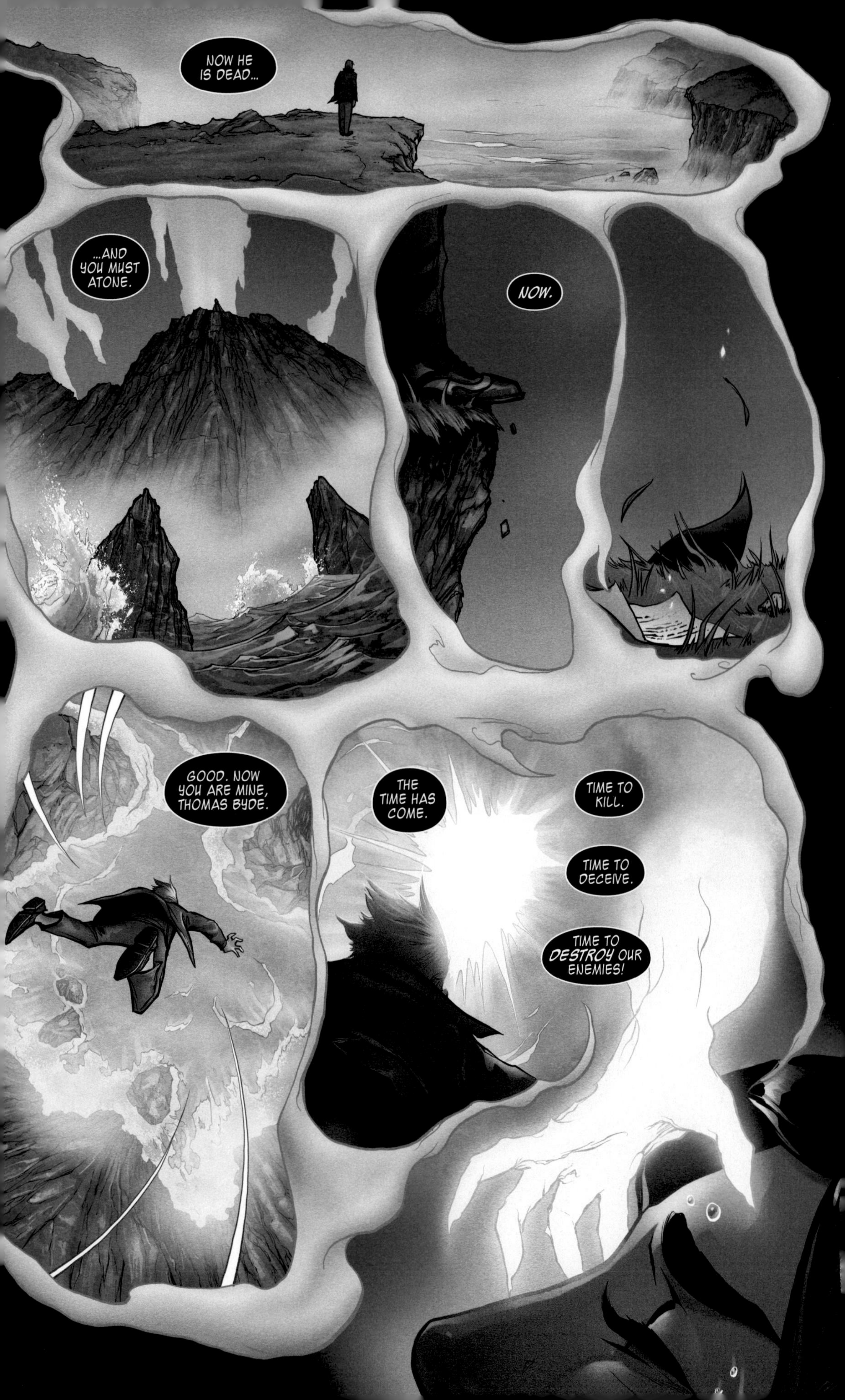
NOW HE IS DEAD...
...AND YOU MUST ATONE.
NOW.
GOOD. NOW YOU ARE MINE, THOMAS BYDE.
THE TIME HAS COME.
TIME TO KILL.
TIME TO DECEIVE.
TIME TO DESTROY OUR ENEMIES!

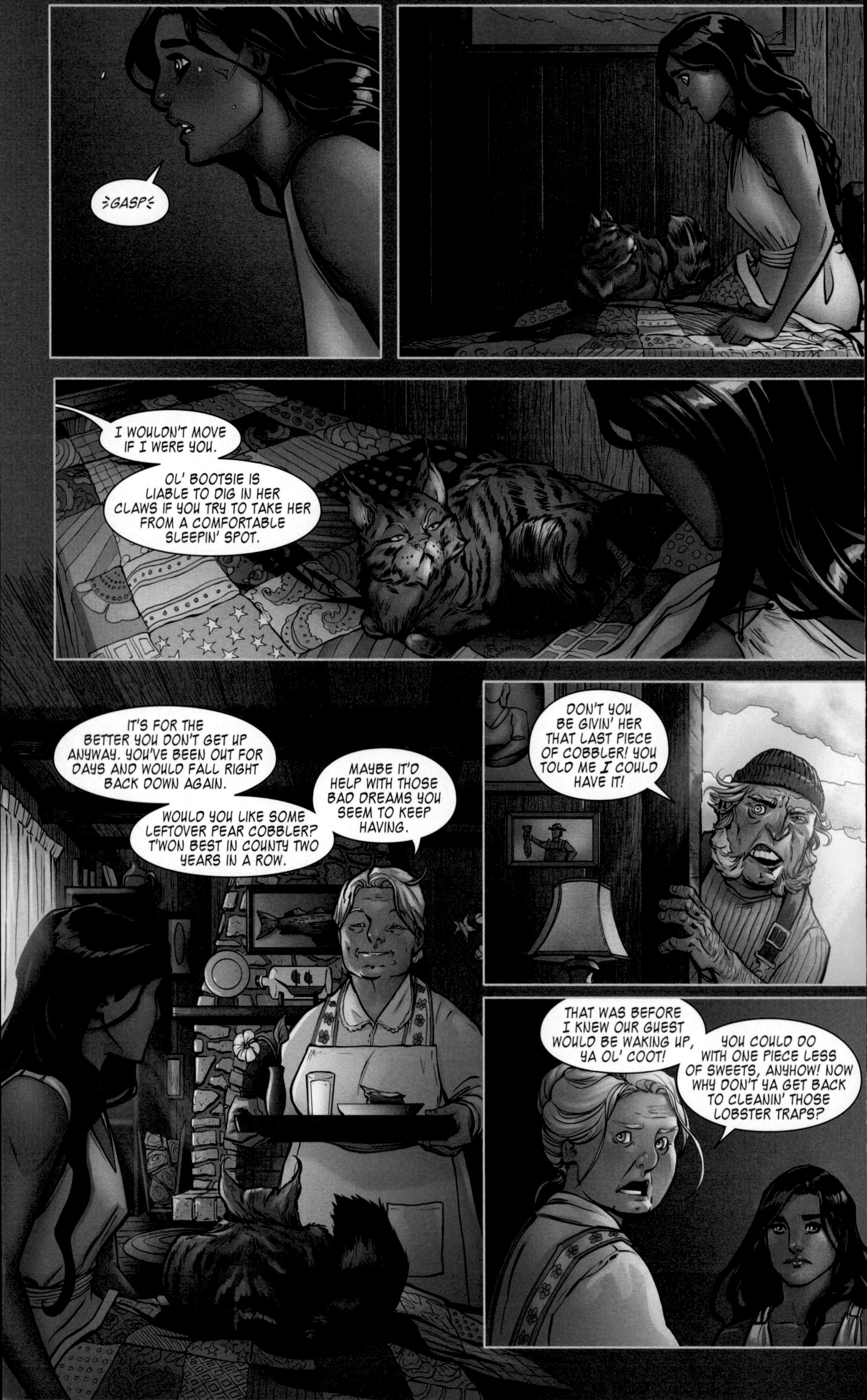
GASP
I WOULDN'T MOVE IF I WERE YOU.
OL' BOOTSIE IS LIABLE TO DIG IN HER CLAWS IF YOU TRY TO TAKE HER FROM A COMFORTABLE SLEEPIN' SPOT.
IT'S FOR THE BETTER YOU DON'T GET UP ANYWAY. YOU'VE BEEN OUT FOR DAYS AND WOULD FALL RIGHT BACK DOWN AGAIN.
WOULD YOU LIKE SOME LEFTOVER PEAR COBBLER? T'WON BEST IN COUNTY TWO YEARS IN A ROW.
MAYBE IT'D HELP WITH THOSE BAD DREAMS YOU SEEM TO KEEP HAVING.
DON'T YOU BE GIVIN' HER THAT LAST PIECE OF COBBLER! YOU TOLD ME I COULD HAVE IT!
THAT WAS BEFORE I KNEW OUR GUEST WOULD BE WAKING UP, YA OL' COOT!
YOU COULD DO WITH ONE PIECE LESS OF SWEETS, ANYHOW! NOW WHY DON'T YA GET BACK TO CLEANIN' THOSE LOBSTER TRAPS?

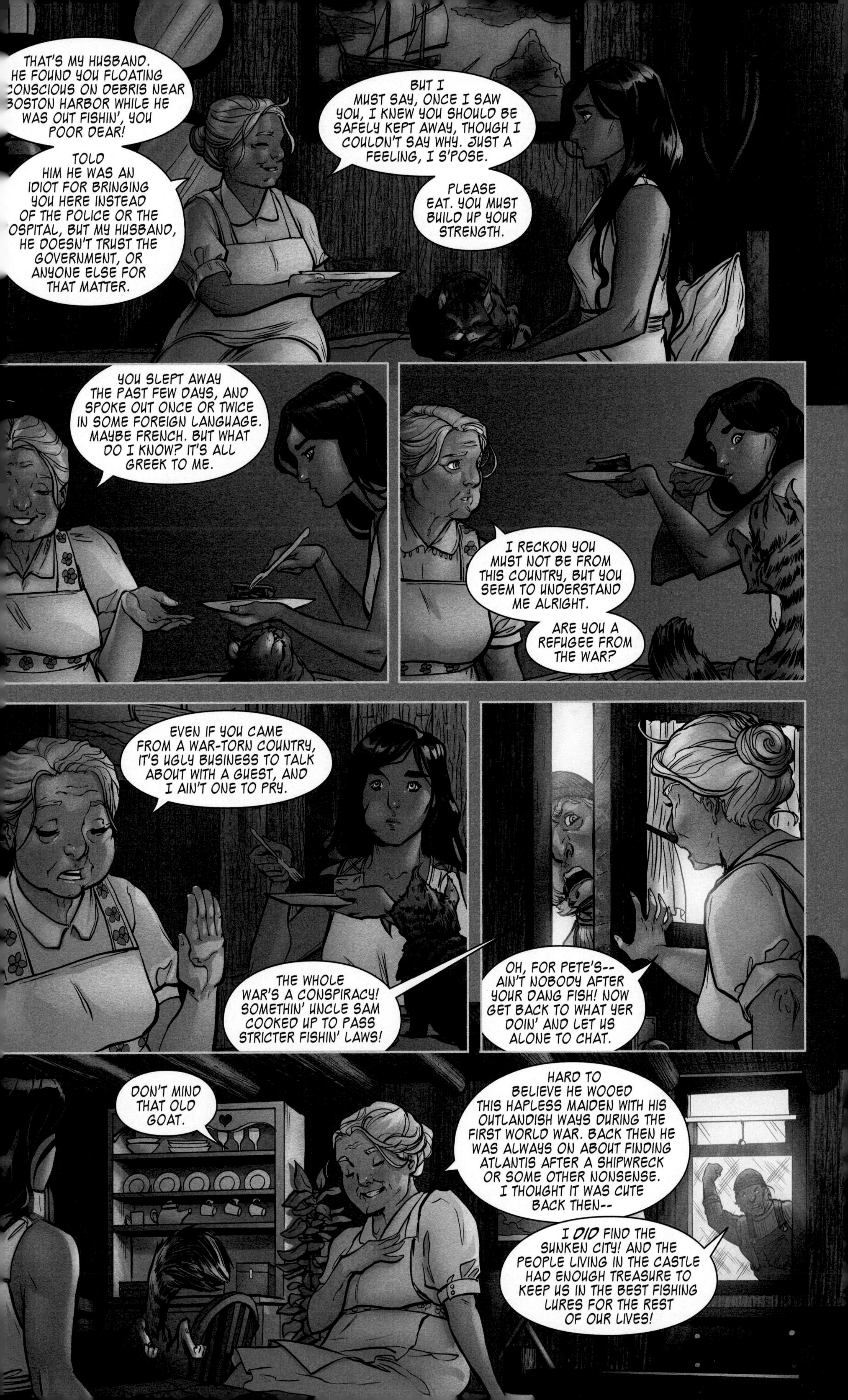
THAT'S MY HUSBAND. HE FOUND YOU FLOATING CONSCIOUS ON DEBRIS NEAR BOSTON HARBOR WHILE HE WAS OUT FISHIN', YOU POOR DEAR!
TOLD HIM HE WAS AN IDIOT FOR BRINGING YOU HERE INSTEAD OF THE POLICE OR THE OSPITAL, BUT MY HUSBAND, HE DOESN'T TRUST THE GOVERNMENT, OR ANYONE ELSE FOR THAT MATTER.
BUT I MUST SAY, ONCE I SAW YOU, I KNEW YOU SHOULD BE SAFELY KEPT AWAY, THOUGH I COULDN'T SAY WHY. JUST A FEELING, I S'POSE.
PLEASE EAT. YOU MUST BUILD UP YOUR STRENGTH.
YOU SLEPT AWAY THE PAST FEW DAYS, AND SPOKE OUT ONCE OR TWICE IN SOME FOREIGN LANGUAGE. MAYBE FRENCH. BUT WHAT DO I KNOW? IT'S ALL GREEK TO ME.
I RECKON YOU MUST NOT BE FROM THIS COUNTRY, BUT YOU SEEM TO UNDERSTAND ME ALRIGHT.
ARE YOU A REFUGEE FROM THE WAR?
EVEN IF YOU CAME FROM A WAR-TORN COUNTRY, IT'S UGLY BUSINESS TO TALK ABOUT WITH A GUEST, AND I AIN'T ONE TO PRY.
THE WHOLE WAR'S A CONSPIRACY! SOMETHIN' UNCLE SAM COOKED UP TO PASS STRICTER FISHIN' LAWS!
OH, FOR PETE'S-- AIN'T NOBODY AFTER YOUR DANG FISH! NOW GET BACK TO WHAT YER DOIN' AND LET US ALONE TO CHAT.
DON'T MIND THAT OLD GOAT.
HARD TO BELIEVE HE WOOED THIS HAPLESS MAIDEN WITH HIS OUTLANDISH WAYS DURING THE FIRST WORLD WAR. BACK THEN HE WAS ALWAYS ON ABOUT FINDING ATLANTIS AFTER A SHIPWRECK OR SOME OTHER NONSENSE. I THOUGHT IT WAS CUTE BACK THEN--
I *DID* FIND THE SUNKEN CITY! AND THE PEOPLE LIVING IN THE CASTLE HAD ENOUGH TREASURE TO KEEP US IN THE BEST FISHING LURES FOR THE REST OF OUR LIVES!

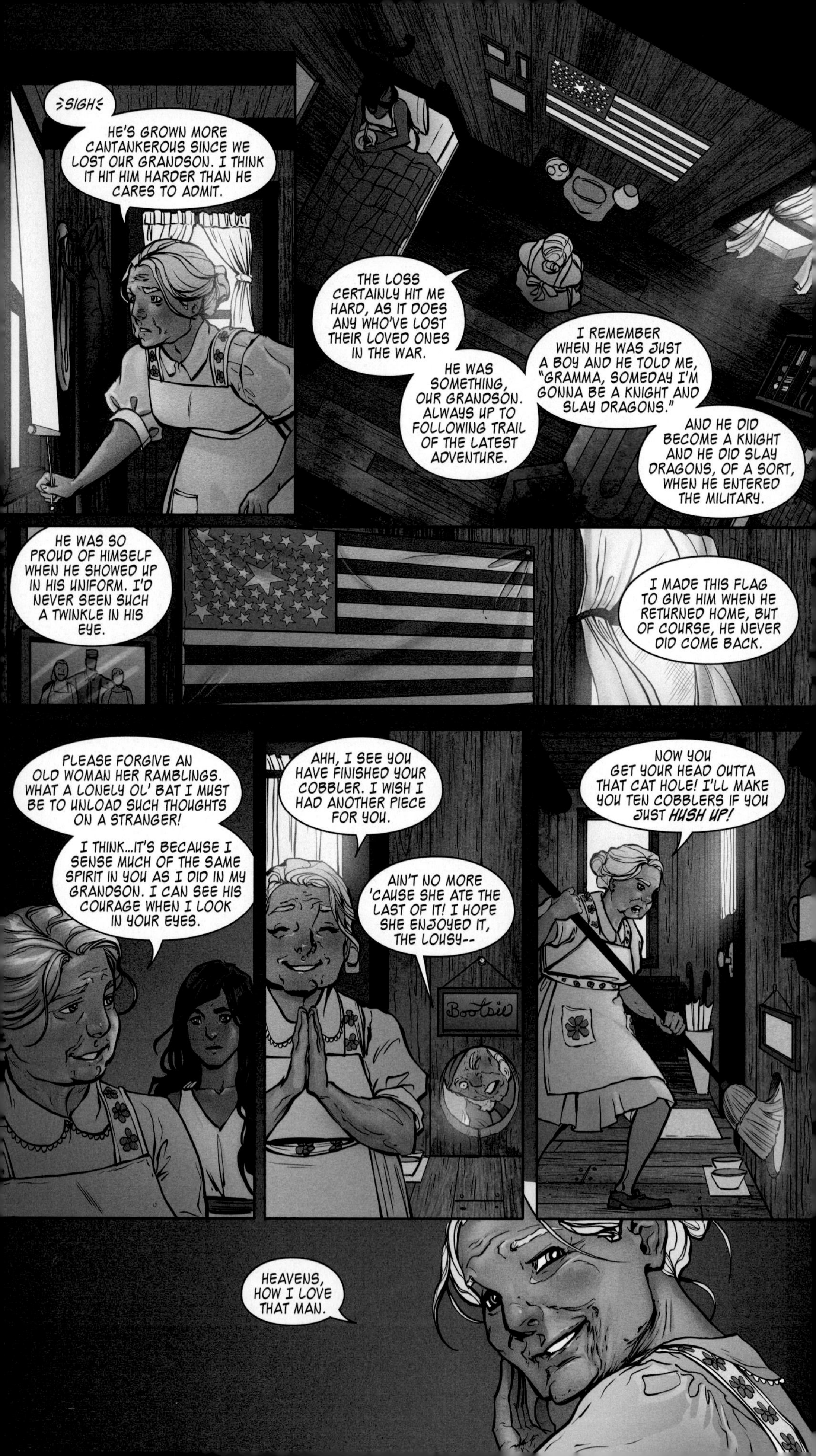

SIGH
HE'S GROWN MORE CANTANKEROUS SINCE WE LOST OUR GRANDSON. I THINK IT HIT HIM HARDER THAN HE CARES TO ADMIT.
THE LOSS CERTAINLY HIT ME HARD, AS IT DOES ANY WHO'VE LOST THEIR LOVED ONES IN THE WAR.
HE WAS SOMETHING, OUR GRANDSON. ALWAYS UP TO FOLLOWING TRAIL OF THE LATEST ADVENTURE.
I REMEMBER WHEN HE WAS JUST A BOY AND HE TOLD ME, "GRAMMA, SOMEDAY I'M GONNA BE A KNIGHT AND SLAY DRAGONS."
AND HE DID BECOME A KNIGHT AND HE DID SLAY DRAGONS, OF A SORT, WHEN HE ENTERED THE MILITARY.
HE WAS SO PROUD OF HIMSELF WHEN HE SHOWED UP IN HIS UNIFORM. I'D NEVER SEEN SUCH A TWINKLE IN HIS EYE.
I MADE THIS FLAG TO GIVE HIM WHEN HE RETURNED HOME, BUT OF COURSE, HE NEVER DID COME BACK.
PLEASE FORGIVE AN OLD WOMAN HER RAMBLINGS. WHAT A LONELY OL' BAT I MUST BE TO UNLOAD SUCH THOUGHTS ON A STRANGER!
I THINK...IT'S BECAUSE I SENSE MUCH OF THE SAME SPIRIT IN YOU AS I DID IN MY GRANDSON. I CAN SEE HIS COURAGE WHEN I LOOK IN YOUR EYES.
AHH, I SEE YOU HAVE FINISHED YOUR COBBLER. I WISH I HAD ANOTHER PIECE FOR YOU.
AIN'T NO MORE 'CAUSE SHE ATE THE LAST OF IT! I HOPE SHE ENJOYED IT, THE LOUSY--
Bootsie
NOW YOU GET YOUR HEAD OUTTA THAT CAT HOLE! I'LL MAKE YOU TEN COBBLERS IF YOU JUST HUSH UP!
HEAVENS, HOW I LOVE THAT MAN.

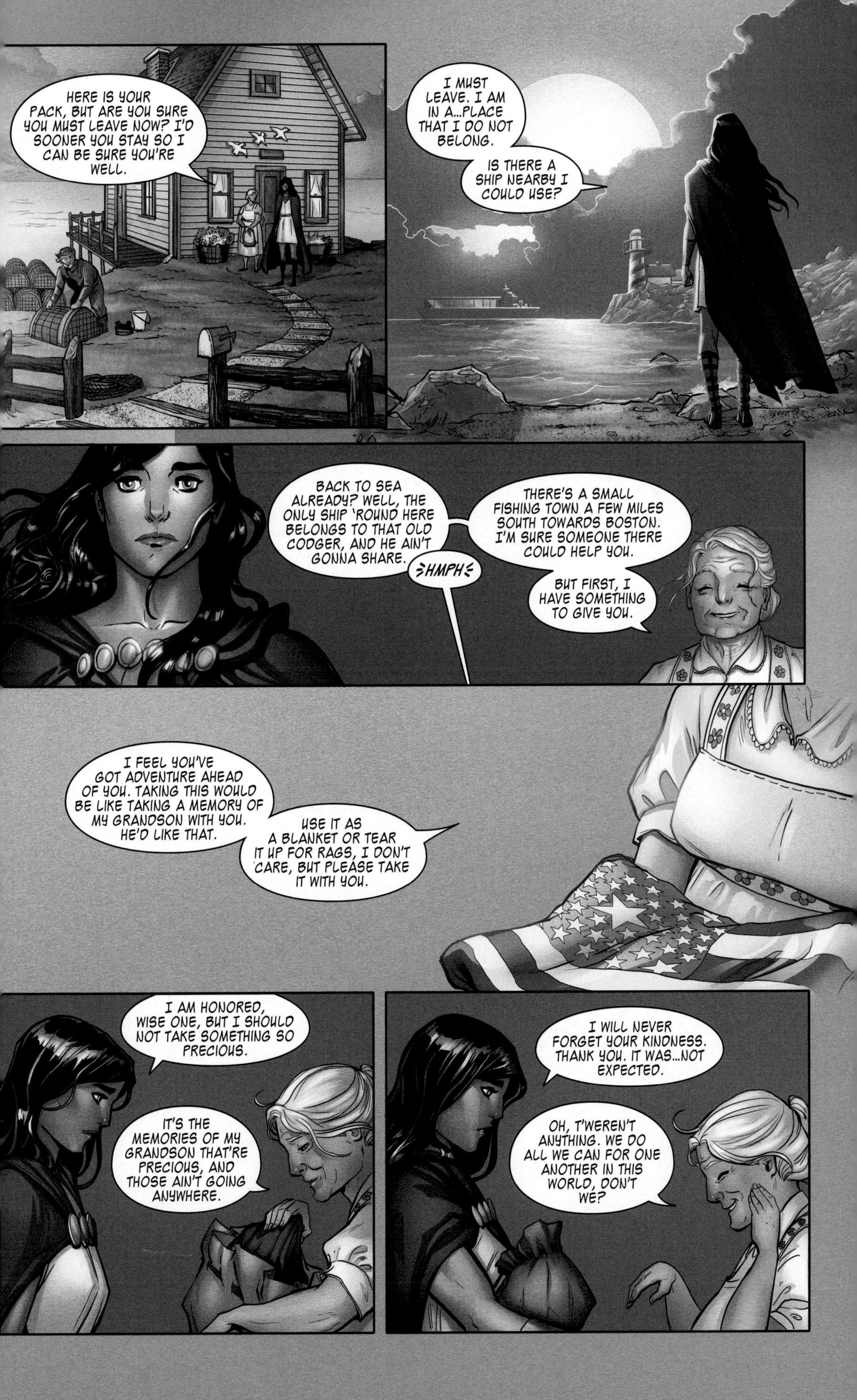
HERE IS YOUR PACK, BUT ARE YOU SURE YOU MUST LEAVE NOW? I'D SOONER YOU STAY SO I CAN BE SURE YOU'RE WELL.
I MUST LEAVE. I AM IN A...PLACE THAT I DO NOT BELONG.
IS THERE A SHIP NEARBY I COULD USE?
BACK TO SEA ALREADY? WELL, THE ONLY SHIP 'ROUND HERE BELONGS TO THAT OLD CODGER, AND HE AIN'T GONNA SHARE.
HMPH
THERE'S A SMALL FISHING TOWN A FEW MILES SOUTH TOWARDS BOSTON. I'M SURE SOMEONE THERE COULD HELP YOU.
BUT FIRST, I HAVE SOMETHING TO GIVE YOU.
I FEEL YOU'VE GOT ADVENTURE AHEAD OF YOU. TAKING THIS WOULD BE LIKE TAKING A MEMORY OF MY GRANDSON WITH YOU. HE'D LIKE THAT.
USE IT AS A BLANKET OR TEAR IT UP FOR RAGS, I DON'T CARE, BUT PLEASE TAKE IT WITH YOU.
I AM HONORED, WISE ONE, BUT I SHOULD NOT TAKE SOMETHING SO PRECIOUS.
IT'S THE MEMORIES OF MY GRANDSON THAT'RE PRECIOUS, AND THOSE AIN'T GOING ANYWHERE.
I WILL NEVER FORGET YOUR KINDNESS. THANK YOU. IT WAS...NOT EXPECTED.
OH, T'WEREN'T ANYTHING. WE DO ALL WE CAN FOR ONE ANOTHER IN THIS WORLD, DON'T WE?

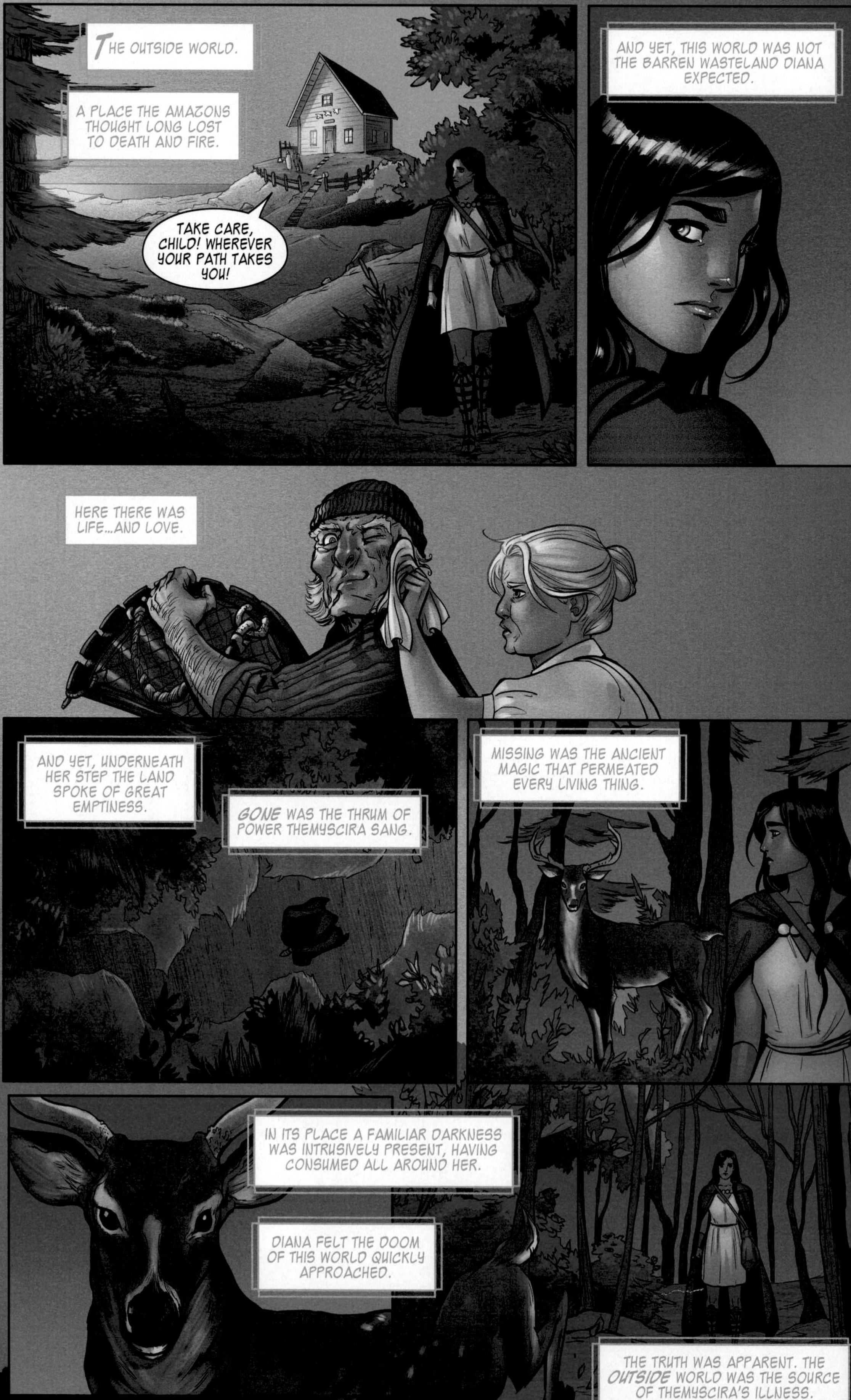
THE OUTSIDE WORLD.
A PLACE THE AMAZONS THOUGHT LONG LOST TO DEATH AND FIRE.
TAKE CARE, CHILD! WHEREVER YOUR PATH TAKES YOU!
AND YET, THIS WORLD WAS NOT THE BARREN WASTELAND DIANA EXPECTED.
HERE THERE WAS LIFE...AND LOVE.
AND YET, UNDERNEATH HER STEP THE LAND SPOKE OF GREAT EMPTINESS.
GONE WAS THE THRUM OF POWER THEMYSCIRA SANG.
MISSING WAS THE ANCIENT MAGIC THAT PERMEATED EVERY LIVING THING.
IN ITS PLACE A FAMILIAR DARKNESS WAS INTRUSIVELY PRESENT, HAVING CONSUMED ALL AROUND HER.
DIANA FELT THE DOOM OF THIS WORLD QUICKLY APPROACHED.
THE TRUTH WAS APPARENT. THE OUTSIDE WORLD WAS THE SOURCE OF THEMYSCIRA'S ILLNESS.

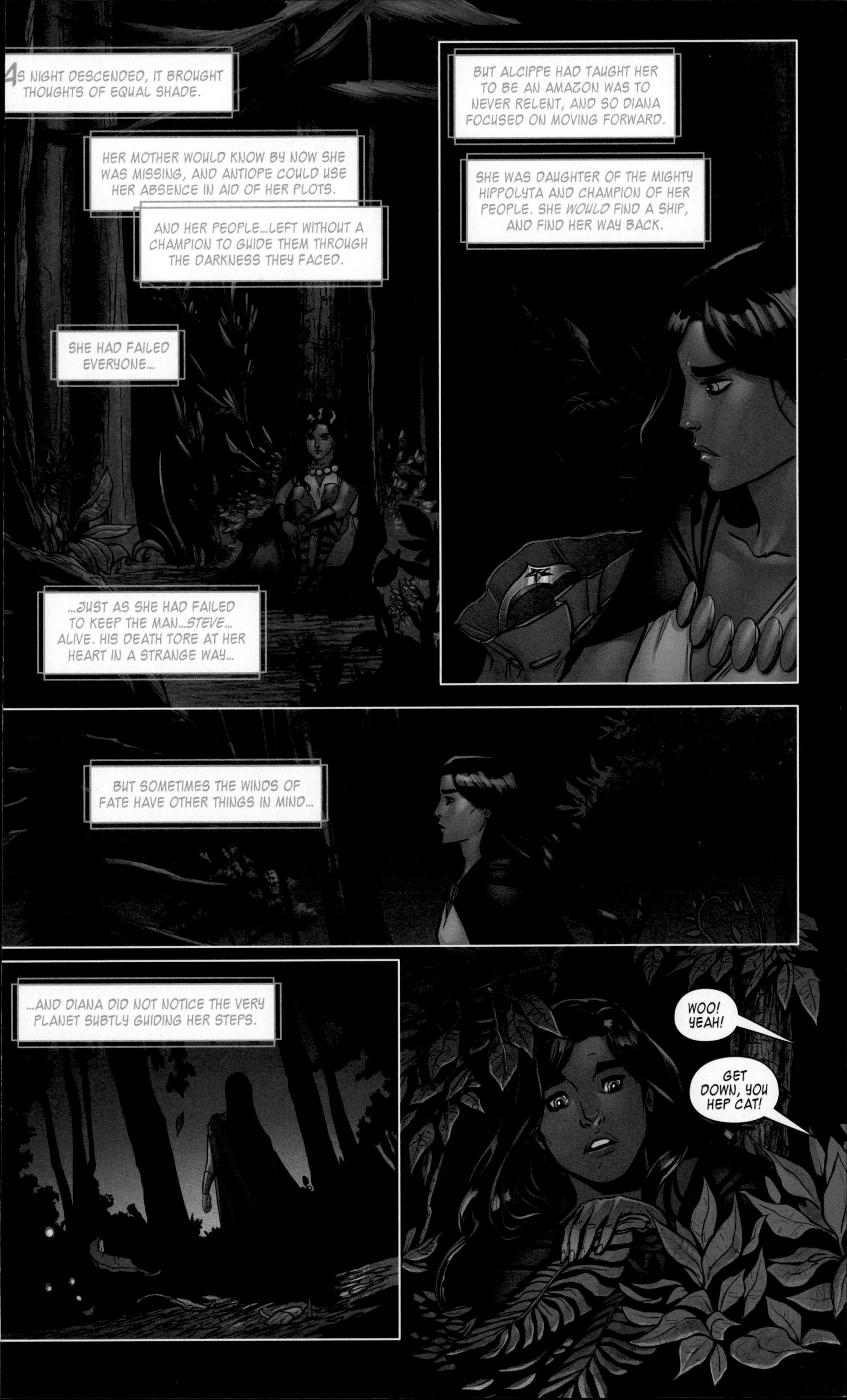
AS NIGHT DESCENDED, IT BROUGHT THOUGHTS OF EQUAL SHADE.
HER MOTHER WOULD KNOW BY NOW SHE WAS MISSING, AND ANTIOPE COULD USE HER ABSENCE IN AID OF HER PLOTS.
AND HER PEOPLE...LEFT WITHOUT A CHAMPION TO GUIDE THEM THROUGH THE DARKNESS THEY FACED.
SHE HAD FAILED EVERYONE...
...JUST AS SHE HAD FAILED TO KEEP THE MAN...STEVE... ALIVE. HIS DEATH TORE AT HER HEART IN A STRANGE WAY...
BUT ALCIPPE HAD TAUGHT HER TO BE AN AMAZON WAS TO NEVER RELENT, AND SO DIANA FOCUSED ON MOVING FORWARD.
SHE WAS DAUGHTER OF THE MIGHTY HIPPOLYTA AND CHAMPION OF HER PEOPLE. SHE WOULD FIND A SHIP, AND FIND HER WAY BACK.
BUT SOMETIMES THE WINDS OF FATE HAVE OTHER THINGS IN MIND...
...AND DIANA DID NOT NOTICE THE VERY PLANET SUBTLY GUIDING HER STEPS.
WOO! YEAH!
GET DOWN, YOU HEP CAT!

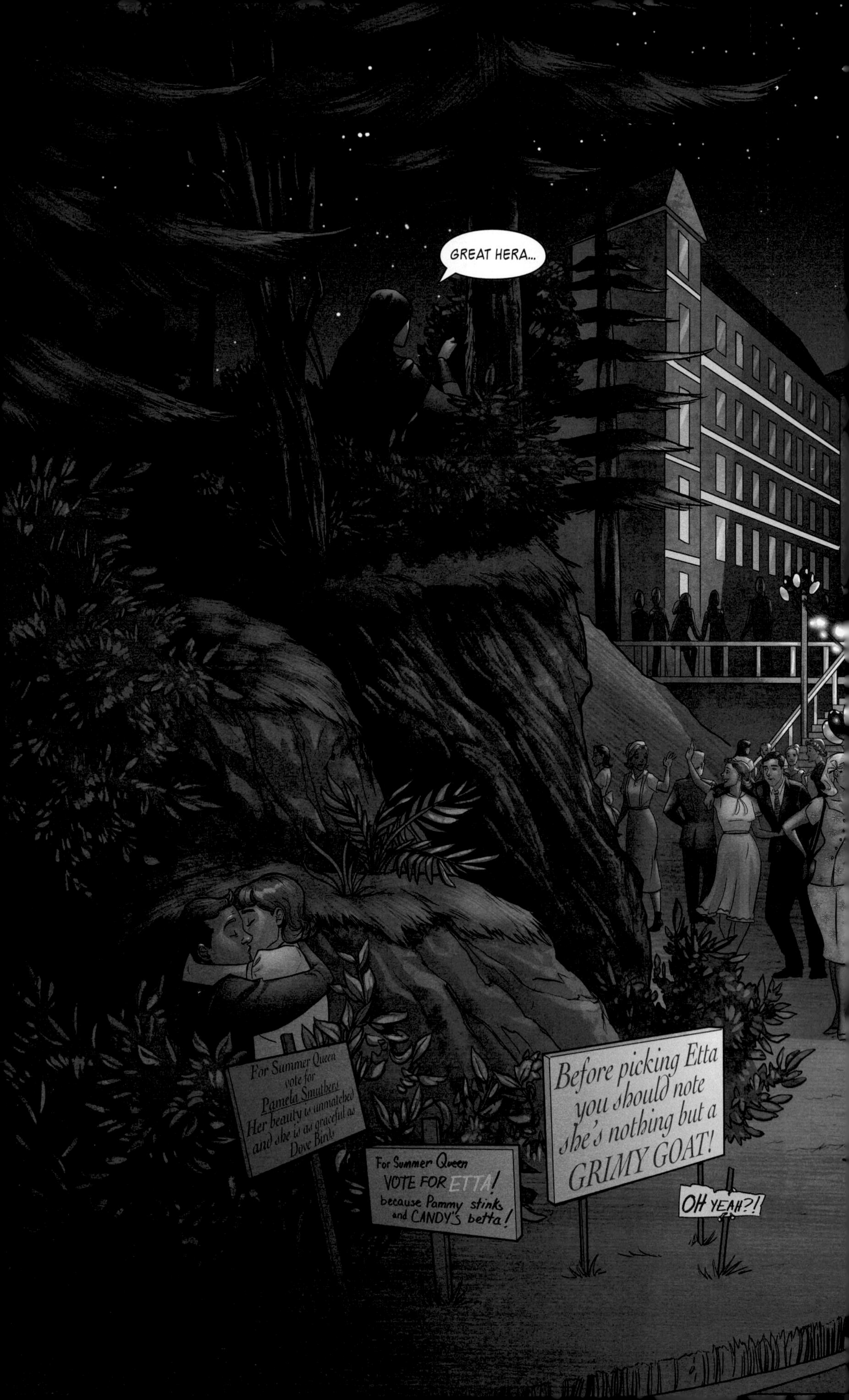
GREAT HERA...
For Summer Queen vote for Pamela Smuthers Her beauty is unmatched and she is as graceful as Dove Birds
For Summer Queen VOTE FOR ETTA! because Pammy stinks and CANDY'S betta!
Before picking Etta you should note she's nothing but a GRIMY GOAT!
OH YEAH?!

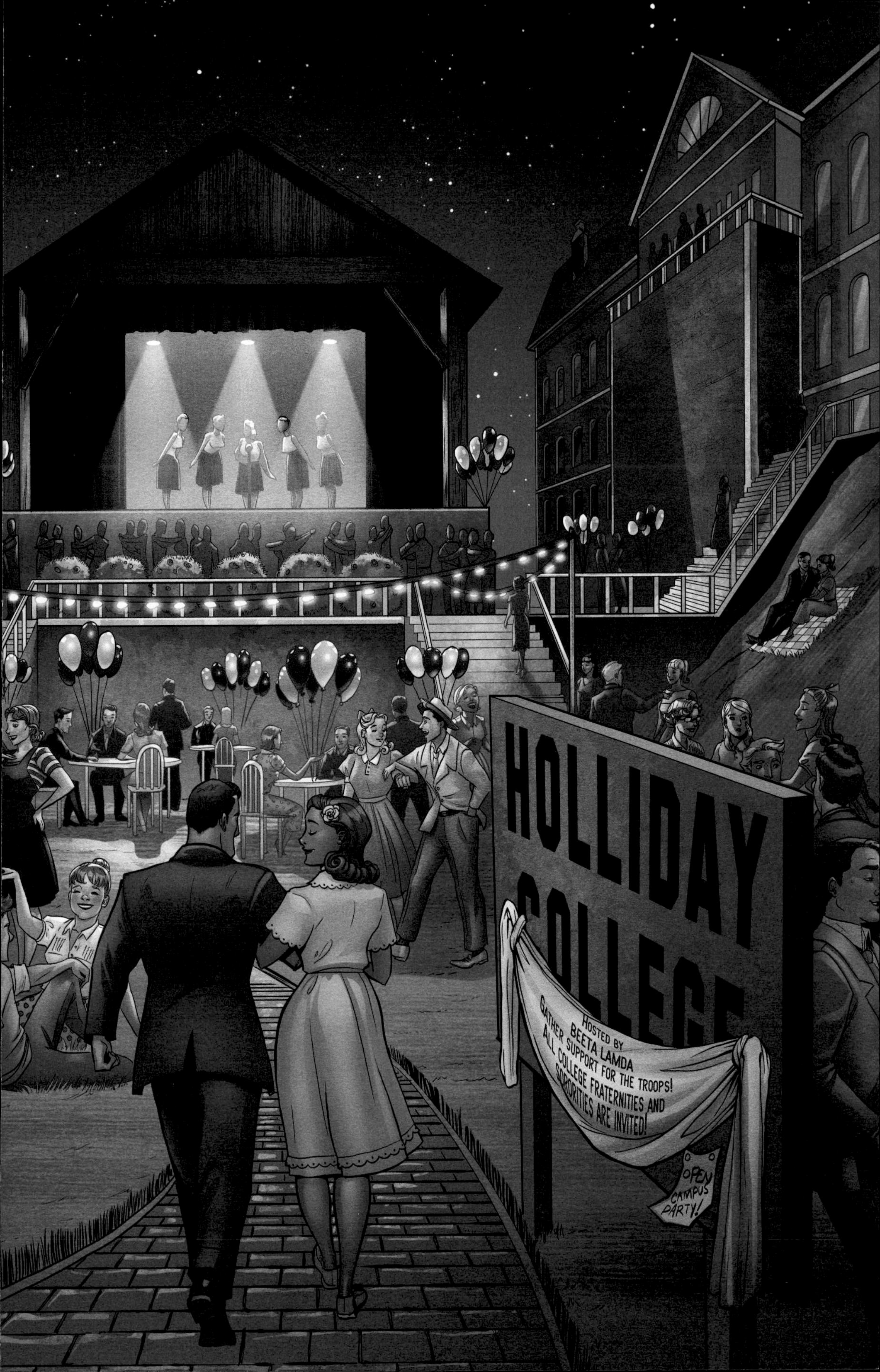
HOLLIDAY
HOSTED BY
BEETA LAMDA
GATHER SUPPORT FOR THE TROOPS!
ALL COLLEGE FRATERNITIES AND
SORORITIES ARE INVITED!
OPEN
CAMPUS
PARTY!

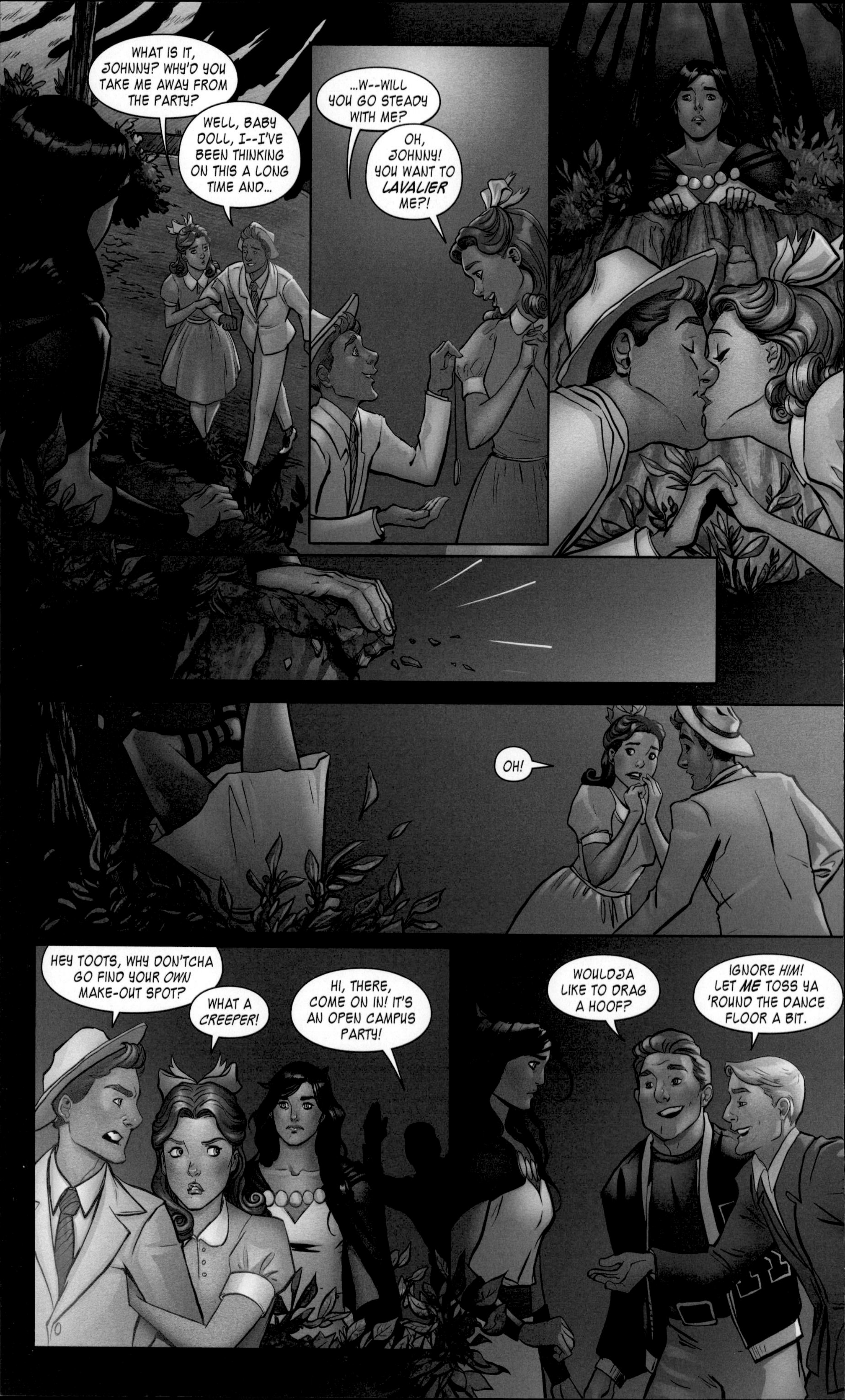
WHAT IS IT, JOHNNY? WHY'D YOU TAKE ME AWAY FROM THE PARTY?
WELL, BABY DOLL, I--I'VE BEEN THINKING ON THIS A LONG TIME AND...
...W--WILL YOU GO STEADY WITH ME?
OH, JOHNNY! YOU WANT TO LAVALIER ME?!
OH!
HEY TOOTS, WHY DON'TCHA GO FIND YOUR OWN MAKE-OUT SPOT?
WHAT A CREEPER!
HI, THERE, COME ON IN! IT'S AN OPEN CAMPUS PARTY!
WOULDJA LIKE TO DRAG A HOOF?
IGNORE HIM! LET ME TOSS YA 'ROUND THE DANCE FLOOR A BIT.

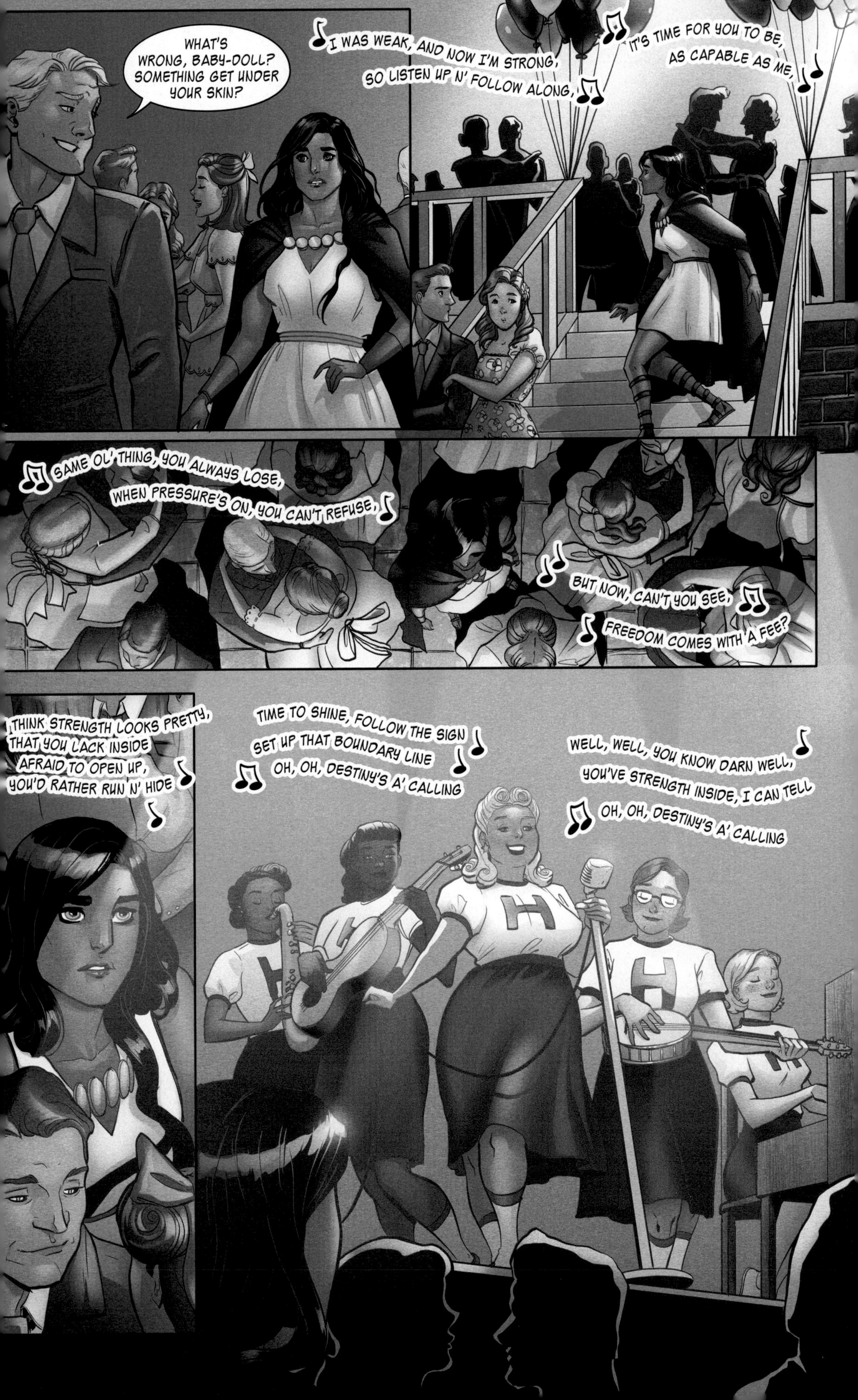
WHAT'S WRONG, BABY-DOLL? SOMETHING GET UNDER YOUR SKIN?
I WAS WEAK, AND NOW I'M STRONG,
SO LISTEN UP N' FOLLOW ALONG,
IT'S TIME FOR YOU TO BE,
AS CAPABLE AS ME,
SAME OL' THING, YOU ALWAYS LOSE,
WHEN PRESSURE'S ON, YOU CAN'T REFUSE,
BUT NOW, CAN'T YOU SEE,
FREEDOM COMES WITH A FEE?
I THINK STRENGTH LOOKS PRETTY,
THAT YOU LACK INSIDE
AFRAID TO OPEN UP,
YOU'D RATHER RUN N' HIDE
TIME TO SHINE, FOLLOW THE SIGN
SET UP THAT BOUNDARY LINE
OH, OH, DESTINY'S A' CALLING
WELL, WELL, YOU KNOW DARN WELL,
YOU'VE STRENGTH INSIDE, I CAN TELL
OH, OH, DESTINY'S A' CALLING

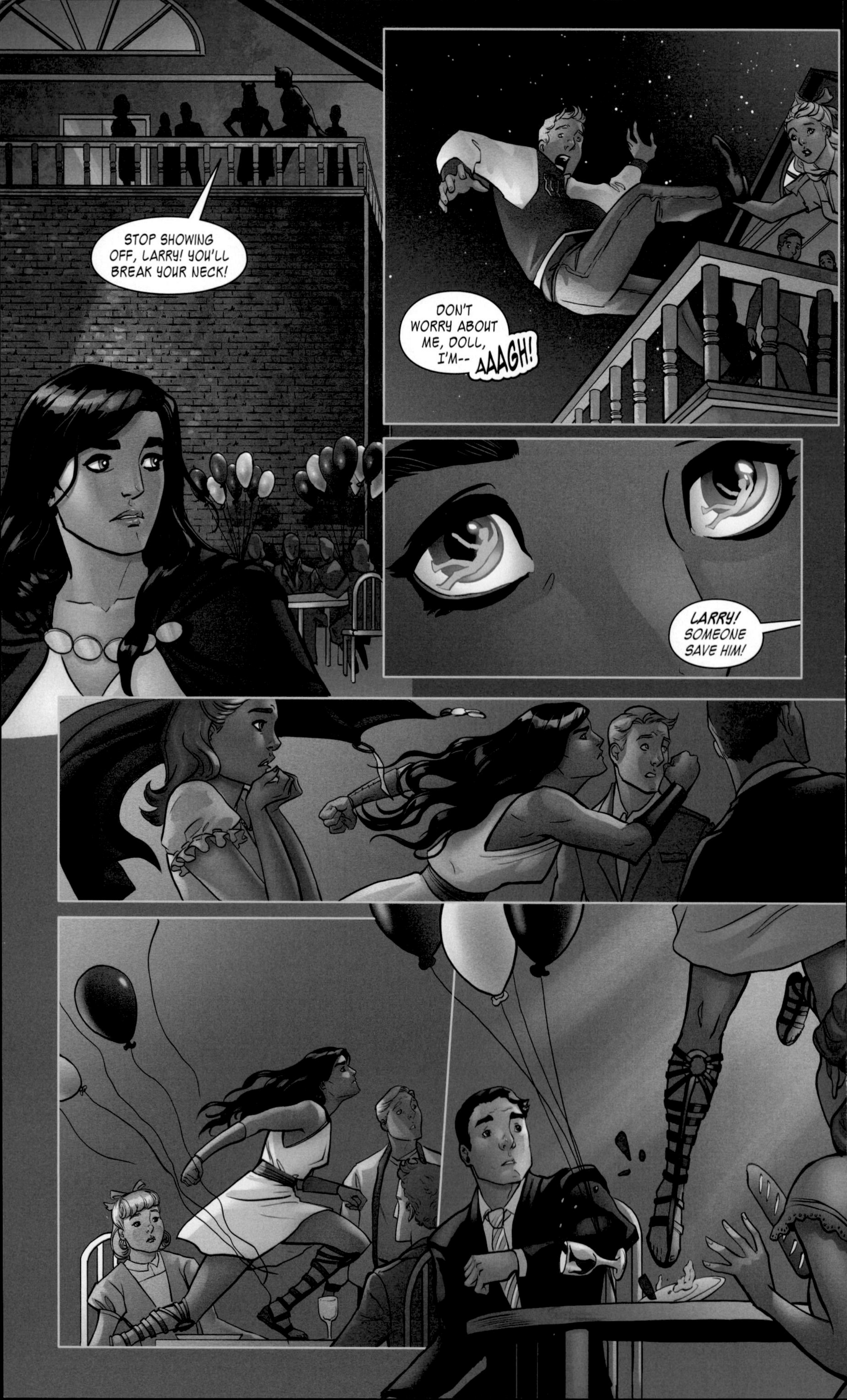
STOP SHOWING OFF, LARRY! YOU'LL BREAK YOUR NECK!
DON'T WORRY ABOUT ME, DOLL, I'M-- AAAGH!
LARRY! SOMEONE SAVE HIM!

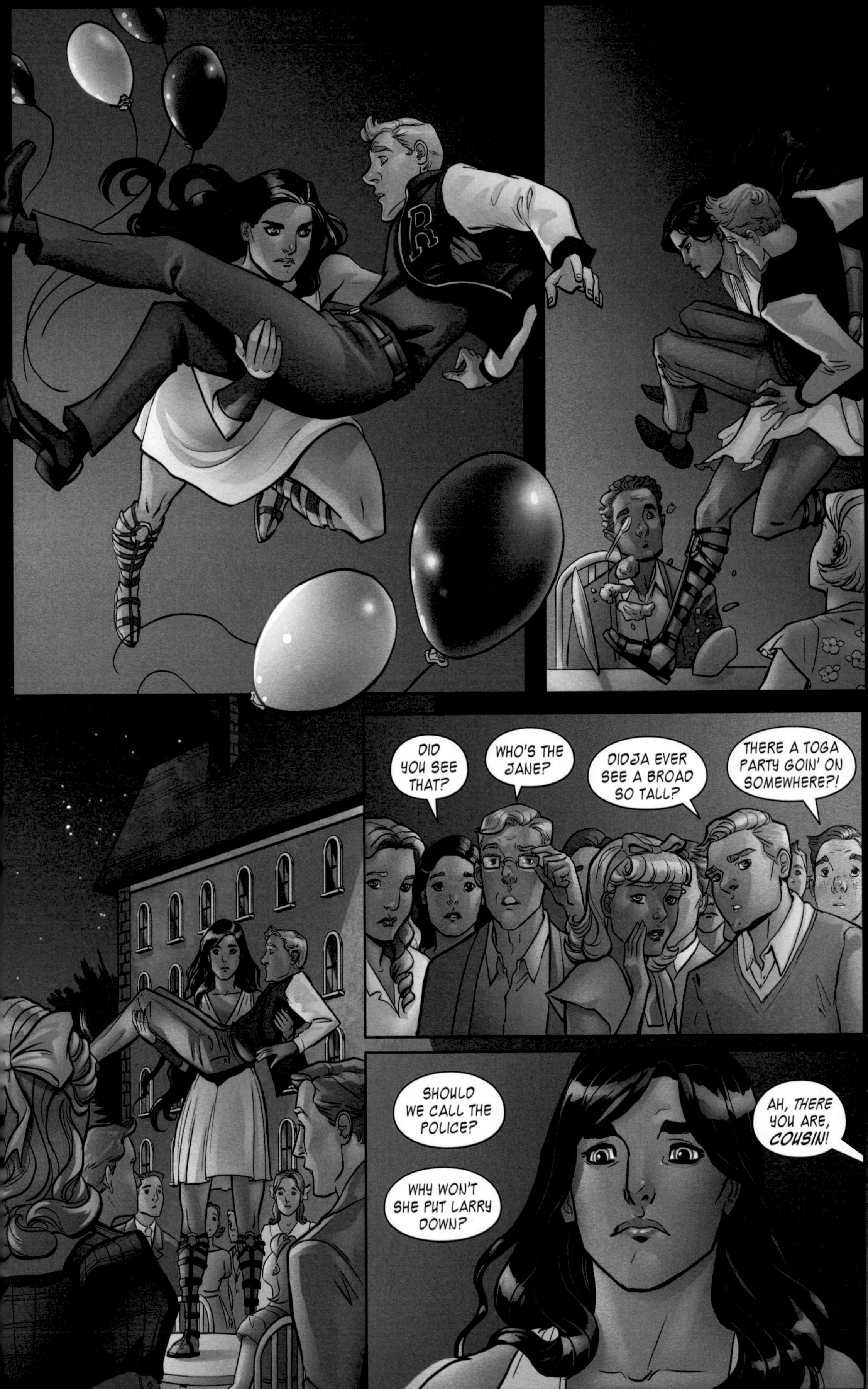
DID YOU SEE THAT?
WHO'S THE JANE?
DIDJA EVER SEE A BROAD SO TALL?
THERE A TOGA PARTY GOIN' ON SOMEWHERE?!
SHOULD WE CALL THE POLICE?
WHY WON'T SHE PUT LARRY DOWN?
AH, THERE YOU ARE, COUSIN!

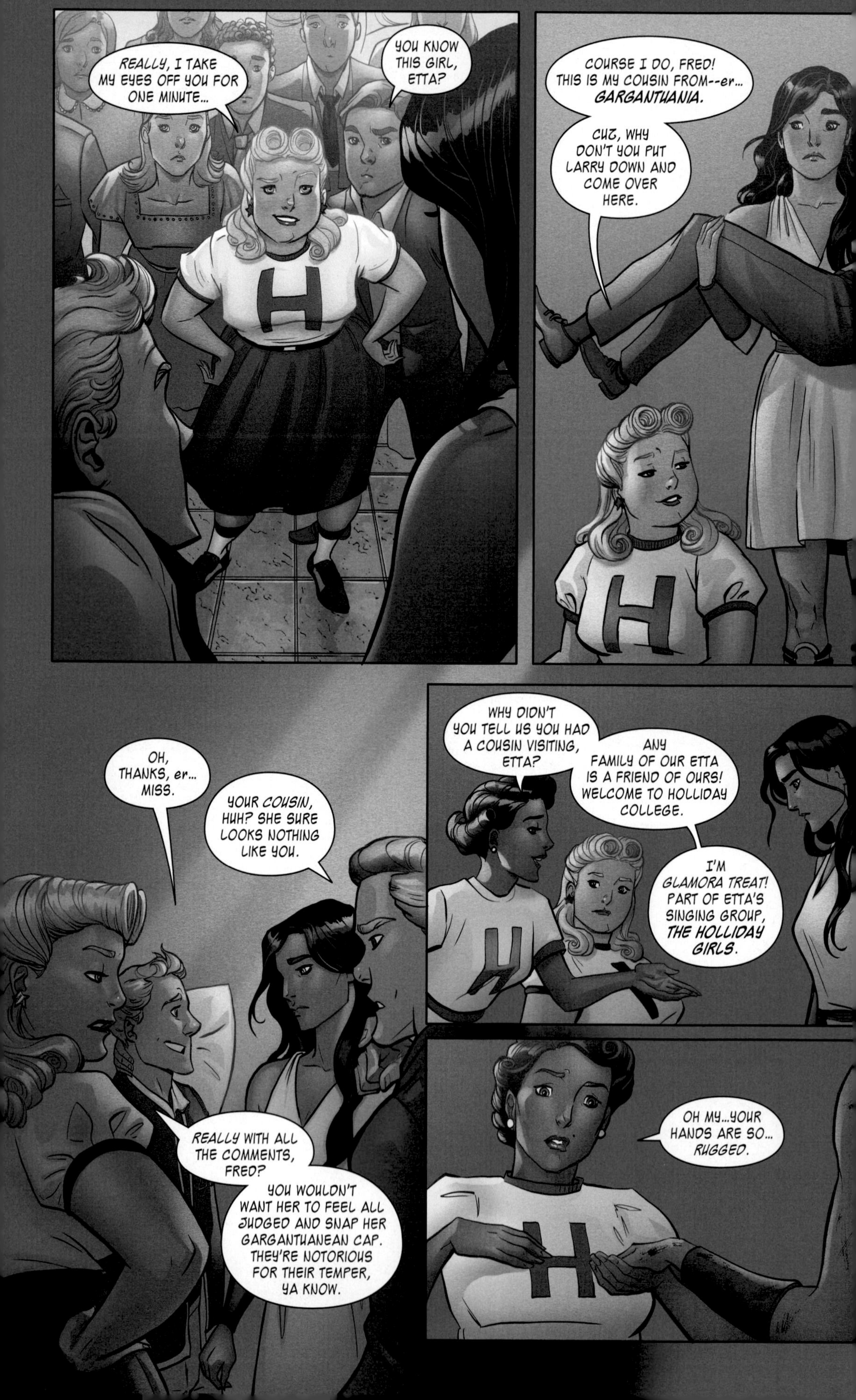
REALLY, I TAKE MY EYES OFF YOU FOR ONE MINUTE...
YOU KNOW THIS GIRL, ETTA?
COURSE I DO, FRED! THIS IS MY COUSIN FROM--er... GARGANTUANIA.
CUZ, WHY DON'T YOU PUT LARRY DOWN AND COME OVER HERE.
OH, THANKS, er... MISS.
YOUR COUSIN, HUH? SHE SURE LOOKS NOTHING LIKE YOU.
REALLY WITH ALL THE COMMENTS, FRED?
YOU WOULDN'T WANT HER TO FEEL ALL JUDGED AND SNAP HER GARGANTUANEAN CAP. THEY'RE NOTORIOUS FOR THEIR TEMPER, YA KNOW.
WHY DIDN'T YOU TELL US YOU HAD A COUSIN VISITING, ETTA?
ANY FAMILY OF OUR ETTA IS A FRIEND OF OURS! WELCOME TO HOLLIDAY COLLEGE.
I'M GLAMORA TREAT! PART OF ETTA'S SINGING GROUP, THE HOLLIDAY GIRLS.
OH MY...YOUR HANDS ARE SO... RUGGED.

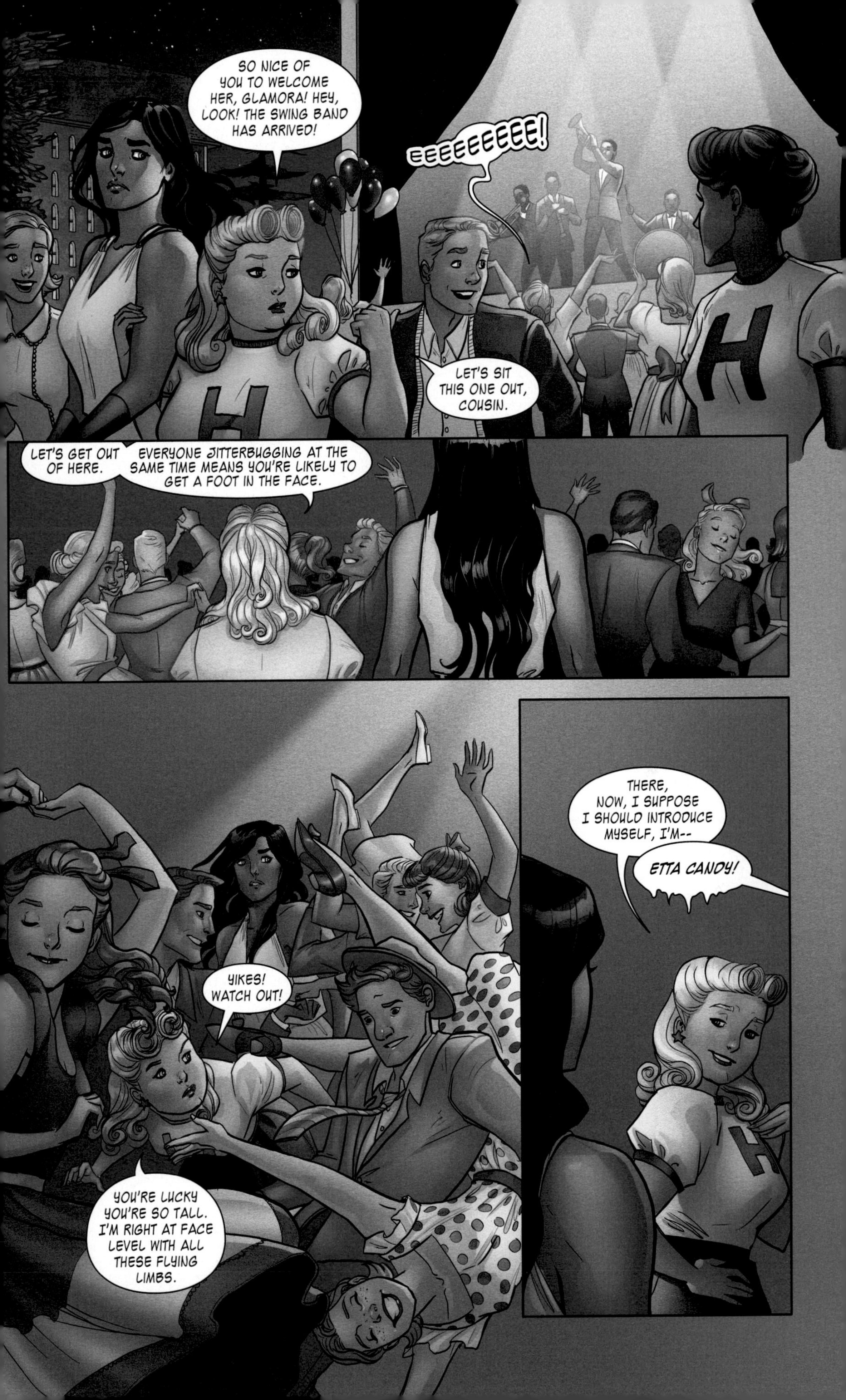

SO NICE OF YOU TO WELCOME HER, GLAMORA! HEY, LOOK! THE SWING BAND HAS ARRIVED!
EEEEEEEEEE!
LET'S SIT THIS ONE OUT, COUSIN.
LET'S GET OUT OF HERE.
EVERYONE JITTERBUGGING AT THE SAME TIME MEANS YOU'RE LIKELY TO GET A FOOT IN THE FACE.
YIKES! WATCH OUT!
YOU'RE LUCKY YOU'RE SO TALL. I'M RIGHT AT FACE LEVEL WITH ALL THESE FLYING LIMBS.
THERE, NOW, I SUPPOSE I SHOULD INTRODUCE MYSELF, I'M--
ETTA CANDY!

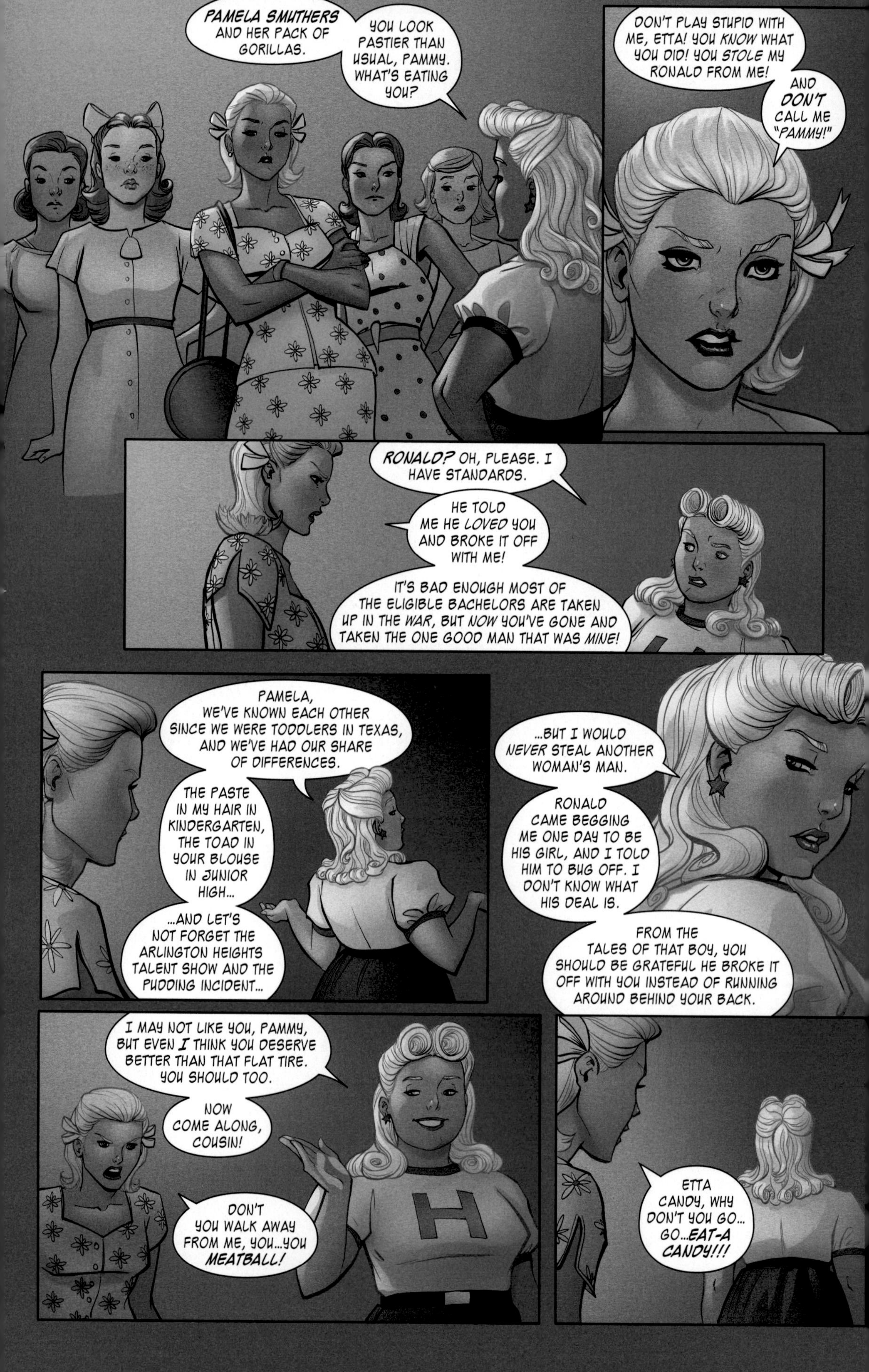

PAMELA SMUTHERS AND HER PACK OF GORILLAS.
YOU LOOK PASTIER THAN USUAL, PAMMY. WHAT'S EATING YOU?
DON'T PLAY STUPID WITH ME, ETTA! YOU KNOW WHAT YOU DID! YOU STOLE MY RONALD FROM ME!
AND DON'T CALL ME "PAMMY!"
RONALD? OH, PLEASE. I HAVE STANDARDS.
HE TOLD ME HE LOVED YOU AND BROKE IT OFF WITH ME!
IT'S BAD ENOUGH MOST OF THE ELIGIBLE BACHELORS ARE TAKEN UP IN THE WAR, BUT NOW YOU'VE GONE AND TAKEN THE ONE GOOD MAN THAT WAS MINE!
PAMELA, WE'VE KNOWN EACH OTHER SINCE WE WERE TODDLERS IN TEXAS, AND WE'VE HAD OUR SHARE OF DIFFERENCES.
THE PASTE IN MY HAIR IN KINDERGARTEN, THE TOAD IN YOUR BLOUSE IN JUNIOR HIGH...
...AND LET'S NOT FORGET THE ARLINGTON HEIGHTS TALENT SHOW AND THE PUDDING INCIDENT...
...BUT I WOULD NEVER STEAL ANOTHER WOMAN'S MAN.
RONALD CAME BEGGING ME ONE DAY TO BE HIS GIRL, AND I TOLD HIM TO BUG OFF. I DON'T KNOW WHAT HIS DEAL IS.
FROM THE TALES OF THAT BOY, YOU SHOULD BE GRATEFUL HE BROKE IT OFF WITH YOU INSTEAD OF RUNNING AROUND BEHIND YOUR BACK.
I MAY NOT LIKE YOU, PAMMY, BUT EVEN I THINK YOU DESERVE BETTER THAN THAT FLAT TIRE. YOU SHOULD TOO.
NOW COME ALONG, COUSIN!
DON'T YOU WALK AWAY FROM ME, YOU...YOU MEATBALL!
ETTA CANDY, WHY DON'T YOU GO... GO...EAT-A CANDY!!!

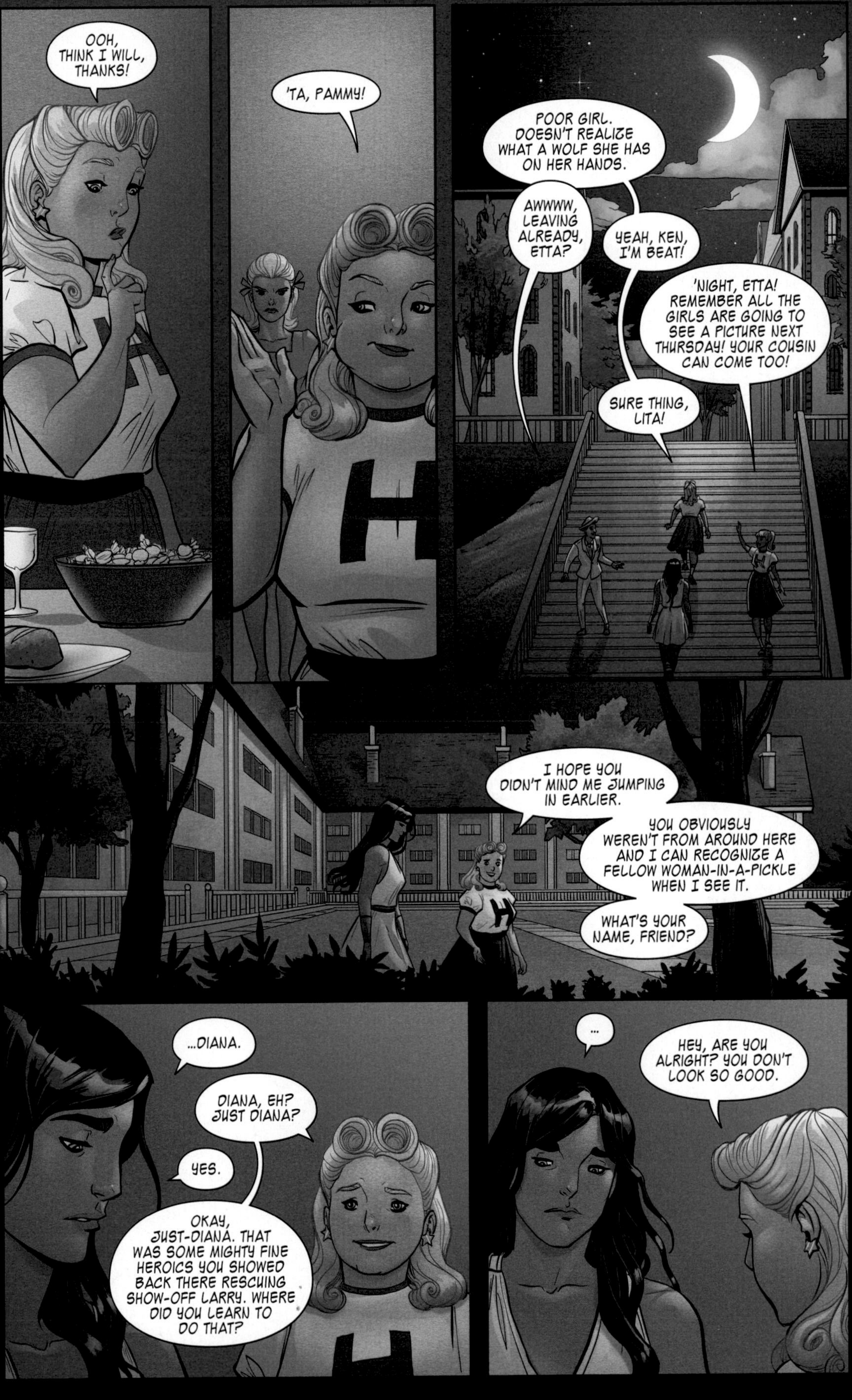
OOH, THINK I WILL, THANKS!
'TA, PAMMY!
POOR GIRL. DOESN'T REALIZE WHAT A WOLF SHE HAS ON HER HANDS.
AWWWW, LEAVING ALREADY, ETTA?
YEAH, KEN, I'M BEAT!
'NIGHT, ETTA! REMEMBER ALL THE GIRLS ARE GOING TO SEE A PICTURE NEXT THURSDAY! YOUR COUSIN CAN COME TOO!
SURE THING, LITA!
I HOPE YOU DIDN'T MIND ME JUMPING IN EARLIER.
YOU OBVIOUSLY WEREN'T FROM AROUND HERE AND I CAN RECOGNIZE A FELLOW WOMAN-IN-A-PICKLE WHEN I SEE IT.
WHAT'S YOUR NAME, FRIEND?
...DIANA.
DIANA, EH? JUST DIANA?
YES.
OKAY, JUST-DIANA. THAT WAS SOME MIGHTY FINE HEROICS YOU SHOWED BACK THERE RESCUING SHOW-OFF LARRY. WHERE DID YOU LEARN TO DO THAT?
...
HEY, ARE YOU ALRIGHT? YOU DON'T LOOK SO GOOD.

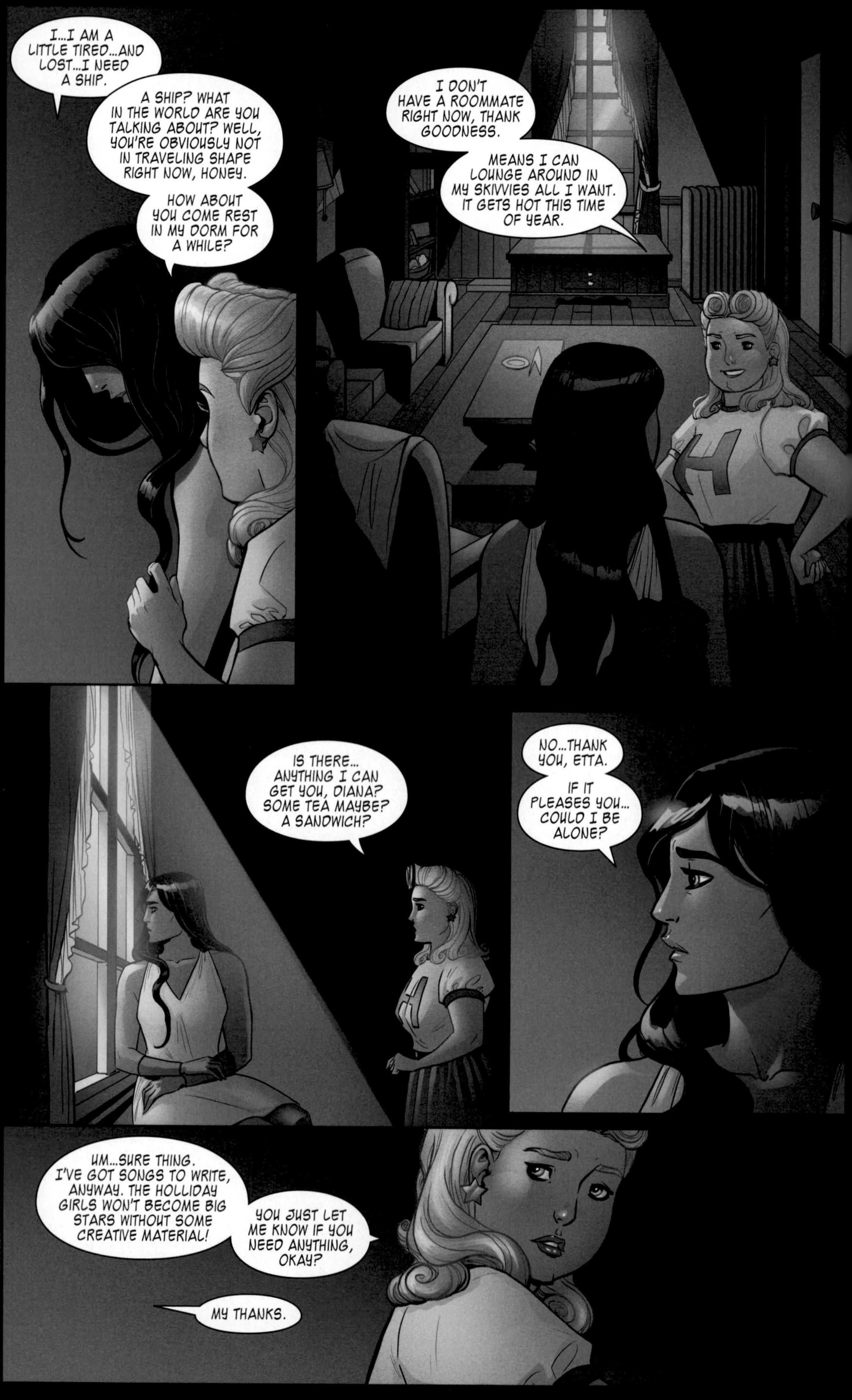

I...I AM A LITTLE TIRED...AND LOST...I NEED A SHIP.
A SHIP? WHAT IN THE WORLD ARE YOU TALKING ABOUT? WELL, YOU'RE OBVIOUSLY NOT IN TRAVELING SHAPE RIGHT NOW, HONEY.
HOW ABOUT YOU COME REST IN MY DORM FOR A WHILE?
I DON'T HAVE A ROOMMATE RIGHT NOW, THANK GOODNESS.
MEANS I CAN LOUNGE AROUND IN MY SKIVVIES ALL I WANT. IT GETS HOT THIS TIME OF YEAR.
IS THERE... ANYTHING I CAN GET YOU, DIANA? SOME TEA MAYBE? A SANDWICH?
NO...THANK YOU, ETTA.
IF IT PLEASES YOU... COULD I BE ALONE?
UM...SURE THING. I'VE GOT SONGS TO WRITE, ANYWAY. THE HOLLIDAY GIRLS WON'T BECOME BIG STARS WITHOUT SOME CREATIVE MATERIAL!
YOU JUST LET ME KNOW IF YOU NEED ANYTHING, OKAY?
MY THANKS.

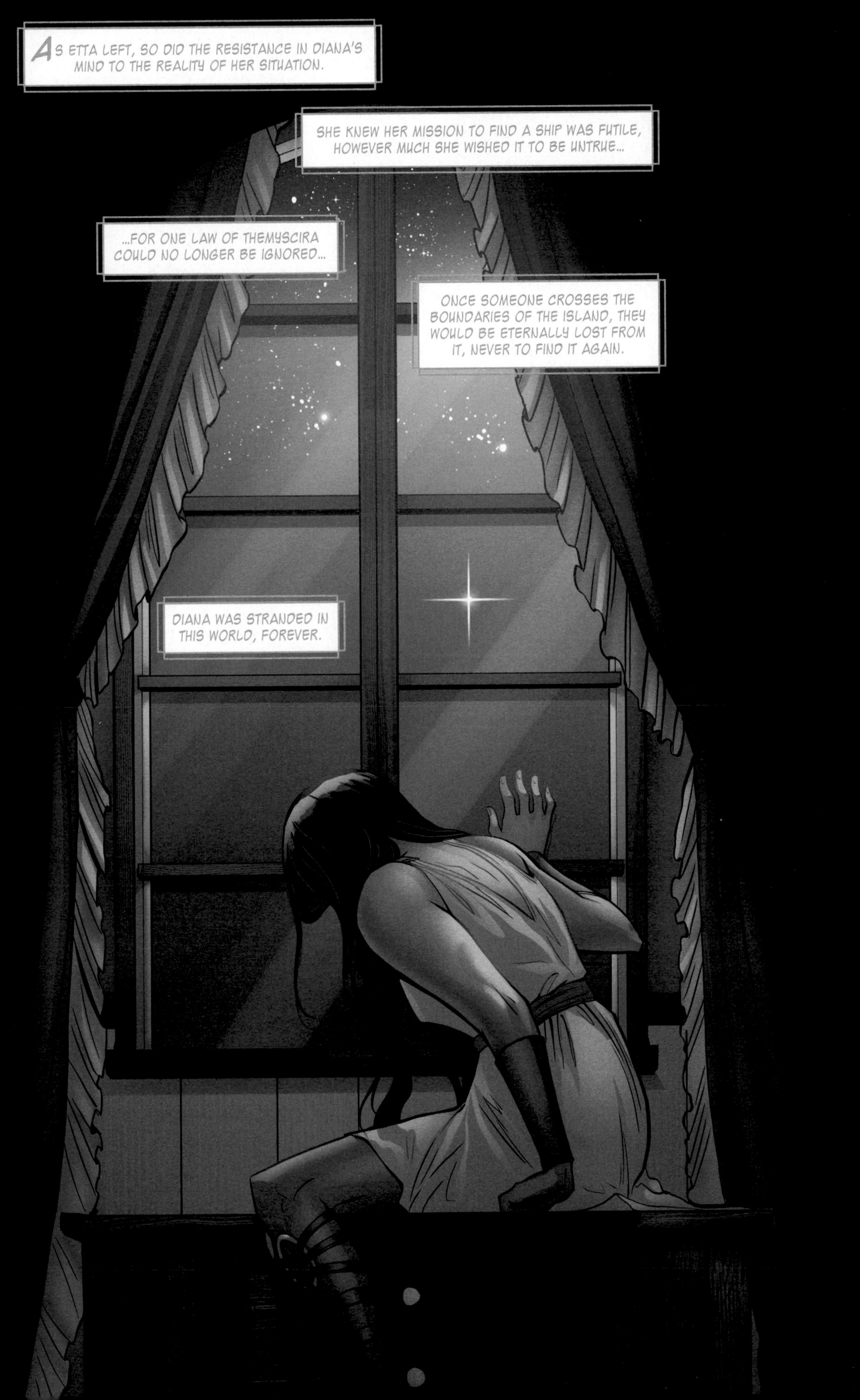
AS ETTA LEFT, SO DID THE RESISTANCE IN DIANA'S MIND TO THE REALITY OF HER SITUATION.
SHE KNEW HER MISSION TO FIND A SHIP WAS FUTILE, HOWEVER MUCH SHE WISHED IT TO BE UNTRUE...
...FOR ONE LAW OF THEMYSCIRA COULD NO LONGER BE IGNORED...
ONCE SOMEONE CROSSES THE BOUNDARIES OF THE ISLAND, THEY WOULD BE ETERNALLY LOST FROM IT, NEVER TO FIND IT AGAIN.
DIANA WAS STRANDED IN THIS WORLD, FOREVER.

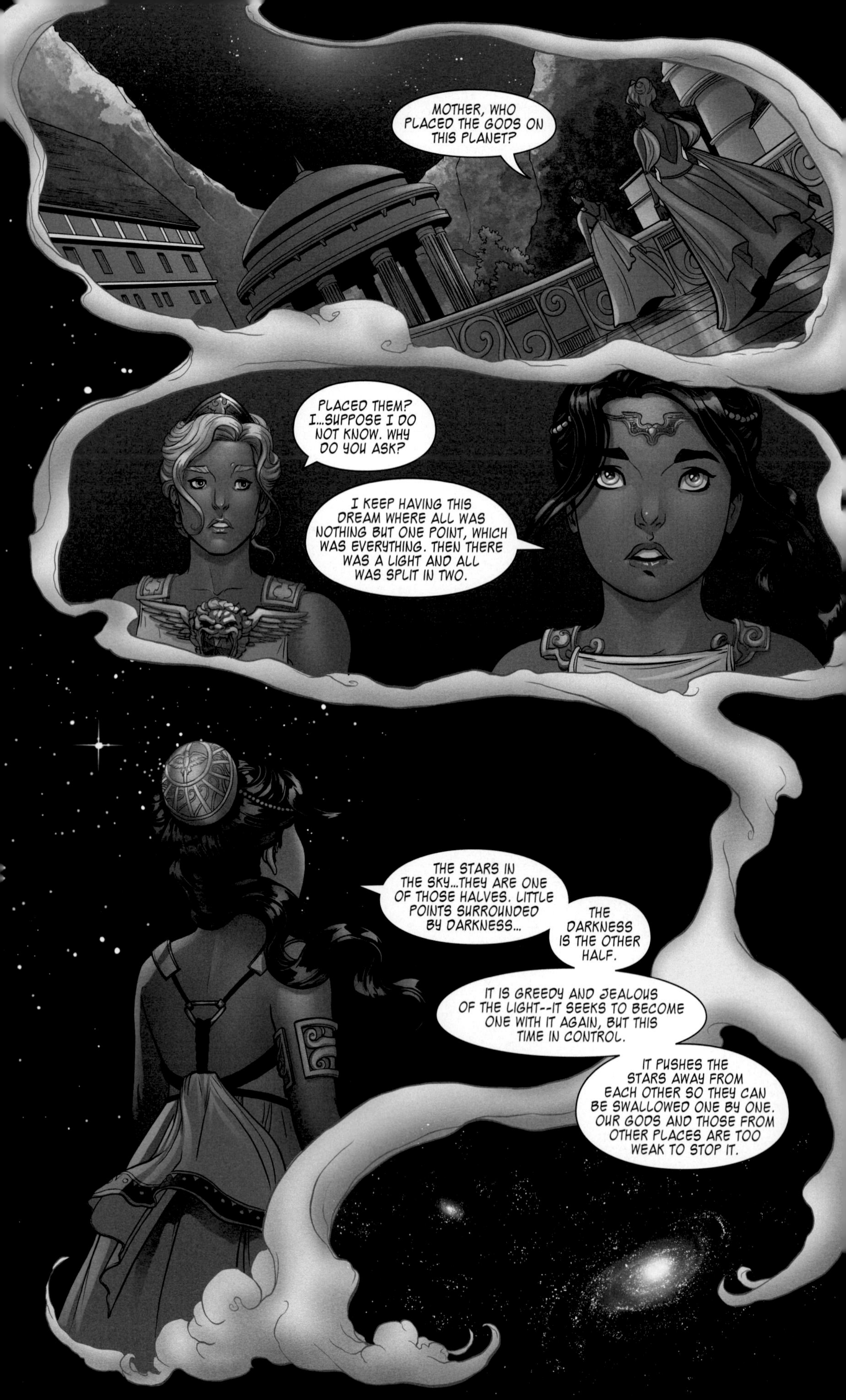
MOTHER, WHO PLACED THE GODS ON THIS PLANET?
PLACED THEM? I...SUPPOSE I DO NOT KNOW. WHY DO YOU ASK?
I KEEP HAVING THIS DREAM WHERE ALL WAS NOTHING BUT ONE POINT, WHICH WAS EVERYTHING. THEN THERE WAS A LIGHT AND ALL WAS SPLIT IN TWO.
THE STARS IN THE SKY...THEY ARE ONE OF THOSE HALVES. LITTLE POINTS SURROUNDED BY DARKNESS...
THE DARKNESS IS THE OTHER HALF.
IT IS GREEDY AND JEALOUS OF THE LIGHT--IT SEEKS TO BECOME ONE WITH IT AGAIN, BUT THIS TIME IN CONTROL.
IT PUSHES THE STARS AWAY FROM EACH OTHER SO THEY CAN BE SWALLOWED ONE BY ONE. OUR GODS AND THOSE FROM OTHER PLACES ARE TOO WEAK TO STOP IT.

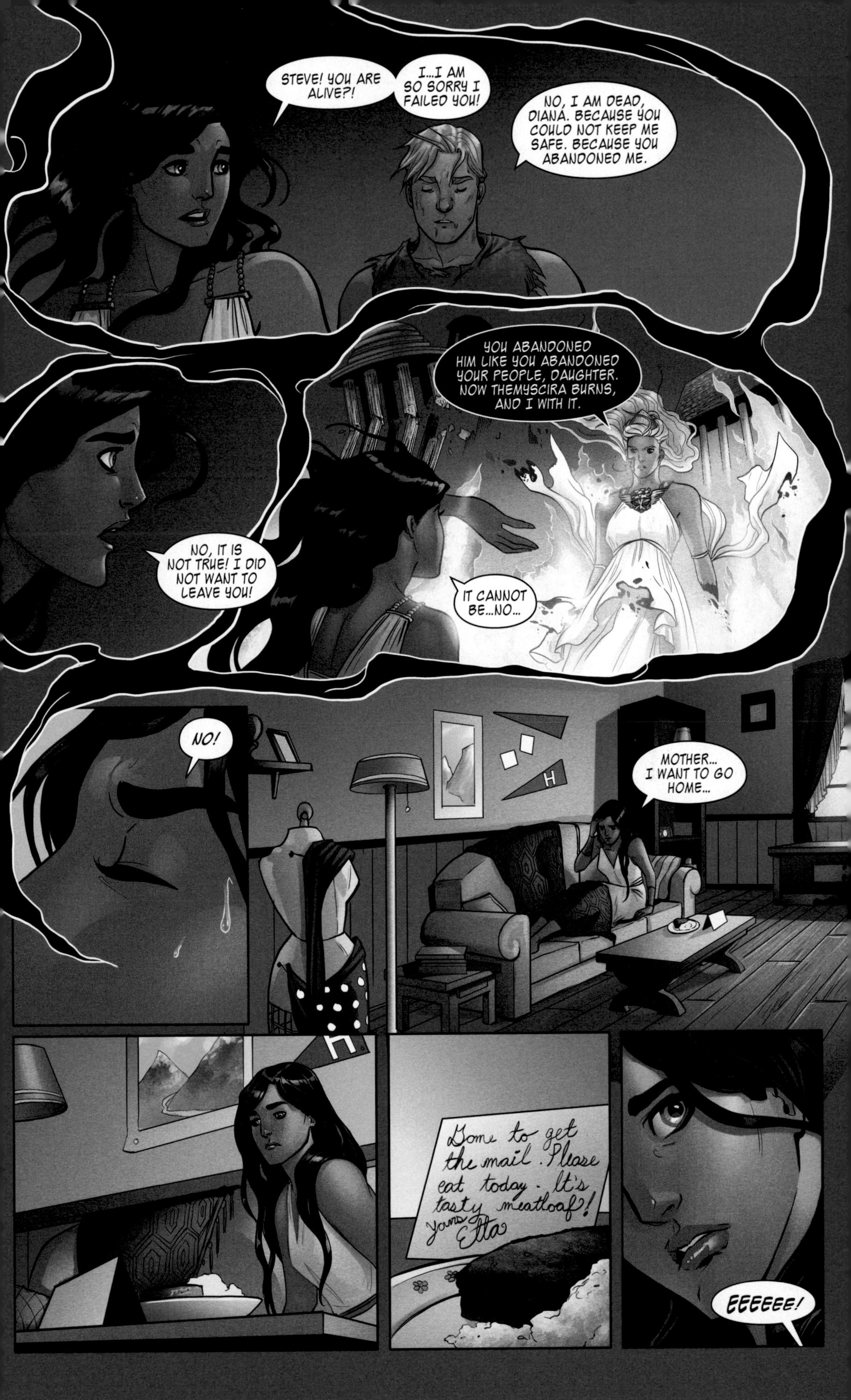
STEVE! YOU ARE ALIVE?!
I...I AM SO SORRY I FAILED YOU!
NO, I AM DEAD, DIANA. BECAUSE YOU COULD NOT KEEP ME SAFE. BECAUSE YOU ABANDONED ME.
YOU ABANDONED HIM LIKE YOU ABANDONED YOUR PEOPLE, DAUGHTER. NOW THEMYSCIRA BURNS, AND I WITH IT.
NO, IT IS NOT TRUE! I DID NOT WANT TO LEAVE YOU!
IT CANNOT BE...NO...
NO!
MOTHER... I WANT TO GO HOME...
Gone to get the mail. Please eat today. It's tasty meatloaf! Yours, Etta
EEEEEE!

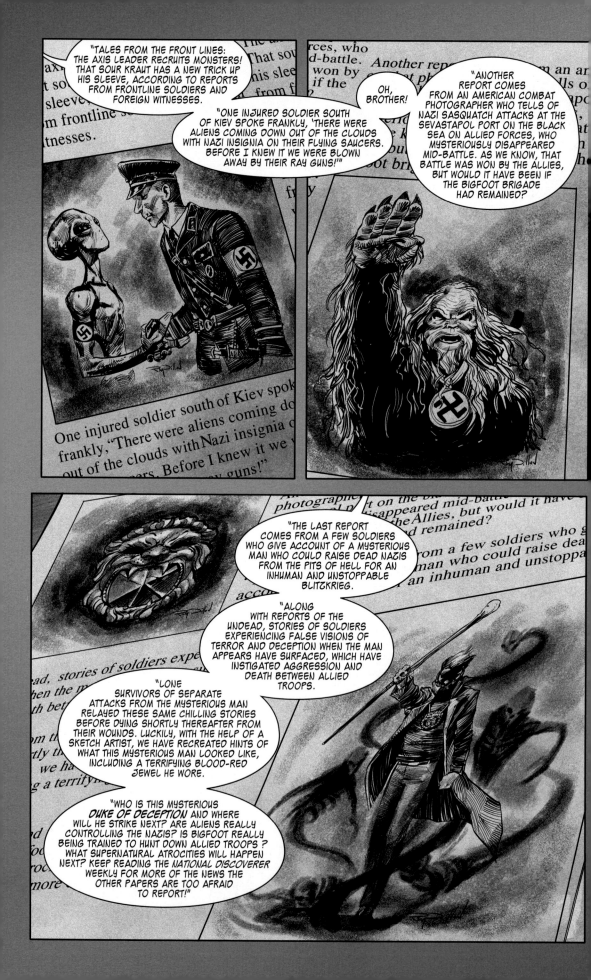

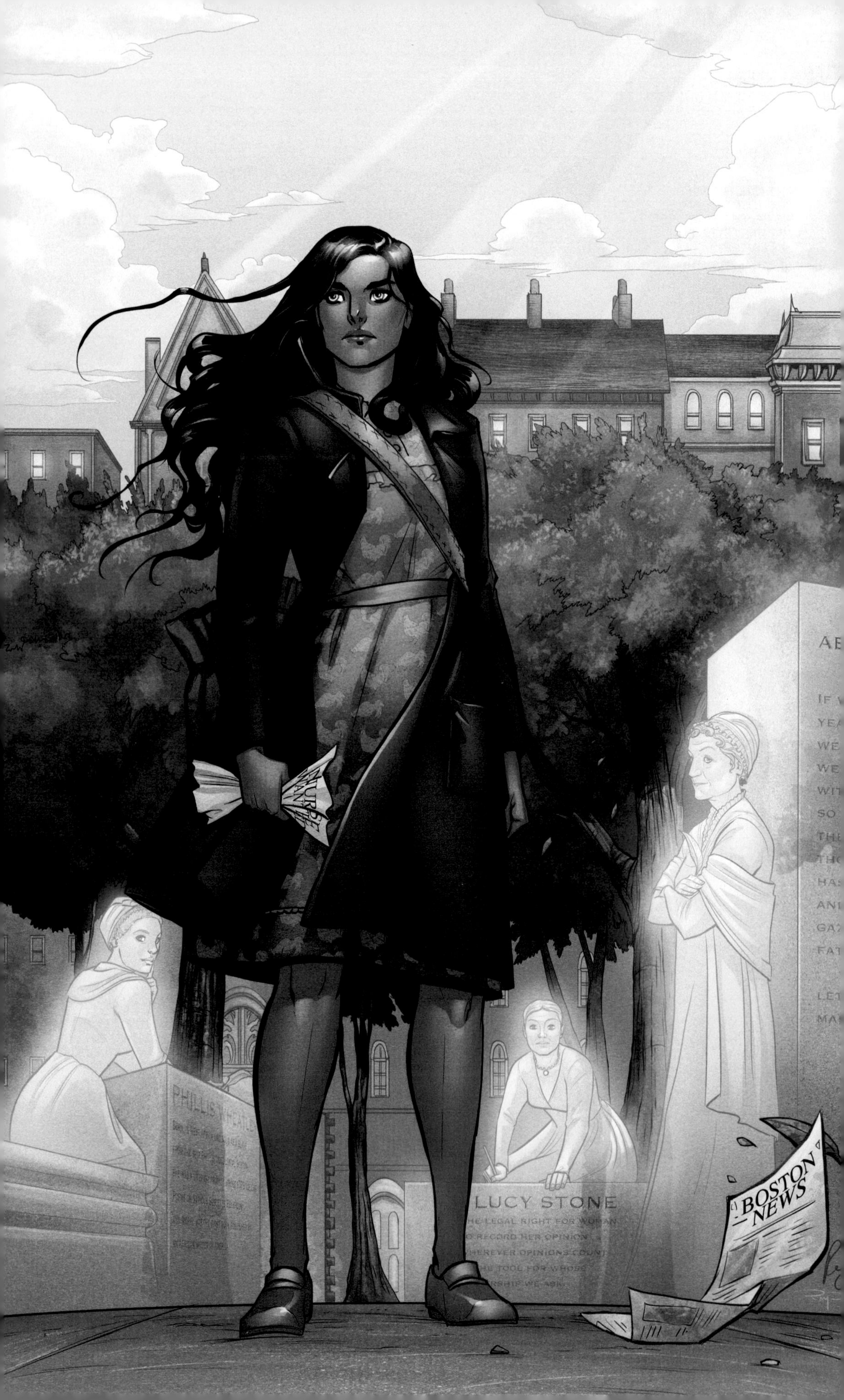
NURSE
LUCY STONE
BOSTON NEWS

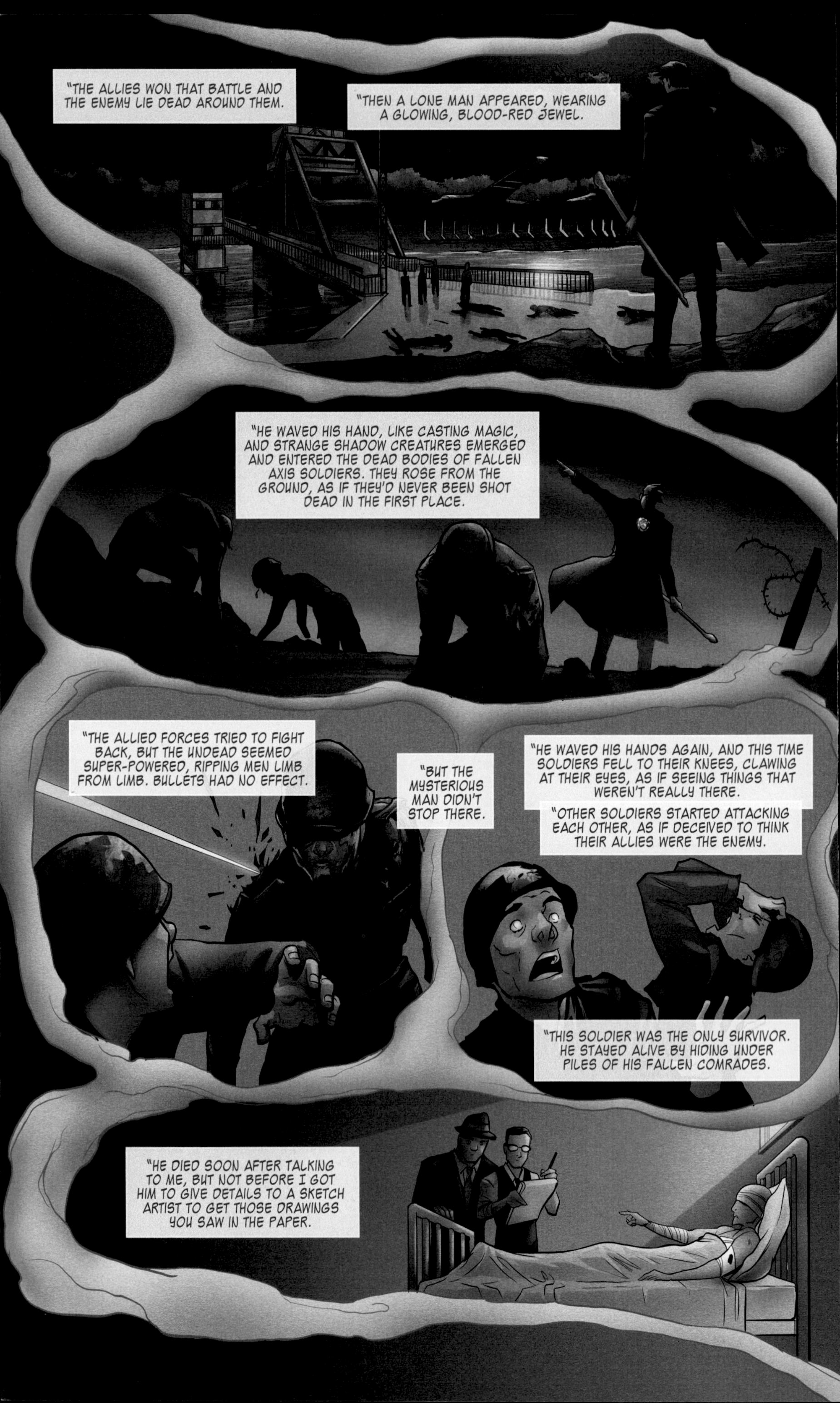
"THE ALLIES WON THAT BATTLE AND THE ENEMY LIE DEAD AROUND THEM.
"THEN A LONE MAN APPEARED, WEARING A GLOWING, BLOOD-RED JEWEL.
"HE WAVED HIS HAND, LIKE CASTING MAGIC, AND STRANGE SHADOW CREATURES EMERGED AND ENTERED THE DEAD BODIES OF FALLEN AXIS SOLDIERS. THEY ROSE FROM THE GROUND, AS IF THEY'D NEVER BEEN SHOT DEAD IN THE FIRST PLACE.
"THE ALLIED FORCES TRIED TO FIGHT BACK, BUT THE UNDEAD SEEMED SUPER-POWERED, RIPPING MEN LIMB FROM LIMB. BULLETS HAD NO EFFECT.
"BUT THE MYSTERIOUS MAN DIDN'T STOP THERE.
"HE WAVED HIS HANDS AGAIN, AND THIS TIME SOLDIERS FELL TO THEIR KNEES, CLAWING AT THEIR EYES, AS IF SEEING THINGS THAT WEREN'T REALLY THERE.
"OTHER SOLDIERS STARTED ATTACKING EACH OTHER, AS IF DECEIVED TO THINK THEIR ALLIES WERE THE ENEMY.
"THIS SOLDIER WAS THE ONLY SURVIVOR. HE STAYED ALIVE BY HIDING UNDER PILES OF HIS FALLEN COMRADES.
"HE DIED SOON AFTER TALKING TO ME, BUT NOT BEFORE I GOT HIM TO GIVE DETAILS TO A SKETCH ARTIST TO GET THOSE DRAWINGS YOU SAW IN THE PAPER.

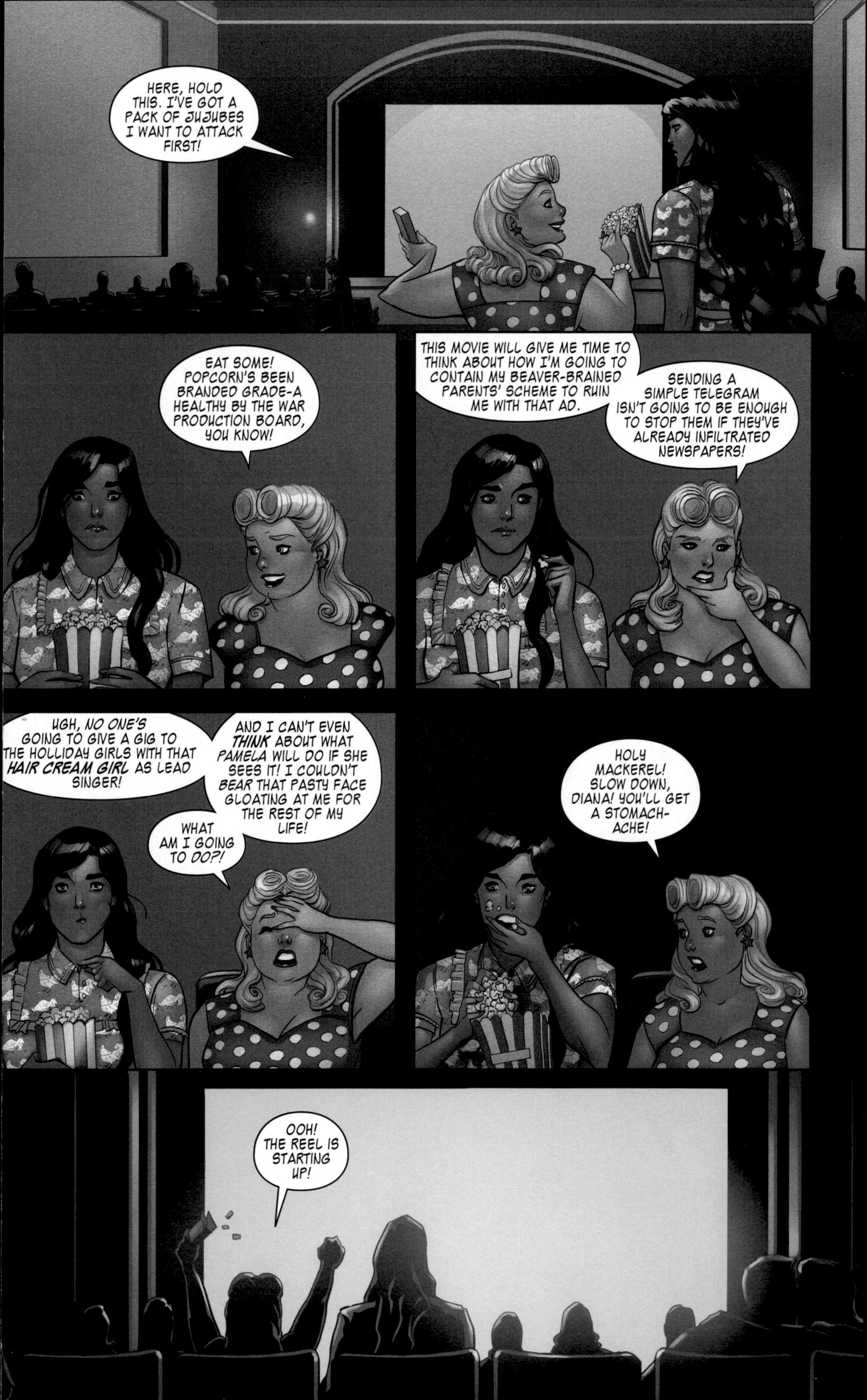
HERE, HOLD THIS. I'VE GOT A PACK OF JUJUBES I WANT TO ATTACK FIRST!
EAT SOME! POPCORN'S BEEN BRANDED GRADE-A HEALTHY BY THE WAR PRODUCTION BOARD, YOU KNOW!
THIS MOVIE WILL GIVE ME TIME TO THINK ABOUT HOW I'M GOING TO CONTAIN MY BEAVER-BRAINED PARENTS' SCHEME TO RUIN ME WITH THAT AD.
SENDING A SIMPLE TELEGRAM ISN'T GOING TO BE ENOUGH TO STOP THEM IF THEY'VE ALREADY INFILTRATED NEWSPAPERS!
UGH, NO ONE'S GOING TO GIVE A GIG TO THE HOLLIDAY GIRLS WITH THAT HAIR CREAM GIRL AS LEAD SINGER!
AND I CAN'T EVEN THINK ABOUT WHAT PAMELA WILL DO IF SHE SEES IT! I COULDN'T BEAR THAT PASTY FACE GLOATING AT ME FOR THE REST OF MY LIFE!
WHAT AM I GOING TO DO?!
HOLY MACKEREL! SLOW DOWN, DIANA! YOU'LL GET A STOMACH-ACHE!
OOH! THE REEL IS STARTING UP!

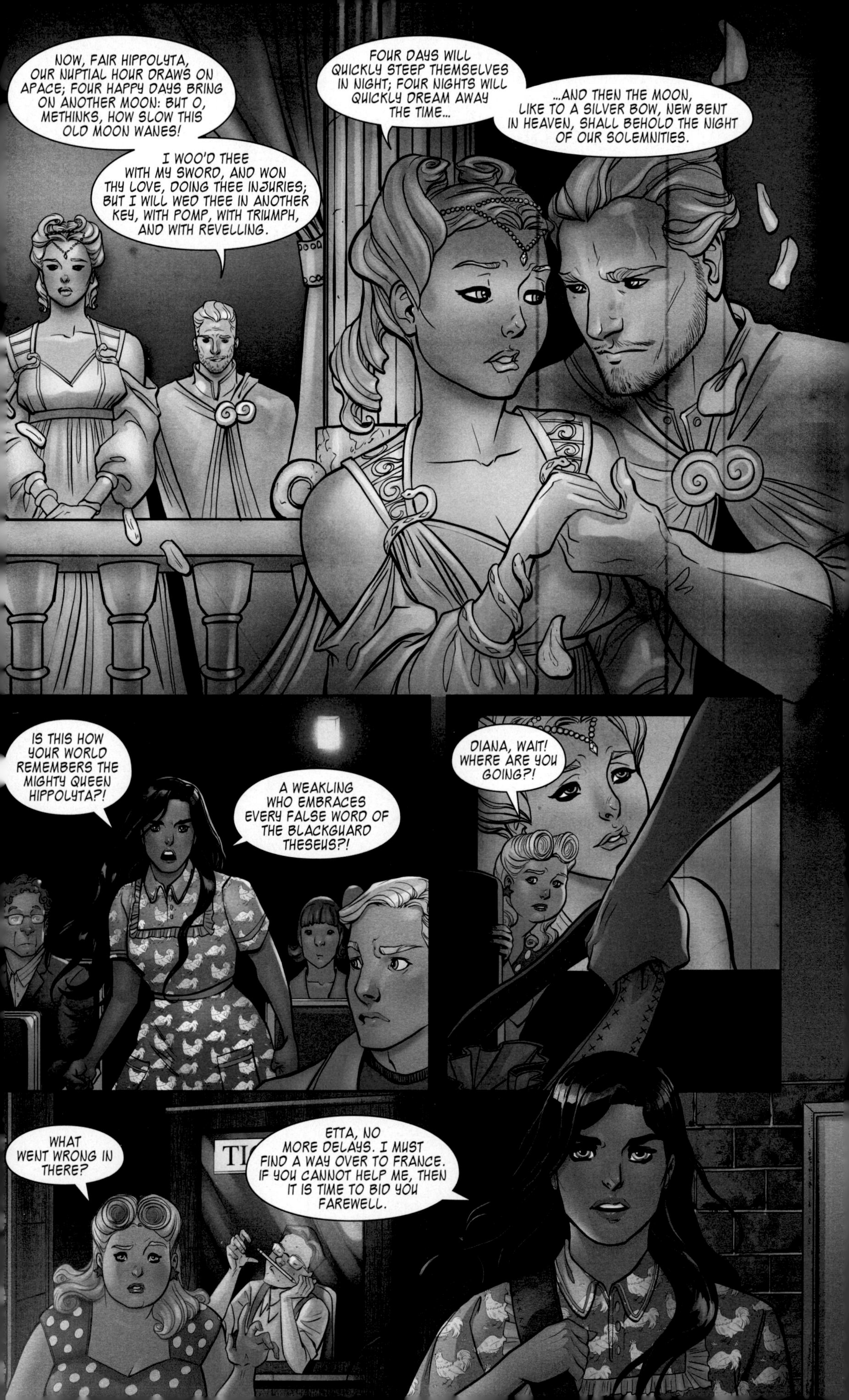
NOW, FAIR HIPPOLYTA, OUR NUPTIAL HOUR DRAWS ON APACE; FOUR HAPPY DAYS BRING ON ANOTHER MOON: BUT O, METHINKS, HOW SLOW THIS OLD MOON WANES!
I WOO'D THEE WITH MY SWORD, AND WON THY LOVE, DOING THEE INJURIES; BUT I WILL WED THEE IN ANOTHER KEY, WITH POMP, WITH TRIUMPH, AND WITH REVELLING.
FOUR DAYS WILL QUICKLY STEEP THEMSELVES IN NIGHT; FOUR NIGHTS WILL QUICKLY DREAM AWAY THE TIME...
...AND THEN THE MOON, LIKE TO A SILVER BOW, NEW BENT IN HEAVEN, SHALL BEHOLD THE NIGHT OF OUR SOLEMNITIES.
IS THIS HOW YOUR WORLD REMEMBERS THE MIGHTY QUEEN HIPPOLYTA?!
A WEAKLING WHO EMBRACES EVERY FALSE WORD OF THE BLACKGUARD THESEUS?!
DIANA, WAIT! WHERE ARE YOU GOING?!
WHAT WENT WRONG IN THERE?
ETTA, NO MORE DELAYS. I MUST FIND A WAY OVER TO FRANCE. IF YOU CANNOT HELP ME, THEN IT IS TIME TO BID YOU FAREWELL.

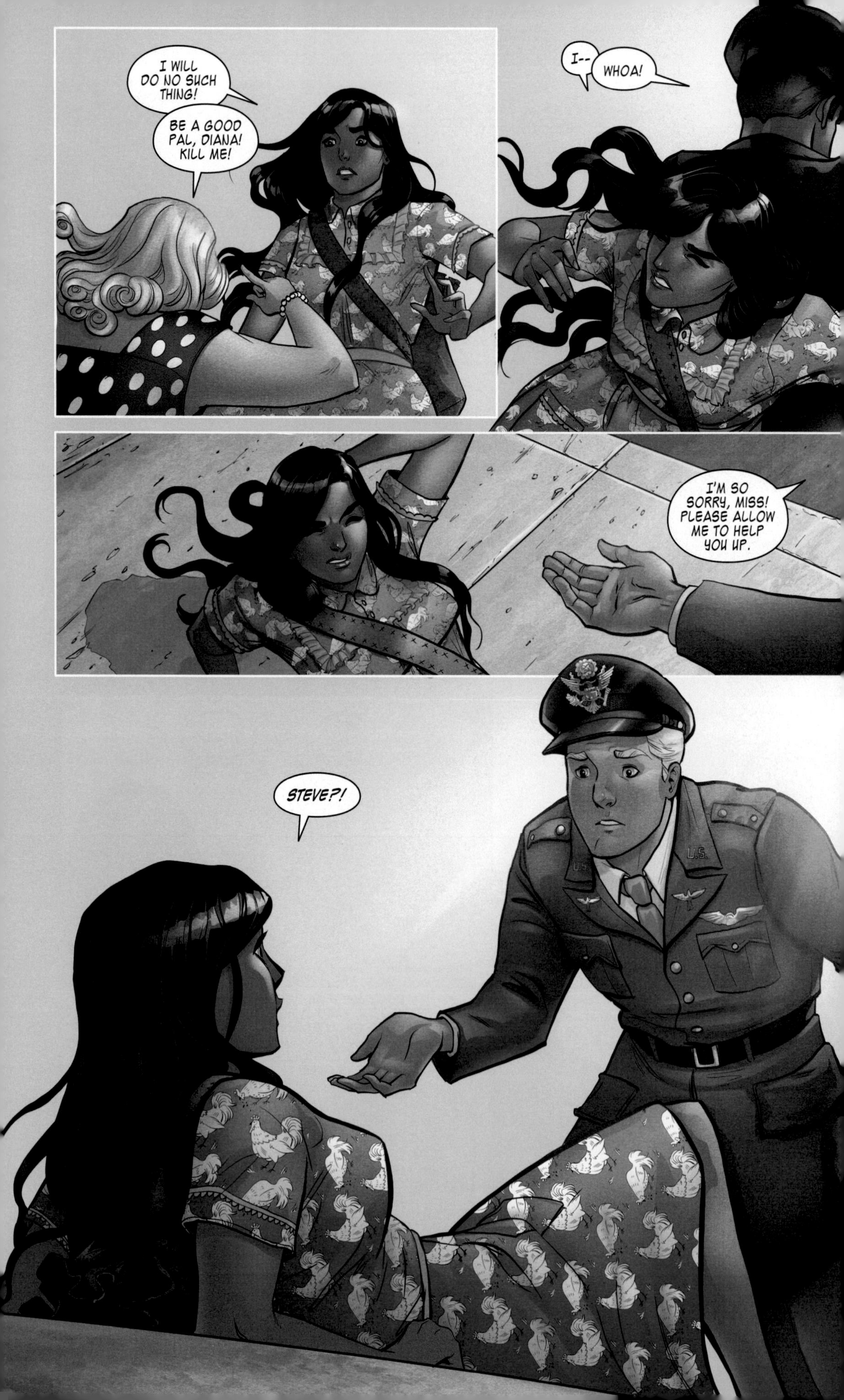
I WILL DO NO SUCH THING!
BE A GOOD PAL, DIANA! KILL ME!
I--
WHOA!
I'M SO SORRY, MISS! PLEASE ALLOW ME TO HELP YOU UP.
STEVE?!

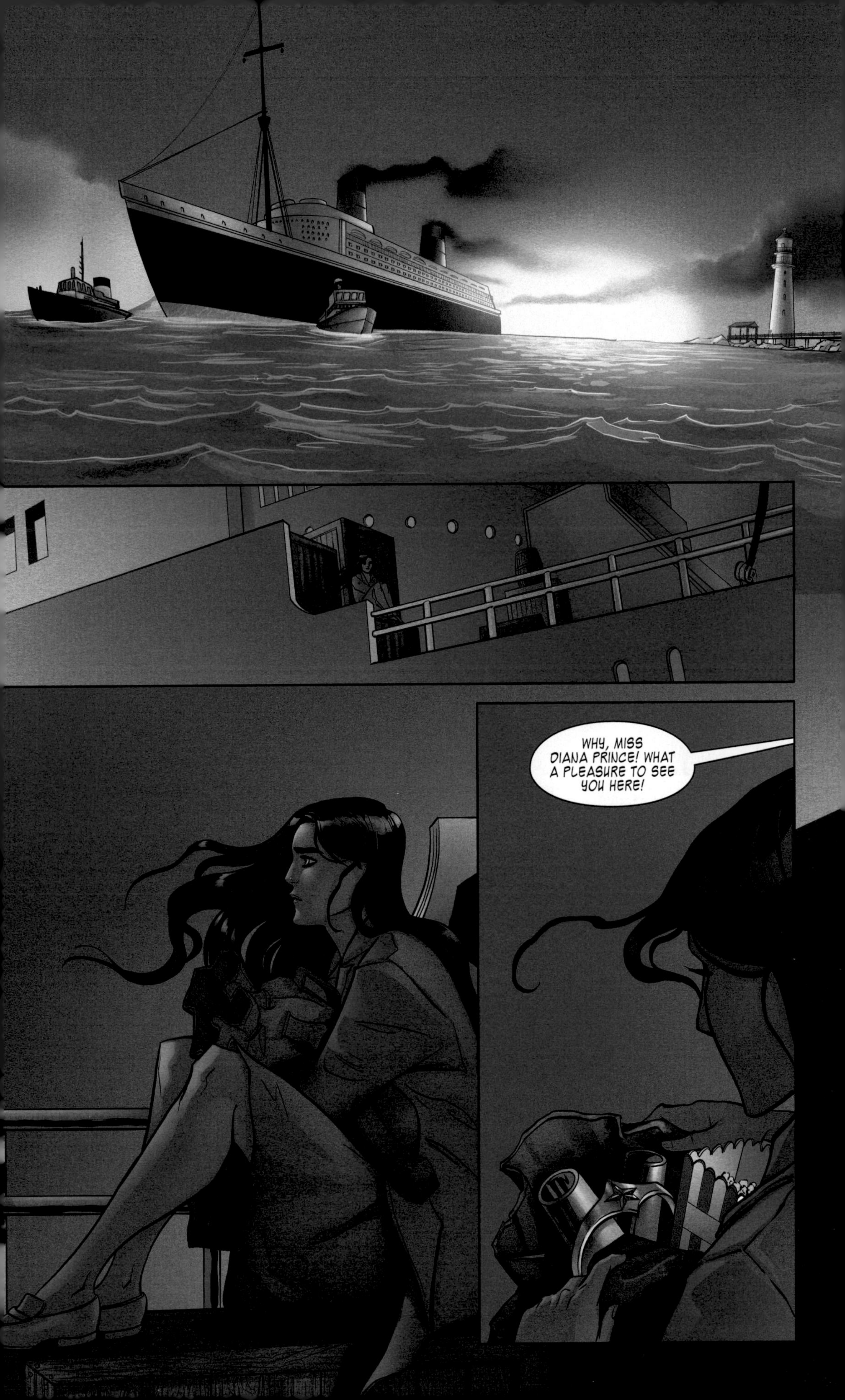
WHY, MISS DIANA PRINCE! WHAT A PLEASURE TO SEE YOU HERE!

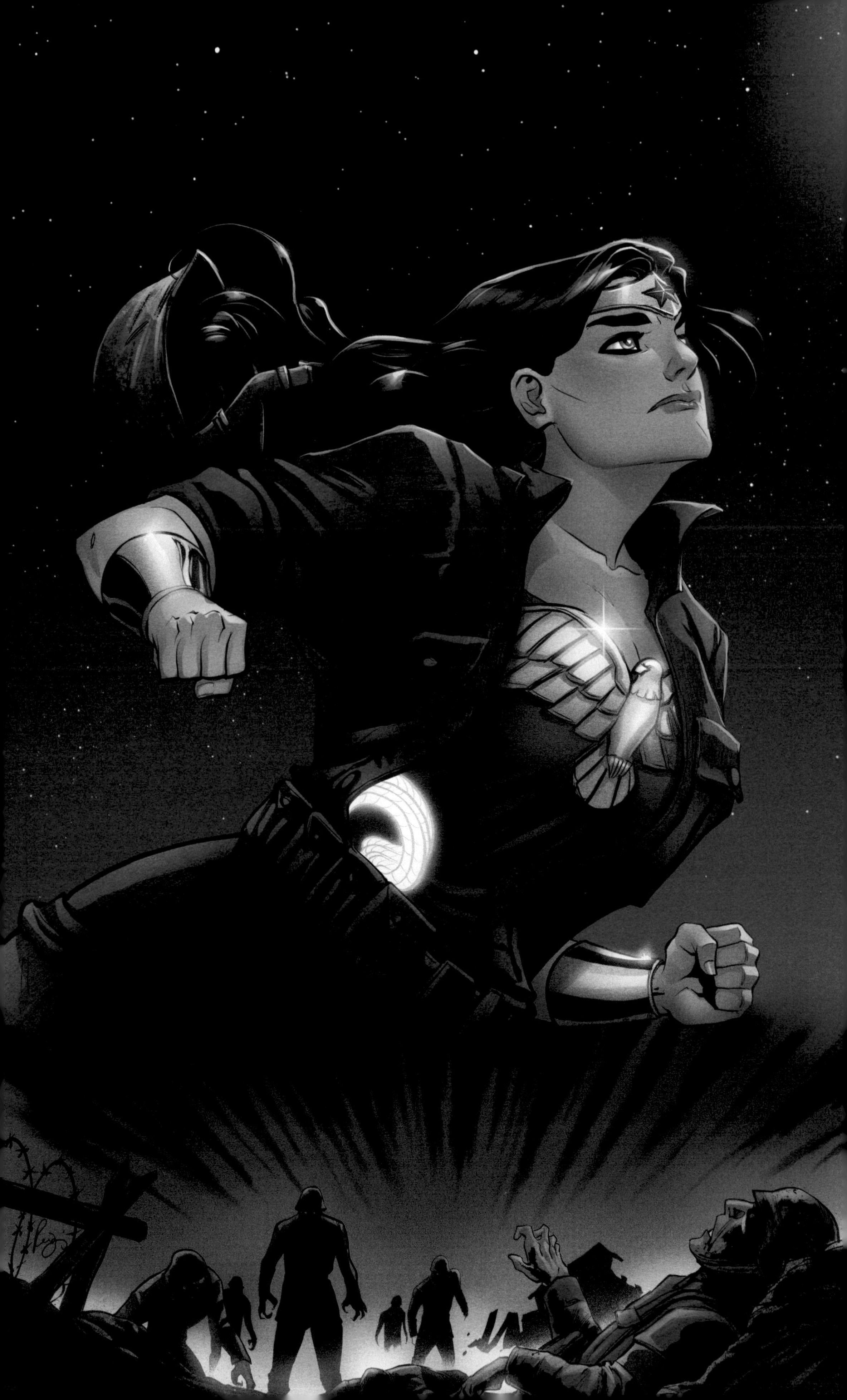

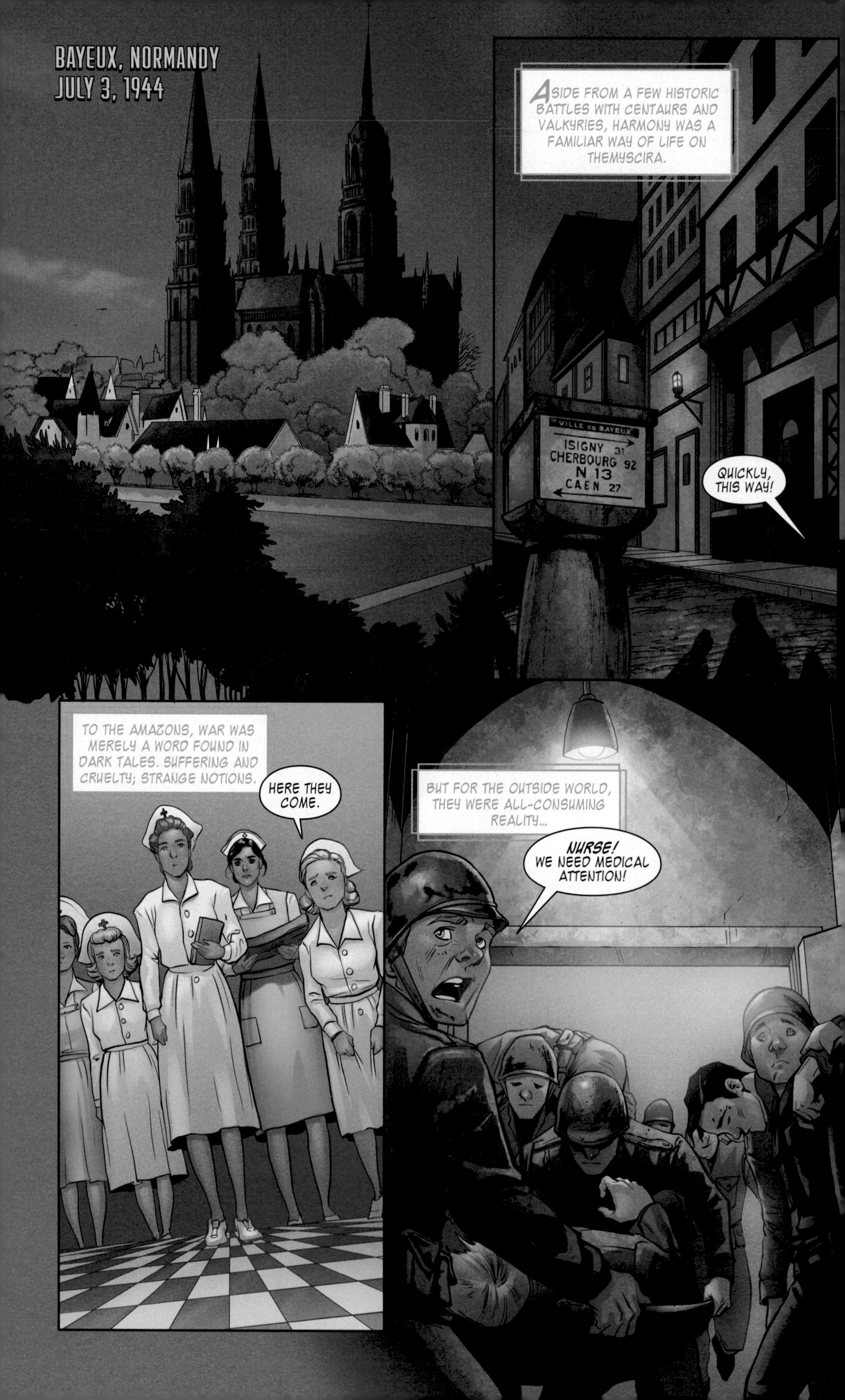
BAYEUX, NORMANDY
JULY 3, 1944
ASIDE FROM A FEW HISTORIC BATTLES WITH CENTAURS AND VALKYRIES, HARMONY WAS A FAMILIAR WAY OF LIFE ON THEMYSCIRA.
VILLE DE BAYEUX
ISIGNY 31
CHERBOURG 92
N 13
CAEN 27
QUICKLY, THIS WAY!
TO THE AMAZONS, WAR WAS MERELY A WORD FOUND IN DARK TALES. SUFFERING AND CRUELTY; STRANGE NOTIONS.
HERE THEY COME.
BUT FOR THE OUTSIDE WORLD, THEY WERE ALL-CONSUMING REALITY...
NURSE! WE NEED MEDICAL ATTENTION!

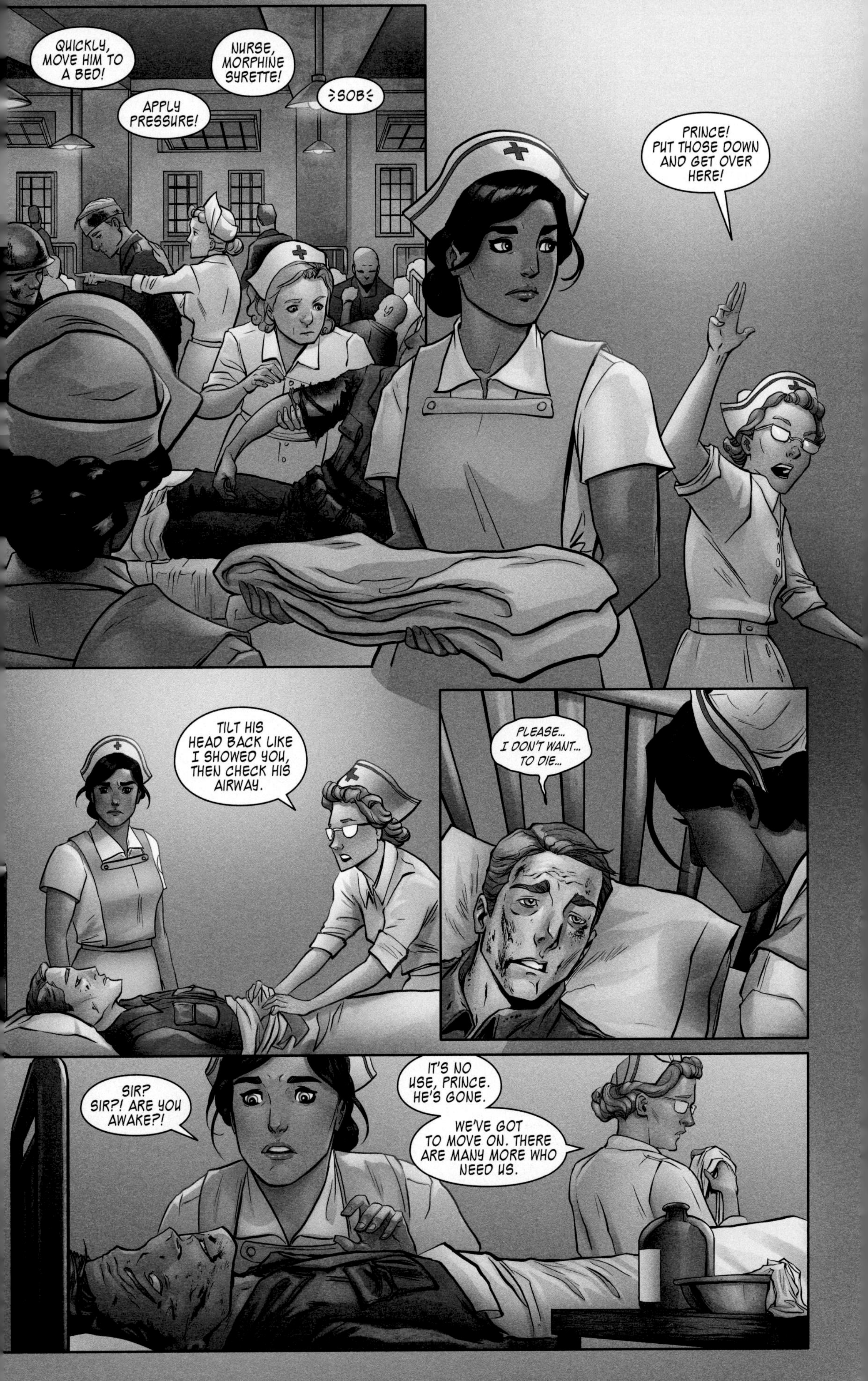
QUICKLY, MOVE HIM TO A BED!
APPLY PRESSURE!
NURSE, MORPHINE SYRETTE!
SOB
PRINCE! PUT THOSE DOWN AND GET OVER HERE!
TILT HIS HEAD BACK LIKE I SHOWED YOU, THEN CHECK HIS AIRWAY.
PLEASE... I DON'T WANT... TO DIE...
SIR? SIR?! ARE YOU AWAKE?!
IT'S NO USE, PRINCE. HE'S GONE.
WE'VE GOT TO MOVE ON. THERE ARE MANY MORE WHO NEED US.

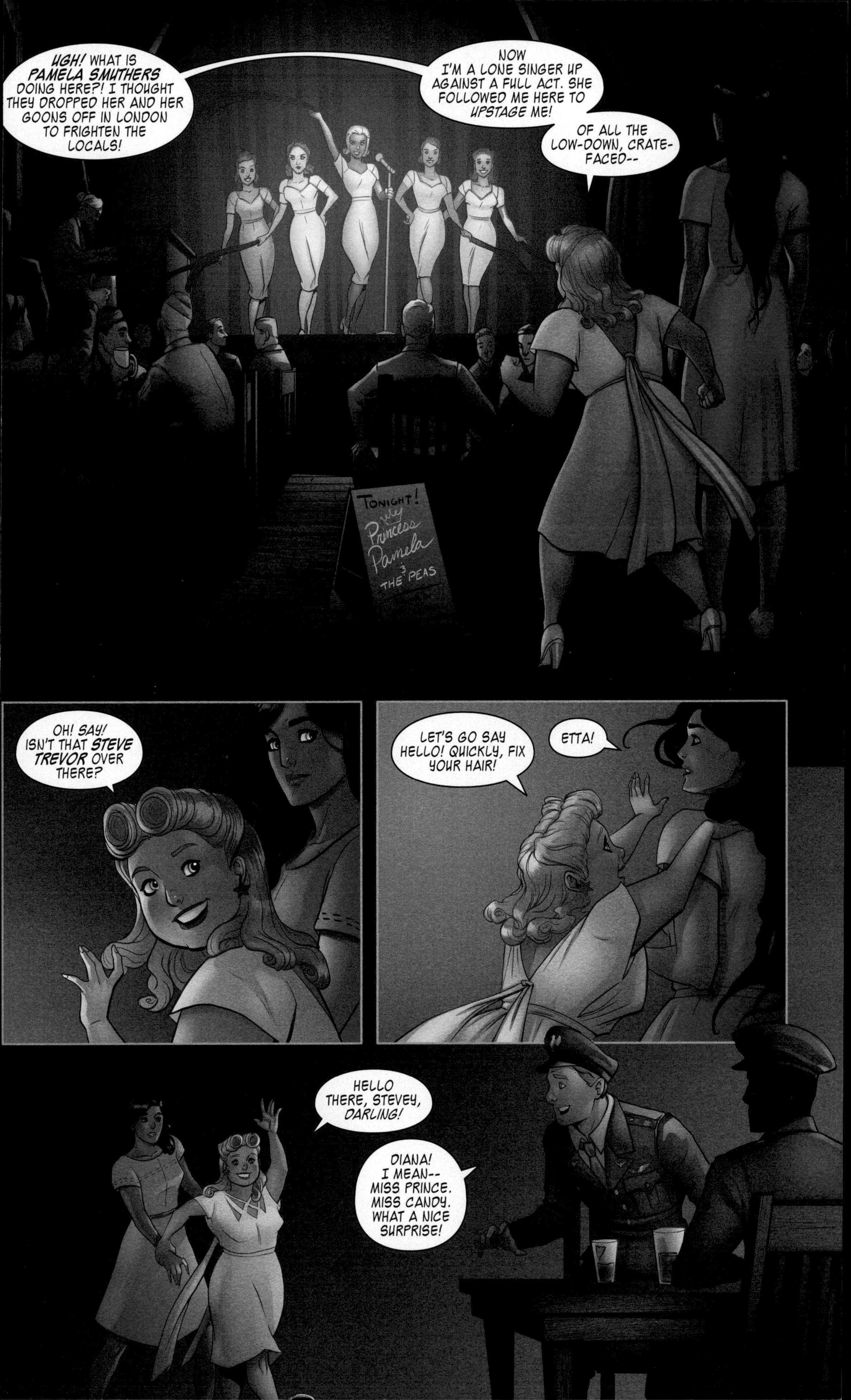
UGH! WHAT IS PAMELA SMUTHERS DOING HERE?! I THOUGHT THEY DROPPED HER AND HER GOONS OFF IN LONDON TO FRIGHTEN THE LOCALS!
NOW I'M A LONE SINGER UP AGAINST A FULL ACT. SHE FOLLOWED ME HERE TO UPSTAGE ME!
OF ALL THE LOW-DOWN, CRATE-FACED--
TONIGHT! Princess Pamela & THE 3 PEAS
OH! SAY! ISN'T THAT STEVE TREVOR OVER THERE?
LET'S GO SAY HELLO! QUICKLY, FIX YOUR HAIR!
ETTA!
HELLO THERE, STEVEY, DARLING!
DIANA! I MEAN-- MISS PRINCE. MISS CANDY. WHAT A NICE SURPRISE!

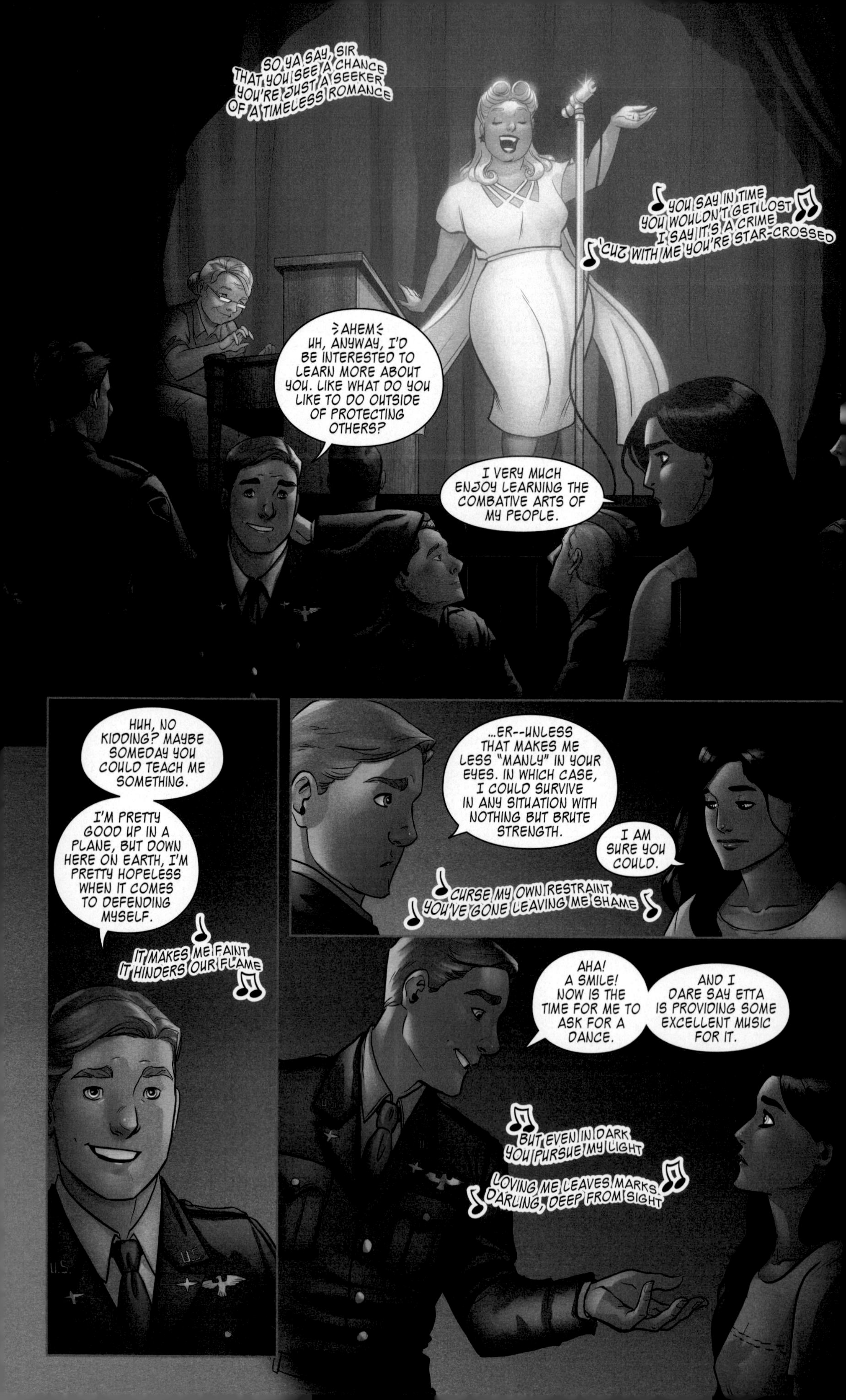
SO YA SAY, SIR
THAT YOU SEE A CHANCE
YOU'RE JUST A SEEKER
OF A TIMELESS ROMANCE
YOU SAY IN TIME
YOU WOULDN'T GET LOST
I SAY IT'S A CRIME
'CUZ WITH ME YOU'RE STAR-CROSSED
AHEM
UH, ANYWAY, I'D BE INTERESTED TO LEARN MORE ABOUT YOU. LIKE WHAT DO YOU LIKE TO DO OUTSIDE OF PROTECTING OTHERS?
I VERY MUCH ENJOY LEARNING THE COMBATIVE ARTS OF MY PEOPLE.
HUH, NO KIDDING? MAYBE SOMEDAY YOU COULD TEACH ME SOMETHING.
I'M PRETTY GOOD UP IN A PLANE, BUT DOWN HERE ON EARTH, I'M PRETTY HOPELESS WHEN IT COMES TO DEFENDING MYSELF.
IT MAKES ME FAINT
IT HINDERS OUR FLAME
...ER--UNLESS THAT MAKES ME LESS "MANLY" IN YOUR EYES. IN WHICH CASE, I COULD SURVIVE IN ANY SITUATION WITH NOTHING BUT BRUTE STRENGTH.
I AM SURE YOU COULD.
CURSE MY OWN RESTRAINT
YOU'VE GONE LEAVING ME SHAME
AHA! A SMILE! NOW IS THE TIME FOR ME TO ASK FOR A DANCE.
AND I DARE SAY ETTA IS PROVIDING SOME EXCELLENT MUSIC FOR IT.
BUT EVEN IN DARK
YOU PURSUE MY LIGHT
LOVING ME LEAVES MARKS,
DARLING, DEEP FROM SIGHT

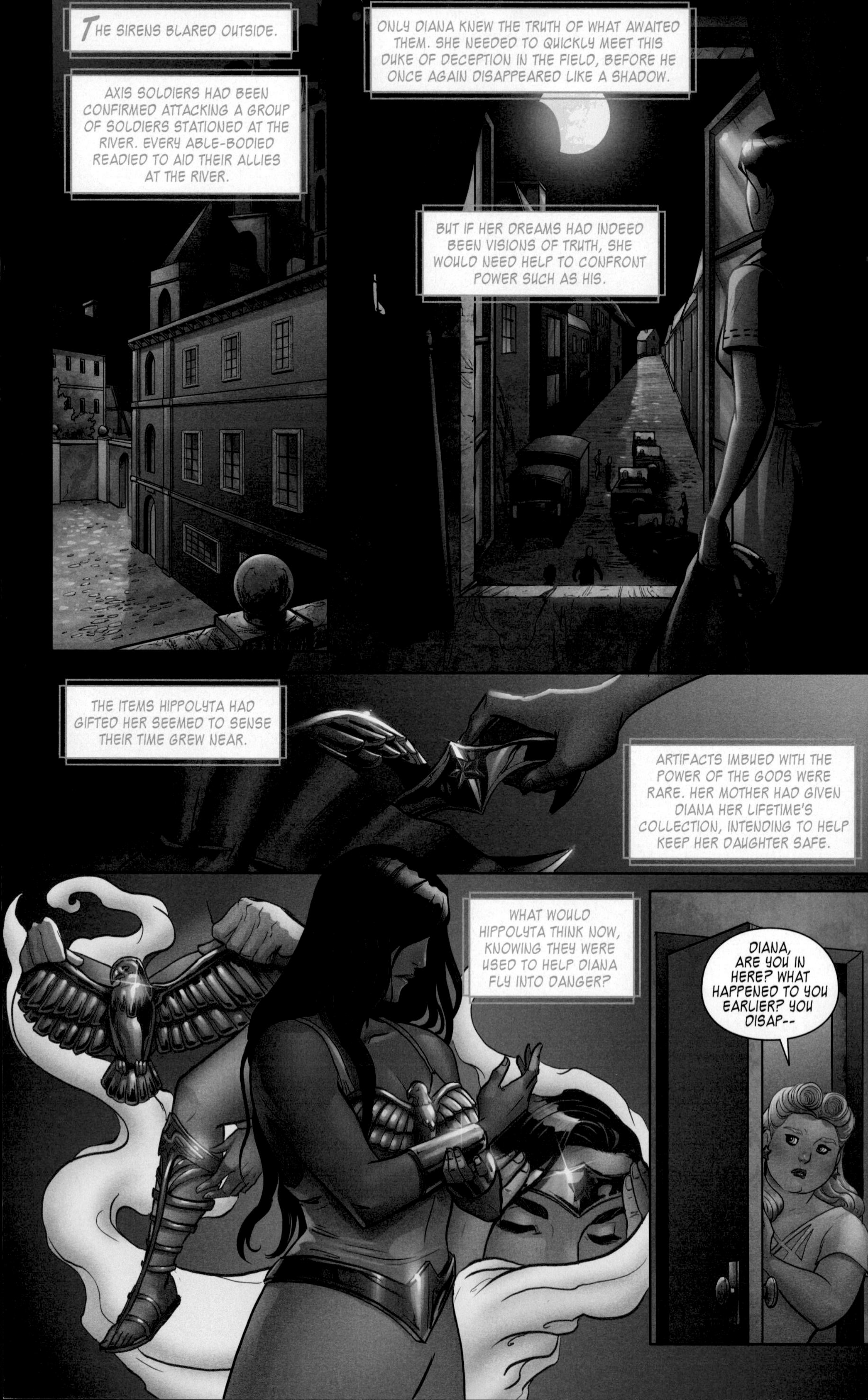
THE SIRENS BLARED OUTSIDE.
AXIS SOLDIERS HAD BEEN CONFIRMED ATTACKING A GROUP OF SOLDIERS STATIONED AT THE RIVER. EVERY ABLE-BODIED READIED TO AID THEIR ALLIES AT THE RIVER.
ONLY DIANA KNEW THE TRUTH OF WHAT AWAITED THEM. SHE NEEDED TO QUICKLY MEET THIS DUKE OF DECEPTION IN THE FIELD, BEFORE HE ONCE AGAIN DISAPPEARED LIKE A SHADOW.
BUT IF HER DREAMS HAD INDEED BEEN VISIONS OF TRUTH, SHE WOULD NEED HELP TO CONFRONT POWER SUCH AS HIS.
THE ITEMS HIPPOLYTA HAD GIFTED HER SEEMED TO SENSE THEIR TIME GREW NEAR.
ARTIFACTS IMBUED WITH THE POWER OF THE GODS WERE RARE. HER MOTHER HAD GIVEN DIANA HER LIFETIME'S COLLECTION, INTENDING TO HELP KEEP HER DAUGHTER SAFE.
WHAT WOULD HIPPOLYTA THINK NOW, KNOWING THEY WERE USED TO HELP DIANA FLY INTO DANGER?
DIANA, ARE YOU IN HERE? WHAT HAPPENED TO YOU EARLIER? YOU DISAP--

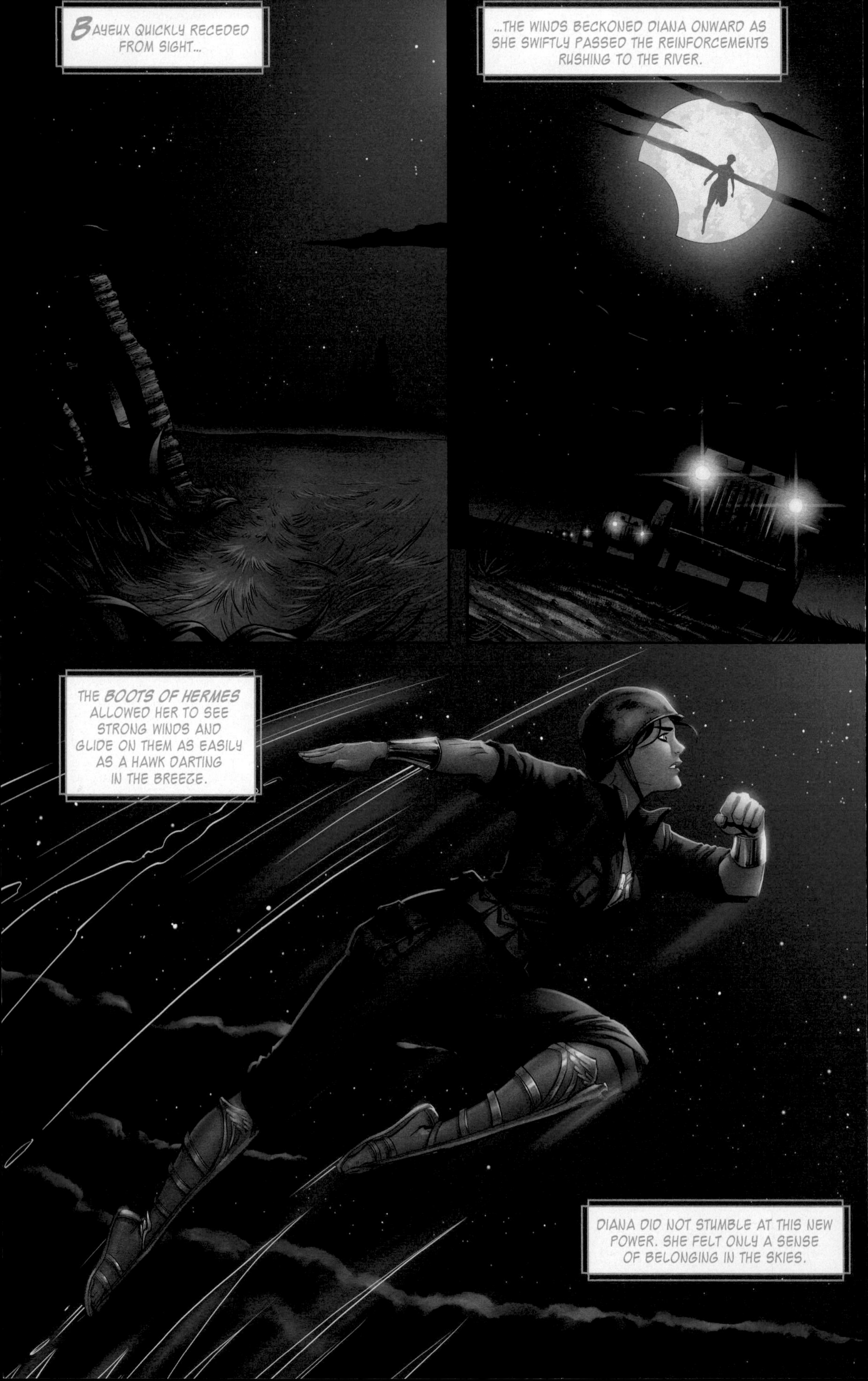
BAYEUX QUICKLY RECEDED FROM SIGHT...
...THE WINDS BECKONED DIANA ONWARD AS SHE SWIFTLY PASSED THE REINFORCEMENTS RUSHING TO THE RIVER.
THE BOOTS OF HERMES ALLOWED HER TO SEE STRONG WINDS AND GLIDE ON THEM AS EASILY AS A HAWK DARTING IN THE BREEZE.
DIANA DID NOT STUMBLE AT THIS NEW POWER. SHE FELT ONLY A SENSE OF BELONGING IN THE SKIES.

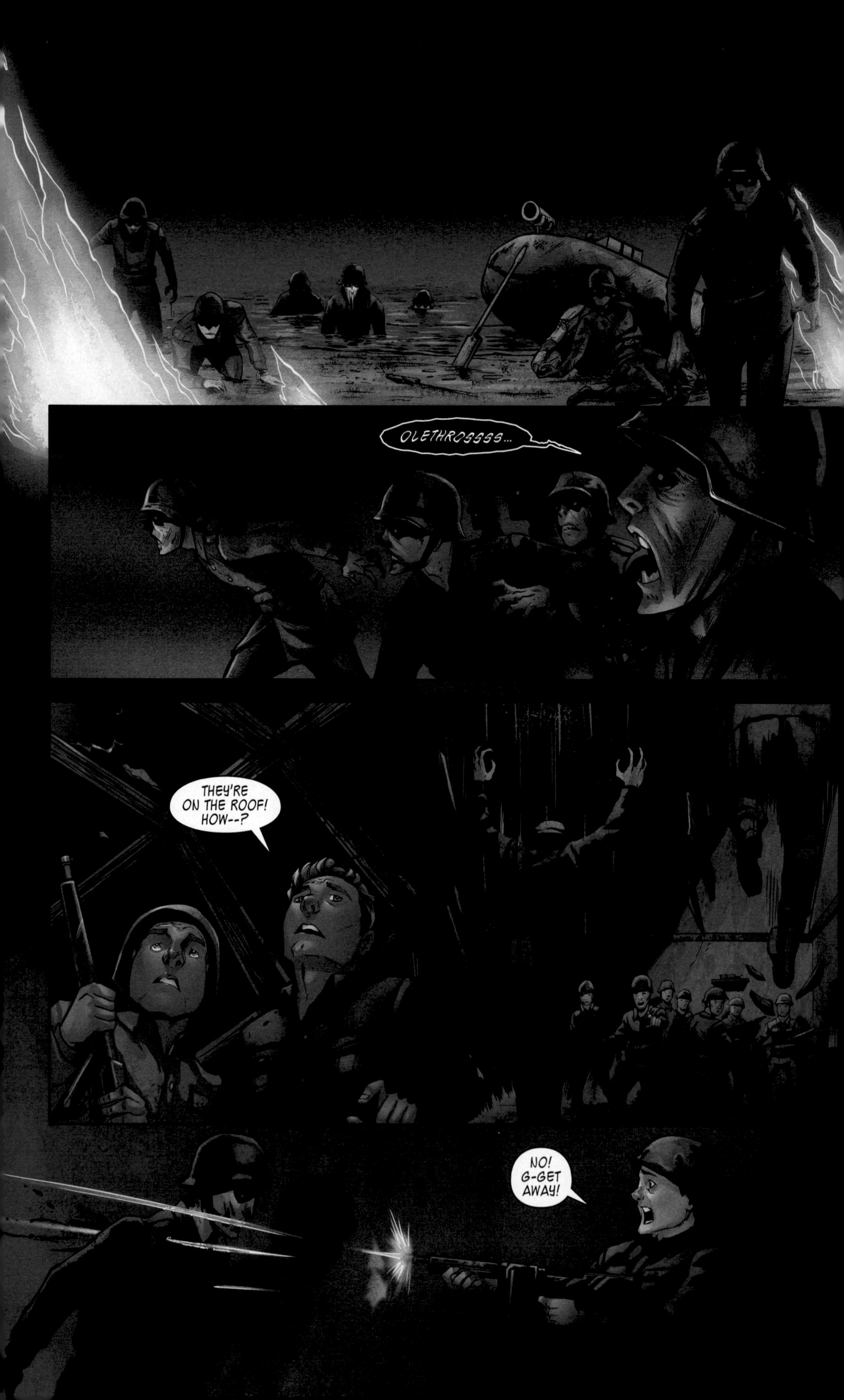
OLETHROSSSS...
THEY'RE ON THE ROOF! HOW--?
NO! G-GET AWAY!

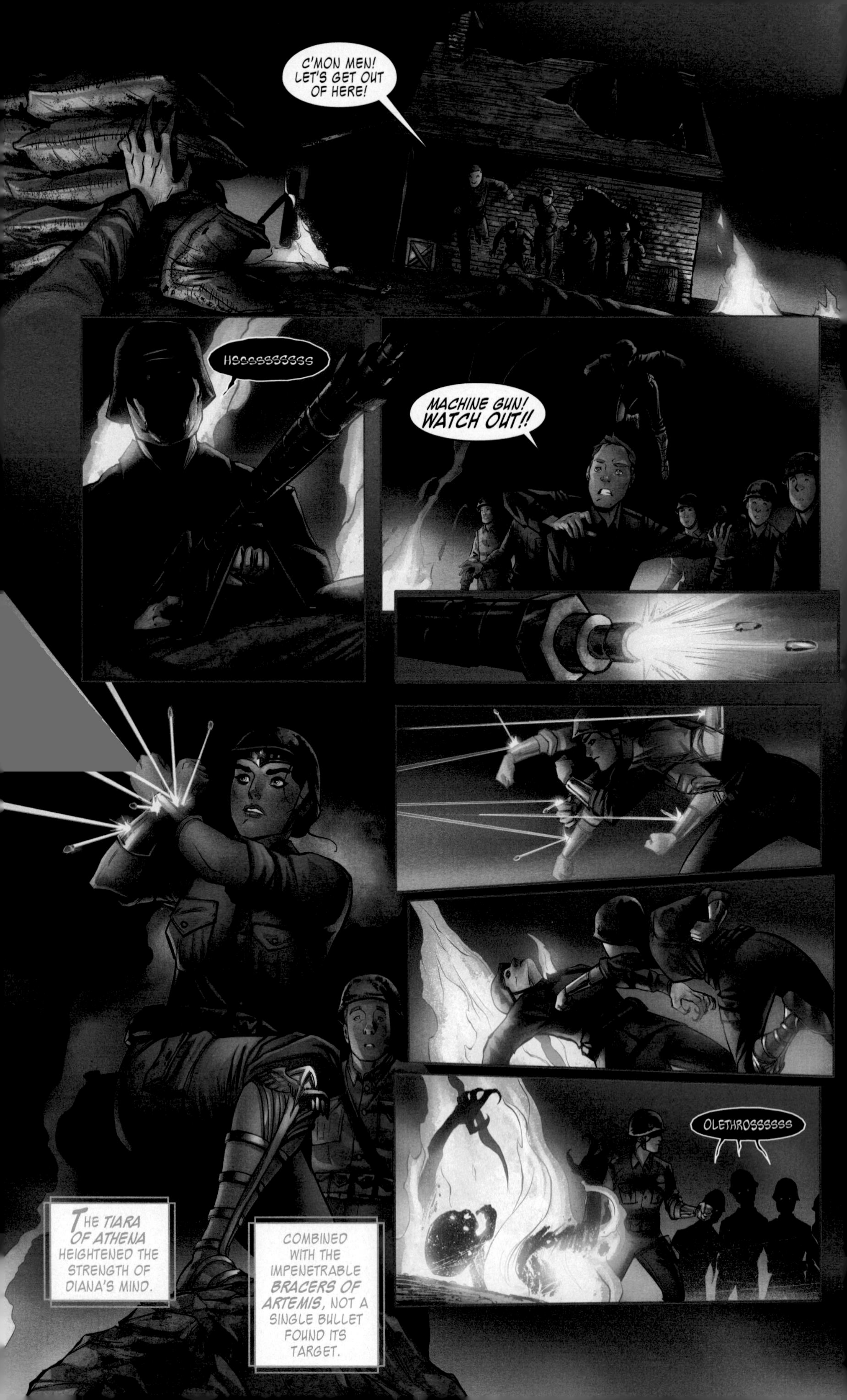
C'MON MEN! LET'S GET OUT OF HERE!
HSSSSSSSSSS
MACHINE GUN! WATCH OUT!!
THE TIARA OF ATHENA HEIGHTENED THE STRENGTH OF DIANA'S MIND.
COMBINED WITH THE IMPENETRABLE BRACERS OF ARTEMIS, NOT A SINGLE BULLET FOUND ITS TARGET.
OLETHROSSSSSS

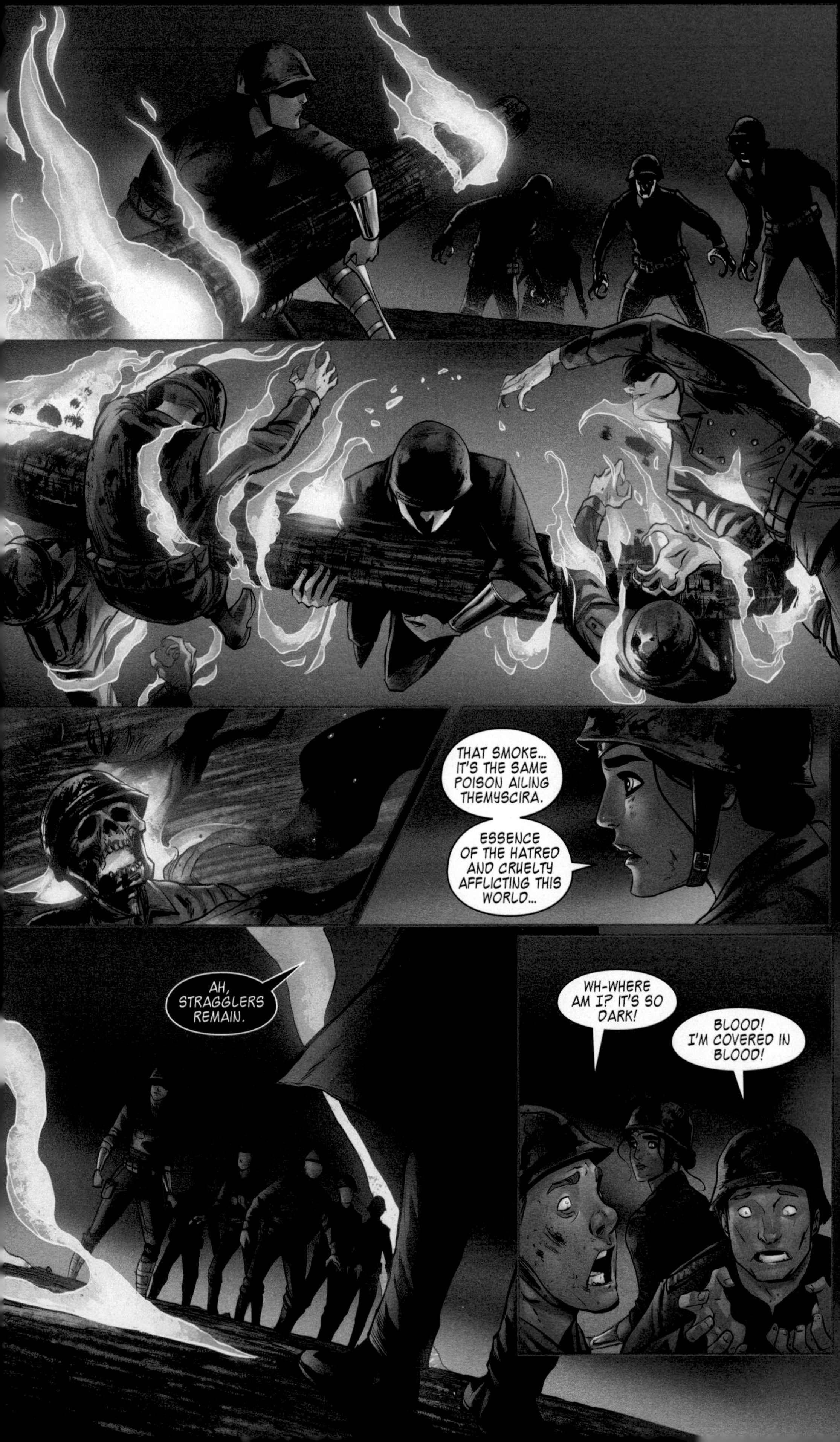
THAT SMOKE... IT'S THE SAME POISON AILING THEMYSCIRA.
ESSENCE OF THE HATRED AND CRUELTY AFFLICTING THIS WORLD...
AH, STRAGGLERS REMAIN.
WH-WHERE AM I? IT'S SO DARK!
BLOOD! I'M COVERED IN BLOOD!

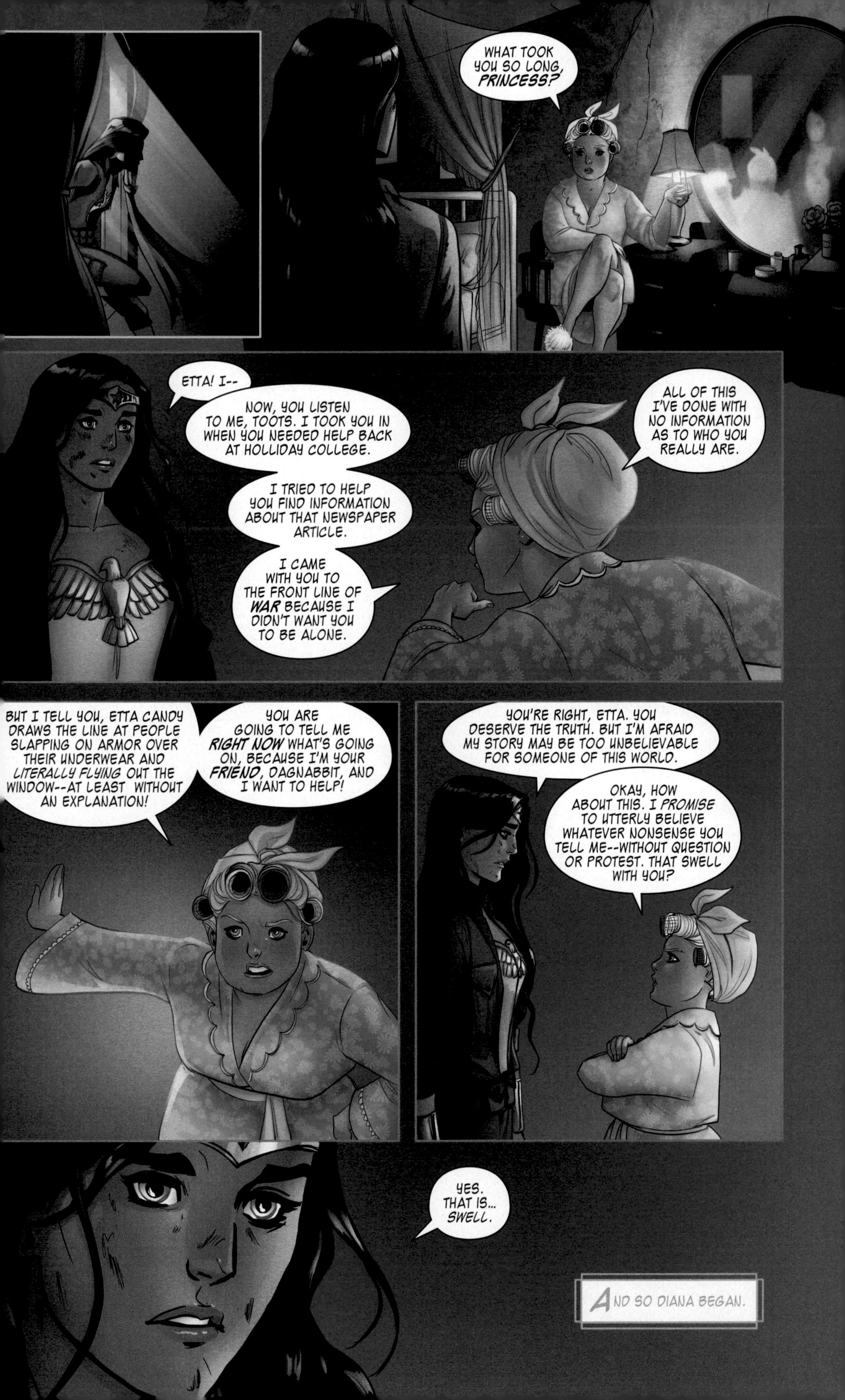
WHAT TOOK YOU SO LONG, PRINCESS?
ETTA! I--
NOW, YOU LISTEN TO ME, TOOTS. I TOOK YOU IN WHEN YOU NEEDED HELP BACK AT HOLLIDAY COLLEGE.
I TRIED TO HELP YOU FIND INFORMATION ABOUT THAT NEWSPAPER ARTICLE.
I CAME WITH YOU TO THE FRONT LINE OF WAR BECAUSE I DIDN'T WANT YOU TO BE ALONE.
ALL OF THIS I'VE DONE WITH NO INFORMATION AS TO WHO YOU REALLY ARE.
BUT I TELL YOU, ETTA CANDY DRAWS THE LINE AT PEOPLE SLAPPING ON ARMOR OVER THEIR UNDERWEAR AND LITERALLY FLYING OUT THE WINDOW--AT LEAST WITHOUT AN EXPLANATION!
YOU ARE GOING TO TELL ME RIGHT NOW WHAT'S GOING ON, BECAUSE I'M YOUR FRIEND, DAGNABBIT, AND I WANT TO HELP!
YOU'RE RIGHT, ETTA. YOU DESERVE THE TRUTH. BUT I'M AFRAID MY STORY MAY BE TOO UNBELIEVABLE FOR SOMEONE OF THIS WORLD.
OKAY, HOW ABOUT THIS. I PROMISE TO UTTERLY BELIEVE WHATEVER NONSENSE YOU TELL ME--WITHOUT QUESTION OR PROTEST. THAT SWELL WITH YOU?
YES. THAT IS... SWELL.
AND SO DIANA BEGAN.

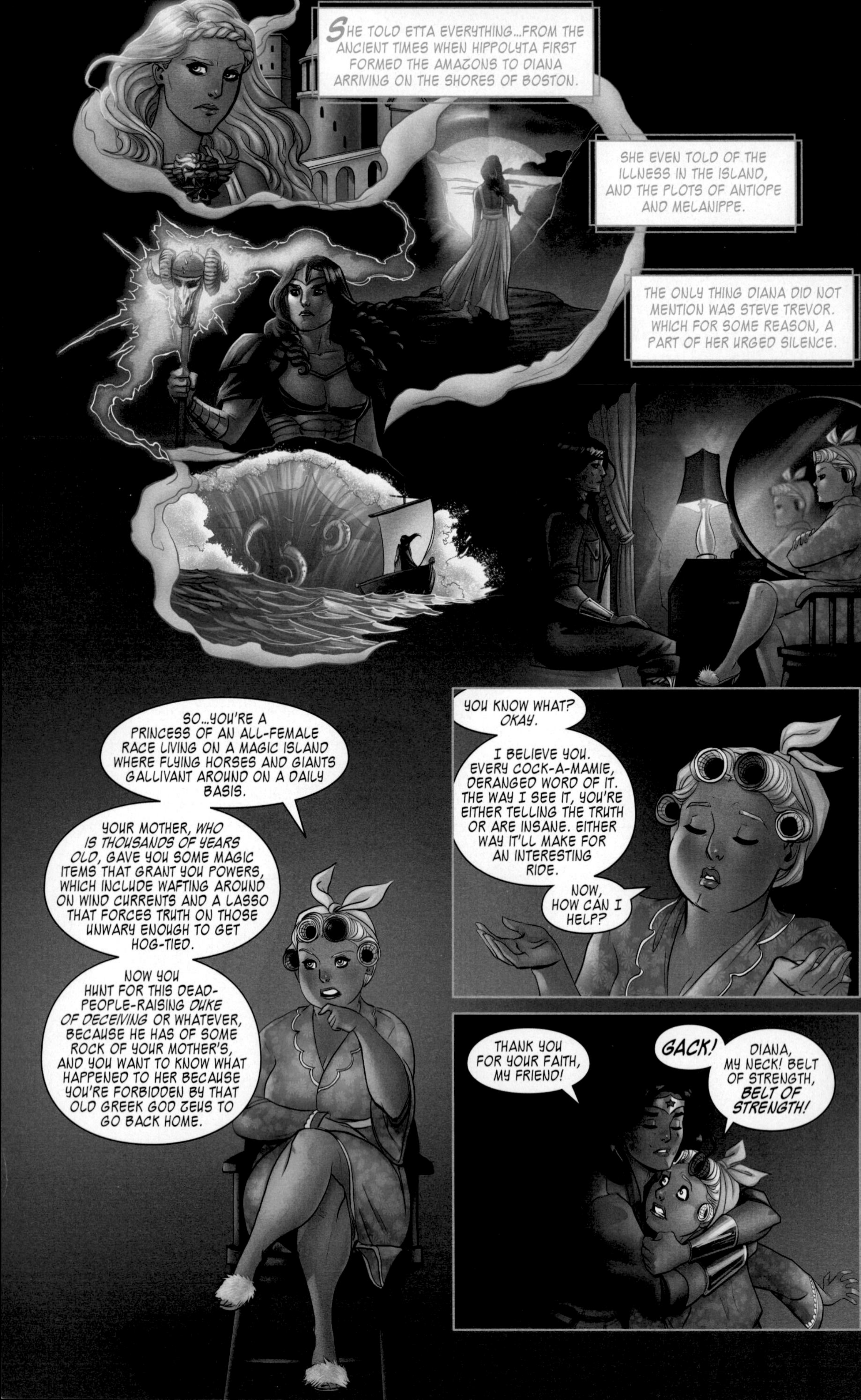
SHE TOLD ETTA EVERYTHING...FROM THE ANCIENT TIMES WHEN HIPPOLYTA FIRST FORMED THE AMAZONS TO DIANA ARRIVING ON THE SHORES OF BOSTON.
SHE EVEN TOLD OF THE ILLNESS IN THE ISLAND, AND THE PLOTS OF ANTIOPE AND MELANIPPE.
THE ONLY THING DIANA DID NOT MENTION WAS STEVE TREVOR. WHICH FOR SOME REASON, A PART OF HER URGED SILENCE.
SO...YOU'RE A PRINCESS OF AN ALL-FEMALE RACE LIVING ON A MAGIC ISLAND WHERE FLYING HORSES AND GIANTS GALLIVANT AROUND ON A DAILY BASIS.
YOUR MOTHER, WHO IS THOUSANDS OF YEARS OLD, GAVE YOU SOME MAGIC ITEMS THAT GRANT YOU POWERS, WHICH INCLUDE WAFTING AROUND ON WIND CURRENTS AND A LASSO THAT FORCES TRUTH ON THOSE UNWARY ENOUGH TO GET HOG-TIED.
NOW YOU HUNT FOR THIS DEAD-PEOPLE-RAISING DUKE OF DECEIVING OR WHATEVER, BECAUSE HE HAS OF SOME ROCK OF YOUR MOTHER'S, AND YOU WANT TO KNOW WHAT HAPPENED TO HER BECAUSE YOU'RE FORBIDDEN BY THAT OLD GREEK GOD ZEUS TO GO BACK HOME.
YOU KNOW WHAT? OKAY.
I BELIEVE YOU. EVERY COCK-A-MAMIE, DERANGED WORD OF IT. THE WAY I SEE IT, YOU'RE EITHER TELLING THE TRUTH OR ARE INSANE. EITHER WAY IT'LL MAKE FOR AN INTERESTING RIDE.
NOW, HOW CAN I HELP?
THANK YOU FOR YOUR FAITH, MY FRIEND!
GACK!
DIANA, MY NECK! BELT OF STRENGTH, BELT OF STRENGTH!

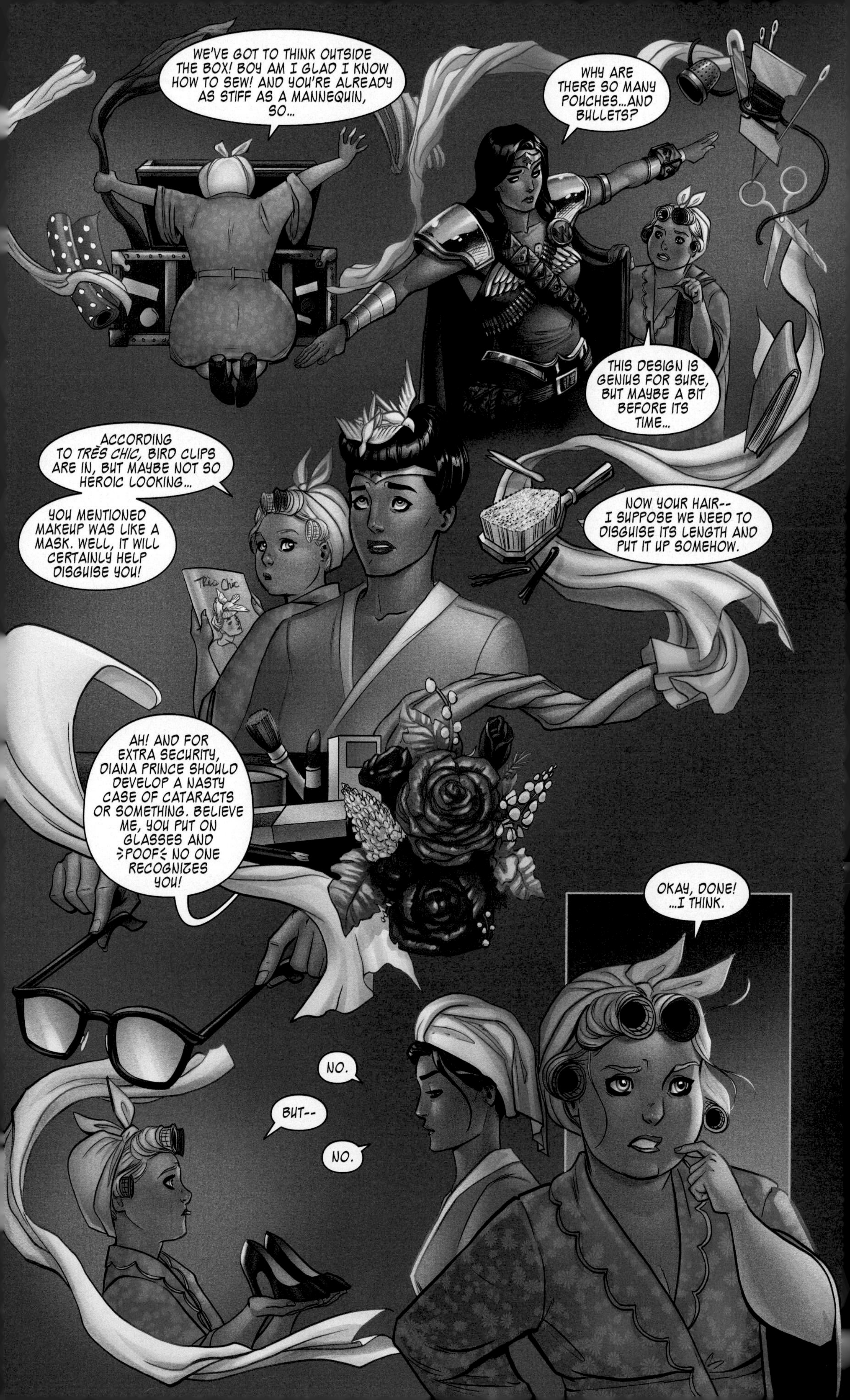
WE'VE GOT TO THINK OUTSIDE THE BOX! BOY AM I GLAD I KNOW HOW TO SEW! AND YOU'RE ALREADY AS STIFF AS A MANNEQUIN, SO...
WHY ARE THERE SO MANY POUCHES...AND BULLETS?
THIS DESIGN IS GENIUS FOR SURE, BUT MAYBE A BIT BEFORE ITS TIME...
ACCORDING TO *TRÈS CHIC*, BIRD CLIPS ARE IN, BUT MAYBE NOT SO HEROIC LOOKING...
YOU MENTIONED MAKEUP WAS LIKE A MASK. WELL, IT WILL CERTAINLY HELP DISGUISE YOU!
TRÈS CHIC
NOW YOUR HAIR-- I SUPPOSE WE NEED TO DISGUISE ITS LENGTH AND PUT IT UP SOMEHOW.
AH! AND FOR EXTRA SECURITY, DIANA PRINCE SHOULD DEVELOP A NASTY CASE OF CATARACTS OR SOMETHING. BELIEVE ME, YOU PUT ON GLASSES AND *POOF* NO ONE RECOGNIZES YOU!
OKAY, DONE! ...I THINK.
NO.
BUT--
NO.

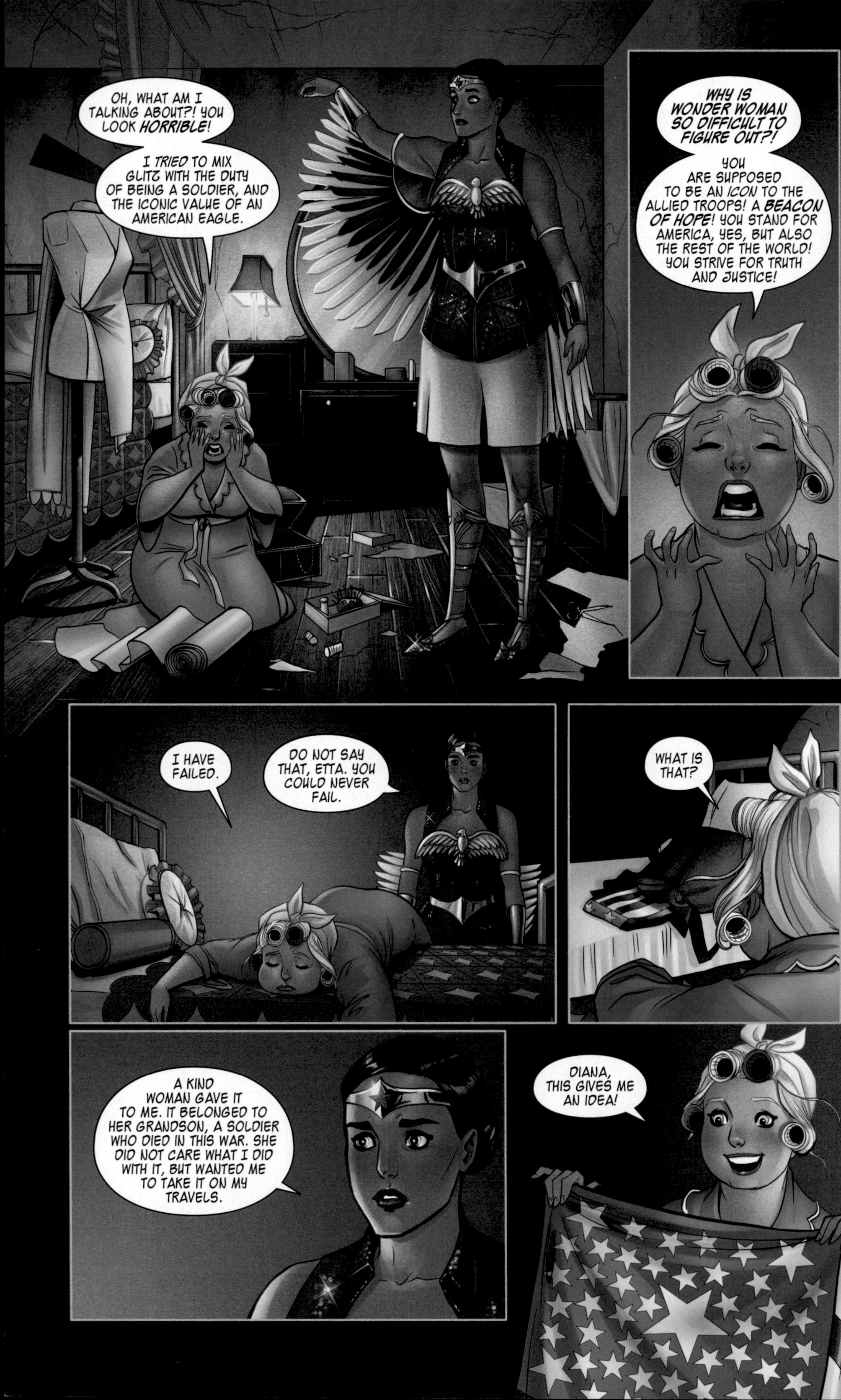
OH, WHAT AM I TALKING ABOUT?! YOU LOOK HORRIBLE!
I TRIED TO MIX GLITZ WITH THE DUTY OF BEING A SOLDIER, AND THE ICONIC VALUE OF AN AMERICAN EAGLE.
WHY IS WONDER WOMAN SO DIFFICULT TO FIGURE OUT?!
YOU ARE SUPPOSED TO BE AN ICON TO THE ALLIED TROOPS! A BEACON OF HOPE! YOU STAND FOR AMERICA, YES, BUT ALSO THE REST OF THE WORLD! YOU STRIVE FOR TRUTH AND JUSTICE!
I HAVE FAILED.
DO NOT SAY THAT, ETTA. YOU COULD NEVER FAIL.
WHAT IS THAT?
A KIND WOMAN GAVE IT TO ME. IT BELONGED TO HER GRANDSON, A SOLDIER WHO DIED IN THIS WAR. SHE DID NOT CARE WHAT I DID WITH IT, BUT WANTED ME TO TAKE IT ON MY TRAVELS.
DIANA, THIS GIVES ME AN IDEA!

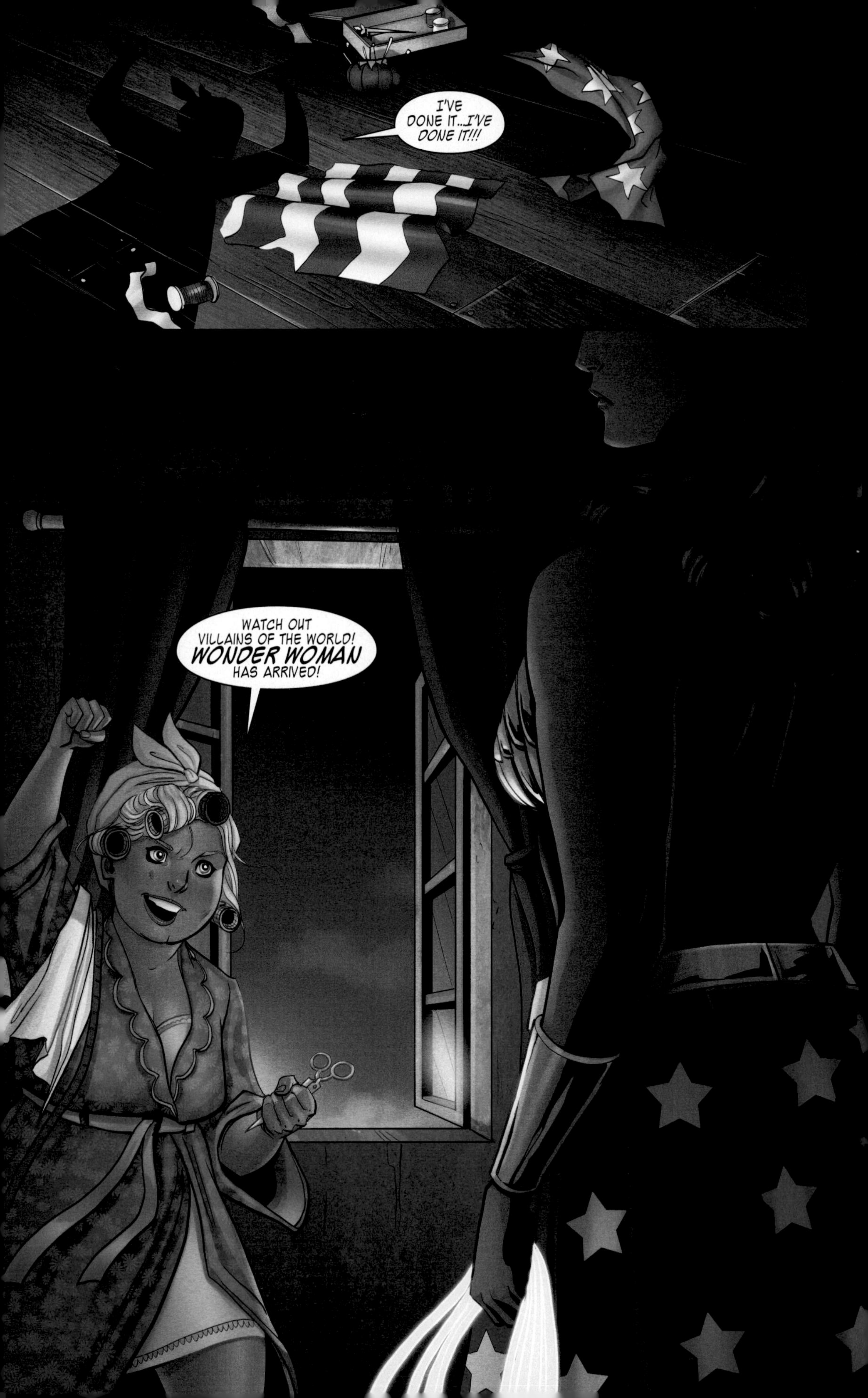
I'VE DONE IT...I'VE DONE IT!!!
WATCH OUT VILLAINS OF THE WORLD! WONDER WOMAN HAS ARRIVED!

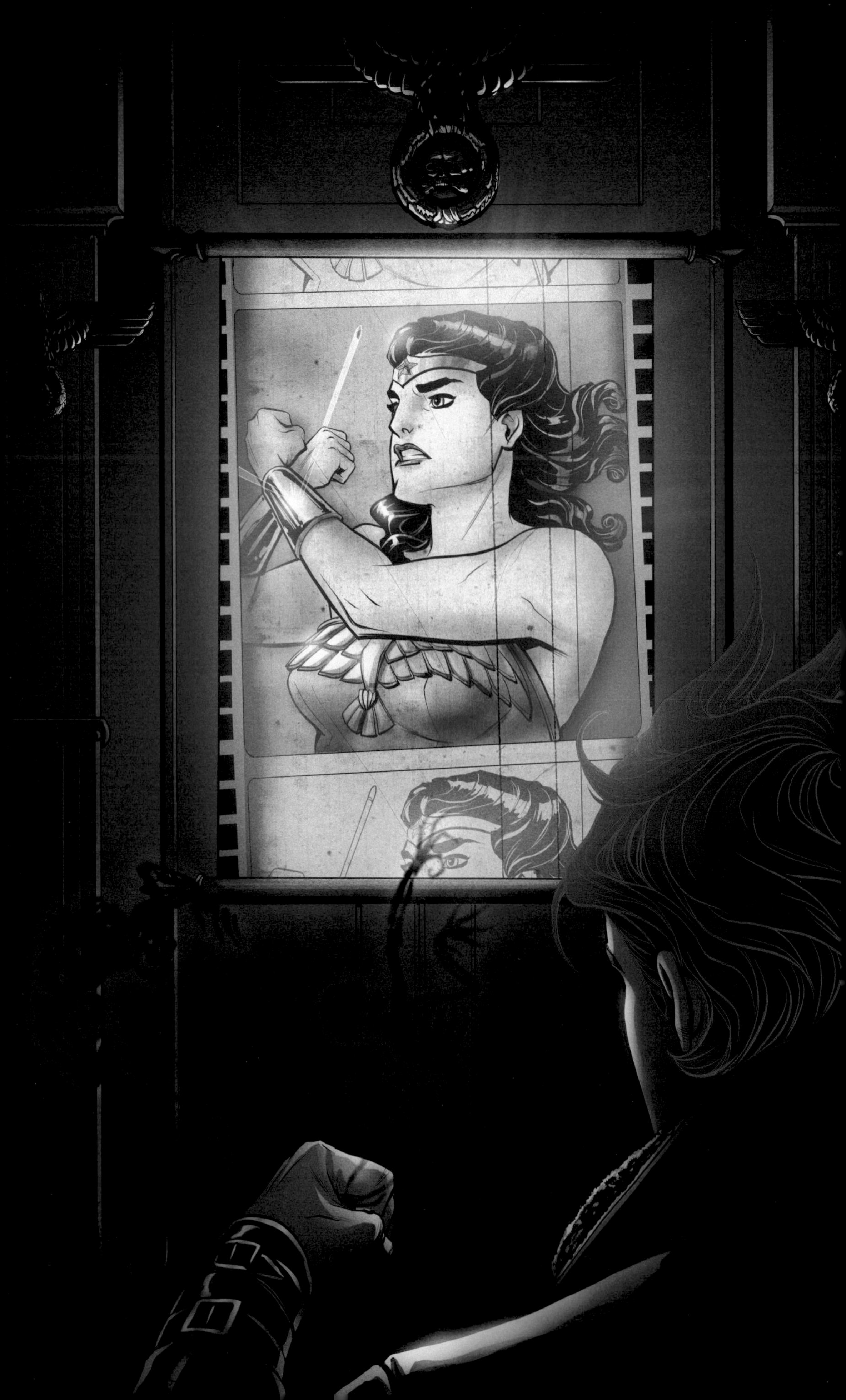

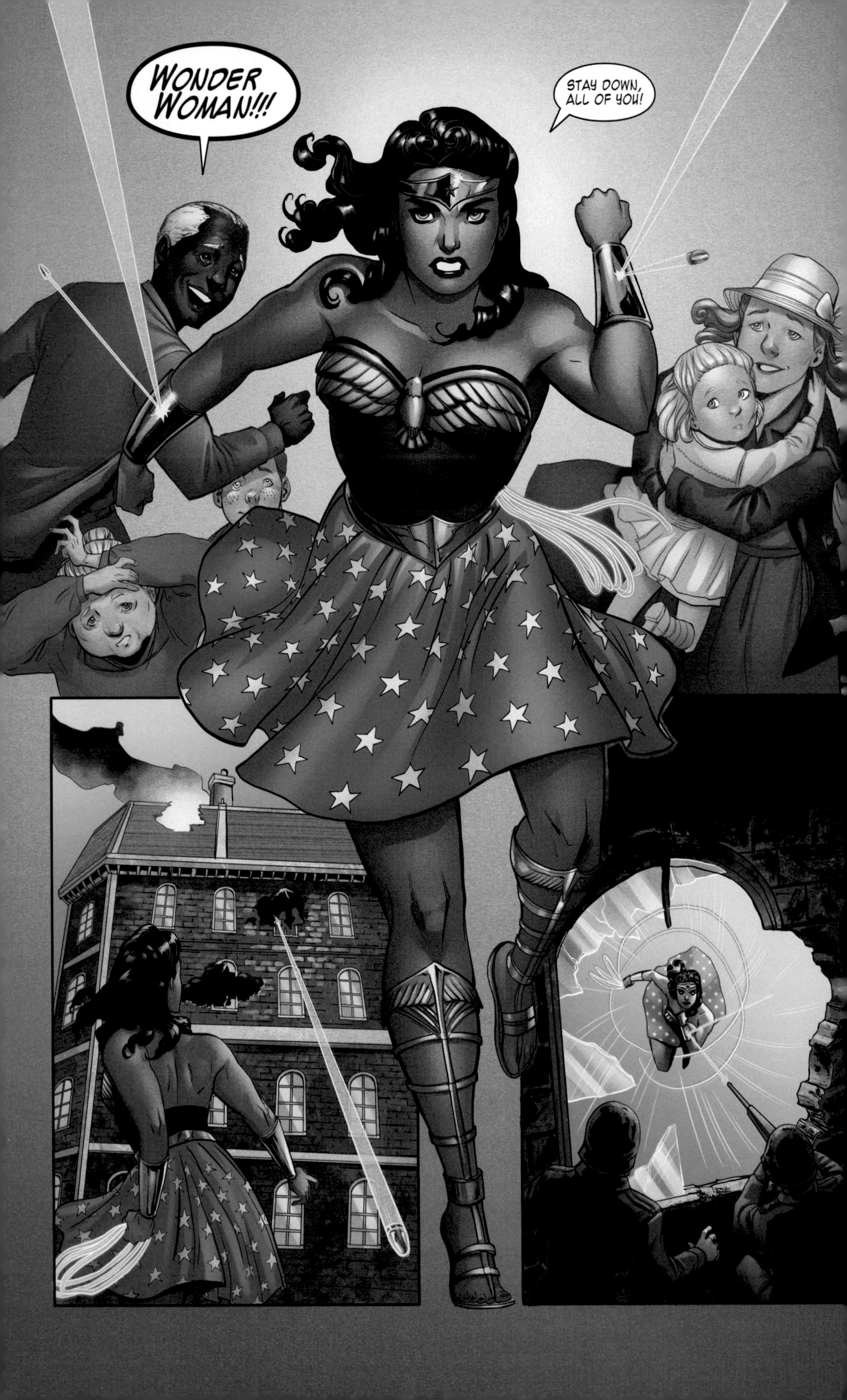
WONDER WOMAN!!!
STAY DOWN, ALL OF YOU!

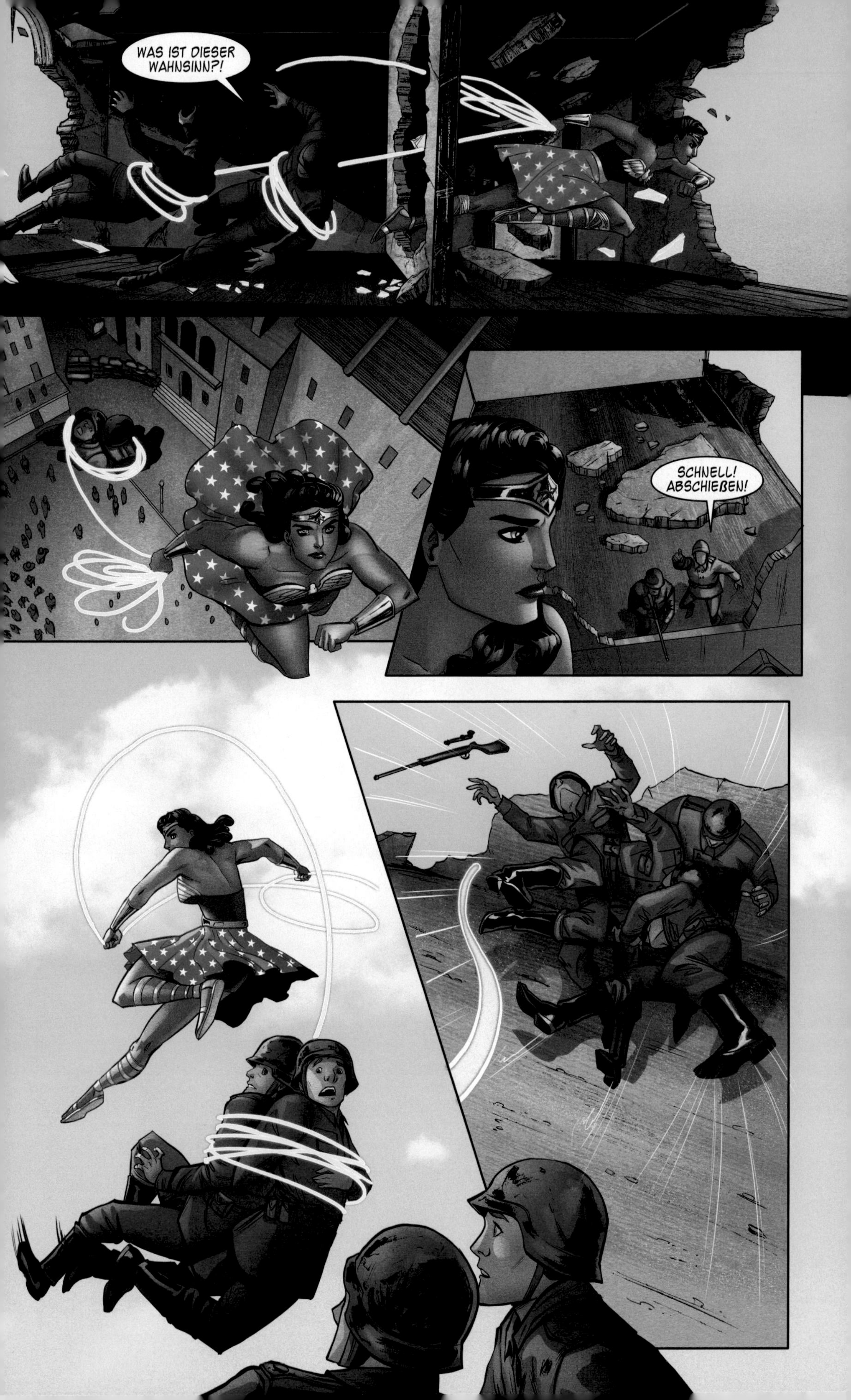
WAS IST DIESER WAHNSINN?!
SCHNELL! ABSCHIEßEN!

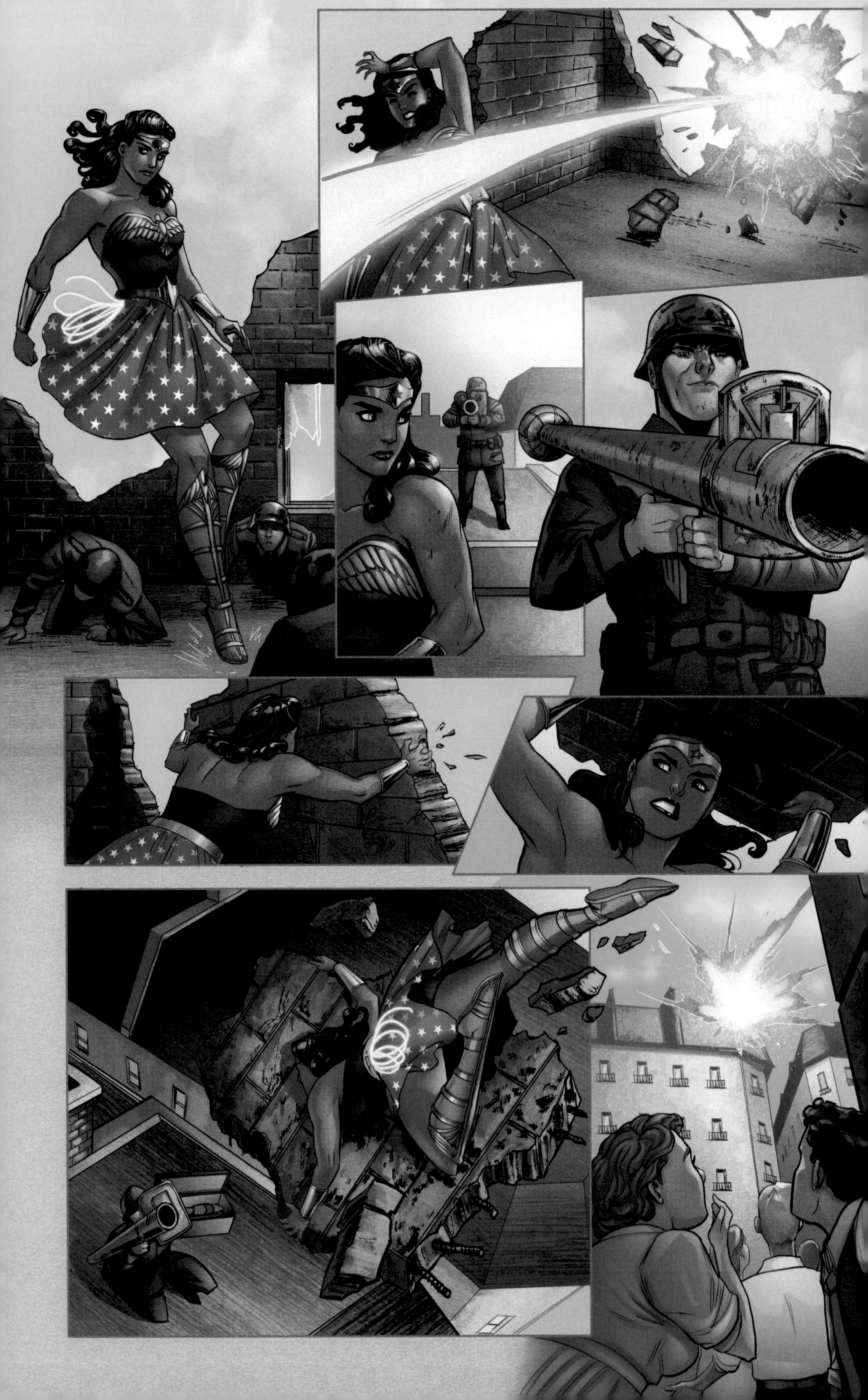

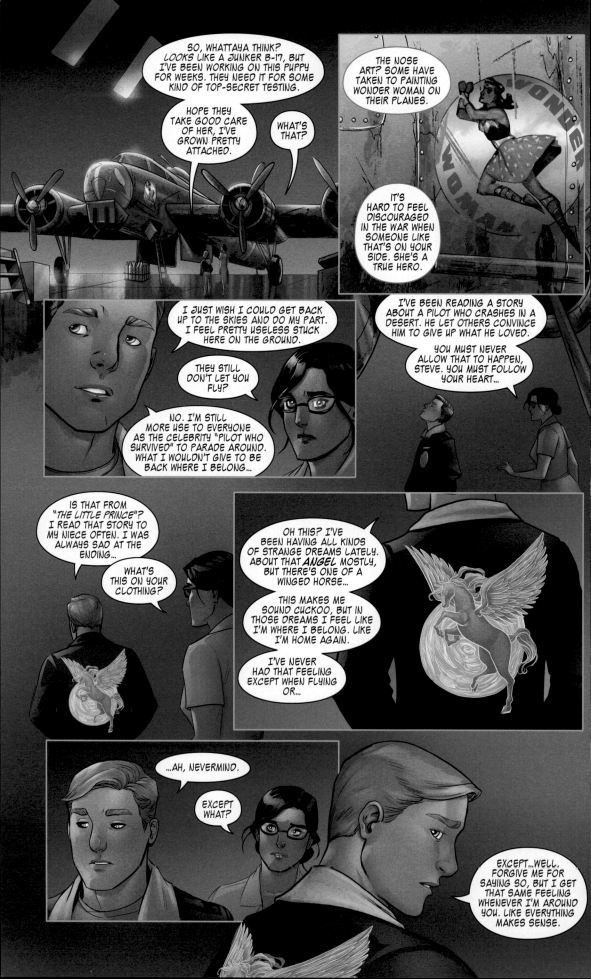

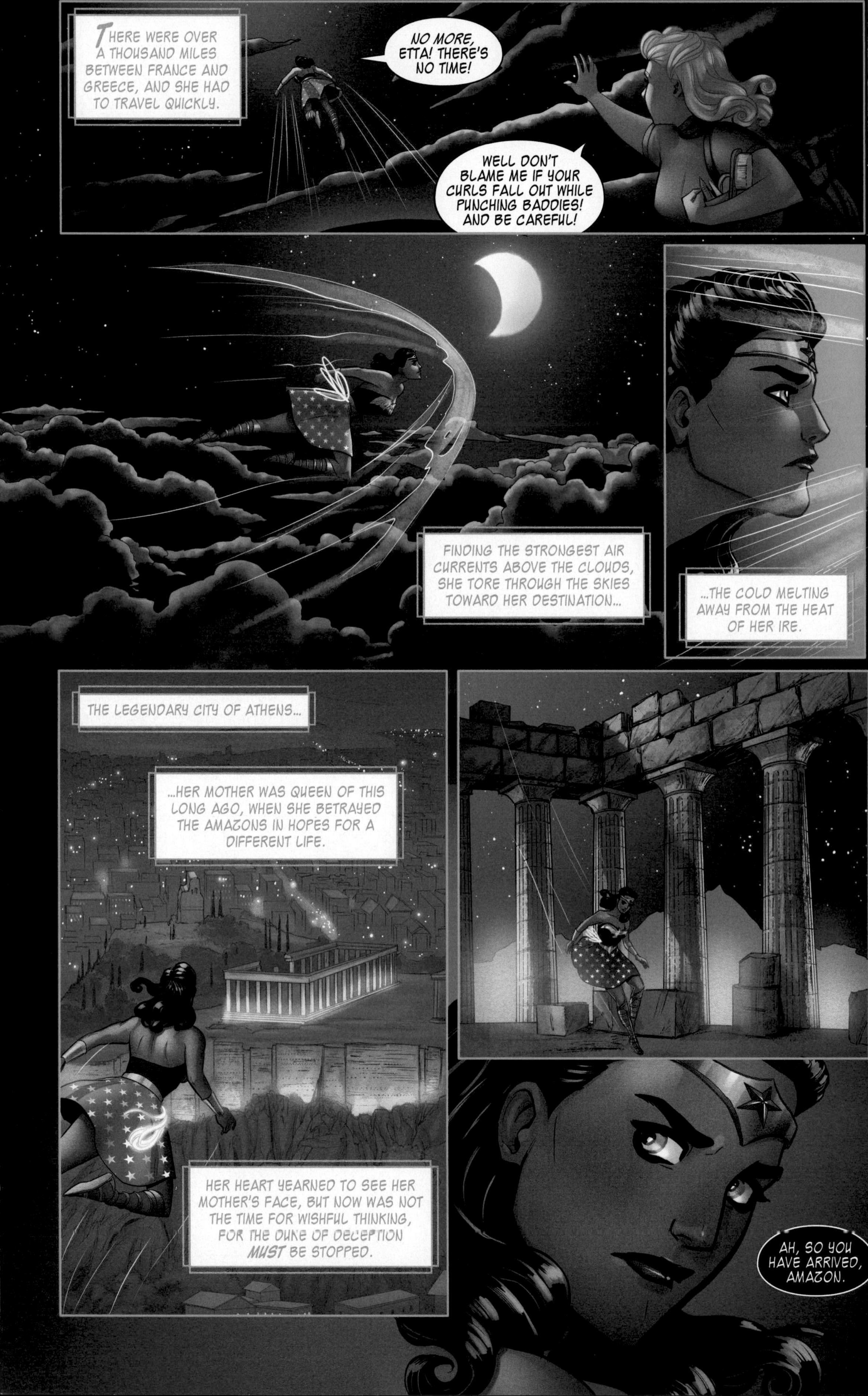
THERE WERE OVER A THOUSAND MILES BETWEEN FRANCE AND GREECE, AND SHE HAD TO TRAVEL QUICKLY.
NO MORE, ETTA! THERE'S NO TIME!
WELL DON'T BLAME ME IF YOUR CURLS FALL OUT WHILE PUNCHING BADDIES! AND BE CAREFUL!
FINDING THE STRONGEST AIR CURRENTS ABOVE THE CLOUDS, SHE TORE THROUGH THE SKIES TOWARD HER DESTINATION...
...THE COLD MELTING AWAY FROM THE HEAT OF HER IRE.
THE LEGENDARY CITY OF ATHENS...
...HER MOTHER WAS QUEEN OF THIS LONG AGO, WHEN SHE BETRAYED THE AMAZONS IN HOPES FOR A DIFFERENT LIFE.
HER HEART YEARNED TO SEE HER MOTHER'S FACE, BUT NOW WAS NOT THE TIME FOR WISHFUL THINKING, FOR THE DUKE OF DECEPTION MUST BE STOPPED.
AH, SO YOU HAVE ARRIVED, AMAZON.

WE BUILT THEMYSCIRA TO SEAL OURSELVES AND THE BAETYLUS AWAY. OUR POWER SUPPORTING A BARRIER AGAINST THE DEVASTATED WORLD.
THE QUEEN OF THE AMAZONS WAS CHOSEN TO SAFEGUARD THE STONE, FOR SURROUNDING IT WITH ETERNAL HARMONY WOULD HALT THE CHARGE OF CHAOS.
FOR CENTURIES THEMYSCIRA THRIVED, AND TIME BURIED THE TITAN IN THE BARREN NORTH OF THE OUTSIDE WORLD.
THEN CAME *CHANGE*.
A WAR OF DISEASED CRUELTY SICKENED THE EARTH, SLOWLY REACHING THEMYSCIRA WITH ITS POISON.
FROM THIS MY SON *ARES* FELT OPPORTUNITY.
DETESTING HIS CHAIN TO THE PEACEFUL THEMYSCIRA, HE PLANNED TO AWAKEN THE TITAN AND LET IT DESTROY THE PLANET, AND WITH IT, THE ISLAND...
HE WOULD THEN BE FREE TO WREST CONTROL FROM ME, AND CREATE A WORLD OF HIS VISION.
HADES JOINED HIS ENDEAVOR, THE TEMPTATION OF DEATH OF SUCH SCALE TOO GREAT.
I OPPOSED THEIR PLAN, BUT TO BATTLE WOULD MEAN OUR DESTRUCTION. THEREFORE, WE ONCE AGAIN AGREED TO THE GAME OF *CHAMPIONS*.

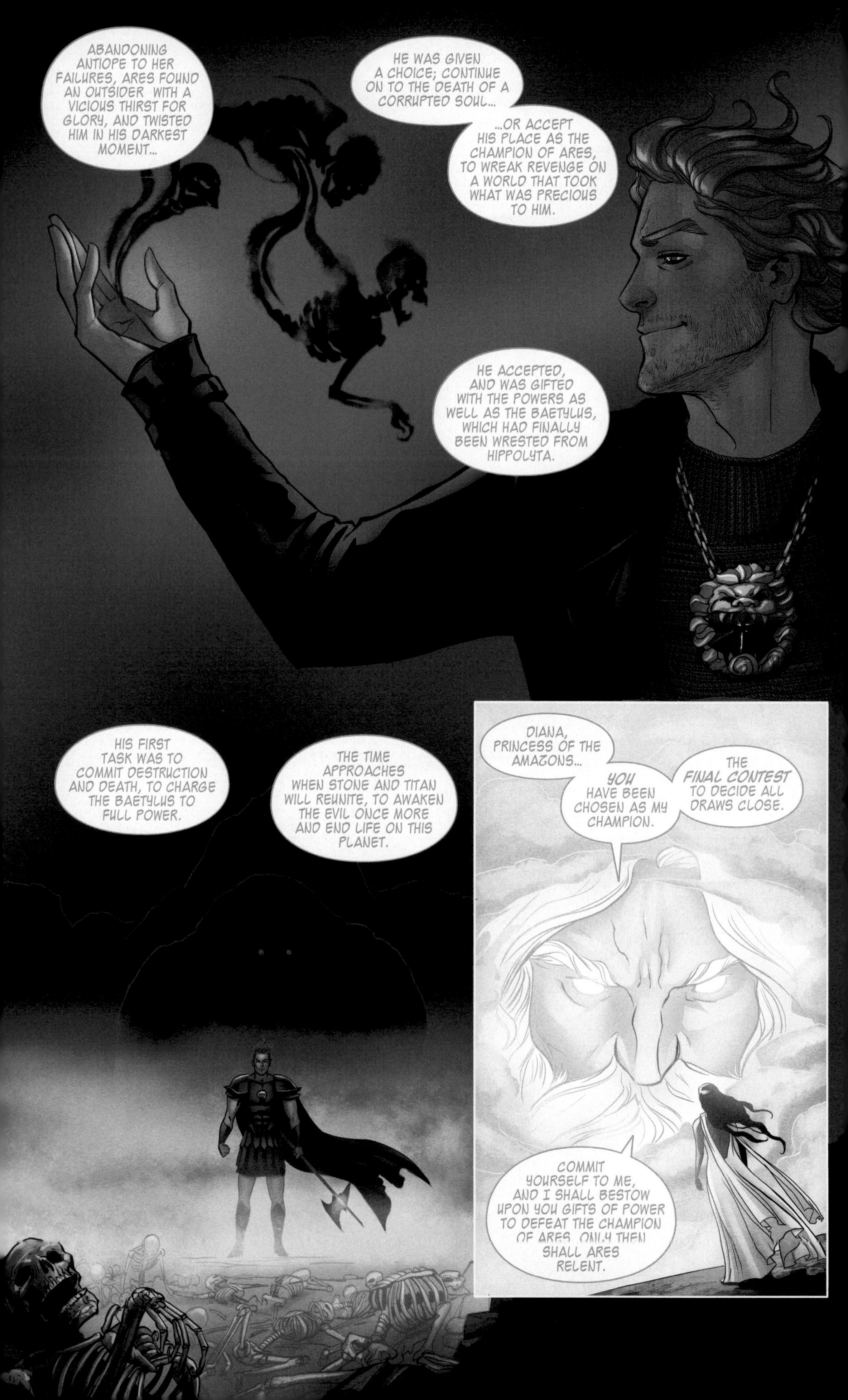
ABANDONING ANTIOPE TO HER FAILURES, ARES FOUND AN OUTSIDER WITH A VICIOUS THIRST FOR GLORY, AND TWISTED HIM IN HIS DARKEST MOMENT...
HE WAS GIVEN A CHOICE; CONTINUE ON TO THE DEATH OF A CORRUPTED SOUL...
...OR ACCEPT HIS PLACE AS THE CHAMPION OF ARES, TO WREAK REVENGE ON A WORLD THAT TOOK WHAT WAS PRECIOUS TO HIM.
HE ACCEPTED, AND WAS GIFTED WITH THE POWERS AS WELL AS THE BAETYLUS, WHICH HAD FINALLY BEEN WRESTED FROM HIPPOLYTA.
HIS FIRST TASK WAS TO COMMIT DESTRUCTION AND DEATH, TO CHARGE THE BAETYLUS TO FULL POWER.
THE TIME APPROACHES WHEN STONE AND TITAN WILL REUNITE, TO AWAKEN THE EVIL ONCE MORE AND END LIFE ON THIS PLANET.
DIANA, PRINCESS OF THE AMAZONS...
YOU HAVE BEEN CHOSEN AS MY CHAMPION.
THE FINAL CONTEST TO DECIDE ALL DRAWS CLOSE.
COMMIT YOURSELF TO ME, AND I SHALL BESTOW UPON YOU GIFTS OF POWER TO DEFEAT THE CHAMPION OF ARES. ONLY THEN SHALL ARES RELENT.

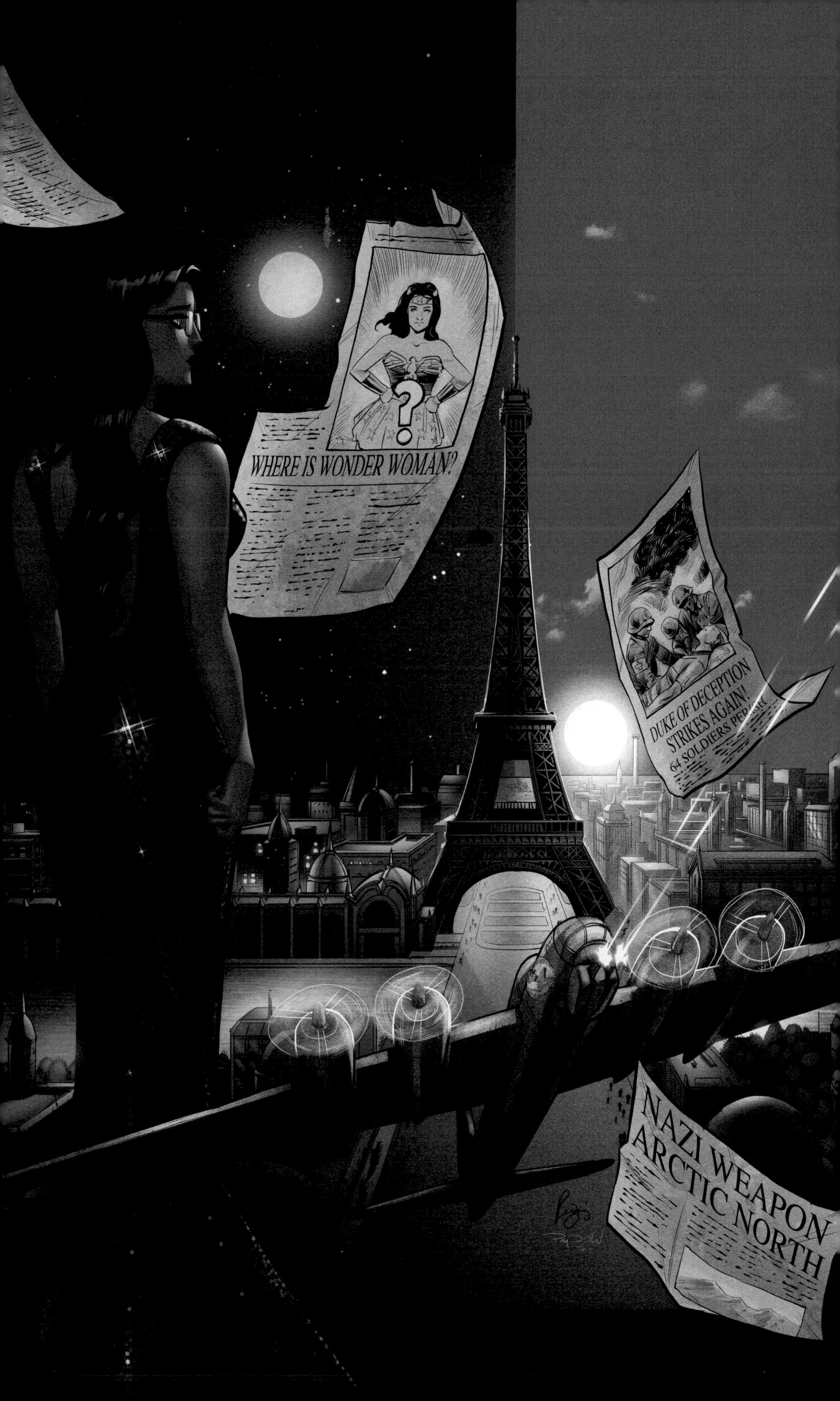
WHERE IS WONDER WOMAN?
DUKE OF DECEPTION STRIKES AGAIN! 64 SOLDIERS PERISH
NAZI WEAPON ARCTIC NORTH

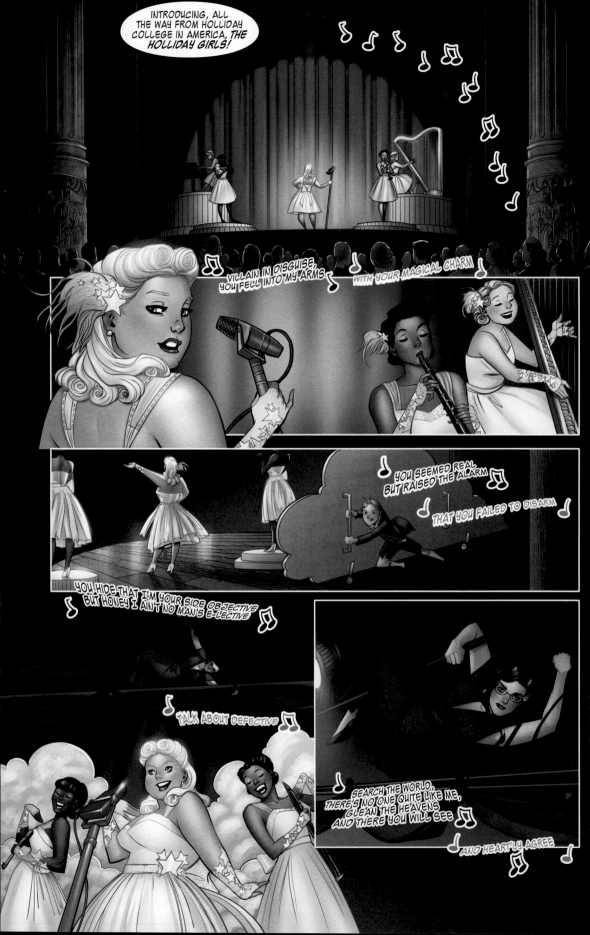

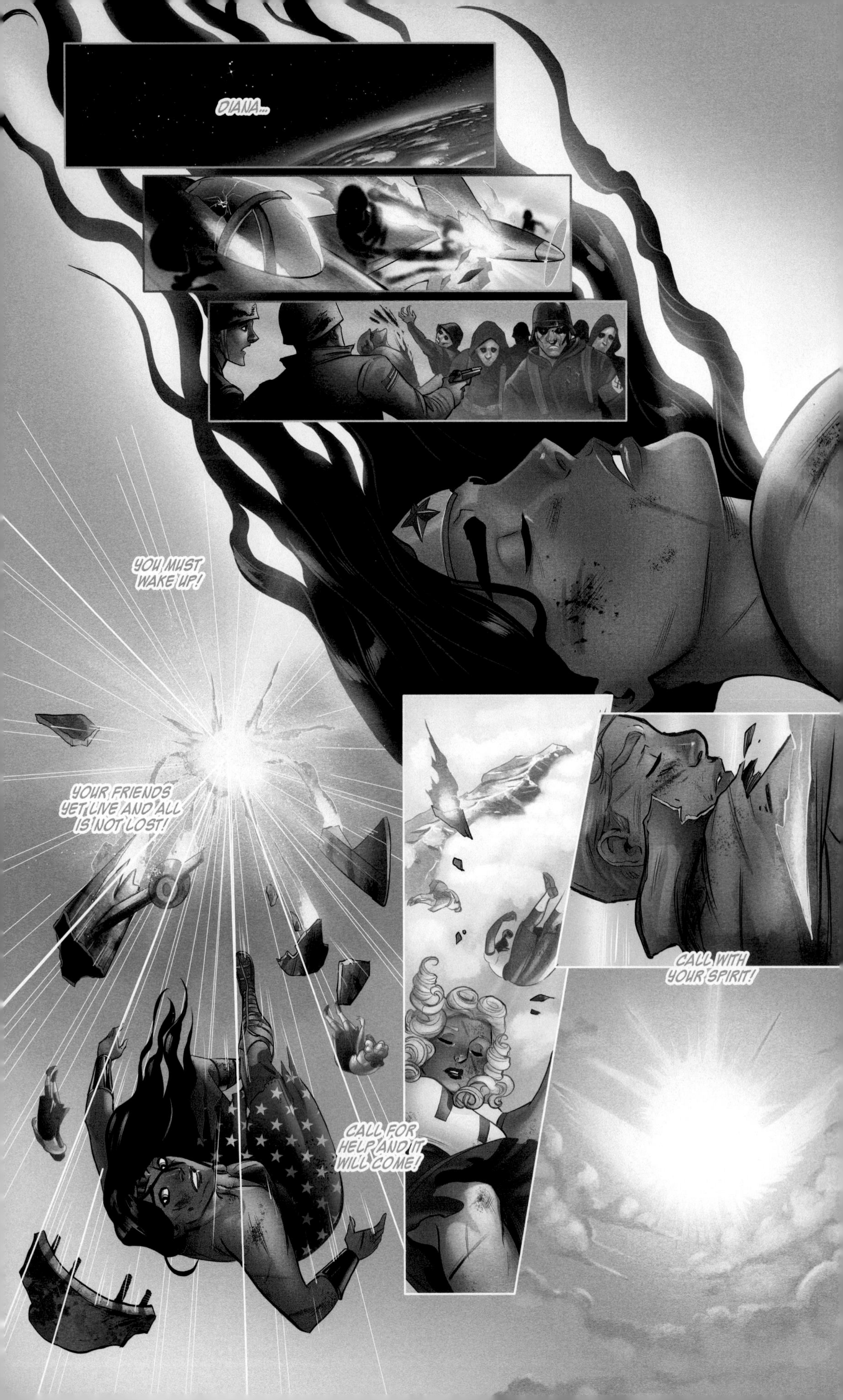
DIANA...
YOU MUST WAKE UP!
YOUR FRIENDS YET LIVE AND ALL IS NOT LOST!
CALL FOR HELP AND IT WILL COME!
CALL WITH YOUR SPIRIT!

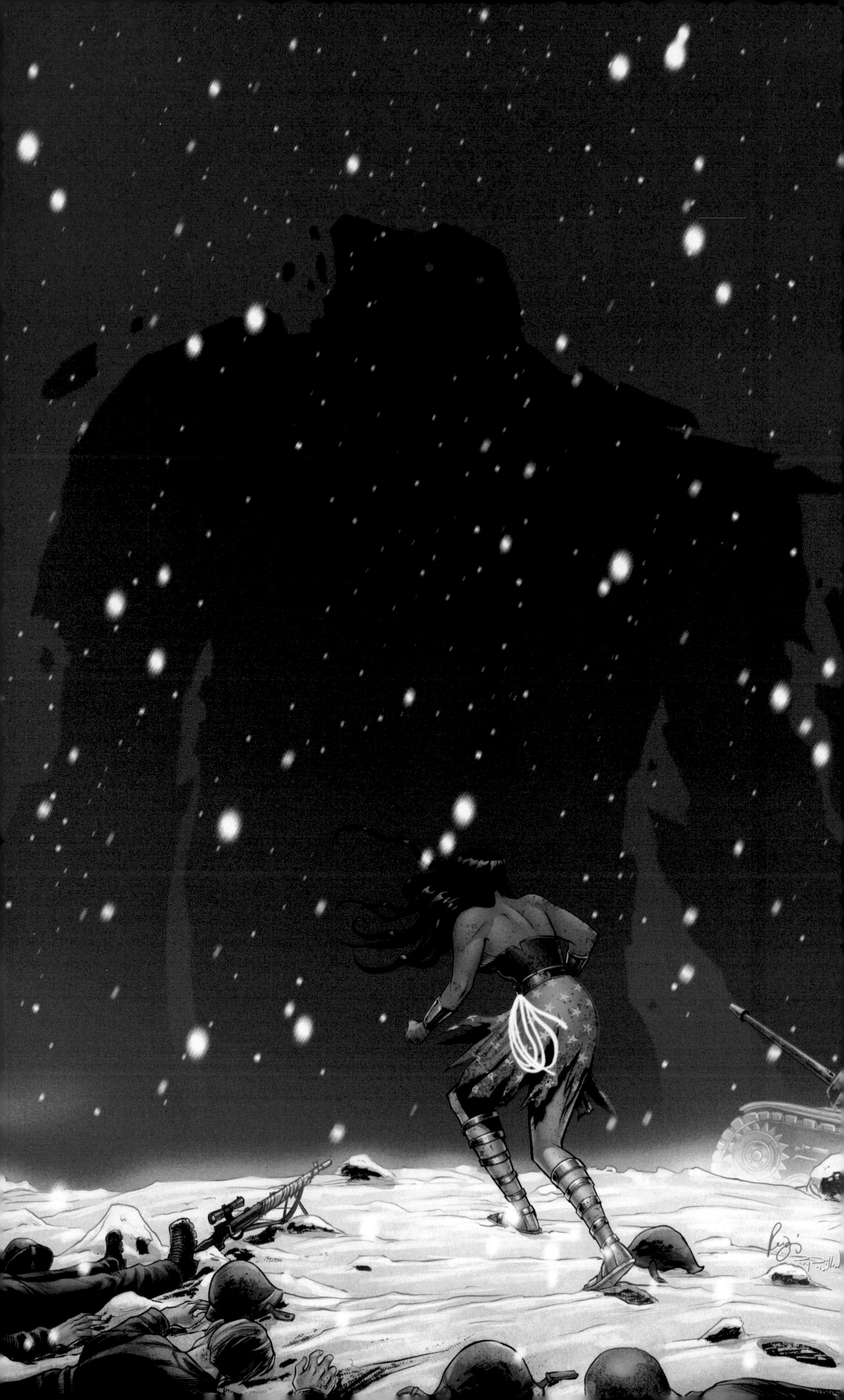

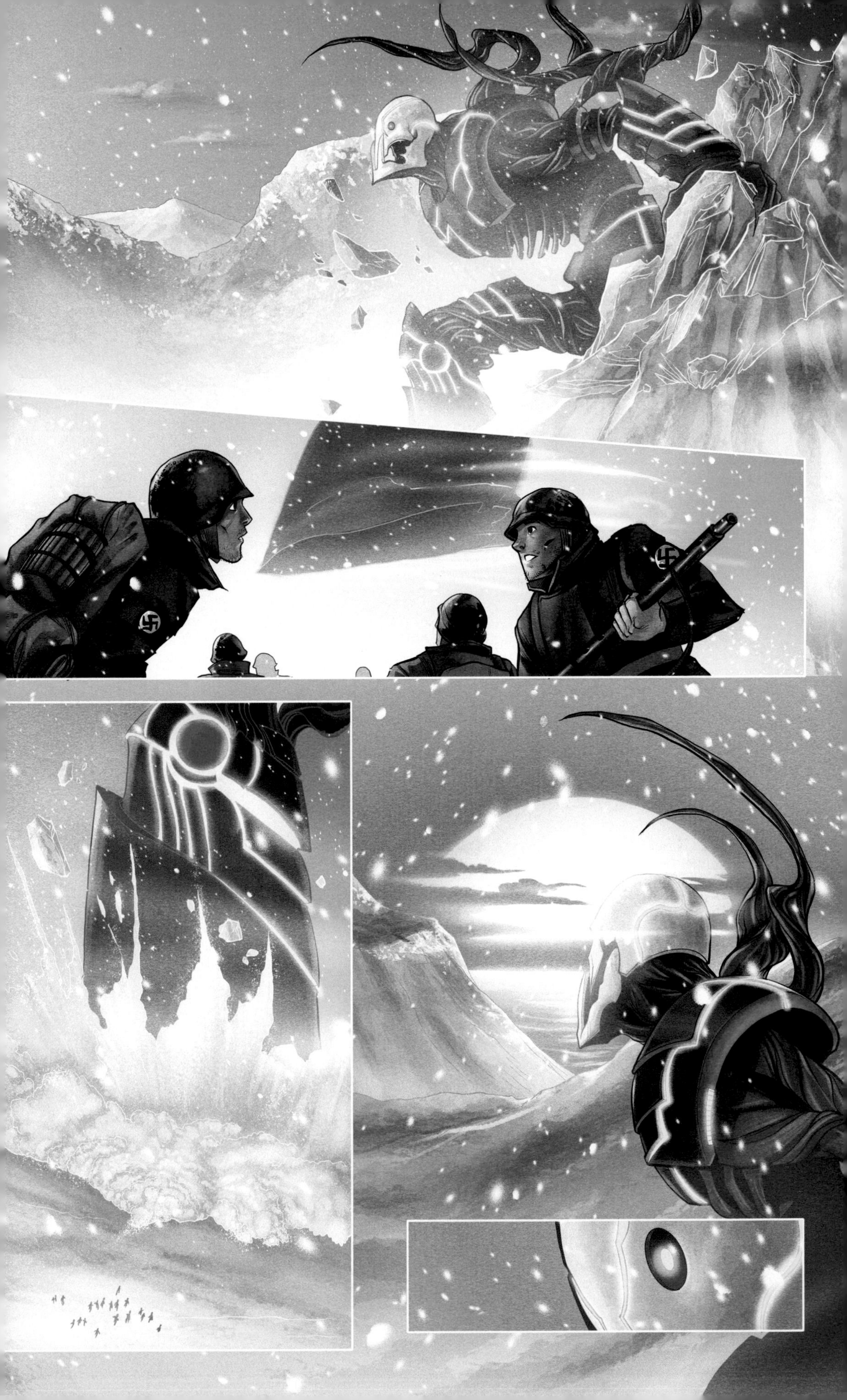

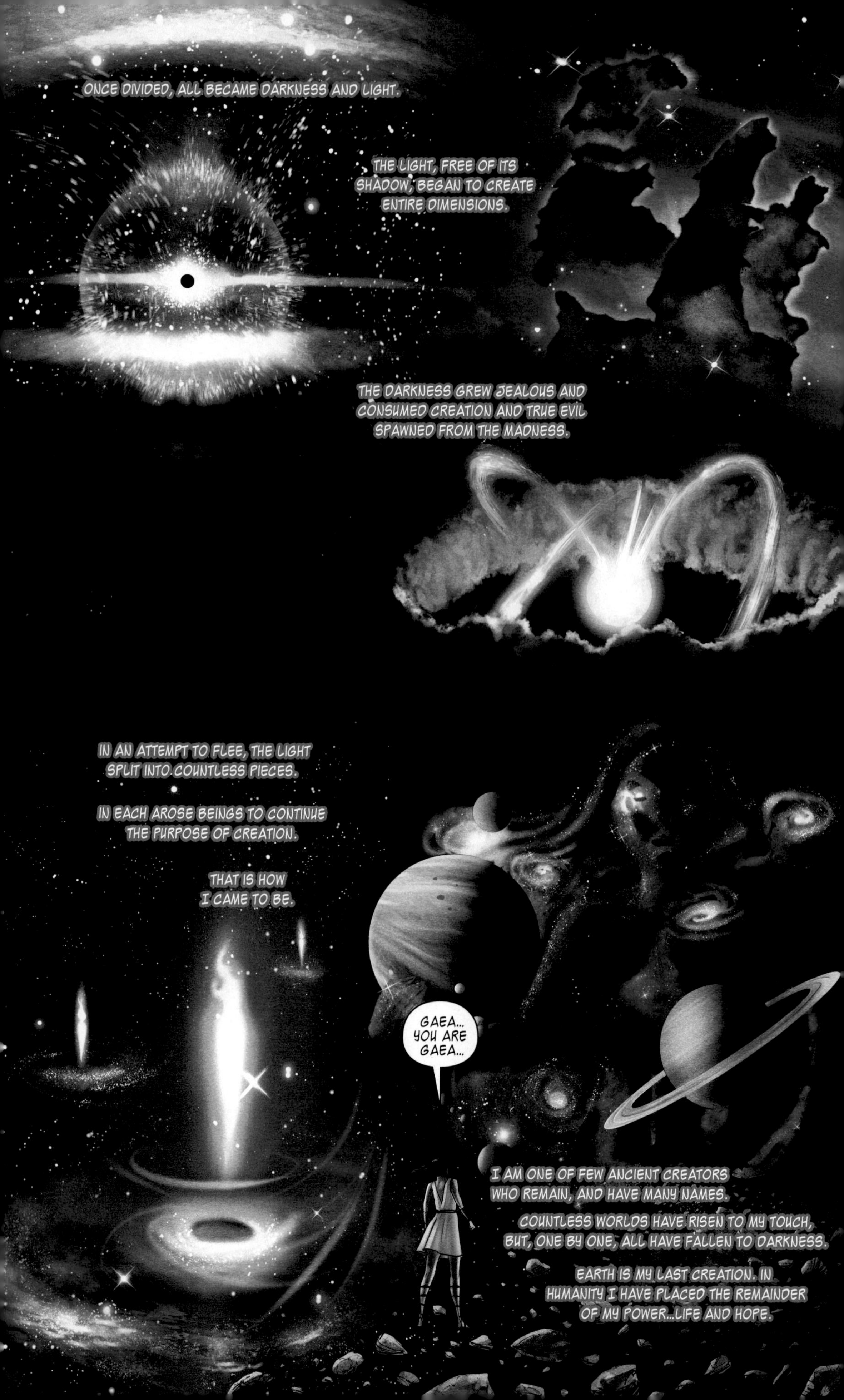
ONCE DIVIDED, ALL BECAME DARKNESS AND LIGHT.
THE LIGHT, FREE OF ITS SHADOW, BEGAN TO CREATE ENTIRE DIMENSIONS.
THE DARKNESS GREW JEALOUS AND CONSUMED CREATION AND TRUE EVIL SPAWNED FROM THE MADNESS.
IN AN ATTEMPT TO FLEE, THE LIGHT SPLIT INTO COUNTLESS PIECES.
IN EACH AROSE BEINGS TO CONTINUE THE PURPOSE OF CREATION.
THAT IS HOW I CAME TO BE.
GAEA... YOU ARE GAEA...
I AM ONE OF FEW ANCIENT CREATORS WHO REMAIN, AND HAVE MANY NAMES.
COUNTLESS WORLDS HAVE RISEN TO MY TOUCH, BUT, ONE BY ONE, ALL HAVE FALLEN TO DARKNESS.
EARTH IS MY LAST CREATION. IN HUMANITY I HAVE PLACED THE REMAINDER OF MY POWER...LIFE AND HOPE.

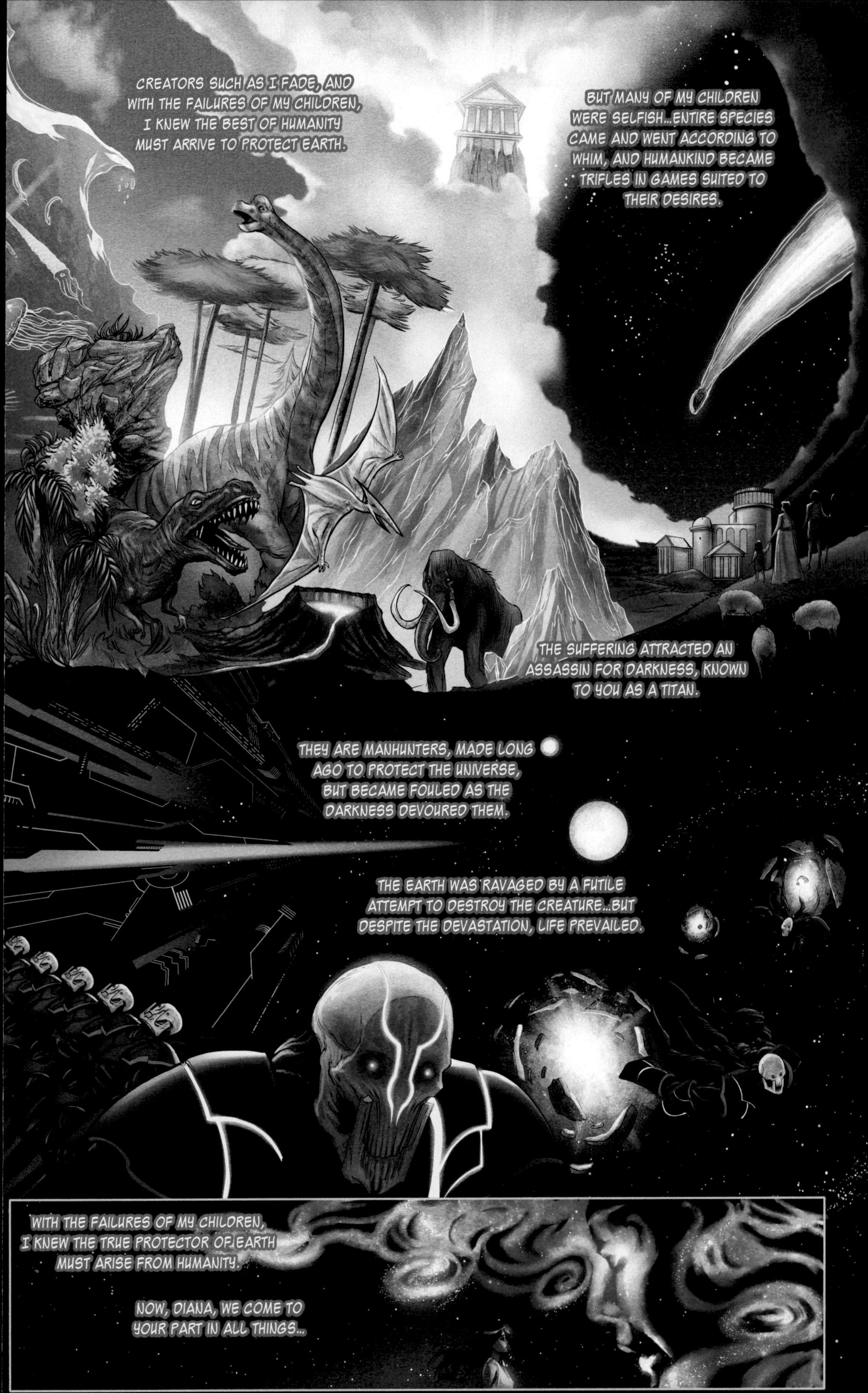
CREATORS SUCH AS I FADE, AND WITH THE FAILURES OF MY CHILDREN, I KNEW THE BEST OF HUMANITY MUST ARRIVE TO PROTECT EARTH.
BUT MANY OF MY CHILDREN WERE SELFISH...ENTIRE SPECIES CAME AND WENT ACCORDING TO WHIM, AND HUMANKIND BECAME TRIFLES IN GAMES SUITED TO THEIR DESIRES.
THE SUFFERING ATTRACTED AN ASSASSIN FOR DARKNESS, KNOWN TO YOU AS A TITAN.
THEY ARE MANHUNTERS, MADE LONG AGO TO PROTECT THE UNIVERSE, BUT BECAME FOULED AS THE DARKNESS DEVOURED THEM.
THE EARTH WAS RAVAGED BY A FUTILE ATTEMPT TO DESTROY THE CREATURE...BUT DESPITE THE DEVASTATION, LIFE PREVAILED.
WITH THE FAILURES OF MY CHILDREN, I KNEW THE TRUE PROTECTOR OF EARTH MUST ARISE FROM HUMANITY.
NOW, DIANA, WE COME TO YOUR PART IN ALL THINGS...

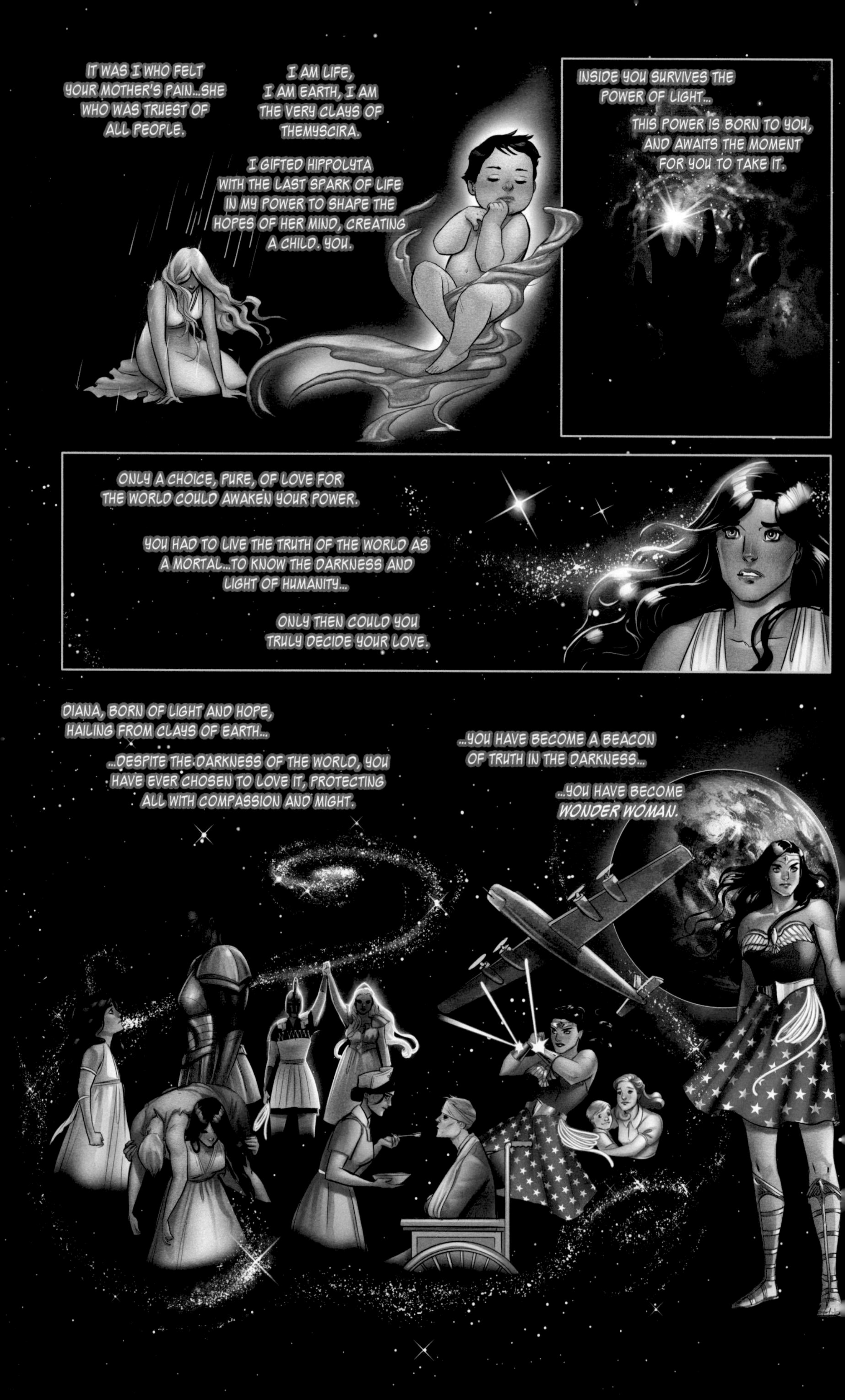
IT WAS I WHO FELT YOUR MOTHER'S PAIN...SHE WHO WAS TRUEST OF ALL PEOPLE.
I AM LIFE, I AM EARTH, I AM THE VERY CLAYS OF THEMYSCIRA.
I GIFTED HIPPOLYTA WITH THE LAST SPARK OF LIFE IN MY POWER TO SHAPE THE HOPES OF HER MIND, CREATING A CHILD. YOU.
INSIDE YOU SURVIVES THE POWER OF LIGHT...
THIS POWER IS BORN TO YOU, AND AWAITS THE MOMENT FOR YOU TO TAKE IT.
ONLY A CHOICE, PURE, OF LOVE FOR THE WORLD COULD AWAKEN YOUR POWER.
YOU HAD TO LIVE THE TRUTH OF THE WORLD AS A MORTAL...TO KNOW THE DARKNESS AND LIGHT OF HUMANITY...
ONLY THEN COULD YOU TRULY DECIDE YOUR LOVE.
DIANA, BORN OF LIGHT AND HOPE, HAILING FROM CLAYS OF EARTH...
...DESPITE THE DARKNESS OF THE WORLD, YOU HAVE EVER CHOSEN TO LOVE IT, PROTECTING ALL WITH COMPASSION AND MIGHT.
...YOU HAVE BECOME A BEACON OF TRUTH IN THE DARKNESS...
...YOU HAVE BECOME *WONDER WOMAN*.

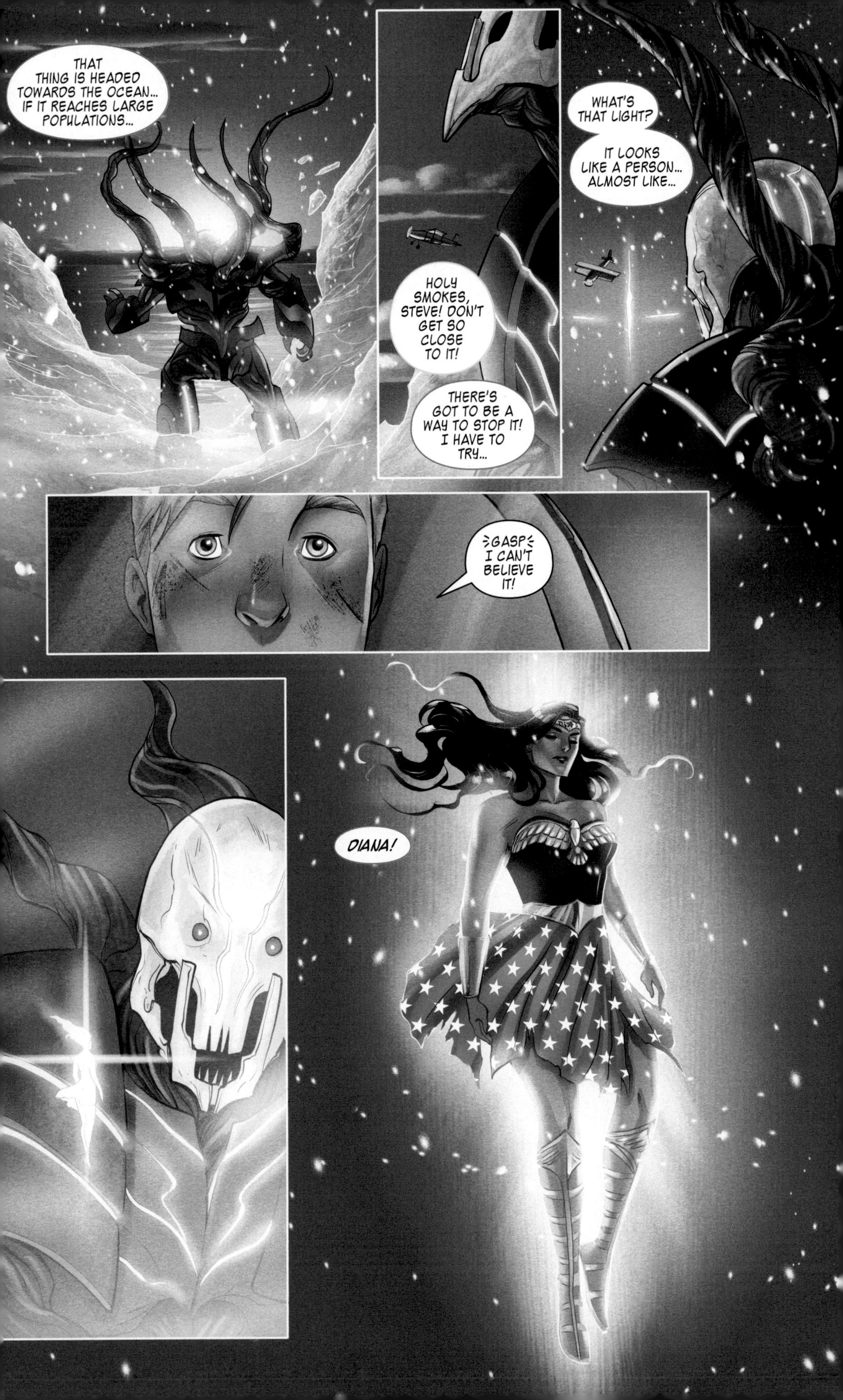
THAT THING IS HEADED TOWARDS THE OCEAN... IF IT REACHES LARGE POPULATIONS...
WHAT'S THAT LIGHT?
IT LOOKS LIKE A PERSON... ALMOST LIKE...
HOLY SMOKES, STEVE! DON'T GET SO CLOSE TO IT!
THERE'S GOT TO BE A WAY TO STOP IT! I HAVE TO TRY...
GASP I CAN'T BELIEVE IT!
DIANA!

THE MOVEMENT OF A BILLION STARS COURSED THROUGH DIANA'S VEINS, THREATENING TO CONSUME HER...

...BUT SHE WOULD MASTER THIS NEW POWER. SHE MUST...

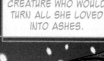 ...FOR HERE WAS A CREATURE WHO WOULD TURN ALL SHE LOVED INTO ASHES.

BUT THE HOUR FOR FEAR HAD PASSED.

IT WAS TIME TO *FIGHT.*

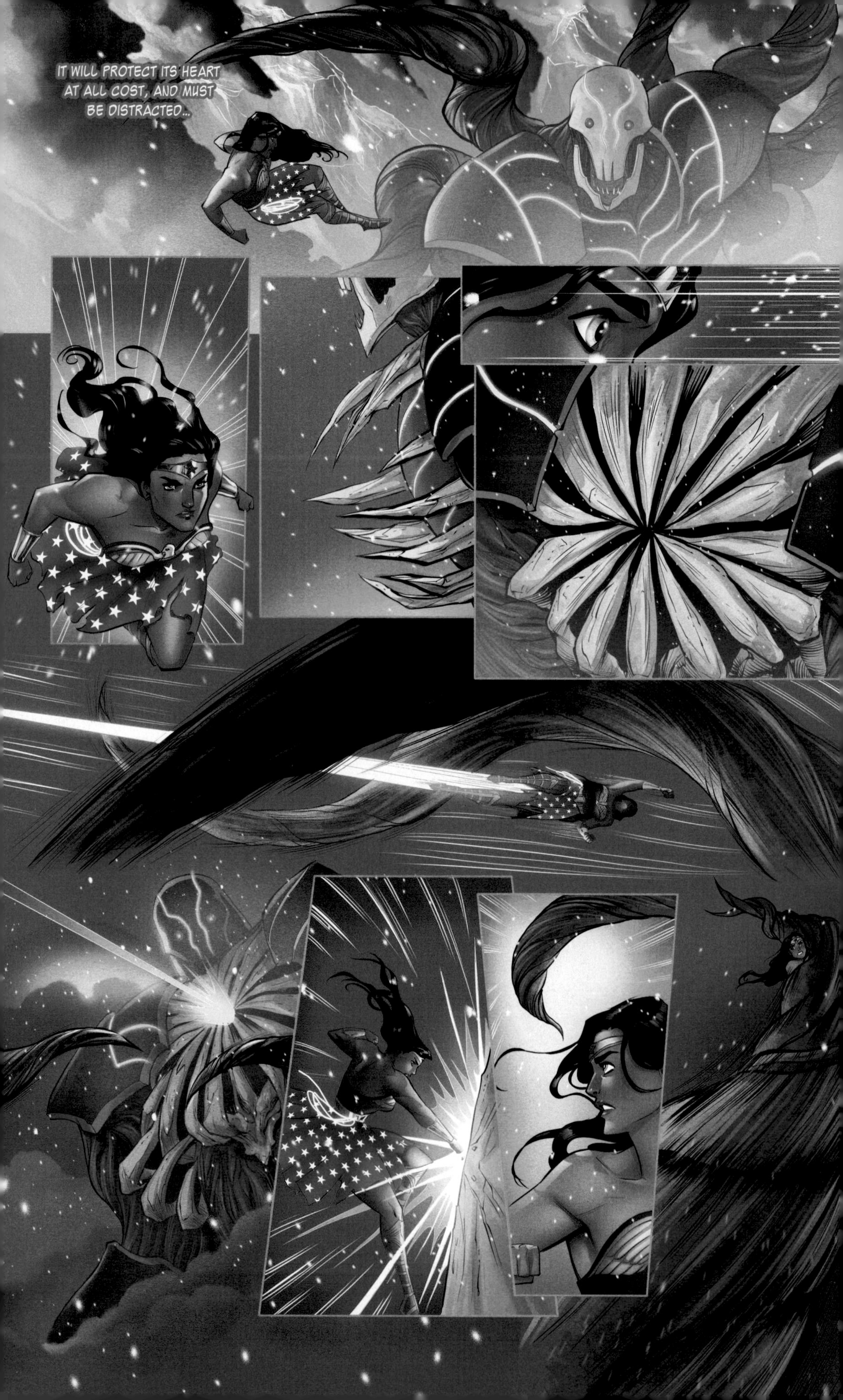
IT WILL PROTECT ITS HEART AT ALL COST, AND MUST BE DISTRACTED...

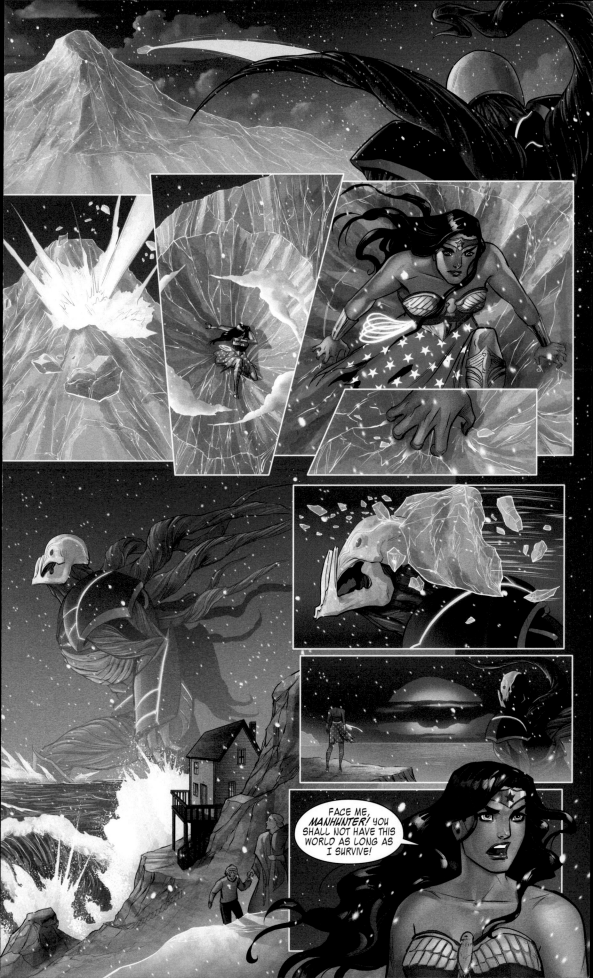

FACE ME, *MANHUNTER!* YOU SHALL NOT HAVE THIS WORLD AS LONG AS I SURVIVE!

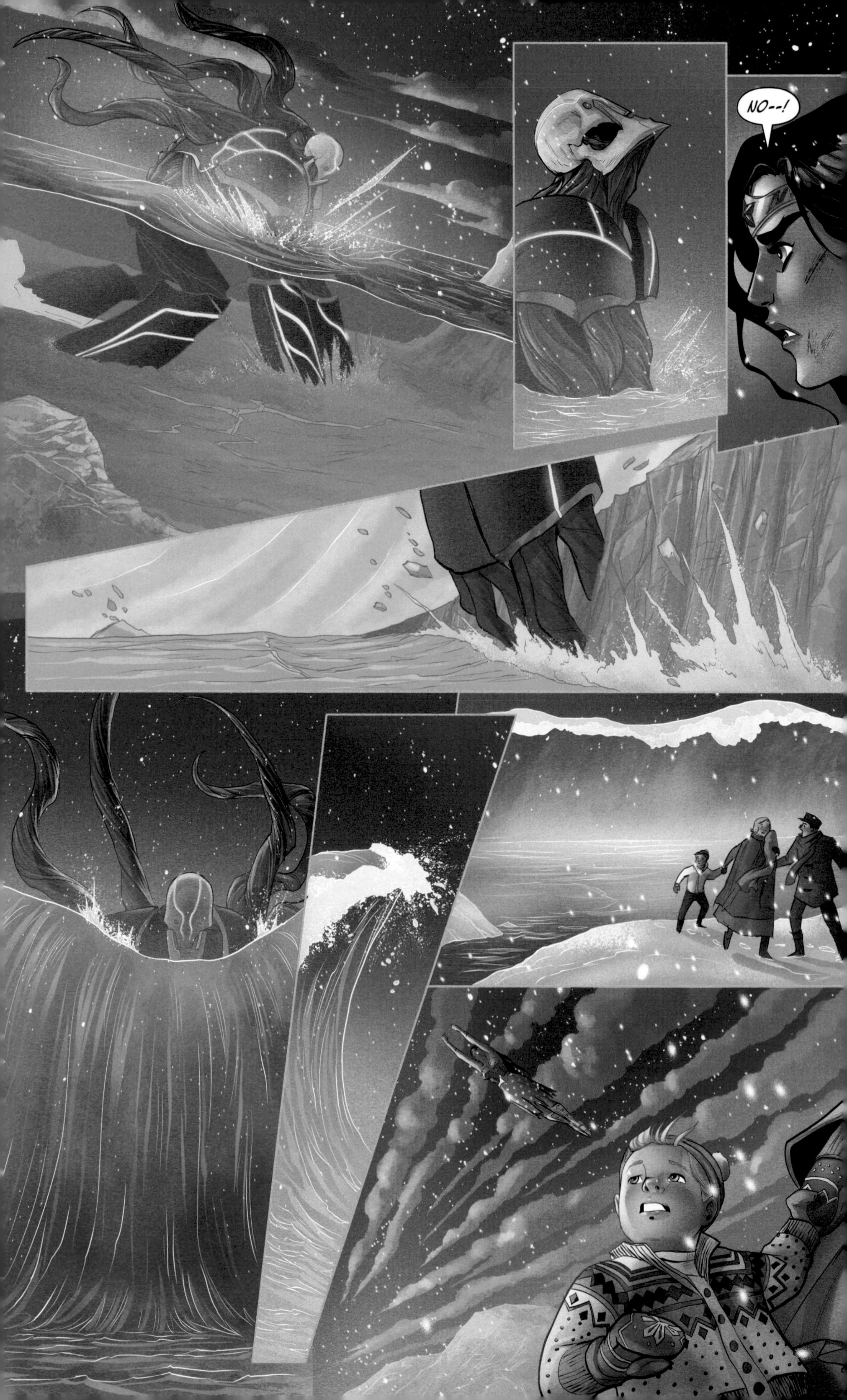
NO--!

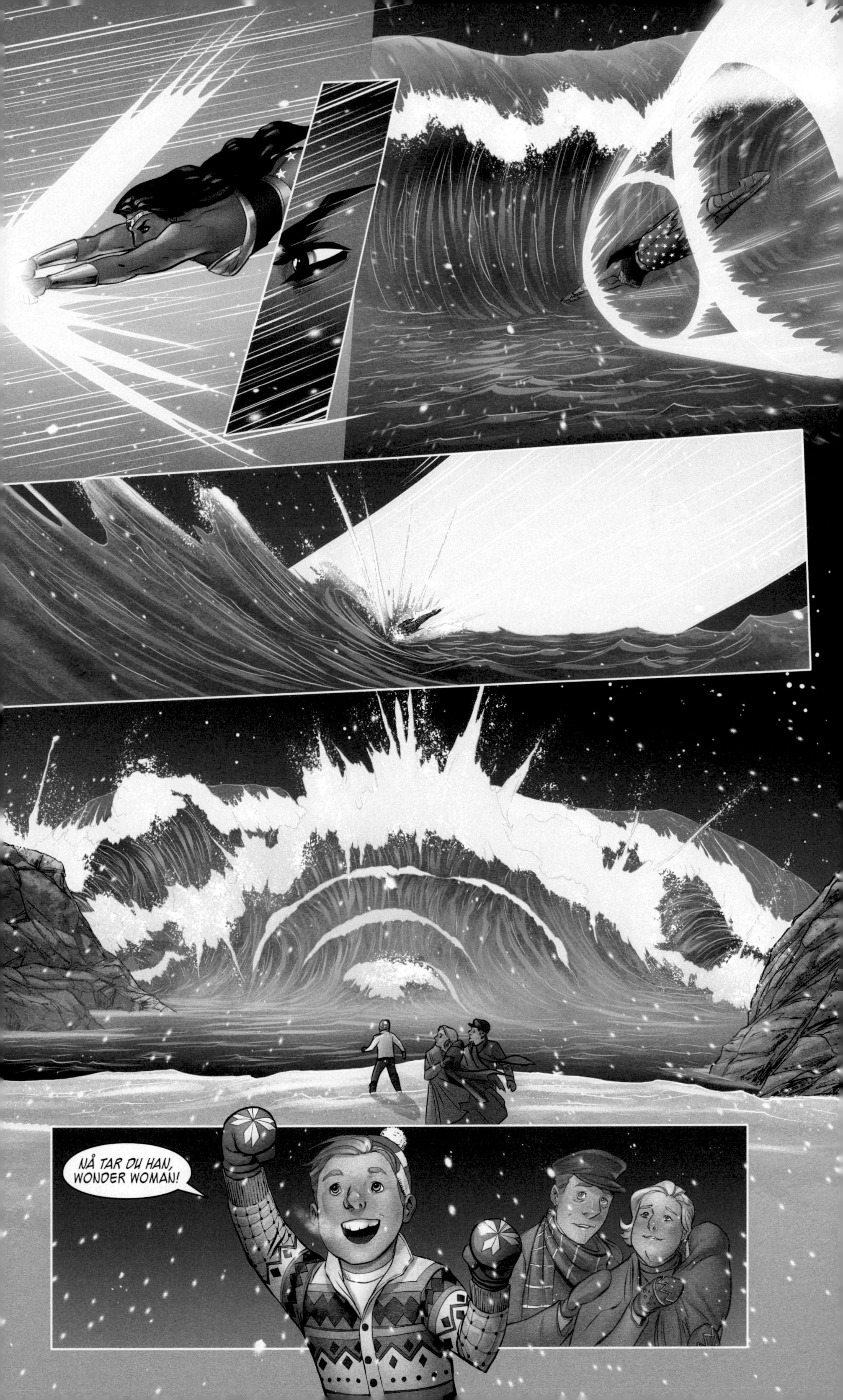
NÅ TAR DU HAN, WONDER WOMAN!

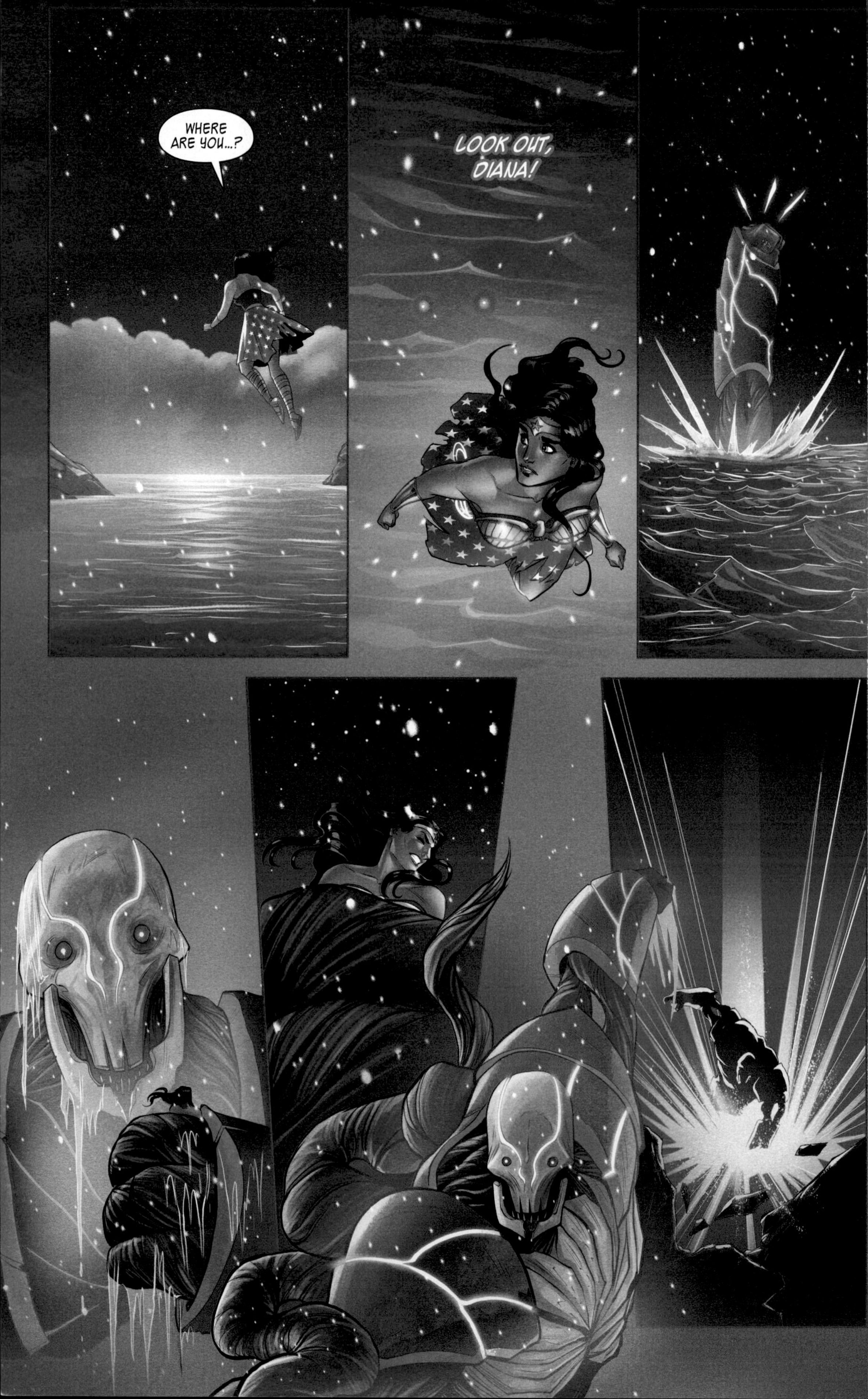
WHERE ARE YOU...?
LOOK OUT, DIANA!

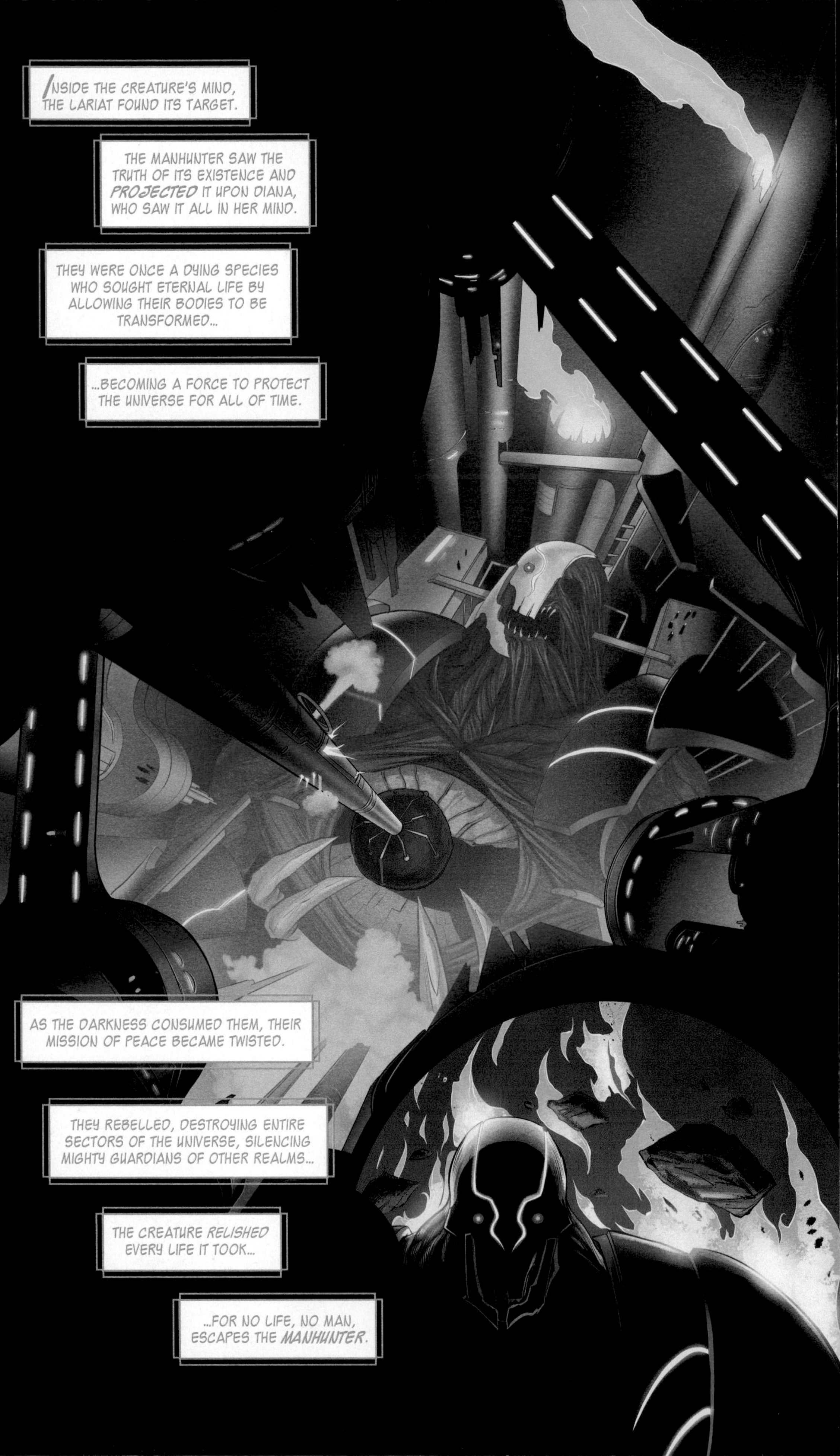
INSIDE THE CREATURE'S MIND, THE LARIAT FOUND ITS TARGET.
THE MANHUNTER SAW THE TRUTH OF ITS EXISTENCE AND *PROJECTED* IT UPON DIANA, WHO SAW IT ALL IN HER MIND.
THEY WERE ONCE A DYING SPECIES WHO SOUGHT ETERNAL LIFE BY ALLOWING THEIR BODIES TO BE TRANSFORMED...
...BECOMING A FORCE TO PROTECT THE UNIVERSE FOR ALL OF TIME.
AS THE DARKNESS CONSUMED THEM, THEIR MISSION OF PEACE BECAME TWISTED.
THEY REBELLED, DESTROYING ENTIRE SECTORS OF THE UNIVERSE, SILENCING MIGHTY GUARDIANS OF OTHER REALMS...
THE CREATURE *RELISHED* EVERY LIFE IT TOOK...
...FOR NO LIFE, NO MAN, ESCAPES THE *MANHUNTER*.

THE LEGEND OF WONDER WOMAN 1
variant cover by Dustin Nguyen

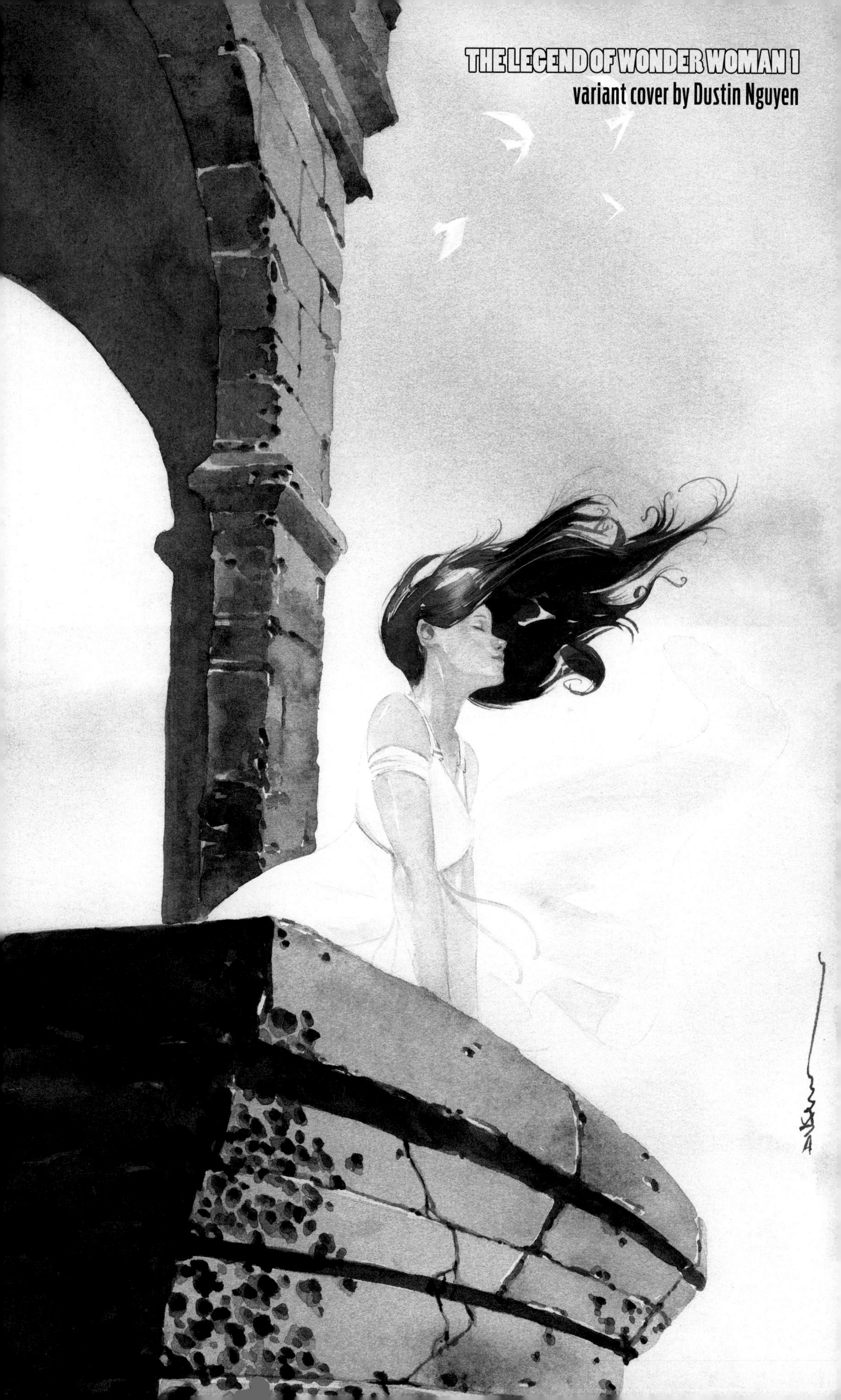

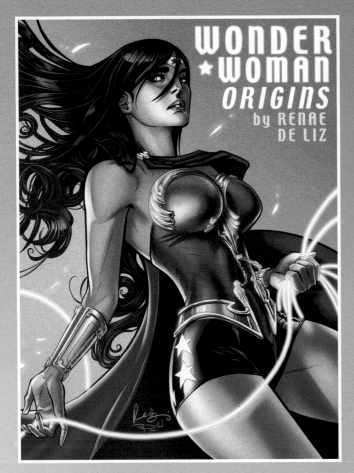

WONDER WOMAN: ORIGINS
ACT 1: CHILD OF THE AMAZON

WONDER WOMAN: ORIGINS
12-issue Series by **Renae De Liz**
(*Womanthology, Peter Pan, The Last Unicorn*)

ACT ONE
CHILD OF THE AMAZON

Through the story of the Immortal Life of Hippolyta, Queen of the Amazons, and her desperate plight to have a child, we discover the Island of Themyscira, the last refuge of mythological creatures and Greek Gods. The Gods finally give her the gift of a baby girl made from clay.

We follow young Princess Diana as she explores the island for adventure but stumbles upon murderous plots orchestrated by Ares and Hades. Circumstances prevent her from telling her mother, so she ignores her wanderlust to be the best heir to her mother's throne.

As Diana reaches womanhood, she witnesses a mysterious fireball crashing into the island and a man in burned rags in the fiery crater who she then hides to keep him safe. His arrival sets off a chain of events that leads to him and Diana leaving the island forever.

At sea, a supernatural storm created by Ares' sect of Amazons engulfs them, and only with the help of Poseidon does she survive. Lost and alone in the dark, Diana floats towards the lights of the Boston Harbor of 1942.

ACT TWO
THE WORLD WAR

A kind fisherman and his wife pull unconscious Diana to shore and nurse her back to health. Before she departs she is given an American flag that belonged to their son who died in the war. She then takes to the woods surrounding Boston, observing this new land when she crosses paths with a brash, outgoing college girl named Etta Candy, who helps her understand the way of this world and gives her a place to stay in the city at the campus of Holiday College.

Here she learns of the world war going on overseas and is devastated by the scale of suffering. She hears wives' tales of Nazis who can raise the dead and a three-headed monster that kills from the shadows. Diana recognizes the work of Ares and Hades and decides to head to the front lines.

Etta suggests joining the army and accompanies Diana to a recruitment facility, where she is shocked to discover women, considered the weaker sex, are not allowed to be soldiers. She runs into the man who crashed on the island. He has no memory of his time there, but does have a sense of her. Etta recognizes him as Steve Trevor, "The Miracle Soldier," a pilot who went missing during the war, but was found months later on the East Coast shore. He helps Diana and Etta join WASP, a new women's Air Force group.

WONDER WOMAN: ORIGINS
ACT 2: THE WORLD WAR

Stationed overseas and being trained as pilots, Steve, Etta, and Diana become close. Steve silently falls in love. Diana is not satisfied to sit by him and train. She dons a uniform (made from the flag she was given by the fisherman and his wife to honor their deceased son) and with the magical items her mother, Hippolyta, had given her, she moonlights as "The Wonder Woman," a name given to her by admirers.

She comes face-to-face with a Nazi General, a disciple of Ares and Hades, who was given powers to aid in his plan to create a war so bloody that it will awaken an ancient Titan to destroy the planet. Diana is not strong enough to stop this, but being half immortal, half human, she is given a choice from the Gods either to embrace their power and fight the evil of the war or to live a mortal life filled with human happiness.

She loves the human side of her life and doesn't want to give that up, but can't let those things be destroyed. Conflicted, she runs away...

ACT THREE
THE TITAN

Diana has fled to a secluded island to think. From the shore she sees the explosions of war and makes her decision: she will no longer be Wonder Woman. She will become mortal and fight the war as only a soldier. She tells the Gods they should be responsible for their own mess. She returns to Boston to an ecstatic Etta and finally gives Steve a hopeful smile, which he happily returns.

A critical battle is coming, one that will decide the final tide of the war. Steve, Etta, and Diana are assigned to fly into battle and hold back enemy bombers. Victory is in their sight...until the Disciple General arrives, unleashing mythical monsters and devouring the Allied Forces on ground and in air. Diana watches as Steve's plane is hit and a creature swiftly descends on her own. Her aircraft explodes and she falls to Earth watching as Steve's and Etta's planes plummet, too. Diana begs the Gods for help.

A burst of light brings forth a ghostly image of Pegasus, her childhood friend from Themyscira. It merges with her battered plane and scoops her up as it turns invisible. She's able to help Steve land but discovers that the Disciple's plan worked and the Titan has been awakened.

Diana flies towards the monster but is still not powerful enough. Confronted by the disciple, Diana battles him as Wonder Woman. Nearly beaten, she calls upon the Gods again, this time accepting her fate and her destined godly powers. She quickly overcomes the evil Disciple and moves on to battle the rampaging Titan. Her powers grow and she defeats it. The war is won and Diana stands victorious and alone. She can no longer live the life of a human.

The Gods surround her to congratulate her, but also to let her know the real battle is coming. They inform her that the resurrected Titan was actually one of the many Signal Men hidden inside planets a millennia ago by a horrible intergalactic force in search of a certain planet that holds the key to keeping the universe together...or the key to destroy it.

The Gods tell Diana she must forever protect the Earth and its people, for someday "The One" who will become the key will be discovered. Now that the Gods are weakened, they rely on Wonder Woman.

Diana faces Steve and Etta in a tearful good-bye. The power unleashed by the Gods will also erase their memories. She flies off into her new life as Protector of the Planet.

WONDER WOMAN: ORIGINS
ACT 3: THE TITAN

COVER SKETCHES
by **RENAE DE LIZ**